Revitalization: Explora
Pietist ;
Series Edi

MW01137821

1. *John Wesley on Religious Affections*, Gregory S. Clapper, 1989.
2. *Gottfried Arnold*, Peter Erb, 1989.
3. *The Presence of God in the Christian Life: John Wesley and the Means of Grace*, Henry H. Knight III, 1992.
4. *Spirituality and Social Liberation: The Message of the Blumhardts in the Light of Wuerttemberg Pietism*, Frank D. Macchia, 1993.
5. *"Gracious Affection" and "True Virtue" according to Jonathan Edwards and John Wesley*, Richard B. Steele, 1994.
6. *Piety and Tolerance: Pennsylvania German Religion, 1700–1850*, Stephen L. Longenecker, 1994.
7. *Early German-American Evangelicalism: Pietist Sources on Discipleship and Sanctification*, J. Steven O'Malley, 1995.
8. *Salvationist Samurai: Gunpei Yamamuro and the Rise of the Salvation Army in Japan*, R. David Rightmire, 1997.
9. *John Bennet and the Origins of Methodism and the Evangelical Revival in England*, Simon Ross Valentine, 1997.
10. *Martin Luther and John Wesley on the Sermon on the Mount*, Tore Meistad, 1999.
11. *John Wesley: His Puritan Heritage*, Robert C. Monk, 1999.
12. *"Heart Religion" in the Methodist Tradition and Related Movements*, Richard B. Steele, 2001.
13. *Singleness of Heart*, Diane Leclerc, 2001.
14. *The Global Impact of the Wesleyan Traditions and Their Related Movement*, Charles Yrigoyen Jr., 2002.
15. *The Meaning of Pentecost in Early Methodism: Rediscovering John Fletcher as John Wesley's Vindicator and Designated Successor*, Laurence W. Wood, 2002.
16. *Holiness Abroad: Nazarene Missions in Asia*, Floyd T. Cunningham, 2003.
17. *"Live While You Preach": The Autobiography of Methodist Revivalist and Abolitionist John Wesley Redfield (1810–1863)*, Howard A. Snyder, 2006.
18. *Living for God: Eighteenth-Century Dutch Pietist Autobiography*, Fred van Lieburg, 2006.
19. *In the Midst of Early Methodism: Lady Huntingdon and Her Correspondence*, John R. Tyson with Boyd S. Schlenther, 2006.
20. *To Be Silent . . . Would Be Criminal: The Antislavery Influence and Writings of Anthony Benezet*, Irv A. Brendlinger, 2007.
21. *E. Stanley Jones Had a Wife: The Life and Mission of Mabel Lossing Jones*, Kathryn Reese Hendershot, 2007.
22. *German Radical Pietism*, Hans Schneider, 2007.
23. *The Making of an American Church: Essays Commemorating the Jubilee Year of the Evangelical United Brethren Church*, Robert L. Frey, 2007.
24. *Foundation for Revival: Anthony Horneck (1641–1697), Religious Societies, and the Construction of an Anglican Pietism*, Scott Thomas Kisker, 2008.
25. *Evangelical Hospitality: Catechetical Evangelism in the Early Church and Its Recovery for Today*, Tory K. Baucum, 2008.
26. *Catholic Spirit: Wesley, Whitefield, and the Quest for Evangelical Unity in Eighteenth-Century British Methodism*, James L. Schwenk, 2008.
27. *John Wesley's Ecclesiology: A Study in Its Sources and Development*, Gwang Seok Oh, 2008.

Revitalization: Explorations in World Christian Movement

This volume is published in collaboration with the Center for the Study of World Christian Revitalization Movements, a cooperative initiative of Asbury Theological Seminary faculty. Building on the work of the previous Wesleyan/Holiness Studies Center at the Seminary, the Center provides a focus for research in the Wesleyan Holiness and other related Christian renewal movements, including Pietism and Pentecostal movements, which have had a world impact. The research seeks to develop analytical models of these movements, including their biblical and theological assessment. Using an interdisciplinary approach, the Center bridges relevant discourses in several areas in order to gain insights for effective Christian mission globally. It recognizes the need for conducting research that combines insights from the history of evangelical renewal and revival movements with anthropological and religious studies literature on revitalization movements. It also networks with similar or related research and study centers around the world, in addition to sponsoring its own research projects.

It is important that the understanding of ecclesiology in Wesley and early Methodism be understood in a larger, more comprehensive trajectory, which places it in the framework of the larger field of movements for world Christian revitalization. This timely study by Dr. Gwang Seok Oh does precisely that. He has produced a resource that will have timely appeal for students and practitioners of the theology of the Wesleys, but especially for those preparing for ministry and membership in United Methodism and other Methodist bodies. Hence, this volume demonstrates congruence with the mission of the Center and serves to advance its research objectives.

The Center for the Study of World
Christian Revitalization Movements
Asbury Theological Seminary
J. Steven O'Malley, Director

John Wesley's Ecclesiology

A Study in Its Sources and Development

Gwang Seok Oh

Revitalization: Explorations in World Christian Movements

Pietist and Wesleyan Studies, No. 27

The Scarecrow Press, Inc.
Lanham, Maryland • Toronto • Plymouth, UK
2008

SCARECROW PRESS, INC.

Published in the United States of America
by Scarecrow Press, Inc.
A wholly owned subsidiary of
The Rowman & Littlefield Publishing Group, Inc.
4501 Forbes Boulevard, Suite 200, Lanham, Maryland 20706
www.scarecrowpress.com

Estover Road
Plymouth PL6 7PY
United Kingdom

British Library Cataloguing in Publication Information Available

Library of Congress Cataloging-in-Publication Data

Oh, Gwang Seok, 1967–
  John Wesley's ecclesiology : a study in its sources and development / Gwang Seok Oh.
    p. cm. — (Revitalization : explorations in world Christian movements) (Pietist and
Wesleyan studies ; no. 27)
  Includes bibliographical references and index.
  ISBN-13: 978-0-8108-5964-7 (pbk. : alk. paper)
  ISBN-10: 0-8108-5964-5 (pbk. : alk. paper)
  1. Wesley, John, 1703–1791. 2. Church. 3. Theology. I. Title.

BX8495.W5O35 2008
262'.07092—dc22

                                                                        2007039252

♾™ The paper used in this publication meets the minimum requirements of
American National Standard for Information Sciences—Permanence of
Paper for Printed Library Materials, ANSI/NISO Z39.48-1992.
Manufactured in the United States of America.

To my parents, Bok-ja Yang and Se-hyuk Oh,
and to my theological and spiritual teacher, John Wesley

Contents

Foreword

There are moments at academic conferences when, as a presenter or as a speaker, I will deliberately describe myself as a pietist. The response is invariably a mixture of consternation and confusion: consternation because colleagues detest pietism, and confusion because they cannot believe that any serious intellectual would identify with such a lowbrow movement. It does not help to insist that I am not a pietist of the higher order. By way of relief I then add that I am an eighteenth century Irish pietist with an Oxford education and an Eastern Orthodox update. This helps soften the tension somewhat. There is method in my strategy. I want to signal that pietism is far more important in the history of theology and society than current ignorance and prejudice allow. After all, a movement that can produce Immanuel Kant and Frederick Schleiermacher in one country in one generation must have something going for it; and a movement that can claim John Wesley as a paid-up member cannot be all-bad. Moreover, a recovery of vital elements of pietism is salutary for our current ecclesial woes. Pietism matters as a historical trajectory and as a resource for the church today.

It is a great joy in these circumstances to welcome this volume of Gwang-Seok Oh on the ecclesiology of John Wesley. It is an additional pleasure to see the pietist side of Wesley taken so seriously by a fine young scholar. Over the last generation we have heard much about Wesley as a proto-liberation theologian, as a great social reformer, as a grand epistemologist of theology, as a folk theologian, as a vital bridge between rival versions of the Christian tradition, and the like. While everybody knows that the heart of the faith for Wesley was the appropriation of the glorious grace of God in the human heart and hand, there has been a deep reluctance to acknowledge his inescapably personalist take on the faith that we associate with pietism. We have wanted to rescue Wesley from the emotionalist riff-raff. Wesley is, of course, sufficiently complex to call forth radically diverse readings of his thought and life. From a distance he can look like an incoherent oddball in need of a good scrub if he is to speak to the current situation. Happily, Gwang-Seok Oh is patient at this point and develops a vision of Wesley that seeks to be faithful to his complexity and oddity. However, I especially welcome the deep corrective to recent scholarship that his stress on the pietist side of Wesley presents to the discerning reader.

Readers need to know immediately that this book is beautifully written. When I first read a research paper from Gwang-Seok Oh, it was so felicitous in expression that I could not believe that English was not his mother tongue. Truth be told, it was so good that I was tempted to think that he could not have written it all by himself. There was no need to disconfirm my suspicion, however, for it was obvious that he wrote with ease and precision without outside help. No doubt his success in this regard was in part derived from his ready love of Wesley and his native ability to enter into Wesley's world. His background in Korean Christianity and his own spiritual pilgrimage fitted him aptly to capture the pietist side of Wesley. In addition he rightly senses that while the ethos and practices of pietism throw light on Wesley, Wesley has much to offer the current recovery of nerve among today's pietists, even if they now fly under very different names and banners.

This is a work in historical theology, so the latter, constructive element necessarily must lie latent. It is crucial to take the time and effort to get the record as straight as we can historically. History is not a wax nose that we can twist to fit our own passions and interests, if we are serious scholars. We all work out of our deepest convictions; but our convictions cannot stand proxy for the canons of evidence and persuasion. The psychology of discovery should not be confused with the logic of evidence and confirmation. I stress this platitude because it is readily scorned in our day. Gwang-Seok Oh has made a thoroughly credible case for his account of the sources and contours of Wesley's ecclesiology. His central claims are clear; they are supported by extensive research; and they deserve to be heard and pondered with care. This historical work is primary here; and it is well done. This work is vital because we can only learn from Wesley, including Wesley the pietist, if we first allow him to speak and act for himself in his own time and place without our whispering what we want to hear in his ear.

The arresting point that strikes me as immediately relevant to our current scene is the tension between Wesley the High-Church Anglican and Wesley the pragmatic, Spirit-led Pietist. Current ecumenical conversations remain bedeviled by the difficulties that gather around these poles. The arrival of evangelicals and Pentecostals on the international and ecumenical scene simply reiterates the long-standing challenge that ran right through the soul of Wesley. Wesley resolved the tension as best he could in his day. His ordinations were an expression of both the catholic and pietist poles of his thinking. He ordained because he believed in catholic institutions and practices; and he ordained because he was convinced that the Spirit was at work in his movement. The more general problem that surrounds this tension is obvious. On the one hand, there is no church without the vibrant life of the Spirit; on the other hand, there is only chaos if there are no institutions to contain and pass on the treasures of the Spirit. Yet pietists, rightly stressing the work of the Spirit, constantly find themselves drifting outside the institutions of the church catholic. They then turn around and immediately invent the functionally equivalent institutions that they resist, or skirt, or leave behind. Sooner or later we will have to find a way to stop this merry-go-round. The key to any lasting resolution has to be the work of the Holy Spirit; surely both sides of this conundrum can sign on to this suggestion. Yet we do not know how to get beyond it as yet. At this point we must stiffen our resolve towards catholic unity, keep our heads, get on our knees, and trust God to do the impossible, that is, to join catholic institutional substance to pietist energy and ingenuity. Gwang-Seok Oh clearly will not allow us to lose the latter. Reading this fine work can help us stay the course in this difficult journey towards the former.

William J. Abraham
Albert Cook Outler Professor of Wesley Studies
Altshuler Distinguished Teaching Professor
Perkins School of Theology, Southern Methodist University

Acknowledgments

Words of gratitude must be expressed to a number of persons who have assisted and encouraged me during this study. Naming all is impossible, but I would like to express special thanks to some of them.

This book is a revision of my doctoral dissertation at Southern Methodist University. I must express my gratitude to Professor William Abraham who was my academic advisor during the doctoral program and encouraged me to publish this work. He was the officiator of my marriage. I am also grateful to other members of my dissertation committee, Professor Bruce Marshall and Dr. Scott Jones. Their constructive criticism and suggestions were very helpful in the revision of this work. Special indebtedness is owed to Professor Richard Heitzenrater of Duke University who gave me the benefits of an unparalleled knowledge of Wesley and the use of special collections of Duke University Library during the "Wesley Summer Seminar." He meticulously read the drafts of selected chapters at the early stage of this study, offering many insightful suggestions. He also provided several historical corrections at the final stage of this work. I must extend grateful appreciation to Dr. William Babcock and Dr. James Kirby who took time from a busy schedule to offer many helpful suggestions. Special thanks also go to Mr. Page Thomas of the Bridwell Library of Southern Methodist University who helped with searching several important materials needed for this study and provided helpful information of the reliability of the materials. Professor Dorothea Wendebourg of Humboldt-Universität zu Berlin also helped with using the theological school library at the final stage of this work. I express my gratitude to Dr. J.

Steven O'Malley, the editor of the Pietist and Wesleyan Studies series, and Ms. April Snider of Scarecrow Press who have worked for the publication of this work.

I owe to my family the personal debts which I cannot repay. My parents and sister have provided constant encouragement, sacrificial love, and unceasing prayer throughout my educational journey. Finally, to my wife Sayako and my daughter Hannah, I acknowledge my deep indebtedness and gratitude for their love and patience, without which I could not have completed this work.

Introduction

The aim of this study is to clarify and identify the sources, nature, and development of John Wesley's ecclesiology. By doing so, the present study seeks to contribute to the understanding of Wesley's ecclesiology. Wesley's ecclesiology is here understood broadly to include his understanding of the church, the ministry, and the sacraments. Although questions concerning the contemporary relevance of Wesley's ecclesiology are important, the concern of this study is to examine possible historical sources for Wesley's ecclesiology and his development under the influences of the sources. More precisely speaking, this study focuses on a historical study more than on a systematic one. It means that this study does not stress the systematic framework of Wesley's ecclesiology but tries to be more faithful to providing the historical sources which assisted Wesley in shaping his ecclesiology and the works of Wesley himself in accord with the chronological development of his ecclesiology.

In light of the large number of studies in Wesley's life and theology, one may well ask, "why do we need this additional study?" Wesley was a significant figure in Christian history whose thought and movement have been remarkably influential not only upon Methodists but upon many other religious groups. The value of Wesley as an evangelist-revivalist, a practical theologian, and the founder of a denominational group on the church history has been largely appreciated by a number of Wesleyan, and even non-Wesleyan, scholars. The significance of Wesley in the Christian tradition cannot be overstated. However, surprisingly, there have been not many studies which comprehensively trace and identify the sources of his ecclesiology in the Christian tradition, while his ecclesiology has been discussed in many interpretative works.[1] Of course scholars have given attention to the sources of Wesley's ecclesiology, investigating his use of materials from patristic, Roman Catholic, Anglican, Puritan, and Pietist sources,[2] but most of the studies have been one-sided historical presentations, whether in Roman Catholicism, Anglicanism, Puritanism, Pietism, or any other tradition. For example, the perhaps most popular description of the root of Wesley's ecclesiology has been to trace the sources of his doctrine in the Church of England. It culminated in the landmark study of Frank Baker, *John Wesley and the Church of England* (1970),[3] which has been the authoritative work on the relation of Wesley to the Church of England. In this work Baker provided an admirably lucid and detailed study of the source and development of Wesley's ecclesiology in relation to the Church of England. But he did not explain the sources and development of Wesley's ecclesiology in a more comprehensive setting. Although it is true that the Church of England was the initial and lifelong, and perhaps greatest, influence upon Wesley, the exposition of Wesley's ecclesiology, if it ends at this point, is one-sided presentation and does not really explore the depth and width of his doctrine. In formulating his ecclesiology, Wesley took multiple traditions which he inherited and sought to appropriate in a creative eclecticism. As Albert Outler suggested, "Wesley must be read in light of his sources—and therefore within the larger ecumenical perspectives of historic Christianity."[4] This fact stands as a relevant reason for a further work to investigate his ecclesiology in a more comprehensive setting. Moreover, while this work is largely a study in the past, it is hoped that Wesley's ecclesiology may, if recovered and reinterpreted, lend identity and direction to the Wesleyan movements today.

Many interpretative works have attempted to rediscover Wesley's ecclesiology and apply his principles and forms to modern expressions of the church. However, the multifaceted Wesley and the complexity of the situation surrounding the origins of Methodism provide warrant for any number of divergent perspectives on the church. Those who see the life of church in the spiritual dynamic of small groups may point to the class meeting and the loose organization of Wesley's Methodist societies for their model of the church. Those who have more institutional and ecumenical concerns may stress Wesley's life-long allegiance to the Church of England and view him as the champion of conciliation and reform from *within* the ecclesiastical structures. Some may point to Wesley's conservative policies regarding the administration of sacraments and use of liturgical forms in their criticism of the free style of worship in many contemporary churches. Others may stress Wesley's willingness to discard the practices of the established church for the flexibility of field preaching and extemporaneous prayers and trace Wesley's heritage in relation to the free church tradition. It would appear that the eclectic nature of Wesley's thought and actions creates the same problem for ecclesiology that also annoys those who endeavor to find some hermeneutical key for his systematic theology.

Wesley did not originally intend to start any sect or church, but to revitalize the established church. Yet he touched off dynamics which resulted in the formation of a separate denominational family. Although the constitution of the Methodists into an independent and autonomous church in England did not take place during his lifetime, Wesley himself eventually did all that was necessary to prepare the way for the separation. In regard to the Methodist Church, Wesley was definitely and unmistakably its architect and its builder. The following questions, then, are raised: What caused Wesley to develop his own interpretation of church? What were the major traditions and sources that shaped his ecclesiology? How did he develop his ecclesiology throughout his life under the influences of the sources? What elements were important for his ecclesiology? What, indeed, was Wesley's ecclesiology? Answering these questions is the purpose of this study.

As a piece of historical research, this study surveys the major traditions or sources of Wesley's ecclesiology. Wesley's concept of church is best understood in light of the sources and background which contributed to his own theological formation, and in light of the events which he faced in the course of his endeavors in the Methodist Revival. Therefore, this study begins its task by examining the possible sources for Wesley's doctrine of the church (Part One) and then moves to the investigation of the development of his ecclesiology in the course of ministry (Part Two). In doing so, this study researches ample primary records: the large number of Wesley's sermons, his journals and pastoral letters, his *Explanatory Notes Upon the New Testament*, the hymnbook, the apologiae for Methodism, the *Minutes* of his conferences, his controversial pamphlets, the brief articles published in his *Arminian Magazine*, and even such tracts and treatises consisting of extracts selected by Wesley from other authorities. The primary sources of the traditions that influenced Wesley are also researched for this study.

This work consists of two parts, each comprising three chapters, and a concluding chapter. Part One investigates the Christian traditions that influenced Wesley's ecclesiology. It does not give any survey of the traditions, but rather it focuses on certain elements in the traditions where we can establish a direct influence on Wesley. Chapter 1 of Part One deals with the traditions of primitive church and medieval Catholicism. This chapter introduces two very different cases: on the one hand, primitive Christianity that was a central influence on and ideal for Wesley, and on the other, medieval Catholicism that shows no more than certain similarities to and no evidence of direct influence upon Wesley's ecclesiology but is useful for understanding of what Wesley's Methodism was like.

Chapter 2 outlines the influence of the reformation tradition upon Wesley's ecclesiology. It shows that although there is no evidence of the reformers' direct influence upon Wesley's ecclesiology, the reformation tradition had an impact on Wesley on the sense that they introduced certain themes—particularly sanctification and discipline—into ecclesiology indirectly through the traditions of the Church of England and the Puritans. Wesley maintained a unique combination of intense dedication to the Church of England and affinity with and sympathy for some aspects of Puritanism. The influence of the Protestant tradition upon Wesley is highlighted in the comparative study of Wesley and the Pietists (Chapter 3).

This study of Wesley's immediate theological heritage such as seventeenth and eighteenth century Anglicanism, Puritanism, and Pietism gives us a feeling for the theological climate into which he was born and raised. Particular attention is given to the catholicity of his sources and the eclecticism in his appropriation of traditional sources.

After investigating the question of possible historical sources, this work turns to the development of ecclesiology in Wesley himself (Part Two). This study presupposes a development in Wesley's ecclesiology. Through his entire life Wesley developed his ecclesiology in reaction to changing circumstances. Accordingly, we may not understand his doctrine of church without understanding his entire life. Hence the present study is developed according to the chronological distinctions: "early Wesley (1703–1738)," "middle Wesley (1738–1765)," and "late Wesley (1766–1791)." Part Two is divided accordingly: "Ecclesiology of the Early Wesley (Chapter 4)," "Ecclesiology of the Middle Wesley (Chapter 5)," and "Ecclesiology of the Late Wesley (Chapter 6)." The purpose of this Part Two is to trace the various elements in Wesley's understanding of the church, the ministry and the sacraments throughout his lifetime and to examine their shifts under the influences of the sources and circumstances he met through his life.

Chapter 4 investigates the early Wesley in Epworth, Oxford, and Georgia who was a High Churchman[5] in the Church of England equipped with a formal ecclesiology. It explores the family background and literary influences he received, and examines the way theological traditions shaped his views of ministry and sacraments.

Chapter 5 deals with the middle Wesley after Aldersgate. It shows how he developed a more pragmatic and functional understanding of ecclesiology to meet the needs of the developing Methodist movement, while it also presents the insoluble tensions between his practical view of ministry after

Aldersgate and his lasting, high-church sacramentalism. In doing so, it also examines some evangelical and simultaneously institutional features of Wesley's view of the sacraments.

Chapter 6 explores the later Wesley. Since Wesley after Aldersgate continued to develop his pragmatic ecclesiology, the middle Wesley and the later Wesley did not differ much in his understanding of the church, the ministry, and the sacraments. Accordingly, this chapter scrutinizes some important issues which arose in the later period of his ministry, that is, the crucial actions and steps Wesley took for Methodism "by necessity" such as his approval of female preaching and his ordinations. It shows that Wesley eventually established a complete ministry and therefore paved a way for the establishment of Methodist Church. It also notes that as far as sacraments are concerned, Wesley maintained his sacerdotal position up till his last days.

Within the framework of these chronological distinctions of Wesley's life and theology, this work examines his doctrine of church as a whole in relation to the concept of salvation, since soteriology took the central place in his understanding of church. Wesley established his understanding of nature and function of the church in relation to the saving work of Christ, and, accordingly, Part Two proposes the development of this evangelical ecclesiology in Wesley's life and ministry. It demonstrates that Wesley, with his highly developed sense of mission, shaped and developed his evangelical, functional understanding of church, responding to the spiritual needs of the people he sought to serve.

In the final chapter, all the analyzed aspects of Wesley's ecclesiology come to synthetic summary statements. A final assessment is made concerning Wesley's place in the Christian tradition on this crucial doctrine.

Notes

1. For the notable interpretative works of Wesley's ecclesiology, see Colin W. Williams, *John Wesley's Theology Today* (New York: Abingdon Press, 1960), 141–166; Reginald Kissack, *Church or No Church? A Study of the Development of the Concept of Church in British Methodism* (London: Epworth Press, 1964); Geoffrey Wainwright, "Methodism's Ecclesial Location and Ecumenical Vocation," *One in Christ* 19. no. 2 (1983): 104–134; Clarence Bence, "Salvation and the Church: The Ecclesiology of John Wesley," in *The Church: An Inquiry into Ecclesiology from a Biblical Theological Perspective*, ed. Melvin E. Dieter and Daniel N. Berg (Anderson, Ind.: Warner Press, 1984), 297–317; Daniel N. Berg, "The Marks of the Church in the Theology of John Wesley," in *The Church: An Inquiry into Ecclesiology from a Biblical Theological Perspective*, 319–331; David L. Cubie, "Separa-

tion or Unity? Sanctification and Love in Wesley's Doctrine of the Church," in *The Church: An Inquiry into Ecclesiology from a Biblical Theological Perspective*, 333–395; Albert C. Outler, "Do Methodists Have a Doctrine of the Church?" in *The Wesleyan Theological Heritage: Essays of Albert C. Outler*, eds. Thomas C. Oden and Leicester R. Longden (Grand Rapids: Zondervan, 1991), 211–226; Howard A. Snyder, *The Radical Wesley and Patterns for Church Renewal* (Eugene, Or.: Wipf and Stock Publishers, 1996).

2. For the notable works which deal with the sources of Wesley's ecclesiology, see Arthur W. Nagler, *Pietism and Methodism, or The Significance of German Pietism in the Origin and Early Development of Methodism* (Nashville: M. E. Church, South, Publishing House, 1918); Herbert B. Workman, *The Place of Methodism in the Catholic Church* (London: Epworth Press, 1921); John Bishop, *Methodist Worship in Relation to Free Church Worship* (London: Epworth Press, 1950) and an enlarged and revised edition in 1975; Clifford W. Towlson, *Moravian and Methodist: Relationships and Influences in the Eighteenth Century* (London, Epworth Press, 1957); John M. Todd, *John Wesley and the Catholic Church* (London: Hodder and Stoughton, 1958); John A. Newton, *Methodism and the Puritans* (London: Friends of Dr. Williams's Library, 1964); Frank Baker, *John Wesley and the Church of England*, (London: Epworth Press, 1970); Robert C. Monk, *John Wesley: His Puritan Heritage* (Nashville: Abingdon Press, 1966) and the second edition in 1999; F. Ernest Stoeffler, "Tradition and Renewal in the Ecclesiology of John Wesley," in *Traditio, Krisis, Renovatio aus Theologischer Sicht: Festshrift Winfried Zeller zum 65. Geburtstag* (Marburg: Elwert, 1976), 298–316; Luke L. Keefer, Jr., *John Wesley: Disciple of Early Christianity*, 2 vols. (Ann Arbor: University Microfilms International, 1981); Howard A. Snyder, *Pietism, Moravianism, and Methodism as Renewal Movements: A Comparative and Thematic Study*, Ph. D. dissertation (Notre Dame University, 1983); Henry D. Rack, "Religious Societies and the Origins of Methodism," *Journal of Ecclesiastical History* 38 (1987): 582–595; Ted A. Campbell, *John Wesley and Christian Antiquity: Religious Vision and Cultural Change* (Nashville: Abingdon, 1991).

3. The second edition of this book was published with the preface by John A. Vickers in 2000.

4. Albert C. Outler, "A New Future for Wesley Studies: An Agenda for 'Phase III,'" in *The Wesleyan Theological Heritage: Essays of Albert C. Outler*, 138.

5. Elastic in meaning, the term "High Church" may today be used in speaking of viewpoints within a number of denominations of Christianity in general, but it is has traditionally been employed in Churches associated with the Anglican tradition in particular. In this work the term is used to imply a general emphasis upon the authority of the church and of its ordained ministers and upon the importance of the sacraments and the other historic rituals and ordinances of the church.

Part One

The Sources of Wesley's Ecclesiology

History is, in a sense, interpreted as a reading of continuities in the received traditions at any given stage. Historical emergents, if carefully analyzed, are seen to be seldom sudden in their development and never totally new.[1] John Wesley is a major figure within that history. In Wesley's reading of the traditions, one can find a demonstrable continuity from the primitive to the contemporary church. The extent of Wesley's familiarity with Christian traditions and contemporary Christian sources is amply demonstrated by the many appeals to and disputations with those sources throughout his writings. Albert Outler noted that "Wesley was a man of tradition," as well as a man of one book [Scripture].[2] In a sense, understanding Wesley entails understanding the whole of the Christian tradition before and in his age. Wesley's readings in Christian traditions, from his own recorded bibliography, included more than 1400 different authors and nearly 3000 separate items from them (ranging from pamphlets to twelve-volume sets). In his printed sermons alone, more than 2500 quotations and allusions have been listed.[3]

Wesley derived his theological heritage from a variety of sources. The major sources of Wesley's ecclesiology were Scripture, the tradition of the primitive church mediated mainly through Anglicanism, and the Protestant tradition mediated mainly through Anglicanism, Puritanism and Pietism. There were, of course, other tributary streams of influence such as Catholicism mediated through Anglicanism. His views on the church were essentially close to those of Anglicanism of seventeenth and eighteenth centuries, but were more catholic and conformed to the church understanding of "the Christian fellowship of believers."

A chronological investigation from the influence of primitivism to the impact of the Pietists has the merit of disclosing development. This study does not attempt to offer any comprehensive survey of the ecclesiologies of the concerned traditions. It, in fact, does not aim at an adequate survey of any of the traditions. It focuses on those elements which can be seen to have directly influenced Wesley in the traditions, searching specific evidence in Wesley's writings.

Primitivism offered a lasting influence on and a continuing model for Wesley's ecclesiology. A strand of primitivism runs through many Christian traditions that influenced Wesley. Wesley strove to revive the primitive spirit of Christianity throughout his life. His primitivism was comprehensive, bringing *together* elements of the early Church that are generally *separated* into the Catholic and Evangelical traditions: the origin of continuity and the model and standard for newness. This amalgamation explains why no traditional label adequately describes his theology; his primitivism was truly ecumenical. Wesley believed that anyone undertaking the task of Christian proclamation should have a working acquaintance with the sources of primitive Christianity. It was to this end that he designed to equip the preachers in the Methodist Connection with a copy of *A Christian Library* (1749–1755), a fifty volume compilation and abridgement of what he felt comprised "the best of divinity" from the beginnings of the church to his own point in time. Indeed, the scope of authors included in these volumes and in references found in his journal and correspondence invites the contemporary Christians to hear his version of the "faith once delivered unto the saints" with eager anticipation.

Medieval Catholicism influenced Wesley through the mystics and indirectly through the Church of England. Special attention must be given to some similarities between the Tertiaries of medieval Catholicism and Methodism. Some of the major issues raised by Luther, Bucer, and Calvin, with an emphasis on discipline, must be dealt with because of their influence upon the Church of England, Puritanism, and Pietism, which became the important sources from which Wesley shaped his doctrine of church. The Church of England was the initial influence upon Wesley, and it made a lasting contribution to his theology. However, it was overshadowed after 1738 by the combined influence of Pietism and Puritanism. Pietism influenced Wesley's soteriology and the creation and development of Methodist Church organization, while Puritanism was a main contributor to Wesley's unorthodox churchmanship after he became a field preacher in 1739.

Notes

1. This interpretation is from F. Ernest Stoeffler, "Tradition and Renewal in the Ecclesiology of John Wesley," 298–316.

2. Albert C. Outler, "John Wesley's Interests in the Early Fathers of the Church," in *The Wesleyan Theological Heritage: Essays of Albert C. Outler*, 109.

3. Albert C. Outler, "John Wesley: Folk Theologian," in *The Wesleyan Theological Heritage: Essays of Albert C. Outler*, 114.

Chapter 1

Primitivism and Catholicism

The Primitive Church and Wesley

Although it might seem desirable to begin our discussion with the Bible's influence upon Wesley, this work does not include a chapter on the Scriptures. This omission doesn't mean that this work denies the importance of the Scriptures for Wesley's ecclesiology. On the contrary, it rather affirms that the research on the relationship between the Bible, particularly the New Testament, and Wesley is so crucial that it requires separate and special consideration. Also, there is a further reason that this study does not deal with the ecclesiologies of the Scriptures and Wesley in a separate chapter. Wesley often loosely referred to the primitive church to mean the church of the Bible, in this case the church of the New Testament. Accordingly, when we deal with the primitive church and Wesley, it in some measure covers the New Testament issue for Wesley.

In the history of the church, there have always been both a quest for the true church and a call for personal and communal reform and renewal. Most frequently the predominant model for this reform and renewal was the *ecclesia primitiva*, an idealized picture of the primitive Christian community, which was most commonly portrayed as a composite of the simple life and teachings of Jesus and his disciples, the allegedly unadulterated gospel of the apostles, and the unselfish common life of the earliest Christians. The notion of the *ecclesia primitiva* in the church history has most frequently referred to the apostolic church as portrayed in such New Testament passages as Acts 4:32ff, but has sometimes been extended to cover either the pre-Constantinian church or the whole patristic period up to the age of

5

Gregory the Great. When the *ecclesia primitiva* was used to cover the pre-
Constantinian church, the idea often suggested that the great divide in the
early church history had been the reign of the first Christian Emperor, Constantine. John Wesley often followed this idea.

The first known use of the term *ecclesia primitiva* dates at least from
the fifth century. The writings of John Cassian (365–435), *The Institutes*
and *The Conferences*, which were important in many ways in the development of Western monasticism, contain the references to the idea of the
primitive church.[1] In particular Cassian, in the *Institutes*, II, 5, actually used
the term *ecclesia primitiva*.[2] Cassian used the idea of the primitive church
as a model by which to form and reform the monastic life of his own day.
Later in the Middle Ages, the model of the *ecclesia primitiva*, particularly
the community of shared material goods, served as the most important basis
for monasticism which in the West became a major vehicle for the Christian
idea of reform.[3]

Furthermore, reform on the model of the primitive church was a primary motive for dissent in the early Middle Ages. It is illustrated in Jeffrey
B. Russell's *Dissent and Reform in the Early Middle Ages*. In his book Russell classifies a variety of types of dissent in the early Middle Ages (c.700 –
c.1150): Reformists, whose enthusiasm for the reform of the Church led
them to extremes; Eccentrics, whose odd and peculiar doctrines took them
far from orthodox traditions; Catharists, who defended doctrines that the
Church had long before condemned; Reactionaries, who were overeager in
their devotion to the past and refused to go along with the development of
newer Christian doctrine and practice; Intellectuals, whose deviations were
philosophical; Reverse heretics, who attacked the authority of the pope and
leveled accusations of heresy against the apostolic see itself. These dissenters, according to Russell, took the primitive church as their model for reform, while they were different in interpreting the ideas and practice of the
primitive church.[4]

The key role played by the *ecclesia primitiva* in religious movements of
dissent in the Middle Ages was most emphatically presented by Herbert
Grundmann. In his *Religiöse Bewegungen im Mittelalter*, Grundmann
wrote,

> In Cologne as well as in Southern France, the idea of Christian poverty
> and apostolic life as a wandering preacher is essential to their stance as
> "heresy," and this idea indeed remains the main theme of heresy until the
> start of the thirteenth century, among Cathars as well as Waldensians.
> Leading the life of the apostles, being true followers of the apostles, is the
> heretics' basic claim, and their break with the Church followed from that.
> . . . No impartial observer can doubt their genuine and passionate convic-

tion that they were reviving and realizing true evangelical and apostolic Christianity in their lives. . . . The first condition for understanding the religious movements of the Middle Ages is to take these convictions and claims seriously.[5]

The dissenters saw the Roman Church as failing in living up to the standards of simplicity and poverty set by the ideal picture of the primitive church. As the Roman hierarchy became more and more unwilling and unable to fulfill the demands for reform imposed by dissenters, it excluded them from the church, labeled them heretical, and sought to repress them by means of the Inquisition. Without delay, these dissenters began to take persecution as one of the essential criteria for claiming equality with the primitive church.

Primitivism, however, was not uniformly rejected, or regarded as heretical, by the medieval Catholic Church. In the Church, there has been always reverence for the primitive church. One may find occasional references to the idea of the *ecclesia primitiva* in Merovingian documents. For example, Bede (c.672–735) in his *The Ecclesiastical History of the English Nation* used several passages which refer to the *ecclesia primitiva*.[6] The perhaps best known passage of them is that from one of the famous responses by Pope Gregory I to the queries by the missionary to the English, St. Augustine of Canterbury, as to how the English Church was to be governed. Here to Augustine's question of "how the bishop is to act in the church," Gregory answers that Augustine must follow the model of the primitive church and practice the common life with their regular clergy.[7] Also, during the Carolingian period, the idea of the *ecclesia primitiva* remained and was used primarily to signify the ideals of the common and apostolic life. The idea was current, especially among those groups interested in the reform of monastic and canonical life. For example, in the *Collectio Isidori Mercatoris* (the so-called Pseudo-Isidorian Decretals), the first manuscript of which dates from the second quarter of the ninth century, the *ecclesia primitiva* was associated with the practice of the common life.[8] Here Isidore Mercator entitled the letter which described the common life of the primitive church "De primitiva ecclesia et sindo nicena," and stated that all succeeding canonists who would use this work would find the idea of the primitive church associated with the practice of the common life.[9] The use of the term *ecclesia primitiva* is seldom found in the tenth-century documents but the idea remained and was widely revived in the middle of the eleventh century and later on was used to promote the ideal of monastic and canonical reform. In most cases, the idea remained associated primarily with the ideal of the common life. As persons searched for right order in both political and personal life, the idea was also associated with

the search for the most perfect form of the Christian life. The idea of the
primitive church further became so common by the middle of the twelfth
century that sometimes it was simply used to refer to the institutions believed to have existed in the early church, very occasionally implying that
in the early church Christianity had not achieved the fullness of its development. For example, in the writings of the canonists of the second half of
the twelfth century, the term *ecclesia primitiva* was so frequently used that
it sometimes lost its special association with reform, the search for Christian perfection, and the practice of the common life, and became simply the
label to describe anything which was thought to have existed in the first age
of the church.[10] However, the idea of the *ecclesia primitiva*, during the
eleventh and twelfth centuries, was most commonly associated with the
following of the apostolic life and the practice of evangelical poverty and
common life. In the first part of the thirteenth century, primitivism gained
official acceptance within the Catholic Church, most notably with the Franciscans.

As the Catholic Church developed the idea of the apostolic succession,
it might well be expected that the primitive church came to gain a more
attention in the Catholic Church, for the apostolic succession cannot be asserted without reference to the validity and authority of the Christian ministry which is derived from the primitive church, more precisely from the
apostles. With the growth of the emphasis on the primacy of the papacy in
the eleventh century, the idea of the papal plenitude of power was often
associated with the primitive church, and later the "Roman Church" and the
"Apostolic Church" began to be used sometimes as interchangeable terms.[11]
Among many Catholics the primitive church has been reverenced as the
first stage in an unbroken tradition of Christian belief and practice.

Although movements within Protestantism distanced themselves from
their Roman Catholic roots, the ideal of the primitive church continued to
be used as a criterion of reform within Protestantism. Appeals to the primitive church as a standard for ecclesiastical life and doctrine have a long
history within Protestantism. Early in the era of the Reformation, Huldreich
Zwingli (1484–1531), the Anabaptists, Heinrich Bullinger (1504–1575),
Martin Bucer (1491–1551), and John Calvin (1509–1564) looked to the
New Testament to restore the primitive Christian faith, taking antiquity as
their standard against the aberrations they were convinced lived in the
church of their day.[12] Even prior to this, the Paulicians, Bogomils,
Waldenses, Lollards, the Unity of the Brethren, and the Christian humanists
had attempted their own versions of restoring the piety of the church, based
on the example of the primitive church. John Wyclif (1328–1384), John
Hus (1373–1415), Erasmus of Rotterdam (1466–1536), and Jacques Lefèvre

d'Etaples (1450–1536) were all attempting in their respective eras and lo-
cales to initiate reform using more or less the ancient precepts and practices
of the early church. Their perceptions of primitive Christianity, ascertained
from the Scriptures, acted in each case as a foundational standard for reform.[13]

Impulses toward restoring the primitive church and seeking a standard
for faith and practice in primitive Christianity were notably present in England during and shortly following the Reformation.[14] During the reign of
Edward VI (1547–1553), Protestant influence, especially from Reformed
sources, infiltrated the Church of England through reformers such as Thomas Cranmer (1489–1556), Nicholas Ridley (1503–1555), and Martin
Bucer, and these precursors of the Elizabethan Settlement, in a sense,
caused a first wave of English primitivistic concern.[15] Primitivism, then,
cannot be entirely separated from the roots of the established Church of
England, despite Anglican tendencies to accentuate its links with Catholic
traditionalism, and despite a penchant on the part of historians to link English appeals to primitive Christianity with the later and better defined Puritan movement.[16] Certainly an interest in following primitive precedents can
be traced in the Elizabethan Settlement and later Anglicanism. In England
in the late-seventeenth and eighteenth centuries (the so-called "Augustan
England"), following the restoration of the Stuarts to the throne in 1660 (in
the person of Charles II), and following the Act of Uniformity in 1662,
there existed a considerable concern on the part of many Anglicans for the
Christianity of antiquity.[17] The expressions "primitive church," "primitive
Christian faith," "primitive Christianity," and "ancient church," were typically used by Anglican restorationists to refer to the characteristics of the
historic church in its various settings as described in the New Testament or
the church of antiquity up through the fourth century. All the expressions
were used to portray primitive Christianity as a perceived "golden age" of
the church, an early time when the church was free from the human accretions which distorted in various ways its doctrine and practice.

A concern for primitive Christianity was also present among the earliest Methodists in eighteenth-century England, and this was particularly so
of John Wesley himself. There is widespread agreement among Wesley
scholars that he had a strong interest in the early church and that this so-
called "primitivism" influenced his theology and practice and offered him a
standard by which to measure the faith and practice of Christians in every
age, at least during certain periods of his life.[18]

In his early days Wesley seems to have contemplated the model of the
ecclesia primitiva, particularly the primitive community of goods, as in
some sense an attainable ideal. For example, the fraternity among the Ox-

ford Methodists, living on a bare minimum, distributing their surplus to the poor, giving and taking among themselves with spontaneity, pointed toward the ideal of the *ecclesia primitiva*, and through the fraternity Wesley seems to have found that the primitive example was one which could be proximately implemented by a Christian community, at least in its smaller groupings. Later, reflecting on the corporate life of the Oxford Methodists, Wesley noted in his sermon: "As to that practice of the apostolic church (which continued till the time of Tertullian, at least in many churches) the 'having all things in common', they [the Oxford Methodists] had no rule, nor any formed design concerning it. But it was so, in effect, and it could not be otherwise; for none could want anything that another could spare."[19] Wesley seems to have seen the primitive community of goods as retaining a prescriptive authority for Christians of all ages. The ideal of primitive communalism later became a rule for Wesley's 'Select Societies': "Every member, till we can all have all things common, will bring once a week, *bona fide*, all he can spare toward a common stock."[20]

Ted A. Campbell sorts out Wesley's uses of Christian antiquity into three groups: polemical, conservative, and programmatic.[21] Richard P. Heitzenrater adds two more: aphoristic and name-dropping.[22] On several occasions, Wesley in a polemical manner used Christian antiquity in order to refute his opponents or contradict an argument. Such an example is shown in his reply to Conyers Middleton or the *Roman Catechism*. He also cited Augustine of Hippo (354–430) and John Chrysostom (347–407) in order to refute the doctrine of predestination. Sometimes Wesley in a conservative or apologetic manner utilized early church material in order to defend certain doctrines, structures, and practices of the Church of England. For example, he defended the Church of England's affirmation of the Nicene doctrine of the Trinity against the challenges of Neo-Arianism, Socinianism, and Deism. Similarly, he defended, at least until the 1740s, the practice of Anglican episcopacy by appeal to patristic precedents and defended the Anglican practices he believed to be consistent with the practices of early Church. Frequently Wesley in a programmatic manner referred to the early Fathers in order to restore ancient beliefs or practices that he considered desirable for the church of his own time, such as "the need to experience persecution as a mark of one's Christian calling," stationary fasts, visitations of the sick, or penitential practices. Also, by reference to "the ancient Christians," he justified some of the distinctive practices of early Methodism such as the watch-night service, class tickets, and the love-feast.[23] On many occasions, Wesley simply name-dropped a person or a group of the early Fathers who agree with him on some particular idea, or listed the Fathers whom he thinks people should read. He quite often used the Fathers' words as proverbial aphorisms, at times quoting them inaccurately or misattributing them.

Clearly Wesley's works reveal that he read Ignatius of Antioch (born around 50; died between 98 and 117), Clement of Rome (c.80 – c.140), Polycarp (69–155), Justin Martyr (c.100 – c.165), Clement of Alexandria (c.150 – c.215), Tertullian (c.160–225), Origen (185–232), Cyprian of Carthage (martyred in 258), Ephraem Syrus (c.306–373), Basil of Caesarea (329–379), John Chrysostom, Jerome (c.340–420), Augustine of Hippo, Pseudo-Macarius, and so on. In Wesley's works, according to Campbell, there are two hundred one references to the ancient Christian works,[24] some of which quote from specific writings, some giving no more than a passing reference by name. Therefore, "[o]ne certainly cannot dismiss the influence of the early church in his life and thought—it is evident in the shape of his theology and the details of his program."[25]

However, formidable methodological problems arise with attempts to show "how early Christian doctrines and church practices were passed down through the tradition" across fourteen to sixteen centuries "to Wesley, and so influenced him."[26] As Campbell points out,

> The demonstration of specific influences of early Christian beliefs or practices on Wesley . . . requires far more than simple comparisons between early Christian writers and his writings: it requires a systematic consideration of all the likely sources for such an influence.
>
> Even when specific influences of early Christian beliefs or practices on John Wesley can be demonstrated. . . . conclusions about Wesley's own understanding of ancient Christianity, or about Wesley's own uses of ancient traditions, do not always follow, because so many ancient Christian ideas and practices came to Wesley in mediated, or indirect, fashion.[27]

Certainly, a great deal of study needs to be done on the specific channels by which the thoughts of early church Fathers were transmitted to John Wesley.[28]

In addition, as Heitzenrater puts it, the strength of Wesley's reliance on primitivism cannot be measured adequately by his quotations from or references to the works of the early church Fathers. Most of the references are very early (between 1726 and 1737) in his letters, journal, and diaries. According to Heitzenrater, the "available data concerning Wesley's references to reading the Fathers . . . reveal a relatively slim bibliography, both in actual numbers and in relative proportion to his vast reading bibliography."[29] Wesley cited them from time to time, especially to support his own doctrinal views.

Wesley's notions of early Christianity were sometimes incorrect. For example, he thought of the "Spiritual Homilies" as actually being the work of the fourth-century Egyptian monk Macarius,[30] and throughout much of his early career he held an exaggerated view of the unity and the holiness of the ancient church.

Campbell and Heitzenrater are right to point scholarship to an exploration of the channels through which the influences of the early church Fathers were transmitted to Wesley. Nevertheless, there are many proofs of the emphasis on primitive Christianity that was present among the early Wesleyan Methodists, particularly John Wesley. We find the proofs in many places of Wesley's works. To give two examples in relation to ecclesiology, first, Wesley placed his brother Charles's hymn "Primitive Christianity" at the end of his "An Earnest Appeal to Men of Reason and Religion" (1743), which poetically expressed an idealized vision of church, revealing the ideas of what is likely to have occurred in primitive Christianity and what the church of the redeemed should look like.[31] He also accepted the account of a genuine Christianity in the *Stromateis* (or Miscellanies) of Clement of Alexandria and echoed it at some length in his treatise "The Character of a Methodist" (1742).[32] In doing so, he saw the continuity between the Methodism of his age and early Christianity. Wesley wanted to restore the nature and characteristics of the primitive church, including its teachings, practices, worship, and, to a lesser extent, its order.

Looking back over forty years of the Methodist Revival, Wesley defined Methodism as "the old religion, the religion of the Bible, the religion of the primitive church, the religion of Church of England."[33] Methodism is

the *religion of the primitive church*, of the whole church in the purest ages. It is clearly expressed even in the small remains of Clemens Romanus, Ignatius, and Polycarp. It is seen more at large in the writings of Tertullian, Origen, Clemens Alexandrinus, and Cyprian. And even in the fourth century it was found in the works of Chrysostom, Basil, Ephrem Syrus, and Macarius. It would be easy to produce a cloud of witnesses testifying the same thing, were not this a point which no one will contest who has the least acquaintance with Christian antiquity.[34]

Martin Schmidt, one of the premier Wesleyan biographers, says,

attachment to primitive Christianity, which John Wesley affirmed with ever-increasing emphasis determined his course. . . . The key to John Wesley's spiritual development is to be found in this living involvement in primitive Christianity.[35]

To his mind, the pristine Christianity of the apostles supplied man's every need. All his zeal was devoted to this. He was utterly convinced that primitive Christianity could be restored in his own day and age, and in every generation. . . . Restoration of the primitive Christian stance in its totality was always his guiding principle; never for a single moment did he diverge from this.[36]

Schmidt's opinion is supported with numerous examples from Wesley's works though they are not in many cases overt references to the term "primitive Christianity." In addressing the subject, Wesley typically referred to "real Christianity" or "scriptural Christianity" and these terms are usually used to appeal to Scripture and to ancient practice.[37]

At this point, there remains one question yet to be answered: What did Wesley mean by the primitive church? Wesley didn't use the term with a fixed meaning. First, as Luke L. Keefer, Jr. puts it, Wesley changed his definition of the primitive church as time went along.[38] Content in his Oxford days to extend the limits of the primitive church through the first five or six centuries of the Christian era, he was later to fix its terminus at Constantine's christianization of the empire. Second, Wesley uses a wide range of expressions to cover the first centuries of the church. Among these are the primitive church or primitive Christianity, the apostolic age, the first ages of the church, the early Christians, scriptural Christianity, old Christianity, and ancient Christianity. These are used loosely to refer to the early Christians, but they do not mean precisely the same thing. Some have a narrow frame of reference, meaning only the first century. Others can be quite elastic and stretch forward for several centuries of Christian history. Thus one must decide upon a standard frame of reference for the "primitive church." Among Wesley scholars there seems to be an agreement that for Wesley the primitive church typically includes the New Testament era through the first three centuries though Wesley saw the pre-Constantinian church as progressively moving further and further away from its pristine purity.[39]

A good example of Wesley's concern for primitive Christianity is that as he worked with the Oxford Methodists in September 1733, he abridged William Wake's *Apostolic Fathers*.[40] Also, at Oxford he studied such works as William Cave's *Primitive Christianity* and Anthony Horneck's *Letter to a Person of Quality concerning the Holy Lives of the Primitive Christians*,[41] which became his primary sourcebooks for patristic spirituality and played an important role in Wesley's intellectual formation. During these Oxford days Wesley earned the title "Mr. Primitive Christianity" among his friends.[42]

Wesley's concern for primitive Christianity is also found in his brief mission to Georgia in 1736–1737. He went to Georgia with the hope that there he could do evangelistic mission work in a context devoid of historical precedent and influences, save those of the earliest Christians. Schmidt says of the trip: "One way for Wesley to return to Primitive Christianity was for him to go to a pristine environment where there was no church. Mission to heathens with no background was viewed by him as parallel to the original church's circumstances."[43] Wesley took a copy of William Cave's *Primitive Christianity* with him to Georgia.

Wesley's interest in primitivism is further found in several places throughout his writings, such as his descriptions of the Wesleyan societies and his instructions regarding ecclesiastical practices and personal discipleship. For instance, in his early essay on the stationary fasts, he appeals to ancient precedent in defense of the fasts which became standard for the Oxford Methodists and the later societies.[44] Describing the validity of appeals to ecclesiastical antiquity for the practice of stationary fasts, Wesley says,

> That the Stations were instituted by the Apostles, is plainly deducible either from the Universality and Antiquity of their observance, or from the express testimony of the earliest writers. . . . The celebrated rule of S. Austin has never yet been controverted, *That which is held by the Universal Church, and was not instituted by Councils, but always was, is delivered down from the Apostles.* The same in sense is the golden rule of Vincentius Lirinensis (as it has been termed for many ages) That is Apostolical, *which has been observed by all men, in all places, at all times.* The reason is plain: Whatever has been at any time received in all parts of the Church Universal, must have been instituted, either by some General Council, or by the Apostles. But if it was so received from the Beginning, before any such Councils were held, then it could not be instituted by any of them, and consequently must be of Apostolical institution.—By all which it appears, that the stations have been observed in all places by all the members of the Church from the Beginning."[45]

Years later in writing his spiritual biography Wesley said, "[1732] I began observing the Wednesday and Friday fasts, commonly observed in the ancient church, tasting no food till three in the afternoon."[46] Wesley read two works on fasting in July 1733. In April 1733 he read Bishop William Beveridge (1637–1708)'s essay on fasting, which was published in Thomas Deacon's work in 1734. In December 1733 he collected Robert Nelson (1656–1715) on fasting, and in February 1734 wrote on fasting. Other examples in which Wesley applies the standards of primitive Christianity to the manner in which a Christian is to live are found in the journal entries for January 21, 1740; May 17, 1740; May 7, 1741; and February 17, 1744.[47]

Meanwhile, the Aldersgate experience influenced Wesley's primitivism. Luke L. Keefer, Jr. notes the significance of Aldersgate for Wesley's primitivism:

> Aldersgate . . . refocused Wesley's primitivism from ecclesiology to soteriology. The wedding of soteriology and primitivism is pervasive throughout the entire course of Wesley's subsequent writings. It is the general perspective in the doctrinal standards of Methodism: his *Standard Sermons* and the *Notes Upon the New Testament*. . . . In Wesley's last sermon before Oxford University, he preached on Acts 4:31: "And they were all filled with the Holy Ghost." His description of salvation in the early church is Aldersgate theology through and through. . . . Bishop Gibson's hand-written summary of what he felt Wesley was saying in this sermon indicates that he understood Wesley's clear implication that apostolic faith was being restored in Methodist evangelism.[48]

The Aldersgate experience invigorated in Wesley the Reformation doctrine of justification by faith, together with its accompanying emphases on assurance, perfection, prayer, confession, and Bible study as the central items in Christian spirituality, as part of a restoration of the Spirit's influence on believers in a manner after the apostolic era. Henry Rack says that Methodism "as a whole, aimed to recover a form of 'primitive Christianity' . . . an apostolic Church with a strongly supernaturalist flavour and centering on the teaching of a version of the Reformation doctrine of justification by faith."[49] Certainly Wesley wanted to experience a renewal of the truth and life of primitive Christianity through the Methodist movement.

In Wesley's *Works*, there are forty-five references to "primitive church" beginning in the early 1740s. In 1756 Wesley wrote "Address to Clergy," and there he commended "those who wrote before the Council of Nice" as "the most authentic commentators on Scripture, as being both nearest the fountain, and eminently endued with that Spirit by whom all Scripture was given."[50] Among the ante-Nicene theologians he considered as particularly worthy guardians of the religion of the primitive church are Clement of Rome, Ignatius, Polycarp, Justin Martyr, Tertullian, Origen, Clement of Alexandria, and Cyprian.[51] He also urged his preachers to have "some acquaintance" with such post-Nicene writers as "St. Chrysostom, Basil, Jerome, Austin; and, above all, the man of a broken heart, Ephraim Syrus."[52] Pragmatically primitivism offered to Methodism the call to apostolic poverty in the lay preachers, the lay preachers' obedience to Wesley (which is expressed in similar terms as the obedience of Timothy to Paul), and the qualifications of lay preachers being judged in terms of their fruitfulness in ministry.[53]

Wesley's use of the expression "Primitive Church" was especially significant when he was using it in 1784, in the twilight of his life. Even near
the end of his long life Wesley was still vitally concerned about practicing
Christianity within the parameters of the ancient faith. Primitivism had become, with time, a primary factor—vis-à-vis Anglican ecclesiastical policy—in determining the course his Methodists in America should take: "As
our American brethren are now totally disentangled both from the State and
from the English hierarchy, we dare not entangle them again either with the
one or the other. They are at full liberty simply to follow the Scriptures and
the Primitive Church. And we judge it best that they should stand fast in
that liberty wherewith God has so strangely made them free."[54]

Wesley's keen interest in the earliest Christian tradition came from the
general Anglican concern of his age and especially from the additional
encouragement of his father, Samuel Wesley, Sr., to study the Eastern
Fathers. For example, in his *Advice to a Young Curate*, Samuel Wesley
highly recommended that clergy read St. John Chrysostom.[55] The influence
of Eastern writers, especially Chrysostom,[56] along with Macarius the
Egyptian (or, more precisely, the writings attributed to him), Ephraem
Syrus and others, is present in John Wesley's soteriology.

The soteriology of Eastern Fathers was closely linked to and revolved
around the concept of *theosis* (or deification). *Theosis* is a mystery difficult
to analyze, and the interpretations of it are various, but simply put, it means
"being deified" or "becoming like God," which connotes participation in
God's nature while maintaining a distinct human nature. The anthropology
in the Christian East is based upon the idea of "participation" in God.[57]
Humans have been not created as an autonomous or self-sufficient being
but created to exist "in God" or "in grace." The participation of humans in
God is not a static givenness. Grace gives humans their "natural" development but humans are called to grow in Divine life. Therefore, Divine life is
on one hand a gift but on the other hand a task which is to be accomplished
by a free human effort. This polarity between the "gift" and the "task" is
often expressed in terms of the distinction between the concepts of "image"
and "likeness." Eastern Fathers distinguished "the Image of God" from "the
Likeness of God." One is the universal human potential for life in God,
while the other is understood as the progressive realization of that potential-
ity. Such realization made only possible by "participation" in Divine life
and grace through dispassion, contemplation, prayer, detachment, discrimi-
nation, worship, sacraments, keeping the commandments of God, and the
like has been often referred to as *theosis*. For Eastern Fathers, humanity's
ultimate goal was the *theosis*, or participation in the Divine life.

The anthropology and soteriology of Eastern Fathers must be understood in reference to the doctrine of *theosis*. Their understanding of original sin differs from that of Western theologians in that Adam and Eve are not responsible, through their sin, for universal guilt, but for universal mortality. Adam's personal sin did not bring condemnation upon all people, but death upon all people. The experience of mortality leads otherwise guiltless individuals to sinful acts, and each person's sin is the result of his or her own choice and not the choice of Adam. Given this idea that humanity's basic problem is mortality, the Eastern view of redemption is much broader than that of the Western church. Western theological tradition emphasizes the judicial aspect of salvation, asserting that in salvation, God is primarily concerned with the remission of sin. The Eastern view is that the gospel is not primarily the solution to humans' problem with personal sin. It is God's provision of divine life in Christ, the beginning of *theosis*. A residual benefit of beginning the process of deification is the remission of sins. Baptism is the means by which the believer enters into this new life. John Meyendorff well summarizes the soteriology in the Eastern theology: "Communion in the risen body of Christ; participation in divine life; sanctification through the energy of God, which penetrates the humanity and restores it to its "natural" state, rather than justification, or remission of inherited guilt—these are at the center of Byzantine understanding of the Christian Gospel."[58]

Eastern Fathers believed that the Fall did not deprive humans "of all grace, or of the accountability for responding to God's offer of restored communion in Christ."[59] Accordingly, they affirmed the synergism or cooperation between the grace of God and human effort even after the Fall. For example, the interaction of grace and human responsibility is clearly portrayed in the *Homilies* of [Pseudo-]Macarius:

> Grace, indeed, is unceasingly present and is rooted in us and mingled with our nature from our earliest years. It is as something natural and real which adheres to a person in various ways, depending on one's cooperation as far as this is given. . . .
> . . . If one does not strive to be good, does not possess the virtues already mentioned [goodness, simplicity, kindness, humility, charity, and prayer] and has not even prepared himself for them, he loses the grace which he has acquired and falls. . . .
> . . . Grace is not extinguished or diminished, but so that your free will and liberty may be put to the test to see which way it tends, grace permits the presence of sin. And then you draw near to the Lord by your free choice and beg that his grace may come upon you. . . . But it is you, if you are neglectful and do not willingly cooperate, who are done in and lose the Spirit. . . . You see that it is up to your will and freedom of choice to

honor the Holy Spirit and not to grieve him. I guarantee you that free choice remains.[60]

According to this view, we do not reach the final stage of spiritual maturity through divine power and grace alone, without ourselves making any effort, while neither on the other hand do we attain the final measure of freedom and purity as a result of our own diligence and strength alone, apart from any divine assistance.

Eastern Fathers' soteriology was focused on *theosis*, a state of the entire human being, transformed by grace, and freely cooperating with it by the efforts of both will and mind. It is the state in which God wanted humans to live and which was restored in Jesus Christ. Accordingly, therapeutic concerns were characteristic of Eastern Christianity while juridical concerns, i.e., "a momentary transaction . . . from guilty to forgiven," were characteristic of the later Western theologians.[61]

Through his exposure to the Anglican patristic revival and some direct reading of Eastern Fathers, Wesley became familiar with the Eastern traditions and shared the early Eastern understanding of the gradual restoration of humanity to God-likeness. Throughout his life Wesley often defined Christian salvation as "a recovery of the divine likeness" or "the renewal of our souls after the image of God."[62] He adopted a soteriology that stresses the dynamic nature of present human spiritual development as much as it stresses justification. This stress on spiritual transformation points toward a basic commonality between Wesley and the therapeutic emphasis characteristic of Eastern Orthodox.

Wesley's emphasis on the spiritual development or transformation in Christian life is most prominent in his doctrine of sanctification, and at this point his doctrine of sanctification was highly continuous with that of the Eastern Fathers.[63] Wesley knew the importance of holiness of life for the Christian, and from the Eastern patristic tradition, especially from the Macarian Homilies,[64] he learned the idea of sanctification or perfection as a process, and "not a goal at which one arrives all at once."[65] The process of sanctification means a participation "in the divine re-creation of the image of God in humanity, namely, that sensitivity which enables us to discern, reflect and image the divine will and purpose in the world."[66] This theme is also found in his mother, Susanna Wesley. In her journal, she said,

> True godliness I think chiefly consisteth in being like God, in being renewed after the image of God in righteousness and true holiness, etc. When the great work of regeneration is effectually begun in the soul and carried on by the Holy Spirit, till the mind is restored to that image of God, that moral goodness in which it was first created, then may such a

person be said to be truly godly: And in proportion to this divine resemblance, a man is more or less godly. 'Tis true there is a vast dissimilitude in the greatest likeness, even as great as there is between infinite and finite, all created good being not so much when in [the] presence of God, as one spark to the whole element of fire; but still the least degree of good is as truly good as the greatest, as one drop of water is as truly and essentially water as the main ocean.[67]

Certainly there is great affinity between John Wesley's doctrine of Christian perfection and the Eastern teaching of *theosis*. Theodore Runyon rightly suggests that "[b]ehind Wesley's understanding of the renewal of the image of God through regeneration lies the Eastern Fathers' notion of "divinization" (*theosis*), mediated to him indirectly through his Anglican tradition and directly from his reading of the Fathers."[68]

The implication of this soteriology for ecclesiology is that the church exists and does what it does to bring souls to salvation, with sanctification as well as justification in view. Wesley affirmed the essential role of the disciplinary function of the church in its proclamation of salvation in Christ. Accordingly, he emphasized the moral accountability of members of his societies and the correction of the community in the life of the members.

In conclusion, primitivism offered a central influence on and a continuing model for Wesley's ecclesiology. Wesley was acquainted with the early church tradition through his direct readings of the Fathers and primarily through his exposure to the Anglican patristic revival. Also, as will be investigated in later chapters, there were the influences of other traditions such as Pietism, especially Moravians, on Wesley's primitivism. Wesley strove to revive the primitive spirit of Christianity throughout his life. He drew from primitive Christianity an ideal of what Christianity and the church should be. For Wesley primitive Christianity was a standard by which to measure the faith and practice of Christians. His practice of stationary fasts is a good example of his efforts to follow the standard of the early church. Primitive Christianity served as a standard of his personal faith and as a model for his Methodist movement. We will further investigate this matter in Part Two. Wesley in part relied on the Eastern Fathers for his own doctrinal construction of "sanctification" or "perfection." What he envisioned as holiness and Christian perfection or entire sanctification reveals his personal vision of what his sources taught about *theosis*. Accordingly, the Eastern patristic tradition was a part of the holy living tradition which offered him the emphasis on holiness—along with other traditions such as mystic writers, the Church of England, Puritans, and Pietists, as shown later in this study. Wesley's concerns for holiness are reflected in his emphasis on the disciplinary function of the church—in the case of Methodism, the discipline in class meetings and societies.

Catholicism and Wesley

At his old age Wesley recollected that from his childhood he was reared to love and reverence the Scripture, the Primitive Church, and the Church of England, and thus in his young age he was strongly attached to them.[69] These three traditions were clearly influential on Wesley. Then, there is a gap of thousand years between the Primitive Church and the Church of England. Was there no influence exerted by medieval Catholicism on Wesley? Although certainly it is difficult to trace the direct influence of medieval Roman Catholicism upon Wesley, some Wesleyan scholars attempted to explore the relationship between Wesley's teaching and the traditional Catholicism of the Roman Catholic Church. John Todd, for example, saw Wesley's faith as "consonant with Catholic doctrine."[70] He says that Wesley believed in such old Catholic doctrines as the Blessed Trinity, the Divinity of Christ, the Incarnation, and the Virginity of Mary before and after the birth of Jesus which the Church of England at his age maintained, and that he held, essentially, the Catholic doctrine of grace. Furthermore, even Wesley's lack of the doctrine of purgatory and his insufficient understanding of the place of Mary in the plan of redemption were "omissions rather than specific doctrinal errors," argues Todd.[71]

Especially in regard to ecclesiology, says Todd, Wesley was close to traditional Catholicism:

> Wesley did not hold to the Protestant conception of a divine inspiration of every man independent of a community, he did not look to an action of the Holy Spirit completely independent of a Church. . . . on the contrary, . . . he believed in the right of the Church to exercise jurisdiction over Christians. . . . he always went out his way to try to avoid a final clash with ecclesiastical authority, and in this he succeeded.[72]

Notably, Todd argues that concerning the sacraments, Wesley held a Catholic conception: "As far as the sacrament of order goes, . . . he believed in the Catholic doctrine of the validity of the sacraments, apart from the worthiness of the priest."[73] To support his view, Todd cites from Wesley's sermon:

> unto false prophets, undeniably such, is frequently committed . . . the administration of the sacraments also. To direct men, therefore, not to hear

them would be in effect to cut them off from the ordinance of God. But this we dare not do, considering the validity of the ordinance doth not depend on the goodness of him that administers, but on the faithfulness of him that ordained it; who will and doth meet us in his appointed ways. . . . Even by these who are under a curse themselves God can and doth give us blessing. For the bread which they break we have experimentally known to be 'the communion of the body of Christ'; and the cup which God blessed, even by their unhallowed lips, was to us the communion of the blood of Christ.[74]

Todd goes on to say that Wesley "believed in the presence of Christ under the appearances of bread and wine" even though "his belief in the real presence may not be philosophically identical with the Catholic definition of transubstantiation."[75]

Wesley, according to Todd, held "to an essentially catholic conception" not only of sacrament but of church order as well. Concerning Wesley's traditional Catholic position on the matter of bishops and the apostolic succession, Todd says, "At Oxford he believed firmly in the bishops as the direct historical successors of the Apostles, and he believed that the Popes did stretch back in an uninterrupted line to St. Peter. . . . Wesley's traditional views on Church order . . . remained substantially unaltered in spite of his subsequent agnosticism on the matter of the succession."[76]

In a letter to his brother-in-law, the Rev. Westley Hall, on December, 1745, Wesley actually showed his traditional view on church order, defending three instances which Hall criticized as not defensible:

1. 'That the *validity* of our *ministry* depends on a *succession* supposed to be from the apostles, and a *commission* derived from the Pope of Rome and his *successors* or *dependents*.'

We believe it would not be right for us to *administer* either Baptism or the Lord's Supper unless we had a commission so to do from those bishops whom we apprehend to be in a *succession* from the apostles. And yet we allow, these bishops are the successors of those who were dependent on the Bishop of Rome. . . .

2. 'That there is an *outward priesthood*, and consequently an *outward sacrifice*, ordained and offered by the Bishop of Rome and his successors or dependents in the Church of England, as *vicars* and vicegerents of Christ.'

We believe there is and always was, in *every* Christian church (whether *dependent* on the Bishop of Rome or not), an *outward priesthood* ordained by Jesus Christ, and an *outward sacrifice* offered therein, by men authorized to act as 'ambassadors of Christ', and 'stewards of the mysteries of God' . . .

3. 'That this *papal hierarchy* and *prelacy* which still continues in the Church of England is of *apostolical institution*, and authorized thereby, though not by the *written Word.*'
We believe that the threefold order of ministers (which you seem to mean by 'papal hierarchy' and 'prelacy') is not only authorized by its 'apostolical institution', but also by the 'written Word.'[77]

Wesley was horrified at the idea of laymen performing liturgical rituals normally confined to the priesthood. Of lay preachers who had given the sacrament at Norwich, which presumably meant that they had carried out the complete Communion service, Wesley wrote: "They did it without any ordination, either by bishops or elders; upon the sole authority of a six-penny licence: nay, all had not that. Do you think they acted right? If the other preachers follow their example, not only separation but general confusion must follow. My soul abhors the thought of separating from the Church of England."[78]

Todd tries to reveal that Wesley was Catholic in many aspects of ecclesiology. He concludes that Wesley in fact was preaching traditional Catholic doctrine while he had a vague, agnostic position of the nature of the Church.[79]

The similarities between Wesley and medieval Catholicism Todd provides are striking. Similarities and parallels, however, are not necessarily proof of direct dependence. In addition, Todd's arguments are incorrect in many points. For example, he is not right in saying that Wesley remained unaltered on the matter of the apostolic succession, even though it is true that Wesley once had a traditional view on church order. After reading Lord Peter King's *An Enquiry into the Constitution, Discipline, Unity, and Worship of the Primitive Church* in 1746, Wesley no longer believed in a literal line of apostolic succession. Also, Wesley clearly stood against the doctrine of transubstantiation. His view was very similar to the Zwinglian doctrine of the Lord's Supper as memorial, together with a Calvinistic emphasis on spiritual reception in the sacrament. He also emphasized the importance of the sacrament as a means of grace. We will further discuss these subjects in the later chapters.

Despite the striking similarities between Wesley and medieval Catholicism that Todd singles out, there is a reason to think that the similarities mean nothing more than that Wesley was an eighteenth-century Anglican.[80] These similarities may be just characteristics of medieval Christianity that carried over into the Anglican tradition. It is difficult to argue that medieval Catholicism, except the mystics as later investigated, had any direct and separate influence on Wesley.

The Anglican tradition's via media between Catholicism and Protestantism is well known. Accordingly, one may consider in some sense Catholicism's influence on Wesley through the Church of England. And it is true that the early Wesley, especially for his high churchmanship, showed some features of an Anglo Catholic. However, attempts to make Wesley an advocator of the Catholic tradition may be misleading.

In the eighteenth century there were some, like George Lavington (1684–1762), Bishop of Exeter, who believed that the Methodists were very close to the Catholics. They accused the Methodists of carrying on the work of Popery in England. While Wesley refuted these accusations, they at least show that the Methodists were often misunderstood as the transmitter of Popery. However, Wesley was not a disciple of the Catholic tradition, particularly for his ecclesiology.

For instance, that Wesley recommended private confession to the band meetings is well known and often pointed to as one of the parallels between Catholicism and Methodism. However, it was by no means similar in Wesley's eyes. For this matter, Wesley wrote in his second letter to Bishop Lavington in 1752: "Therefore every unprejudiced person must see that there is no analogy between the Popish confession to a Priest, and our 'confessing our faults one to another, and praying one for another', as St. James directs."[81]

Likewise, it would not be difficult to show that Wesley did not believe the Church to be what the Roman Catholic Church defines itself to be. In his *Popery Calmly Considered*, Wesley discussed the Church of Rome which, in the Roman Catechism, is said to be that Society of Christians who professes "it necessary to salvation to be subject to the Pope, as the one visible head of the Church."[82] Against such a Catholic ecclesiology, Wesley argues that Christ alone is the Head of the Church. He says,

> The Scripture does not mention any visible head of the Church; much less does it mention the Pope as such; and least of all does it say, that it is necessary to salvation to be subject to him. . . . The Papists say, The Pope is Christ's Vicar, St. Peter's successor, and has the supreme power on earth over the whole Church. We answer, Christ gave no such power to St. Peter himself. He gave no Apostle pre-eminence over the rest.[83]

Wesley continues,

> The Church of Rome is no more the Church in general, than the Church of England is. It is only one particular branch of the catholic or universal Church of Christ, which is the whole body of believers in Christ, scattered over the whole earth. . . . We therefore see no reason to refer any matter in

dispute to the Church of Rome, more than any other Church; especially as
we know, neither the Bishop nor the Church of Rome is any more infallible than ourselves. . . . In all cases, the Church is to be judged by the
Scripture, not the Scripture by the Church.[84]

In general Wesley's strictures against the Roman Catholicism were centered
on the Catholics' adherence to the primacy of the Pope.

While reading Wesley as a Catholic is misleading, dominantly Protestant readings of Wesley are also inadequate, for it is true that there were
clearly typical "Catholic" themes in his thought and practice. Indeed, there
have been several appreciative readings of Wesley from the Roman Catholic tradition. Besides Todd, such Catholic scholars as Maximin Piette and
Michael Hurley S. J. detected and documented Wesley's links to Roman
Catholicism.[85] Several Methodist scholars like Herbert B. Workman, R.
Newton Flew, William R. Cannon, and Charles W. Brockwell, Jr. attempted
to compare Wesley with the Catholic Tradition.[86] Wesley was a person of
the Church of England. "[G]iven Wesley's Anglican affiliation and training,
and Anglicanism's self-professed goal of being a via media," as Randy L.
Maddox suggests, "a Protestant/Catholic synthesis should have been expected."[87]

In attempts to explore Roman Catholicism's influence upon Wesley,
mysticism must not be overlooked. The debt of Wesley, especially in his
early period, to mysticism is well known. From the time Wesley entered
Oxford until his return from Georgia in 1738, he became familiar with
many mystical works. Some were more influential than others but all of
them left a lasting imprint on his spiritual life.[88]

Martin Schmidt, emphasizing the "significance of the Romanic mystics
for England" and Wesley, says that "the Romanic mystics with which he
[Wesley] was familiar . . . introduced him to a particular type of spiritual
culture. . . . The type of spiritual culture which was founded . . . by the
Romanic mystics . . . helped to mould John Wesley."[89]

Albert Outler suggests that three distinct mystical traditions influenced
Wesley.[90] The first is the *voluntaristic* mysticism represented by such mystics as Thomas à Kempis (c.1380–1471), William Law (1686–1761) and
Lorenzo Scupoli (1530–1610), which was "a mysticism of a will that issues
in a strenuous program of self-denigration aimed at total resignation."[91]
Naturally this *voluntaristic* mysticism emphasized asceticism and self-
abasement. The second is the *quietistic* mysticism represented by persons
like François de Sales (1567–1622), Michael (or Miguel) de Molinos
(1640–1696), and Madame Guyon (1648–1717). The *quietistic* mystics employed a stillness and waiting on God. And the third is the mysticism of

early and Eastern spirituality like Macarius the Egyptian and Ephraem Syrus. These three mystical traditions offered a lasting impact on Wesley's spiritual life. Particularly "his experimentation with the *voluntaristic* mysticism . . . and with the *quietistic* mysticism of the Molinists . . . drove Wesley to the pitch of futile striving which was such a vivid agony in his early years."[92]

The early Wesley seemed greatly influenced by his mother Susanna in that she encouraged all her children to read the books which she chose and many of which had a mystical emphasis. Many of the devotional books being read by pious Christians during the first part of the eighteenth century were written by the Roman Catholic mystics. Devotional reading was an important part of Susanna's discipline for her children. Wesley's earliest devotional reading accelerated his appreciation of asceticism held by the mystics and also by puritans.[93]

In fact many mystical writers from the fourth through to the eighteenth century influenced Wesley. [Pseudo-]Macarius the Egyptian and Ephraem Syrus of the fourth century influenced Wesley's concept of perfection as a dynamic process rather than a static state, and in his the *Christian Library* Wesley published an abridgment of *The Homilies of* [Pseudo-]*Macarius.*[94] Wesley in the *Christian Library* also published such other works of mystics as B. Lawrence's *Practice of the Presence of God*, Juan d'Avila's *The Spiritual Letters*, and Michael de Molinos' *Spiritual Guide which Disentangles the Soul.*

In *A Plain Account of Christian Perfection*, Wesley mentioned Jeremy Taylor (1613–1667), Thomas à Kempis, and William Law as the writers who had made a significant impact upon his early spiritual development.[95] While Wesley did not agree with everything written by these mystics, they certainly deepened his sense of inward holiness. Through reading à Kempis's *Christian Pattern* Wesley "began to see that true religion was seated in the heart and that God's law extended to all our thoughts as well as words and actions."[96] Law's *Christian Perfection* and *Serious Call* convinced Wesley more than ever "of the absolute impossibility of being half a Christian"[97] and "of the exceeding height and breadth and depth of the law of God."[98] After reading these works, to him "everything appeared in a new view."[99] Particularly, "Law introduced Wesley to the medieval mystical treatise *Theologia Germanica*, which marked the beginning of Wesley's contact with a wide range of continental Catholic mystic writings."[100] Wesley "was exceedingly affected" by Taylor's *Rule and Exercises of Holy Living and Dying*, in particular the "part which relates to purity of intention."[101] Reflecting on Taylor's impact upon his spirituality, Wesley wrote, "Instantly I resolved to dedicate all my life to God, all my thoughts, and words, and actions; being thoroughly convinced, there was no medium; but that every part of my life (not some only) must either be a sacrifice to God, or myself, that is, in effect, to the devil."[102] It is certain that Wesley learned from these mystics the innerness of religion, the uncompromising call to a wholehearted Christian commitment, and the importance of purity of intention.

French Count Gaston Jean-Baptiste De Renty (1611–1649) was a mystic who Wesley and his parents liked and valued highly. De Renty was the energetic organizer of the various branches of the 'Compagnie du Saint-Sacrement' (or Company of the Holy Sacrament), which were little groups of believers who helped to build each other up by spiritual discussions,[103] and the weekly gatherings of which were akin to the Methodist class-meetings. De Renty, "a significant and effective example of Romanic mysticism," was also a mystic who valued mystic solitude and through self-discipline "felt himself one with the true believers of all ages in a real and deep communion of the saints."[104] Wesley knew Père de Saint-Jure's *The Life of Monsieur De Renty* through his father, and he kept it while in Georgia.[105] Thereafter it stayed with him his whole life and his works show frequent allusions to Renty's simple life and extraordinary intimacy of the union with God. In 1741 Wesley published an abridged version of *The Life of Monsieur De Renty* written in December 1738. He also had *The Life of Monsieur De Renty* read in the sixth class of Kingswood School.[106] Throughout his life Wesley used and emphasized Renty's "experimental verity" of the Trinity as one of his principal arguments against the Arians.[107] To Wesley, "De Renty was an individual witness, just as the Herrnhutters had been a corporate one, to the fact that primitive Christianity could be realized in the present."[108]

Madame Guyon was a mystic writer Wesley kept close contact with throughout his life. Wesley read Guyon's works such as *A Short and Easy Method of Prayer* and *Les Torrents Spirituelles*,[109] and he was so deeply moved by her life and books that even after his repudiation of mysticism, he wrote favorably of her.[110] For example, in 1776 Wesley published *An Extract of the Life of Madam Guion* and in its preface he said of her,

> As to Madam Guion herself, I believe she was not only a good woman, but good in an eminent degree; deeply devoted to God. . . . What a depth of religion did she enjoy! Of the mind that was in Christ Jesus! What heights of righteousness, and peace, and joy in the Holy Ghost! How few such instances do we find, of exalted love to God and our neighbor; of genuine humility; of invincible meekness, and unbounded resignation! So that, upon the whole, I know not whether we may not search many centuries to find another woman who was such a pattern of true holiness.[111]

Wesley recommended "all serious persons" that they read the "Life of Madam Guion" while he warned of her quietistic tendencies.[112] Situated within the apophatic or non-discursive mystical tradition, Guyon, in her writings, attempted to qualify the nature of the experience of abandonment to the divine will.[113] Guyon's stress on total commitment of the "will" to God and on effort for an intimacy with God, which was beyond nominal Christianity and sheer rationalism, might have especially caught Wesley's eye. Guyon, however, paid little attention to the nature of the disciplines of Christian life and practice, primarily because of her emphasis on contemplative prayer and the inner experience of love.

Besides, Lorenzo Scupoli's *Pugna Spiritualis*[114] was a favorite of Wesley and his mother. For study with the Oxford Methodists, Wesley also used many works of mystic writers like James Garden's *Theologia Comparativa cum Adjectis*, Peter Heylin's *Historical and Miscellaneous Tracts*, François De Sales' *An Introduction to a Devout Life*, Henry Scougal's *The Life of God in the Soul of Man*, William Spurstowe's *The Spiritual Chymist*, and *Theologia Germanica*.[115] Moreover, Wesley read many mystics such as François Fénelon's works,[116] Richard Lucas' *An Enquiry after Hapiness*, Alonso Rodriguez' *A Treatise of Humilitie*, John Scott's *The Christian Life, from its Beginning to its Consummation in Glory*, Nathaniel Spinckes' *The True Church of England Man's Companion in the Closet*,[117] and so on. Of these mystic writers, Wesley later published Scougal, Lucas, and Spinckes.

However, Wesley was not always favorably disposed to mysticism. Wesley did often have difficulty with mysticism. Wesley was struggling with mysticism at one time in Georgia. In a letter to his brother Samuel on November 23, 1736, he said, "I think the rock on which I had the nearest made shipwreck of the faith was the writings of the mystics, under which term I comprehend all, and only those, who slight any of the means of grace."[118] Perhaps Wesley, as James H. Rigg suggested, in his desire to find rest, was oscillating between mysticism and ritualism.[119]

Wesley himself wrote of this period before Aldersgate,

These considerations insensibly stole upon me as I grew acquainted with the mystic writers, whose noble descriptions of union with God and internal religion made everything else appear mean, flat, and insipid. But in truth they made good works appear so too; yea, and faith itself, and what not? They gave me an entire new view of religion, nothing like any I had had before. But alas! It was nothing like that religion which Christ and his apostles loved and taught. . . . I had no heart, no vigour, no zeal in obeying; continually doubting whether I was right or wrong, and never out of perplexities and entanglements.[120]

Wesley's move to withdraw from mysticism is clearly seen in his preface to *Hymns and Sacred Poems*, which he published in 1739. "Some verses, it may be observed, in the following Collection, were wrote upon the scheme of the Mystic Divines. And these, it is owned, we had once in great veneration, as the best explainers of the gospel of Christ. But we are now convinced, that we therein greatly erred, not knowing the Scriptures, neither the power of God."[121] In his later years, commenting on some of Charles' poems, John Wesley also says, "some still savour of that poisonous mysticism with which we were both not a little tainted before we went to America. This gave a gloomy cast, first to his mind and then to many of his verses. This made him frequently describe religion as a melancholy thing. This so often sounded in his ears, 'To the desert,' and strongly persuaded in favour of solitude."[122]

Wesley disliked mysticism as solitary religion. Wesley stood against the mystics' tendency to privatize the revelation of God. Wesley opposed the "solitary religion," arguing that "'[h]oly solitaries' is a phrase no more consistent with the gospel than holy adulterers."[123] Wesley believed that one cannot serve God alone and must therefore find companions or make them. "The gospel of Christ knows of no religion, but social; no holiness but social holiness."[124] Social holiness for Wesley means Christian fellowship. Thus, avoiding solitary religion was at the heart of Wesley's reservations about mysticism.

Wesley's antipathy to mysticism is probably best expressed in the following denouncement:

> Nor can I at this hour give a distinct account how or when I came a little back toward the right way. Only my present sense is this: all the other enemies of Christianity are triflers; the mystics are the most dangerous of all its enemies. They stab it in the vitals, and its most serious professors are most likely to fall by them. May I praise him who hath snatched me out of this fire likewise, by warning all others that it is set on fire of hell.[125]

This statement seems to reveal that now Wesley rejected mysticism completely.

Wesley seems to have begun to withdraw from mysticism from the mid-1730s. However, "Wesley's anti-mysticism did not wholly persist."[126] He continued to read selected mystical writings throughout his life. "[T]he Catholic and even the mystical literature and biographies continued to attract Wesley."[127] Wesley shared the mystics' concern for holy living throughout his life. He published some of the mystics' books in his *Christian Library* as late as 1756. Wesley was probably more influenced by mysticism than he was aware. As Henry Bett puts it, "the deeply mystical character of many of the hymns of Methodism should not be forgotten. . . . It can hardly be denied, then, that Wesley and early Methodism were considerably influenced, directly and indirectly, by the mystics."[128] Therefore, the question of mysticism should be treated as an influence that remained even after Wesley rejected mysticism as "the worst enemy of Christianity."

Perhaps the influence of the mystics on Wesley is finally to be reduced to no more than an emphasis on inward religion and inward relation to God. Then, the question arises as to how their influence is to be distinguished from the influence of the Pietists who stressed the same things. Wesley himself knew the things in common between mystics and Pietists. He actually criticized the Moravian Pietists for being mystic. "The errors which had crept in among the Moravians in London at that time, were a refined species of Antinomianism, and mystic notions of ceasing from ordinances and waiting for faith in stillness."[129] In a letter to the Moravians in Herrnhut, Wesley wrote,

> you receive not the *ancients* but the *modern mystics* as the best interpreters of Scripture, and in conformity to these you mix much of man's wisdom with the wisdom of God; you greatly refine the plain religion taught by the letter of Holy Writ and philosophize on almost every part of it to accommodate it to the *mystic* theory. . . .
> . . . In conformity to the *mystics* you likewise greatly check joy in the Holy Ghost by which cautions against *sensible comforts* as have no title of Scripture to support them.[130]

We will discuss the Moravian Pietists later in Chapter 3. Here notable point is that Wesley separated from the Moravians for their excessive mysticism, that is, quietism. The most disputed parts of quietism were the lesser importance of exterior acts or works and an emphasis on passivity and the control of the will by God that could permit irresponsible behavior.

Bishop Lavington of Exeter in 1747 produced a work regarded by the eighteenth century as a triumph of logic, *The Enthusiasm of Methodists and Papists Considered.*[131] Here he accused Wesley of "doing the Papists' work" in England and agreeing "with them in some of their Principles."[132] One method by which Wesley had done this work was by the recommending of mystics' books such as the life of de Renty and the work of François de Sales. While we are not hesitant to deny his main impeachment, Bishop Lavington was right in his analysis of Roman mysticism and Methodism; mysticism and Methodism were both built upon the foundation, not of argument or observation or memory, or of the power to analyze and synthesize, but of conscious spiritual experience.

It is interesting to compare Wesley's Methodism with medieval Western monasticism. In his *The Place of Methodism in the Catholic Church*, Herbert B. Workman observed six similarities between the monasticism of medieval Western Catholicism and Wesley's Methodism. First, both monasticism and early Methodism, according to Workman, emphasized the need for discipline, "the importance of the conquest of self, in other words, of renunciation, as the one condition of effective work for God."[133] For both of them, without discipline there can be no holiness.

Secondly, both identified themselves as a social religion. Workman says, "Monasticism, as worked out by St. Benedict, and developed by his successors . . . was essentially a social religion; men were to help each other to the spiritual life under leadership and a rule. Nor was this fellowship limited to the affairs of the soul: it extended, far more completely than has ever been realized in Methodism."[134]

Thirdly, in both "holiness" was "a fact of character rather than an imputed act."[135] Since St. Cyprian the Church had laid its foundations on "the doctrines of apostolic succession and a mediating priesthood."[136] Such doctrines stressed the coming of grace from without, through channels other than the man himself. Against this sacerdotal view, the monk was a silent but constant protest. Workman says,

> Monasticism never forgot that personal holiness . . . is something far higher than any succession can bestow. Instead of intermediate communion with God through priests and sacraments, the monk upheld the ideal of the direct intercourse of the soul with its Maker. Thus in its origin Monasticism lay over against the Catholic Church, with an ideal other than, possibly higher than, that of the Church.[137]

Fourthly, in both monasticism and Methodism, says Workman, one can see an emphasis on the priesthood of the laity and anti-sacerdotalism. "Monasticism," from its early days, "was the protest that the laity also are priests unto God."[138] The earlier monks, including St. Anthony, the founder of monasticism, were generally laymen. In the course of time the monks were forced to join the priesthood under the pressure of the bishops who "felt the danger of communities of laymen growing up within the Church, which proclaimed to the world, by their very existence, an ideal of religious life opposite to that sacramental and sacerdotal theory on which their episcopal authority rested."[139] Nevertheless, the monks, at least in theory, were not necessarily priests, and their abbot was only a presbyter though often classified as the equal of a bishop by papal sanction. A good example of this anti-sacerdotalism is represented in St. Benedict's *Little Rule for Beginners*. Here "[c]onfession was not made to a priest, nor to the monastic chaplain, but to the abbot or to the whole brotherhood, even though they were laymen."[140] John Wesley wrote for his Helpers rules which in their trenchant simplicities recall the *Rule* of St. Benedict. With regard to the important role of laymen in Methodism, Workman says that "the anti-sacerdotalism of Methodism is but the development, under a new form, of this constant protest of Monasticism."[141]

Fifthly, monasticism and Methodism see the sacrifice of praise and thanksgiving as important. "In every monastery the service of God in the church was the supreme duty."[142] This service was "a continuous sacrifice of prayer and thanksgiving" rather than "the adoration of the mass."[143] The monks laid a great emphasis upon prayer over against external and sacerdotal religion. Even after the dissolution of monasticism, "this spirit survived in the Nonconformity of England," especially in Methodism, "with its consistent protest against any sacerdotal conception of the Church."[144]

Finally and perhaps most importantly, Workman observed a considerable similarity of organization between monasticism and Methodism. Both of them were in connexionalism. Wesley's connexionalism is well known. Although the old monasteries of Cistercians and Friars were isolated and independent of all others, they were also in connection with each other. Workman says that "the Cistercians and the Friars were the founders of connexionalism."[145]

Although Workman's analogy between monasticism and Methodism is striking, his weakness is that he is dealing with no more than similarities. Workman does not present any evidence that Wesley knew anything of or had read anything about the history of the Franciscans and their organizational structure. In fact, for the similarities between the two movements we may catalogue more. The *Rules* Wesley wrote for his Helpers and St. Benedict's *Little Rule for Beginners* have often been compared.[146] Also, Methodists, and Cistercians and the Friars had a similar conference. For instance, although each Cistercian monastery was an independent unit, Cistercians kept up the connexional spirit by enforcing everywhere a unity of usage, and by an annual chapter or conference in September at Citeaux attended by the abbots of all Cistercian foundations. Discipline was maintained not only by this conference but by giving to the abbot of Citeaux a prevailing voice in the congregation of which he was the president, with also the right of visiting any monastery at will.[147] Each abbot also had the duty of visiting the daughter houses of his own foundation. In this organizational structure of Cistercians we see striking similarities with that of the Methodists, but we must admit that we cannot find no stated evidence in Wesley's works that he referred to the medieval Teritaries for his Methodist organization.

We know that there are many cases where although similarities seem evident, the similarities are only similarities and actual relationship is thin.

Workman's studies certainly require critical assessment. However, they are useful for understanding of what Wesley's Methodist organization was like. For that reason, the further investigation of the organizational similarities of Methodism and medieval monasticism will be given in this section.

W. H. Fitchett in *Wesley and His Century* noted the parallel between the medieval friars and Wesley's preachers saying that "Wesley had gathered round himself, and was training in his helpers, a new order of Christian workers, in some respects curiously like the preaching friars of the Middle Ages."[148] But Fitchett didn't take note of the Conference in the medieval monasticism when he proposed that "the Conference . . . is perhaps the most original contribution that Methodism has made to church history."[149] Seeing the organizations of Methodism and of the Friars, one is surprised at their closeness. A good illustration is provided by Workman:

> The Franciscans . . . were divided into 'Provinces,' over each of which was a 'Provincial Minister,' among the Dominicans elected for four years only. The 'Provinces' were again divided into 'Custodies,' under the charge of 'Custodians,' who possessed general rights of supervision for their districts. Every year Chapters-General were held—the first at Michaelmas, the second and more important at Whitsuntide. The annual Dominican chapter-general was held alternately at Paris and Bologna; among the Franciscans, as in Methodism, it roamed about. In many of its powers this Whitsuntide gathering corresponded with the Methodist Conference. The original purpose of both Chapter-General and Conference was the same: the forgathering of brethren from far and near that they might gain new enthusiasm by the communion of saints.[150]

As they grew, the Friars restricted the Chapter-General to the delegates of the 'provinces'; Wesley excluded all but a select band of preachers, the 'Legal Hundred.' Both Friars and Wesley found that this common government by a central court united the whole body into a compact effective instrument.

A church historian like Henry Offley Wakeman saw Wesley as "the S. Francis of the eighteenth century," saying that

> The Methodist, like the friar minor, took the world as his parish. He planted himself in the crowded cities and among the outcast population. His mission was to the poor, the unlearned, and the neglected. He cared not for boundaries of parish or country. Borne on the wings of love, he crossed the seas bringing to all who would hear at the churchyard cross, on the village green, in the streets, and on the moors, the glad tidings of

forgiveness. Indeed, with due allowance for the differences of the time, the methods as well as the objects of Wesley were singularly like those of S. Francis. There was a similar use of colloquial and simple sermons, similar reiteration of a few all-important truths, similar renunciation of all pomp and splendour of service or building, similar religious use of hymns and music. Even the obstacles which they encountered and the difficulties which they raised were similar. The sneer of the worldly, the accusation of fanaticism, the dread of the orderly, the dislike of the parish clergy, the timidity of the bishops, the self-sufficiency of the members of the society themselves, were trials common to both. That the sons of S. Francis, with all his individuality, remained devoted children of the Church, that the sons of Wesley, with all his personal loyalty, found their natural sphere outside the Church, was due, under God to the circumstances of the time.[151]

We do well to remember that Wesley's Helpers and the Little Poor Brothers of St. Francis were both originally lay-persons. The new place of the laity was emphasized by St. Francis in the foundation of his Tertiaries, or great guild of the Brothers and Sisters of Penitence. Wesley found his Tertiaries in the development of his class-meetings. Only slowly has there grown up in Methodism a difference of spiritual rank between its local preachers and its itinerant ministers. No one conversant with Methodism would deny that the key to its influence was its appeal to the laity. Deprived of its lay workers Methodism would assuredly have died. Methodism was in essence a lay movement. The lay persons served as the itinerant preachers or the members of the Societies. Indeed, not merely the *bene esse* (well being) of Methodism, but its *esse* (essence—being), lay in their service.

Methodism was not designed as a substitute for the Anglican or any other church. It was auxiliary to the church, supporting her mission by enriching and deepening the spiritual life of the members who used its services. At this point, Wesley's Methodism most clearly resembled "Tertiaries" or "Third Orders" of High medieval Western Catholicism,[152] which had been auxiliary to and not independent of the Catholic Church. Since Methodism did not provide for communal living or encourage celibacy, there was no element of strict monasticism about it, but Methodism sought to enrich the spiritual life of the members through fasting, prayer, worship, and service as did the Catholic Third Orders, composed as they were of men and women engaged in ordinary occupations.

In conclusion, Wesley does not seem to have read in or to have conceptualized medieval Catholicism in the way he did primitive Christianity. In fact, it is difficult to trace and identify direct influence of medieval Catholicism on him. One exception is the case of the mystics. There is clear evidence that Wesley read many mystics and was to some extent influenced by them, even after he came to reject the mystics and mysticism generally. Wesley learned from the mystics the religion of heart or inward religion. He also shared the mystics' concern for holy living throughout his life. Such an emphasis on the religion of heart and the holy living is also shared by the Pietists who were more influential upon Wesley than mystics as we will later see. At this point one may not say that Wesley derived the concepts of religion of heart and holy living only from the mystics. Wesley possibly drew them from both the mystics and the Pietists.

This chapter dealt with two very different cases in regard to Wesley's ecclesiology: primitive Christianity which was a central influence on and ideal for Wesley, on the one hand, and on the other, medieval Catholicism which shows no more than certain similarities to Wesley. Primitive church offered Wesley an ideal of what the church should be, and therefore was a key tradition in the shaping of Wesley's ecclesiology. On the contrary, it is difficult to prove that medieval Catholicism is a tradition which was directly influential upon Wesley's ecclesiology. It is possible that he was influenced by Catholicism through the medieval influences on Anglicanism. For example, the Church of England, even after the dissolution of the monasteries in the English Reformation, retained the monastic ideal of morning and evening prayer in its prayer book. That practice clearly affected Wesley's rules for Methodists. However, Wesley did not borrow it directly from the historic monastic tradition. In fact, it is difficult to present any evidence of direct influence from medieval Catholicism that Wesley acknowledges—except the mystics.

Notes

1. For example, see *John Cassian: The Institutes*, Translated and Annotated by Boniface Ramsey (New York: The Newman Press, 2000), 39ff; *John Cassian: The Conferences*, Translated and Annotated by Boniface Ramsey (New York: Paulist Press, 1997), 637ff, 742f.

2. *John Cassian: The Institutes*, 40. From the earlier writers on monasticism such as Eusebius of Caesarea (c.260 – c.340), Pachomius (c.292 – c.346), Basil of Caesarea (329–379), and Jerome (c.340–420), Cassian fashioned two versions of what is called the "myth of apostolic origin of cenobitism": the Alexandrian and the Jerusalem version. One "traced the origins of Egyptian monasticism to the apostolic community under the evangelist St. Mark at Alexandria" while the other, of much greater influence in the medieval age, traced monasticism directly to the primitive Christian community at Jerusalem portrayed in Acts 4:32ff, "thus 'monasticizing' the history of the early church." Both versions agree that Acts 4:32ff. describes the life of the believers of the primitive church while the Alexandrian version specifi-

cally associates the perfection of the practice of the common life with the *ecclesia primitiva*. Also, both agree that shortly after the apostolic age there began a falling away, so the primitive church is primarily associated with the apostolic age. Though in the medieval age and the later period, the primitive church was sometimes extended in time beyond the apostolic period, there was already present in Cassian the notion that the spread and success of Christianity destroyed or injured the purity of her primitive practices. See Glenn Olsen, "The Idea of the *Ecclesia Primitiva* in the Writings of the Twelfth-Century Canonists," *Traditio: Studies in Ancient and Medieval History, Thought, and Religion*, vol. xxv (New York: Fordham University Press, 1969), 67–68.

3. For the *ecclesia primitiva* as a model of reform in the history of church, see Gerhart B. Ladner, *The Idea of Reform: Its impact on Christian Thought and Action in the Age of the Fathers* (Cambridge: Harvard University Press, 1959). Here Ladner suggests "monasticism as a vehicle of the Christian idea of reform in the age of the fathers" (319ff).

4. Jeffrey B. Russell, *Dissent and Reform in the Early Middle Ages* (Berkeley: University of California Press, 1965).

5. Herbert Grundmann, *Religiöse Bewegungen im Mittelalter: Untersuchungen über die geschichtlichen Zusammenhänge zwischen der Ketzerei, den Bettelorden und der religiösen Frauenbewegung im 12. und 13. Jahrhundert, und über die geschichtlichen Grundlagen der Deutschen Mystik* (Darmstadt: Wissenschaftliche Buchgesellschaft, 1970), 21–22.

> Der Gedanke der christlichen Armut und des apostolischen Lebens als Wanderprediger ist der wesentliche Gehalt der Ketzerei sowohl in Köln als in Südfrankreich, und dieser Gedanke ist tatsächlich das Hauptmotiv der Ketzerei bis in den Anfang des 13. Jahrhunderts, bei den Katharen wie bei den Waldensern, immer geblieben. Das Leben der Apostel zu führen, die echten Nachfolger der Apostel zu sein, das ist der eigentliche Anspruch der Ketzer, und aus ihm hat sich ihr Bruch mit der Kirche entwickelt. . . . Ihre echte und leidenschaftliche Überzeugung, das wahre evangelische und apostolische Christentum in ihrem Leben erneuert und verwirklicht zu haben, läßt sich bei unbefangener Betrachtung gar nicht bezweifeln. . . . Diese Überzeugung und diesen Anspruch ernst zu nehmen und gelten zu lassen ist die erste Voraussetzung für jedes Verständnis der religiösen Bewegungen des Mittelalters.

For an English translation, see Steven Rowan, trans., *Religious Movements in the Middle Ages* (University of Norte Dame Press, 1995), 11.

This theme has been pursued in detail for the later Middle Ages by Gordon Leff. See Gordon Leff, *Heresy in the Later Middle Ages: The Relation of Heterodoxy to Dissent, c.1250 – c.1450*, 2 vols. (Manchester: Manchester U.P.; New York: Barnes & Noble, 1967); "The Apostolic Ideal in Later Medieval Ecclesiology," *Journal of Theological Studies* 18 (April, 1967): 58–82; "The Making of the Myth of a True Church in the Later Middle Ages," *Journal of Medieval and Renaissance Studies* 1 (1971): 1–15.

6. See Venerable Bede, *The Ecclesiastical History of the English Nation, From the Coming of Julius Caesar into This Island, in the Sixtieth Year Before the Incarnation of Christ, Till the Year of Our Lord 731, Carefully Revised and Corrected from the Translation of Mr. Stevens, by the Rev. J.A. Giles* (London: E. Lumley, 56, Chancery Lane, 1840), Book I, Chapter 26 (44) and 27 (46); Book IV, Chapter 23 (243) and 27 (258).

7. Bede, *The Ecclesiastical History of the English Nation*, 45–46. Gregory says that, being under monastic rules, Augustine must not live apart from his clergy in the English Church, and that he must "follow that course of life which our forefathers did in the time of the primitive church, when none of them said any thing that he possessed was his own, but all things were in common among them."

There has been among scholars discussions of the problem of the authenticity of the answers given by Gregory I and the form of life practiced at Canterbury in the time of Gregory. For this matter, see Dom David Knowles, *The Monastic Order in England*, 2d ed. (Cambridge: Cambridge University Press, 1963), 619–620 and 758, note K; Ladner, *The Idea of Reform*, 399–400; Margaret Deanesly, "The Capitular Text of the Responsiones of Pope Gregory I to St. Augustine," *Journal of Ecclesiastical History* 12, no. 2 (October 1961): 231–234.

8. Olsen, "The Idea of the *Ecclesia Primitiva* in the Writings of the Twelfth-Century Canonists," 69.

9. Olsen, "The Idea of the *Ecclesia Primitiva* in the Writings of the Twelfth-Century Canonists," 69.

10. Olsen, "The Idea of the *Ecclesia Primitiva* in the Writings of the Twelfth-Century Canonists," 70–71.

11. The best example of this is found in the *Quaestiones Stuttgardienses* (c.1154–1179) the anonymous author of which argued that in the primitive church the Roman pontiff had all right and authority of binding and loosing. This view attributed to the primitive church the idea that all powers within the Church are derived from the authority of the pope, and the idea that the primates and bishops, established to act as the deputies of the pope, therefore appeared later in time than the papacy. Olsen, "The Idea of the *Ecclesia Primitiva* in the Writings of the Twelfth-Century Canonists," 75–76.

12. See Paul D. L. Avis, "'The True Church' in Reformation Theology," *Scottish Journal of Theology* 30 (1977): 319–345; D. F. Wright, trans. and ed., *Common Places of Martin Bucer*, The Courtenay Library of Reformation Classics 4 (Abingdon, England: Sutton Courtenay Press, 1972), intro. 39–41; also see C. Leonard Allen and Richard T. Hughes, *Discovering Our Roots: The Ancestry of Churches of Christ* (Abilene, Tex.: ACU Press, 1988), 21–34.

13. See Monroe Hawley, *The Focus of Our Faith* (Nashville: 20th Century Christian, 1985), 29–66 for a description of these groups as restorationists. Cf. Abraham Friesen, "The Impulse Toward Restitutionist Thought in Christian Humanism," *Journal of the American Academy of Religion* 44 (March, 1976): 29–45; Allen and Hughes, *Discovering Our Roots*, 11–20.

14. Cf. William P. Haugaard, "Renaissance Patristic Scholarship and Theology in Sixteenth-Century England," *Sixteenth-Century Journal* 10, no. 3 (Fall 1979): 37–60.

15. During this period, continental reformers exerted a significant influence in England. Pursuing reformation, King Edward directed Cranmer to seek advice from continental reformers. Bullinger, Zwingli's successor at Zurich, responded to Cranmer's inquiry by urging England to restore the primitive church. Bullinger also influenced John Hooper (1495–1555), Bishop of Gloucester, who had lived with Bullinger in Zurich for eight years, and after returning to England exerted a wide influence for primitive practices in the church. Some influential reformers came from the continent to England to escape persecution and tried to drive the Church of England toward further Protestant reformation. Most influential among them was Martin Bucer, who later assumed a chair of theology at Cambridge University. Bucer influenced such influential figures in the Church of England as Cranmer, Ridley, Edmund Grindal (1519–1583) and Matthew Parker (1504–1575). His book *The Reign of Christ* frequently used the theme of restoration of primitivism. In it Bucer suggested that the restoration of the purity of the ancient church played a key role in a nation's welfare. The primitive Christianity Bucer sought to restore was not so much the apostolic age. Rather he sought to restore the model of the Constantinian church in the early fourth century, when the church was protected and overseen by a Christian ruler. This ideal of a restored godly commonwealth, with stress upon ecclesiastical forms and moral discipline, was to become one of the hallmarks of Puritanism. See Allen and Hughes, *Discovering Our Roots*, 21–48.

16. Primitivism was clearly a main constituent of Puritanism. In fact, a call for primitive Christianity is typically associated with Puritan reform. For the primitivism in Puritanism, see Theodore D. Bozeman, *To Live Ancient Lives: The Primitivist Dimension of Puritanism* (Chapel Hill, NC: Published for the Institute of Early American History and Culture, Williamsburg, Virginia, by the University of North Carolina Press, 1988). Noting such Puritan terms as imitation, pattern, model, example, primitive, old, ancient, first, purity, and simplicity, Bozeman sees a "peculiar rallying to an ancient and primitive standard" (12) as characteristic to Puritanism. Cf. Allen and Hughes, *Discovering Our Roots*, 35–48; C. Leonard Allen and Richard T. Hughes, *Illusions of Innocence: Protestant Primitivism in America, 1630–1875*, with a Foreword by Robert N. Bellah (Chicago: University of Chicago Press, 1988).

17. See Campbell, *John Wesley and Christian Antiquity*, 9–21. Campbell divides Anglican primitivists into "conservative" and "programmatic." Both groups affirmed "Christian antiquity as an authority for Christian doctrine and practice." However, the conservative primitivists are those who wished to defend the Anglicanism of their day "by the appeal to Christian antiquity" and viewed "the ancient church's life as a pattern realized in the faith and practice of Anglicans," while programmatic primitivists also wished to defend Anglicanism, but were willing to change the liturgy and piety of their day by reinstituting, renewing, or reviving the model of the ancient church's life. Classifying Wesley as "more programmatic than conservative" primitivist, Campbell asserts that Wesley's interests in Christian an-

tiquity were mostly "inspired by programmtic concerns about the reform of the church" (20, 23).

18. Cf. Martin Schmidt, *John Wesley: A Theological Biography*, trans. Norman P. Goldhawk, 2 vols. (Nashville: Abingdon Press, 1962), vol. i, 134, 222; Martin Schmidt, *John Wesley: A Theological Biography*, trans. Denis Inman (Nashville: Abingdon Press, 1973), vol. ii, part ii, 191–192; Baker, *John Wesley and the Church of England*, especially 30–34; Outler, "John Wesley's Interests in the Early Fathers of the Church" in *The Wesleyan Theological Heritage: Essays of Albert C. Outler*, 97–110; Keefer, *John Wesley: Disciple of Early Christianity*; Henry D. Rack, *Reasonable Enthusiast: John Wesley and the Rise of Methodism* (London: Epworth Press, 1989), 78, 90, 114, 158, 175, 514; Campbell, *John Wesley and Christian Antiquity*; Randy L. Maddox, *Responsible Grace: John Wesley's Practical Theology* (Nashville: Kingswood Books, 1994), 22–23, 28–29, 42–43, 66–67, 91, 97–98, 138–139; Michael J. Christensen, "Theosis and Sanctification: John Wesley's Reformulation of a Patristic Doctrine," *Wesleyan Theological Journal* 31 (Fall 1996): 71–94; Theodore Runyon, *The New Creation: John Wesley's Theology Today* (Nashville: Abingdon Press, 1998), 13, 46, 80–81, 117, 213–214.

19. John Wesley, Sermon "On Laying the Foundation of the New Chapel," I, 3, in *The Bicentennial Edition of The Works of John Wesley* (Nashville: Abingdon Press, 1984–), vol. iii, 582. Hereinafter cited as *Works*.

20. *Minutes of the Methodist Conferences, from the First, Held in London by the Late Rev. John Wesley, A.M., in the Year 1744*, 5 vols. (London: John Mason, at the Wesleyan Conference Office, 1862–1864), vol. i, 23; cf. *Works*, ix, 270.

21. Campbell, *John Wesley and Christian Antiquity* , 104–108.

22. Richard P. Heitzenrater, "John Wesley's Reading of and Reference to the Early Church Fathers," in *Orthodox and Wesleyan Spirituality*, ed. S. T. Kimbrough, Jr. (Crestwood, N.Y.: St. Vladimir's Seminary Press, 2002), 30.

23. *Works*, ix, 264–268.

24. Campbell misses a few entries, and actually, in Wesley's works there are a few more references to the Fathers. Cf. Heitzenrater, "John Wesley's Reading of and Reference to the Early Church Fathers," 31, note 12.

25. Heitzenrater, "John Wesley's Reading of and Reference to the Early Church Fathers," 31.

26. Campbell, *John Wesley and Christian Antiquity*, 3.

27. Campbell, *John Wesley and Christian Antiquity*, 3.

28. Heitzenrater, "John Wesley's Reading of and Reference to the Early Church Fathers," 31.

29. Heitzenrater, "John Wesley's Reading of and Reference to the Early Church Fathers," 27.

30. While the precise identity of the author of the "Spiritual Homilies" is a mystery, there is today general agreement that the Homilies has no connection with the coptic Desert Father, St. Macarius of Egypt (300–390) for the milieu presupposed in the Homilies is definitely Syria rather than Egypt. The author used highly distinctive Syrian vocabulary and imagery though he wrote it in Greek. Cf. Pseudo-Macarius, *The Fifty Spiritual Homilies and The Great Letter*, Translated, Edited,

and with an Introduction by George A. Maloney, Preface by Kallistos Ware (New York: Paulist Press, 1992), xi–xii.

31. *Works*, xi, 90–94.

32. *Works*, ix, 31–42. According to Ted Campbell, although Wesley's description does not follow Clement's *Stromateis* precisely, Wesley's model for an ideal Methodist "was consciously inspired" by Clement's description of a perfect Christian Gnostic in the book seven of the *Stromateis*. Campbell offers some common elements between Wesley and Clement as follows: "both stress the hope of immortality, prayer without ceasing, love of one's neighbor, obedience to God's commandments, and freedom from worldly desires as characteristics of the ideal Christian (Gnostic or Methodist!)." Campbell, *John Wesley and Christian Antiquity*, 42. Wesley himself later acknowledged that he had referred to Clement's *Stromateis* for his "The Character of a Methodist":

> Five or six and thirty years ago I much admired the character of a perfect Christian drawn by Clemens Alexandrinus. Five or six and twenty years ago, a thought came into my mind of drawing such a character myself, only in a more scriptural manner and mostly in the very words of Scripture. This I entitled the 'Character of a Methodist' (Letter "To the Editor of Lloyd's Evening Post," March 26, 1767, in *Works*, xxii, 72).

John Wesley, earlier in the *Hymns and Sacred Poems* (1739) which he and his brother Charles published, included a poem entitled "On Clemens Alexandrinus's Description of a Perfect Christian." The poem is based on Clement's *Stromateis*. *The Poetical Works of John and Charles Wesley: Reprinted from the Originals, with the Last Corrections of the Authors; Together with the Poems of Charles Wesley Not Before Published*. Collected and arranged by G. Osborn, 13 vols. (London: Wesleyan-Methodist Conference Office, 1869), vol. i, 34–36. Hereinafter cited as *The Poetical Works*.

For the further study of Wesley's adoption of Clement, see Neil D. Anderson, *A Definitive Study of Evidence Concerning John Wesley's Appropriation of the Thought of Clement of Alexandria* (Lewiston, N.Y.: Edwin Mellen Press, 2004).

33. Wesley, Sermon "On Laying the Foundation of the New Chapel," II. 1–4, in *Works*, iii, 585–586.

34. *Works*, iii, 586.

35. Schmidt, *John Wesley: A Theological Biography*, vol. i, 222.

36. Schmidt, *John Wesley: A Theological Biography*, vol. ii, part ii, 191–192.

37. See Wesley, Sermon "Scriptural Christianity," in *Works*, i, 159–180; Sermon "Causes of the Inefficacy of Christianity," 7, in *Works*, iv, 90; Sermon "On a Single Eye," 3, in *Works*, iv, 121–122; "An Earnest Appeal to Men of Reason and Religion," in *Works*, xi, 54.

38. Keefer, *John Wesley: Disciple of Early Christianity*, 3–4.

39. See Campbell, *John Wesley and Christian Antiquity*, 46–53; Outler, "John Wesley's Interest in the Early Church Fathers," 102; Keefer, *John Wesley: Disciple of Early Christianity*, 4.

40. *The Journal of the Rev. John Wesley, A.M.*, ed. Nehemiah Curnock, 8 vols. (London: Epworth Press, 1938), vol. i, 37 and 89 footnote 4. Hereinafter cited as *Journal*.

41. Richard P. Heitzenrater, *John Wesley and the Oxford Methodists, 1725–1735*, Ph. D. dissertation (Duke University, 1972), 499 and 508. The full title of Cave's work is Primitive *Christianity; or, The Religion of the Ancient Christians in the First Ages of the Gospel* (London, 1763), and the full title of Horneck's work is *The Happy Ascetick, or, The Best Exercise, Together with Prayers Suitable to Each Exercise: To Which Is Added a Letter to a Person of Quality, concerning the Holy Lives of the Primitive Christians* (London, 1681). Wesley subsequently abridged and reprinted Cave and Horneck in his *Christian Library*.

42. Wesley was actually awarded the nickname "Primitive Christianity" by Mrs. Pendarves. *Works*, xxv, 246 n., 286 n.; also see Baker, *John Wesley and the Church of England*, 34.

43. Schmidt, *John Wesley: A Theological Biography*, vol. i, 132. Cf. "He saw in missionary activity the key to the original meaning of the gospel, the rebirth of primitive Christianity, the existential way towards his own salvation." Schmidt, *John Wesley: A Theological Biography*, vol. i, 134.

44. "Mr. Wesley's Essay upon the Stationary Fasts," Thomas Deacon, *A Compleat Collection of Devotions, both Publick and Private, Taken from the Apostolical Constitutions, the Ancient Liturgies and the Common Prayer Book of the Church of England* (London, 1734), appendix, 72–78.

45. "Mr. Wesley's Essay upon the Stationary Fasts," 72–73. Further, for the appeals to antiquity, Wesley indicates the "value of ecclesiastical antiquity" by citing some passages extracted from such books as "*Dr. Waterland's The Importance of the doctrine of the Holy Trinity . . . Mr. Chillingworth's Religion of Protestants . . . Daillée's Use of the Fathers . . . Archbishop Tillotson's vol. I. serm. 44 . . . Dr. Sherlock's present state of the Socinian controversy . . . Bishop Patrick on Tradition . . . Dr. Cave's epist. Apologet.*" "Mr. Wesley's Essay upon the Stationary Fasts," 74–78.

46. Wesley, Journal, 24th May 1738, in *Works*, xviii, 245. Wesley's observance of stationary fasts began on 2nd June 1732 under the influence of John Clayton (1709–1773) who had the High Church tendencies. The stationary fasts greatly strengthened Wesley's interest in the primitive church, and especially in the Eastern Church. *Works*, xviii, note 44; Baker, *John Wesley and the Church of England*, 32.

47. *Works*, xix, 135–136, 149, 193–194; *Works* xx, 10; Cf. Schmidt, *John Wesley: A Theological Biography*, vol. ii, part i, 190.

48. Luke L. Keefer, Jr., "John Wesley: Disciple of Early Christianity," *Wesleyan Theological Journal* 19, no. 1 (Spring 1984): 25.

49. Rack, "Religious Societies and the Origins of Methodism," 590.

50. *The Works of the Rev. John Wesley, M.A.*, ed. Thomas Jackson, 14 vols., 3d ed. (London: Wesleyan Conference Office, 1872), vol. x, 484. Hereinafter cited as *The Works* (Jackson).

51. *The Works* (Jackson), x, 492.

52. *The Works* (Jackson), x, 484. In other place, Wesley commended Ephraem Syrus as "the most awakening writer . . . of all the ancients." See Journal of October 12, 1736, in *Works*, xviii, 172. Wesley sometimes used the form "Ephrem" or "Ephraim" instead of "Ephraem."

53. Schmidt, *John Wesley: A Theological Biography*, vol. ii, part i, 107, 125, 136.

54. Wesley, "To 'Our Brethren in America'" (September, 1784), in *The Letters of the Rev. John Wesley, A.M.*, ed. John Telford, B.A., 8 vols. (London: Epworth Press, 1931), vol. vii, 239. Hereinafter cited as *Letters*.

55. Heitzenrater, "John Wesley's Reading of and Reference to the Early Church Fathers," 31.

56. The data by Heitzenrater shows that there are Wesley's thirteen references to Chrysostom including the references to Chrysostom's specific writings and passing references. Heitzenrater, "John Wesley's Reading of and Reference to the Early Church Fathers," 28.

57. For the concise, yet effective, exposition of the anthropology of Eastern Christianity, see John Meyendorff, *Byzantine Theology: Historical Trends and Doctrinal Themes* (New York: Fordham University Press, 1979), 138–150; Daniel B. Clendenin, *Eastern Orthodox Christianity: A Western Perspective*, 2d ed. (Grand Rapids: Baker Academic, 2003), 117–137. Also, Randy L. Maddox well summarizes the anthropology of Eastern Christianity in relation to Wesley in his *Responsible Grace: John Wesley's Practical Theology*, 65–67.

58. John Meyendorff, *Byzantine Theology*, 146.

59. Maddox, *Responsible Grace*, 66.

60. Pseudo-Macarius, *The Fifty Spiritual Homilies and The Great Letter*, 81, 148, 177–178.

61. Maddox, *Responsible Grace*, 67.

62. For example, see Wesley's "Letter to Richard Morgan" (January 15, 1734), in *Works*, xxv, 369; "A Farther Appeal to Men of Reason and Religion" (1745), Part I, 3, in *Works*, xi, 106; Sermon "Original Sin" (1759), III, 5, in *Works*, ii, 185; Wesley's note on II Peter 1:4, in John Wesley, *Explanatory Notes upon the New Testament* (London: Epworth Press, 1958), 890. Hereinafter cited as *Explanatory Notes upon the New Testament*. This *Notes* was first published by Wesley in 1755. This definition of salvation is also implied in Sermon "The Witness of Our Own Spirit" (1746), 15, in *Works*, i, 309; "A Plain Account of Genuine Christianity," II, 12, in Albert C. Outler, *John Wesley* (New York: Oxford University Press, 1964), 191.

63. Cf. Outler, "Wesley's Interest in the Early Fathers," 107–108.

64. Wesley commended [Pseudo-]Macarius as an excellent model of Christian perfection and stated in his introduction to the *Homilies*: "Whatever he insists upon is essential, is durable, is necessary." John Wesley, *A Christian Library: Consisting of Extracts from and Abridgments of the Choicest Pieces of Practical Divinity, Which have been publish'd in the English Tongue. In Fifty Volumes* (Bristol: Printed by Felix Farley, 1749–1755), vol. i, 83. Hereinafter cited as *Christian Library*. As Theodore Runyon puts it, "the core idea of *theosis*—participating in, and

transformation by, the creative energy of the Spirit—was central to Wesley's understanding of regeneration and sanctification," while the translation of the Macarian *Homilies* which Wesley used avoided translating *theosis* with "deification" or "divinization," often using instead "sanctification" or "perfection," probably because it was thought that the term "deification" or "divinization" was either unfamiliar or too subject to misunderstanding. Runyon, *The New Creation*, 245, n. 35.

65. Roberta Bondi, "The Meeting of Oriental Orthodoxy and United Methodism," in *Christ in East and West*, eds., Paul Fries and Tiran Nersoyan, and intro. Jeffrey Gros (Macon, GA: Mercer University Press, 1987), 175–176. Also, for the study of Wesley's use of the Macarian Homilies see Mark T. Kurowski, "The First Step Toward Grace: John Wesley's Use of the Spiritual Homilies of Macarius the Great," *Methodist History* 36, no. 2 (January 1998): 113–124.

66. Runyon, *The New Creation*, 80.

67. Charles Wallace Jr., ed., *Susanna Wesley: The Complete Writings* (New York: Oxford University Press, 1997), 263–264.

68. Runyon, *The New Creation*, 80.

69. Wesley, "Farther Thoughts on Separation from the Church" (1789), 1, in *Works*, ix, 538.

70. Todd, *John Wesley and the Catholic Church*, 12.

71. Todd, *John Wesley and the Catholic Church*, 18–19.

72. Todd, *John Wesley and the Catholic Church*, 17.

73. Todd, *John Wesley and the Catholic Church*, 175.

74. Wesley, Sermon "Upon our Lord's Sermon on the Mount, XII," III, 8, in *Works*, i, 682–683.

75. Todd, *John Wesley and the Catholic Church*, 18–19.

76. Todd, *John Wesley and the Catholic Church*, 170–171.

77. *Works*, xxvi, 173–174.

78. Cited from Todd, *John Wesley and the Catholic Church*, 173. These preachers were Paul Greenwood, Thomas Mitchell, and John Murlin. They began to administer the Lord's Supper to the society in 1760. See John C. Bowmer, *The Sacrament of the Lord's Supper in Early Methodism* (London: Dacre Press, 1951), 151.

79. Todd, *John Wesley and the Catholic Church*, 170.

80. This work will follow Frank Baker in using the term "Anglican" for that which pertains to the Church of England, even though that term was very seldom used in the eighteenth century. Baker, *John Wesley and the Church of England*, 6.

81. *Works*, xi, 424.

82. Earlier in 1302, the bull *Unam Sanctam* of Boniface VIII promulgated: "We say, define, and pronounce, that it is absolutely necessary to salvation, for every man to be subject to the Pope of Rome." Cited from David Butler, *Methodists and Papists: John Wesley and the Catholic Church in the Eighteenth Century* (London: Darton, Longman and Todd, 1995), 105.

83. *The Works* (Jackson), x, 140.

84. *The Works* (Jackson), x, 142.

85. Maximin Piette, *John Wesley in the Evolution of Protestantism* (London: Sheed and Ward, 1937); Michael Hurley S. J., "Salvation Today and Wesley Today," in *The Place of Wesley in the Christian Tradition: Essays delivered at Drew University in Celebration of the Commencement of the Publication of the Oxford Edition of the Works of John Wesley*, ed. Kenneth E. Rowe (Metuchen, N. J.: The Scarecrow Press, 1976), 94–116. Particularly, in his work Piette proposes a brave thesis that Wesley represented a Catholic reaction to the Protestant extremes of Luther and Calvin, turning back to historic Catholic understandings of sanctity.

86. Workman, *The Place of Methodism in the Catholic Church*; R. Newton Flew, "Methodism and the Catholic Tradition," in *Northern Catholicism: Centenary Studies in the Oxford and Parallel Movements*, eds. N. P. Williams and Charles Harris (London: SPCK, 1933), 515–530; William R. Cannon, "John Wesley and the Catholic Tradition" (paper delivered at World Methodist Council Executive Committee, Toronto, Canada, 24 September 1980); Charles W. Brockwell Jr., "Methodist Discipline: From Rule of Life to Canon Law," *The Drew Gateway* 54, no 2–3 (1984): 1–24.

87. Randy L. Maddox, "John Wesley and Eastern Orthodoxy: Influences, Convergences and Differences," *The Asbury Theological Journal* 45, no. 2 (Fall 1990): 29.

88. See Jean Orcibal, "The Theological Originality of John Wesley and Continental Spirituality," in *A History of the Methodist Church in Great Britain*, eds. Rupert Davies, A. Raymond George and Gordon Rupp, 4 vols. (London: Epworth Press, 1965–1988), vol. i, 83–111; Robert G. Tuttle, Jr., *John Wesley: His Life and Theology* (Grand Rapids: Zondervan Publishing House, 1978). Particularly Jean Orcibal shows that the French Catholic mystics constantly influenced upon Wesley's theology throughout his life.

89. Schmidt, *John Wesley: A Theological Biography*, vol. i, 13–14.

90. Outler, *John Wesley*, 251f.

91. Outler, *John Wesley*, 252.

92. Outler, *John Wesley*, 252.

93. Tuttle, *John Wesley: His Life and Theology*, 46.

94. "In 1721, an English edition of the *Homilies* of [Pseudo-]Macarius was published and quickly came into Wesley's hands. From then on, both before and after Aldersgate in 1738, Wesley apparently returned periodically to Macarius." Howard Snyder, "John Wesley and Macarius the Egyptian," *The Asbury Theological Journal* 45, no. 2 (Fall 1990): 55.

95. *The Works* (Jackson), xi, 366ff.

96. *Works*, xviii, 243.

97. *The Works* (Jackson), xi, 367.

98. *Works*, xviii, 244.

99. *Works*, xviii, 244.

100. Richard P. Heitzenrater, *Wesley and the People Called Methodists* (Nashville: Abingdon Press, 1995), 72–73.

101. *The Works* (Jackson), xi, 366.

102. *The Works* (Jackson), xi, 366.

103. Orcibal, "The Theological Originality of John Wesley and Continental Spirituality," 88–90.

104. Schmidt, *John Wesley: A Theological Biography*, vol. i, 213, 215.

105. See the diary of May 20, 1736 in Georgia, in *Works*, xviii, 386.

106. Wesley, "A Short Account of the School in Kingswood, Near Bristol," in *The Works* (Jackson), xiii, 284.

107. For example, see Wesley, Sermon "On the Trinity" (1775), in *Works*, ii, 374–386; Letter to Miss Hester Ann Roe on June 2, 1776, in *The Works* (Jackson), xiii, 77; Letter to Miss Ritchie on August 2, 1777, in *The Works* (Jackson), xiii, 59; Journal, March 1, 1786, in *Works*, xxiii, 386.

108. Schmidt, *John Wesley: A Theological Biography*, vol. i, 216.

109. Cf. *The Works* (Jackson), i, 404; Heitzenrater, *John Wesley and the Oxford Methodists*, 506.

110. Howard F. VanValin, "Mysticism in Wesley," *The Asbury Seminarian* 12, no. 2 (Spring-Summer 1958): 7.

111. *The Works* (Jackson), xiv, 385–386.

112. *The Works* (Jackson), xiv, 384–386.

113. Cf. Patricia A. Ward, "Madame Guyon (1648–1717)," in *The Pietist Theologians: An Introduction to Theology in the Seventeenth and Eighteenth Centuries*, ed. Carter Lindberg (Malden, MA: Blackwell Publishing, 2005), 161–174.

114. In Wesley's time, Juan de Castaniza (c.1536–1599) was credited with the book (the original full title is *De pugna spiritualis; tractatus vere aureus de perfectione vitae christianae* [1599]). Castaniza was a Spanish Benedictine monk. The *De pugna spiritualis* was translated into English in 1698 by Richard Lucas, under the title *The Spiritual Combat; or the Christian Pilgrim in His Spiritual Conflict and Conquest*. Recently it is attributed to Lorenzo Scupoli. See Outler, *John Wesley*, 107–108, note 8 and Schmidt, *John Wesley: A Theological Biography*, vol. i, 48.

115. Heitzenrater, *John Wesley and the Oxford Methodists*, 505, 507, 517, 518, 520 and 522. The full title of Scougal's work is *The Life of God in the Soul of Man, or the Nature and Excellency of the Christian Religion, with the Method of Obtaining the Happiness it Purposes*. The intention of this book was to stimulate a sincere interest in the vital, inward feeling of religion as opposed to the legalism prevalent in a more formal religious experience, showing that true religion is not in the form of religion but in the union of the soul with God, Christ literally formed in us. Susanna Wesley read this book and was influential in securing its effect in John Wesley. John Wesley was so taken by the book that he abridged the original edition and had it printed no less than seven times for distribution. The full title of Spurstowe's work is *The Spiritual Chymist; or, Six Decads of Divine Meditations on Several Subjects (Σατανα νοηματα: or, The Wiles of Satan, in a Discourse)*.

116. Wesley read Fénelon's *Of Simplicity* (on December 1726), *The Archbishop of Cambray's Pastoral Letter* (on January 1733), and *The Maxims of the Saints Explained, concerning the Interiour Life* (on July 1733). Of these *The Archbishop of Cambray's Pastoral Letter* was used by Wesley for study with the Oxford Methodists. Heitzenrater, *John Wesley and the Oxford Methodists*, 504.

117. Heitzenrater, *John Wesley and the Oxford Methodists*, 511, 517, 518 and 519. The full title of Spinckes' work is *The True Church of England Man's Companion in the Closet; or, A Complete Manual of Private Devotions*.

118. *Works*, xxv, 487.

119. James. R. Rigg, *The Living Wesley, As He Was in His Youth and in His Prime*, With an introduction by John F. Hurst (New York: Nelson & Phillips, 1874), 154–155.

120. It comes from a memorandum of Wesley's, written on January 25, 1738, in which stating on his spiritual condition, he wrote of different views of Christianity, including the mystics. *Works*, xviii, 212f.

121. *The Works* (Jackson), xiv, 319.

122. Journal on December 15, 1788, in *Works*, xxiv, 117.

123. *The Works* (Jackson), xiv, 321.

124. *The Works* (Jackson), xiv, 321.

125. *Works*, xviii, 213.

126. Gordon S. Wakefield, *Methodist Devotion: The Spiritual Life in the Methodist Tradition, 1791–1945* (London: Epworth Press, 1966), 23.

127. Rack, *Reasonable Enthusiast*, 401.

128. Henry Bett, *The Spirit of Methodism* (London: Epworth Press, 1937), 61–63.

129. "The Life of the Rev. John Wesley," in *The Works* (Jackson), v, 514.

130. *Works*, xix, 219.

131. Wesley in his response called it *The Enthusiasm of Methodists and Papists Compar'd*, and wrote several letters about the book disclaiming any similarities.

132. George Lavington, *The Enthusiasm of Methodists and Papists Compar'd* (London: Printed for J. and P. Knapton, 1749), Part I, ← 2.

133. Workman, *The Place of Methodism in the Catholic Church*, 61.

134. Workman, *The Place of Methodism in the Catholic Church*, 62.

135. Workman, *The Place of Methodism in the Catholic Church*, 62.

136. Workman, *The Place of Methodism in the Catholic Church*, 62.

137. Workman, *The Place of Methodism in the Catholic Church*, 62.

138. Workman, *The Place of Methodism in the Catholic Church*, 62.

139. Workman, *The Place of Methodism in the Catholic Church*, 63.

140. Workman, *The Place of Methodism in the Catholic Church*, 63.

141. Workman, *The Place of Methodism in the Catholic Church*, 63.

142. Workman, *The Place of Methodism in the Catholic Church*, 63.

143. Workman, *The Place of Methodism in the Catholic Church*, 63.

144. Workman, *The Place of Methodism in the Catholic Church*, 63.

145. Workman, *The Place of Methodism in the Catholic Church*, 64.

146. For example, see Gordon Rupp, "Introductory Essay," *A History of the Methodist Church in Great Britain*, eds., Rupert Davies and Gordon Rupp, 4 vols. (London: Epworth Press, 1965), vol. i, xxxvi.

147. Herbert B. Workman, *The Evolution of the Monastic Ideal: From the Earliest Times Down to the Coming of the Friars, a Second Chapter in the History of Christian Renunciation* (Boston: Beacon Press, 1962), 243.

148. W. H. Fitchett, *Wesley and His Century: A Study in Spiritual Forces* (New York: Abingdon Press, 1917), 346.

149. Fitchett, *Wesley and His Century*, 343.

150. Workman, *The Place of Methodism in the Catholic Church*, 64–65.

151. Henry Offley Wakeman, *An Introduction to the History of the Church of England: From the Earliest Times to the Present Day*, revised, with an Additional Chapter, by S. L. Ollard (London: Rivingtons, 1919), 439.

152. The High Medieval Age in Western Catholicism designates the period of c.1050 – c.1300, the epoch of the flowering of the Medieval Ages.

Chapter 2

Reformation Tradition

Reformers and Wesley

The main concern of this section is to trace the areas where Wesley may have been influenced by the reformers. This work does not attempt to amount to any sort of survey of reformers' ecclesiologies. It focuses on certain elements in reformers' ecclesiologies rather than others because those are elements where we can trace the reformers' possible influences on Wesley.

Martin Luther (1483–1546) was inspired by the teaching and example of men such as Hus and shared their longing for a return to Scripture and the authenticity of the primitive church. Luther's original intention was not to create a new church but to restore the existing one to pristine purity. As he saw it, the true Church of the apostles had been obscured by a heavy overlay of ecclesiastical bureaucracy and popular piety symbolized by the practice of indulgences. Above all, the visible, hierarchical Church had lost sight of the central doctrine of faith as set forth by Paul in his letter to the Romans. Of Luther and of the reformers in general it has been said that "[w]hat they saw in the teaching of the Roman Catholic Church was the undue stress upon works, and the answer to this was the justification of the sinner by divine grace through faith alone."[1]

A direct corollary of Luther's doctrine of justification was his conception of the church as essentially the congregation of those who have faith. The faith of believers is evoked and sustained by the word of God. In Luther's thought, the word of God assumes an authority greater than and even in conflict with the authority of tradition, the magisterium, and the pope.

For Luther, the genuine sacraments of Christ are not the seven proclaimed by the pope but only those whose institution by Christ is explicit in
the Gospels: baptism and the eucharist. According to Luther, the word of
God comes to us first of all in Jesus Christ. But, in a derivative sense, it
comes also through Scripture, through the preaching of the gospel, and
through the sacraments. The sacraments are physical acts that God has chosen to be signs of His promise. They are intimately connected with faith and
with the Word, for their function is precisely to be another form in which
the Word is heard in faith. In order to qualify as a sacrament, an act must
have been instituted by Christ and must be bound up with the promise of
the gospel. Therefore, there are only two sacraments.[2]

Luther's understanding of the church is essentially and fundamentally
evangelical and Christological. On the one hand, it is evangelical in the
sense that the evangel, the gospel, constitutes the reality of the church and
is the one thing needful to ensure its existence. Luther lists in *On the Councils and the Church* seven marks of the church as the public and external
signs by which the true church may be recognized. The first three of them,
by which the existence of the church in the world can be noticed externally,
are the possession of the Word of God, baptism, and eucharist.[3]

> First, the holy Christian people are recognized by their possession of the
> holy word of God.
> Second, God's people or the Christian holy people are recognized by the
> holy sacrament of baptism, wherever it is taught, believed, and adminis-
> tered correctly according to Christ's ordinance . . .
> Third, God's people, or Christian holy people, are recognized by the holy
> sacrament of the altar, wherever it is rightly administered, believed and
> received, according to Christ's institution.[4]

Most important is the first of these marks: the Church's possession of the
word of God in a greater or lesser degree of purity. Luther says, "God's
word cannot be without God's people, and conversely, God's people cannot
be without God's word."[5] Therefore, the word of God is the starting point
of Luther's ecclesiology. "Where the word is, there is faith; and where faith
is, there is the true church."[6] By the word of God Luther means the gospel.
And the gospel is also the preached gospel. He states,

> For the gospel is before bread and baptism the unique, most certain and
> noblest symbol of the church, because through the gospel alone is the
> church conceived, formed, nourished, generated, instructed, fed, clothed,
> ornamented, strengthened, armed, preserved—in short the entire life and
> substance of the church is in the word of God. . . . Nor am I speaking

about the written word but rather voice of the gospel . . . only by the vocal
and public voice of the gospel can it be known where is the church and the
mystery of the kingdom of heaven.[7]

. . . we are speaking of the external word, preached orally . . . for this is
what Christ left behind as an external sign, by which his church, or his
Christian people in the world, should be recognized . . . wherever you hear
or see this word preached, believed, professed, and lived, do not doubt
that the true *ecclesia sancta catholica*, "a Christian holy people" must be
there, even though their number is very small.[8]

Luther laid down this principle in his monumental "Ninety-Five Theses":
"The true treasure of the Church is the Holy Gospel of the glory and grace
of God."[9] For Luther the meaning of the church can not be arrived at in
terms of tradition, structure, teaching authority, or canon law, but solely in
terms of the gospel. The church is where the gospel is. The gospel means
justification: administered in absolution, received by faith, experienced as
forgiveness, and worked out in mutual service in the priesthood of every
Christian.

On the other hand, because Christ is the gospel, the church is where
Christ is. In that sense Luther's ecclesiology is Christological. Christ is the
living Word who is made manifest in the preached Word and in the sacraments, and the Church is that place in which the Word is truly preached and
the sacraments are rightly celebrated. In other words, the church is the
mode of Christ's saving presence in the world, communicating his life to
men through its ministries and sacraments. The church is truly known only
by faith, through baptism, the Lord's Supper, and the preaching of the
Word. As Luther put it: "The church is a high, deep, hidden thing which
one may neither perceive nor see, but must grasp only by faith, through
baptism, sacrament and word."[10]

Luther is associated with the Aldersgate event of John Wesley. While
listening to a reading of "Luther's Preface to the Epistle to the Romans," at
Aldersgate Street, on May 24, 1738, Wesley felt his heart "strangely
warmed" and was given assurance of salvation.[11] Leo G. Cox says, "until
1738, when Wesley was thirty five, he was not much interested (in) Luther
and made no reference to any of his writings."[12] Cox, however, does not
take note of the fact that Wesley studied Luther and Calvin at Charterhouse.
In addition, Wesley had interest in something of Luther's thought through
his contact with the Moravians before Aldersgate. But it is true that after
Aldersgate, Wesley showed increased awareness of Luther as a man to be
reckoned with. In a sermon preached at St. Mary's, Oxford, on June 11,

1738, for instance, he praised Luther as "that glorious champion of the Lord of Hosts" and "that man of God."[13]

About a year later, April 4, 1739, however, Wesley recorded his negative impression of Luther. In his *Journal* of that date, he mentions three women (Mrs. Norman, Mrs. Grevil, and Mrs. Panou) who "agreed to meet together weekly '[t]o confess their faults one to another and pray one for another, that may be healed,'" according to James 5:16. He then asks, "How dare any man deny this to be (as to the substance of it) a means of grace, ordained by God? Unless he will affirm (with Luther in the fury of his solifidianism) that St. James's Epistle is 'an epistle of straw'?"[14] Another negative reference to Luther comes from Wesley's *Journal* entries of June 15–16, 1741. Here he records his severe criticism of Luther's *Lectures on Galatians*:

> I set out for London and read over in the way that celebrated book, Martin Luther's Comment on the Epistle to the Galatians. I was utterly ashamed. How have I esteemed this book, only because I had heard it commended by others! Or, at best, because I had read some excellent sentences occasionally quoted from it. But what shall I say, now I judge for myself? Now I see with my own eyes? Why, not only that the author makes nothing out, clears up not one considerable difficulty; that he is quite shallow in his remarks on many passages, and muddy and confused almost on all; but that he is deeply tinctured with *mysticism* throughout, and hence often fundamentally wrong. To instance only in one or two points. How does he (almost in the words of Tauler) decry *reason*, right or wrong, as an irreconcilable enemy to the gospel of Christ! Whereas, what is *reason* (the faculty so called) but the power of apprehending, judging, and discoursing? Which power is no more to be condemned in the gross than seeing, hearing, or feeling. Again, how blasphemously does he speak of good works and of the law of God! Constantly coupling the law with sin, death, hell, or the devil! And teaching that Christ 'delivers us from' them all alike. Whereas it can no more be proved by Scripture that Christ 'delivers us from the law of God' than that he delivers us *from holiness* or *from heaven*. Here (I apprehend) is the real spring of the grand error of the Moravians. They follow Luther, for better, for worse. Hence their 'No works, no law, no commandments.' But who art thou that 'speakest evil of the law, and judgest the law'?
> . . . In the evening I came to London and preached on those words, 'In Christ Jesus neither circumcision availeth anything, nor uncircumcision, but faith which worketh by love.' After reading Luther's miserable comment upon the text, I thought it my bounden duty openly to warn the congregation against that dangerous treatise and to retract whatever recommendation I might ignorantly have given of it.[15]

Wesley's later references to Luther are ambivalent. On the one hand, Wesley admires Luther and appreciates his work. He translated *Martin Luther's Life*[16] from a German edition by John Daniel Herrnschmid and inserted it in the first volume of his *Arminian Magazine* (1778).[17] But on the other hand, he hated and rebuked Luther's ignorance of the doctrine of sanctification. In his sermon "On God's Vineyard" (1787), he wrote,

> Who has wrote more ably than Martin Luther on justification by faith alone? And who was more ignorant of the doctrine of sanctification, or more confused in his conceptions of it? In order to be thoroughly convinced of this, of his total ignorance with regard to sanctification, there needs no more than to read over, without prejudice, his celebrated comment on the Epistle to the Galatians.[18]

Wesley certainly missed Luther's emphasis on righteous living, but it is true that for Wesley a holy life became a far more reliable sign of salvation than for Luther.

While Wesley declared his detestation of Luther's ignorance of the doctrine of sanctification, he certainly owed Luther the fundamental doctrine of justification by faith alone. The doctrine of justification was Wesley's first point of contact with Luther, and Wesley, like Luther, saw it as *articulus stantis vel cadentis ecclesiae* ("the doctrine on which the church stands or falls").[19] Wesley received Luther's doctrine of justification from the Moravians and preached it to the Methodists as "the pillar and ground of that faith of which alone cometh salvation."[20]

In his doctrine of the church, Wesley followed the Thirty-Nine Articles of Religion of the Church of England with minor alterations,[21] and the doctrine of the Church in the Thirty-Nine Articles may be traced ultimately to the Confession of Augsburg. Article XIX, "Of the Church," of Thirty-Nine Articles is "partly Lutheran in tenor"[22] because of the influence of the Augsburg Confession. Article VII of the Augsburg Confession says, "The Church is the congregation of saints [the assembly of all believers], in which the Gospel is rightly taught [*purely preached*] and the sacraments rightly administered [according to the Gospel]."[23] Article XIX of the Church of England says, "The Visible Church of Christ is a Congregation of faithful men, in the which the pure Word of God is preached, and the Sacraments be duly administered according to Christ's Ordinance, in all those things that of necessity are requisite to the same."[24] Wesley followed Article XIX of the Thirty-Nine Articles with the omission of the closing part (errors of the churches).

Gordon E. Rupp was right in saying that "The question which was asked in the 16th century, 'where was your church before Luther?', and in the 18th century, 'where was your church before Wesley?' has gotten its appropriate answer in the Augsburg Confession: 'we existed in one holy Christian church which was from the beginning.'"[25] The most significant common element between Luther and Wesley, reflecting the Augsburg Confession, is that the Church is primarily a *congregation of holy people of God.* Luther says, "God's word cannot be without God's people, and conversely, God's people cannot be without God's word."[26] But perhaps, "Luther laid more stress on the second half of his sentence, Wesley on the first."[27]

Luther, as Gordon Rupp points out, was not concerned with defining the circumference of the church, but with proclaiming the essence of the church. After his death, Protestantism came to wrestle with "the intricate question of circumference."[28] Reformers after Luther "added to Word and Sacrament another dimension, 'The Discipline of Christ.'"[29]

This development was represented by Martin Bucer, John Calvin, John Knox (1505–1572), the Puritans and the Separatists, who stressed discipline.[30] Martin Bucer says, "There cannot be a Church without Church discipline (*ein ban*)."[31] "Any . . . people in the Church are to be kept in check by excommunication and every form of discipline."[32] The word alone is not enough; it must be heard with joy and obeyed with zeal. The quality of Christian discipleship becomes a mark of the church. Love and discipline must be added to word and sacrament. The Church of the Lord must be restored "through his holy word, sacraments and discipline."[33] Bucer lists as the marks of the church: hearing the voice of its Shepherd, the ministry of teaching, the possession of suitable ministers, the lawful dispensation of the sacraments, and righteousness and holiness of life.[34] Including discipline under the lawful dispensation of the sacraments, Bucer argues that discipline has been "commanded by Christ," and that the "[c]orruption of discipline ruins the entire ministry of teaching and sacraments." Discipline is "the final aspect of mutual intercourse in the Church."[35] He concludes, "The Church which lacks these aforesaid marks is not to be called the body of Christ. Although it may contain many members of Christ, it is not a fellowship gathered by the Spirit of Christ, comprising [clergy], ministers and people."[36]

Bucer's theology suggests many parallels with Wesley in terms of the emphasis on discipline, the missionary outlook, the stress on the necessity of inward Christian experience and personal holiness, the role of the small cell of Christian laymen (the Christian *Gemeinschaft*), the great stress on hymn-singing, and the relative prominence he gives to the ministry of the Holy Spirit. Actually, some scholars depicted Bucer as "the Pietist among the Reformers," and even traced a straight line of community from him to Methodism.[37]

In John Calvin we also find a stress on discipline.[38] Paul Bassett pointed out that a major cause of divergent ecclesiological understandings between Luther and Calvin is the latter's teaching on "a third mark of the Church," that is discipline.[39] For Luther, what makes the church the church is the gospel. The church, in Luther's view, was created by the presence of Christ through the gospel. Where the gospel is found, Christ is present, and where Christ is present, the church must truly exist. This conviction is equally important for Calvin. Luther and Calvin were both prepared to sacrifice the visible unity of the Western Church if only by so doing they could save the gospel. But in Calvin there was an effort to make Luther's doctrine of the church more practicable. For Luther the church is constituted and defined solely by reference to the gospel. It is the gospel that is believed, the gospel that is preached, and the gospel that regulates the administration of the sacraments. But in Calvin, we find a rather more external and formal doctrine of the marks of the church than in Luther. Like Luther, Calvin joins the Word and the sacraments as the marks of the church. But while for Luther the Word means the gospel or absolution, for Calvin it is more suggestive of correct doctrine and proper church order. Sometimes Calvin links very closely the Word itself and the ministry of the Word. Perhaps this is reminiscent of Luther's doctrine of the Word as the Word preached. But for Calvin, preaching carries a stronger underlying emphasis on church order. Calvin makes the Word constitutive, not only of the church itself, but also of the ministry. Calvin describes the ministry of the Word as the true mark of the church. This is not a movement away from the Christological center that we find in Luther towards a clerical ecclesiology, for Calvin's doctrine is to be interpreted in a Christological way (through perhaps the Christ of the law as well as of the gospel). Calvin's position may be interpreted as transitional between that of Luther with its radical holding to the Christological center, and that of the later Reformed tradition with its stress on discipline. Calvin's view gave him a more positive doctrine of sanctification and an important place for discipline in the church.[40] For Calvin, the church is the place where the elect are perfected.

Wesley was closer to Bucer and Calvin than to Luther, with respect to the emphasis on sanctification and discipline. In his notes on Acts 5:11, Wesley describes the church as "a company of men, called by the gospel, grafted into Christ by baptism, animated by love, united by all kinds of fellowship, and disciplined by the death of Ananias and Sapphira." Here Wesley, along with other elements of biblical preaching, the sacraments, unity, and fellowship, introduces the element of discipline. Furthermore, in his sermon "Of the Church," he finds in the exhortation to "Walk worthy of the vocation wherewith we are called" a basis for stressing the importance of a disciplined life as essential to the church being the church.[41] A powerful theological support for his inclusion of discipline as an important element in the church is the place of sanctification in his soteriology. Sanctification would entail a call for the church to be a holy community.

In conclusion, Wesley seems to have read little of the reformers. The reformers do not count as an influence on Wesley in any sense similar to that in which primitive Christianity became an influence on and an ideal for him. Rather they had an influence on Wesley on the sense that they introduced certain themes—particularly sanctification and discipline—into ecclesiology which were to have an impact on Wesley not through any encounter with the works of the reformers themselves, but primarily through the way in which those themes played themselves out in the Anglican and Puritan traditions. Therefore, one may conclude that the reformers, with the themes of sanctification and discipline they put stress on, had an impact on Wesley's ecclesiology through the traditions of English Protestantism (the Church of England and the Puritans) and not in any direct way.

The Church of England and Wesley

The Church of England at its outset was aptly described by Horton Davies as "non-Papal and nationalistic Catholicism."[42] The theology of Henry VIII (1491–1547), even when he separated from Rome, was Catholic. Similarly, the first apologists for the Church of England broke little new theological ground, changing largely their ecclesiology and politics. Henry, for all his cynicism and hatred of the papacy, remained attached to much of the traditional framework of Catholicism. Also, for his people at large, Catholic piety continued in the midst of all the political changes. At least by the 1530s, in England "the vigour, richness, and creativity of late medieval religion was undiminished, and continued to hold the imagination and elicit the loyalty of the majority of the population."[43] The English Reformation, in a sense, did not come from popular uprising against Roman authority, but was imposed from the top by force on a largely unwilling public.

In the midst of the reformation, the numbers of committed Protestants were growing to become a force to be reckoned with. They pressed for a closer affinity between the reforming English Church and the churches of the Continental Reformation.

The early English Reformers' ecclesiology tended to follow developments on the Continent. Thomas Cranmer, the first non-Roman Catholic

Archbishop of Canterbury, states the problem as the English Reformers saw it:

> If we shall allow them for the true church of God, that appear to be the visible and outward church, consisting of the ordinary succession of bishops, then shall we make Christ, which is an innocent lamb without spot, and in whom is found no guile, to be the head of ungodly and disobedient members. . . . if we allow the pope, his cardinals, bishops, priests, monks, canons, friars, and the whole rabble of the clergy, to the will and commandment of Christ, left and expressed in his word written; then make we him a sinner, and his word of no effect. For as sweet agreeth with sour, black with white, darkness with light, and evil with good; even so this outward, seen, and visible church [of Rome], consisting of the ordinary succession of bishops, agreeth with Christ.[44]

The attempt is therefore made by the English Reformers to identify the true church differently from Rome and in the Continental Reformation manner. As John Hooper (1495–1555) writes, "the true church is known by these two marks; the pure preaching of the gospel, and the right use of the sacraments."[45] Others add discipline in an effort to make the marks a more reliable guide. So Nicholas Ridley says, "The holy catholic church...is the communion of saints....The marks whereby this church is known unto me in this dark world, and in the midst of this crooked and forward generation, are these—the sincere preaching of God's word; the due administration of the sacraments; charity; and faithful observing of ecclesiastical discipline according to the word of God."[46] The catechism of 1553 lists the marks: "first, pure preaching of the gospel: then brotherly love . . . thirdly, upright and uncorrupted use of the Lord's sacraments, according to the ordinance of the gospel: last of all, brotherly correction and excommunication, or banishing those out of the church, that will not amend their lives."[47]

However, ultimately, England did not go in the direction of Wittenburg or Geneva, much to the displeasure of some of the Puritans. Also, England did not completely return to Rome, though it did for a while during Mary's reign (1553–1558). Eventually, an attempt at the *via media* was made with the desire to preserve the best of the Christian tradition as corrected by the freshly opened Scriptures. The major theological task was to define this middle ground in such a way as to avoid undue antagonisms from either side of Puritans or Roman Catholics.

The task of defining the direction of this *via media* largely fell into the hands of John Jewel (1522–1571). In his *Apology* (1564), although he assigned the most part of his work to attack the Romanists, Jewel clearly had in mind two types of opponents (that is, Roman Catholics and Puritans),

with major arguments targeted for each of them. Against the Roman side of
the conflict, Jewel is concerned to show that the Roman Catholic Church is
not the true church by the common standards of judgment, by the examples
of the Scriptures and the primitive church "which we doubt not but was
indeed the true catholic church."[48] He further contends for the jurisdiction
of the prince over the church. Jewel first cites the Scriptural precedent for
the authority of temporal political powers, appealing especially to the Old
Testament monarchy.[49] He then moves to the writings of the early Fathers,
who used this argument in support of giving the same deference to the political rulers in all subsequent ages.[50] The jurisdiction of the prince over the
church is also argued against his second opponent, the Puritans. Against the
Puritan side, Jewel argues that Scripture demands a specific form of polity
for all times and places. He also denies that the Church of England "allow
every man to be a priest, to be a teacher, and to be an interpreter of the
Scriptures."[51]

Although his views were widely accepted by the leaders of the Continental Reformation whom he met during the Marian exile,[52] Jewel did not
feel compelled to throw out everything having the slightest connection with
the "papist religion." The *sola scriptura* principle was accepted, but so were
the interpretive authority of the primitive church and a belief in the continuity of that church, and hence its authority, through the ages. This led to a
position which accepted the validity of varying types of church order,[53]
though preferring episcopal order—a position Puritans found unsupported
by the New Testament, to which alone appeal was to be made for the legitimacy of any and all practices. For Puritans, church order must be drawn
directly from the New Testament.

Albert C. Outler summarized Jewel's ecclesiology as part of the Anglican ethos in which Wesley would later live and think, offering the following five principles:

> (1) The church's subordination to Scripture; (2) The church's unity in
> Christ and in the essentials of doctrine; (3) The notion that paradigmata
> for ecclesiology should be drawn from the patristic age; (4) The apostolic
> doctrine [with the conviction that apostolic authority adheres in the conti-
> nuity of apostolic teaching, rather than in apostolic persons]; (5) The idea
> of a *functional* episcopacy (as belonging to the church's well being rather
> than to its essence).[54]

The first, fourth and fifth of the principles take issue with the Roman
Catholic Church; the third and fifth argue against the Puritans. The second
would find agreement with both of the opponents, but would be differently
interpreted by all three parties, that is, Roman Catholics, Puritans, and An-

glicans. Together the ideas convey the Anglican sentiment that the Church of England was not at all a new church, unlike some of the Reformed expressions, nor was it a church gone astray from the foundational doctrines of Christian antiquity, as was the Church of Rome; rather, it was part of the truly Catholic Church within which all churches practicing the "faith once delivered unto the saints" are contained.[55]

Without question, Jewel was the major spokesman for Anglican ecclesiology. His *Apology* helped to shape the Thirty-Nine Articles of Religion (1571) which dealt specifically with the doctrine of the Church. The Articles, as Eric Jay points out, have to do only with questions of the visible Church and its ministry, preaching, sacraments and discipline while the English reformers generally followed Calvin in thinking about the concept of the invisible Church.[56] Brief attention should be given to the Articles, particularly in light of the interpretation to be given to them later by Wesley in defending his views and his movement.

In the Thirty-Nine Articles of Religion, the definition of the Church is given in Article XIX, "Of the Church":

> The Visible Church of Christ is a Congregation of faithful men, in the which the pure Word of God is preached, and the Sacraments be duly administered according to Christ's Ordinance, in all those things that of necessity are requisite to the same.
>
> As the Church of Jerusalem, Alexandria, and Antioch, have erred, so also the Church of Rome hath erred, not only in their living and manner of Ceremonies, but also in matters of Faith.[57]

A standard interpretation of the Articles in Wesley's day was that of Bishop Gilbert Burnet (1643–1715). Although his comments were made more than a century later, Burnet was consistent with the thought of John Jewel in his 1699 exposition of the nineteenth Article. Here, he clearly saw the distinction between Roman teaching and Anglican thought: "This Article, together with some that follow it, relates to the fundamental difference between us and the church of Rome: they teaching that we are to judge of doctrines by the authority and the decisions of the church; whereas we affirm, that we are first to examine the doctrine, and according to that to judge of the purity of a church."[58] Here is the outworking of the *sola scriptura* principle. The fact that the Scripture was recognized in the Church of England as the final authority in all matters of doctrine and practice[59] was certainly not lost upon the conscientious young Wesley as he pored over the Articles of Religion in preparation for his ordination. Further, the very action of subscribing to the Articles at that time is a very strong indicator that Wesley was beginning to make the Bible his complete rule in matters of religious authority.

The Catholic way to understand the church, as described by Burnet, is that of a self-defining institution while the common Protestant alternative is that of a body itself subject to unalterable truths which precede it. The danger in this Catholic approach, not lost on Roman apologists such as Robert Bellarmine (1542–1621), is the possibility of erecting temporally bound human judgment concerning that which is true doctrine in a place above all the judgments of the Church. This danger is addressed in Article XX, "Of the Authority of the Church" (along with Articles VI and VII, of the Scriptures), placing the Church under Scripture on matters the Scriptures address and leaving to the Church the authority to decree rites and ceremonies; and in Article XXI, "Of the Authority of the General Councils," and Article VIII, "Of the Three Creeds."

Another great apologist of the Church of England who defined the direction of Anglican ecclesiology was Richard Hooker (1554–1600). Hooker gloried in a church freed of the superstition of Rome and the scrupulosity and intensity of Geneva. His work *Of the Laws of Ecclesiastical Polity* evidences a significant shift away from an apology focused on Rome and toward a polemic against the Puritans.[60] In the preface to the *Laws*, Hooker outlined the themes of his eight projected books and made clear the purpose of the work. It was a defense, based on Scripture, the pure traditions of the primitive and undivided church, and reason,[61] of Queen Elizabeth's settlement of the Church of England against the radical Puritans. The latter sought to overthrow the settlement by abolishing the royal supremacy, episcopacy, and the *Book of Common Prayer* and to substitute a Presbyterian system of church government and discipline modeled on Calvin's church at Geneva.

Book VI of the *Laws* attracts our attention in relation to the disciplinary system of the Church of England. Therein Hooker ostensibly refutes the charge made by certain Puritans that Anglican laws were corrupt for their non-inclusion of lay-elders as agents directly responsible for discipline. Those Puritans, according to Hooker, argue: *"by the law of God there must bee for ever in all congregations certaine Layelders ministers of Ecclesiasticall Jurisdiction, in as much as our Lord and Saviour by testament . . . hath left all ministers or Pastors in the Church executors equally, to the whole power of spirituall Jurisdiction, and with them hath joyned the people as Colleagues."*[62] Against this argument, Hooker defends the right, or authority, of the ordained clergy to do discipline in the Church. He especially appeals to the early church Fathers and early church practice for authorization of penitential discipline. Hooker upholds the discipline of repentance as the rightful exercise of the keys given to the apostles (Matt 16:19) and to their successors (1 Tim 1:20),[63] and not to an unprecedented office of lay eldership, as many of the Puritans were advocating. He says in such a *via media* manner as the times and circumstance dictated:

> For they that have the keyes of the kingdome of heaven are thereby signi-fied to be stewards of the house of God, under whome they guide, com-mand, judge and correct his family. The soules of men are Gods treasure, committed to the trust and fidelity of such, as must render a strict account for the very least which is under their custodie. . . .
>
> And because their office herein consisteth of sundry functions, some belonging to doctrine, some to discipline, all conteyned in the name of the keyes: they have for matters of discipline . . . their Courts and Consisto-ries erected by the heavenly authority. . . . Against rebellious and contu-macious persons, which refuse to obey their sentence, armed they are with power to eject such out of the Church. . . .
>
> . . . This is that grand originall warrant, by force whereof the guides and Prelates in Gods Church, first his Apostles, and afterwards others fol-lowing them successively, did both use and uphold that discipline, the end whereof is to heale mens consciences, to cure theyr sinnes, to reclayme of-fendors from iniquitie, and to make them by repentance just.
>
> Neyther hath it of ancient tymes for any other respect beene accus-tomed, to bind to Ecclesiasticall censures, to retayne soe bound, till tokens of manifest repentance appeared, and upon apparent repentance to release, saving only because this was received, as a most expedient method, for the cure of sinne.[64]

The last portion indicates the major change from Catholicism; the clergy is indeed charged with the disciplinary function, but the means of carrying out that function are not themselves divinely instituted. Instead certain means had developed because they were answerable to the need.

Hooker, like Jewel, was unwilling to hold with the argument that Rome is the only meaningful sense in which the Church can be identified. And equally he was cautious about throwing full support to the continental em-phasis on invisibility.

As might be expected, however, there were varying opinions expressed by English clerics on these subjects. As seen above, early Anglican apolo-gists had given much attention to the doctrine of the Church in the sixteenth and seventeenth centuries. What emerged as a result of conflicts both with Rome and with a potentially emergent free-church ecclesiology was clearly removed from the institutional model, at least in theory and in the minds of men like John Jewel and, to an even greater degree, Burnet and the other Latitudinarians. This group, which also included Edward Stillingfleet, John

Tillotson, and Lord Peter King, was more directly drawn to the principles of Continental Protestantism than were the generality of English Churchmen. Most notable among their views was an indifference toward direct apostolic succession and toward distinctions between bishops and other presbyters— notable, that is, because of its later impact upon Wesley, as will be seen later in this study.[65]

The consideration of Anglican ecclesiology is very important in order to understand Wesley's perspective on the church. Studying Wesley's ecclesiology, Wesleyan scholars often have focused on his relationship with the Church of England. Frank Baker, for instance, argued that Wesley "firmly accepted the *via media* of the Church of England, as incorporated in Cranmer's *Book of Common Prayer*, expounded in turn by Jewel as the fulfillment of Scripture and the Fathers and by Hooker as the crown of human reasoning."[66] There is no doubt that Wesley argued for ecclesiology in an Anglican manner—that is, the church as "a congregation of faithful men, in the which the pure word of God is preached, and the Sacraments be duly administered according to Christ's ordinance, in all those things that of necessity are requisite to the same." John Wesley did indeed live and die a member of the Church of England,[67] defending it at times to the dismay of his own collaborators. This Church, defined by John Jewel and Richard Hooker, provided Wesley with a venue from which to repudiate the accumulation of Roman practices with questionable scriptural pedigree while at the same time laying claim to continuity with the defining centuries of Christian doctrine.

During the early years of his ministry, John Wesley was an ardent supporter of the Church of England. Wesley's interest in the early church was in large measure developed through his studies for ordination in the Church of England, and was encouraged further by his father Samuel. Even at the end of his life, after many charges against him and deviations from official standards by him, both his indebtedness and his loyalty to the Church of England were evident in his thinking regarding the Church and its discipline. Although Wesley himself may have been the only one to believe so, the Church of England remained his professed home until the day he died. This loyalty came in spite of persecution from the established Church itself and opposition from his own Methodist colleagues, with some awkward moments as Charles Wesley points out. Although he had been barred from the pulpits of the Church and spurned by the overwhelming majority of her clergy for over forty years, Wesley, in 1780, could still say: "I am fully convinced that our own Church, with all her blemishes, is nearer the scriptural plan than any other in Europe."[68] Three years later he said that "[i]f ever the Methodists in general were to leave the Church, I must leave them,"[69] while he did some unusual things in the eyes of the majority of clergy of the Church.

Not only did he have reverence for the tradition of the Church of England, but he claimed also to be her follower in doctrine. In 1739 when he was asked in which doctrines the Methodists differed from the Church of England, he answered, "To the best of my knowledge, in none. The doctrines we preach are the doctrines of the Church of England; indeed, the fundamental doctrines of the Church, clearly laid down, both in her Prayers, Articles, and Homilies."[70] And in 1773, he maintained: "The Methodists, so called, observe more of the Articles, Rubrics, and Canons of the Church than any other people in the three Kingdoms."[71]

However, it is notable that there is a profound ambiguity at the heart of his opinions on the established Church. On the one hand he valued the ecclesiastical discipline, historical traditions (including the writings of great Anglican churchmen) and social utility of the Church of England, while on the other hand he regarded state patronage of religion as one of the "mysteries of iniquity" that destroyed the spirituality of the early church. Therefore, Wesley's support of the Church of England, which was always more impressive in thought and expression than in deed, was neither static nor entirely unconditional. This is because Wesley viewed the Church of England as primarily an instrument of the gospel, not a divine right institution of state.

In conclusion, the Church of England provided Wesley with the themes of the *via media*, the primacy of Scripture, the *ecclesia primitiva*, and a functional episcopacy. It also helped Wesley to have a sacerdotal view of sacraments, as will be seen later in this study. The Church of England was the initial and a lasting influence upon Wesley's ecclesiology while he had a critical eye on the iniquities of the established Church, which in a sense led to his Methodist movement. The impact of the Church of England on Wesley will be further demonstrated in Part Two.

Puritans and Wesley

Anglican voices regarding ecclesiology were not the only ones Wesley heard in England. England in the eighteenth century had come to accept the presence of nonconforming churches, though reluctantly. The Puritan presence has a history as long as that of the Church of England itself. The Church of England consciously defined itself on one hand against Rome and on the other against those who would fashion the English Reformation after that on the continent. The Puritans have their origins in the latter group while their types were so varied as to make it difficult for them to form one cohesive company. The relationship of Wesley to the Puritans and to Puritan ideas is somewhat curious, probably in large measure explained by a family history of dissenting pastors as grandfathers, but with parents who separately returned to the established church and became its staunch defenders. This work does not trace the whole history of Puritanism. Concern is focused on its contribution to the eighteenth century religious environment in which Wesley lived.

A portion of that contribution, albeit indirect, is in the very shape of the inherited Anglicanism. The origins of the Puritans as an informal party within the Church of England virtually parallels the Elizabethan Settlement (1559).[72] The Church of England marked its borders in terms of its opponents and its competing impulses. Most prominent among such impulses was the influence of Geneva, particularly through those who had spent the years of the Marian exile imbibing its ethos. Upon their return to England under Elizabeth, they found themselves divided over the best approach to continuing reform in the national church. The dominant group, largely accepting in theory the ecclesiology articulated by Jewel, pressed for continual reform from within the establishment. A second group pressed for the more radical solution of separation, calling for an entirely different form of church. Although it is this second form of the protest which came to carry forward the name "Puritan" in English history after the seventeenth century, it is the former group that truly earned the title.

From the beginning the Puritans complained of a Church "only halfway reformed" in association with the Settlement.[73] Of the major subjects of contention, the nature of the Church and its discipline were especially prominent. In his *The Character of an old English Puritane, or Non-Conformist* (1646), John Geree (c.1601–1649) gave a brief but comprehensive description of the initial Puritans:

> The Old English Puritan....did not what was good in his own, but in God's sight, making the word of God his rule in worship. He highly esteemed order in the House of God: but would not under color of that submit to superstitious rites, which are superfluous, and perish in their use. He reverenced Authority keeping within its sphere: but durst not under pretence of this subjection to the higher powers, worship God after the traditions of men. He made conscience of all God's ordinances, though some he esteemed of more consequence. He was much in prayer; with it he began and closed the day. In it he was exercised in his closet, family, and public assembly. He esteemed that manner of prayer best, where by the gift of God, expressions were varied according to present wants and occasions; yet did he not account set forms unlawful. Therefore in that circumstance of the Church he did not wholly reject the Liturgy, but the corruption of it.

... He accounted preaching as necessary now as in the Primitive Church. ... He was a man of good spiritual appetite, and could not be contented with one meal a day. An afternoon sermon did relish as well to him as one in the morning. ... The Lord's day he esteemed a divine ordinance, and rest on it necessary, so far as it conduced to holiness. He was very conscientious in observance of that day as the mart day of the Soul. ...

He endeavored to have the scandalous cast out of Communion: but he cast not out himself. ... He condemned that superstition and vanity of Popish mock-fast: yet neglected not on occasion to humble his soul by right fasting: He abhorred the popish doctrine of *opus operatum* in the notion. And in practice rested in no performance, but what was done in spirit and truth. He thought God had left a rule in his word for discipline. ... Right discipline he judged pertaining not to the being, but well-being of a Church. Therefore he esteemed those Churches most pure where the government is by Elders, yet unchurched not those where it was other ways. Perfection in Churches he thought a thing rather to be desired, than hoped for. And so he expected not a Church state without all defects. The corruptions that were in Churches he thought his duty to bewail, with endeavors of amendment: yet would he not separate, where he might partake in the worship, and not in the corruption. ... Just laws and commands he willingly obeyed not only for fear but for conscience also; But such as were unjust he refused to observe, choosing rather to obey God than man: yet his refusal was modest and with submission to penalties, unless he could procure indulgence from authority.[74]

The list of names involved in the early Puritanism includes Miles Coverdale (1488–1569), John Foxe (1516–1587), Thomas Sampson (1517–1589), Laurence Humphrey (c.1527–1590), Thomas Cartwright (1535–1603), John Field (1545–1588), William Perkins (1558–1602), Robert Bolton (1572–1631), Joseph Hall (1574–1656), Richard Sibbes (1577–1635), William Whateley (1583–1639), John Preston (1587–1628), John Geree, and so on.[75] The characteristic of these Puritans was the "combination of piety and realism, of humility and self-assertion, of deference and rebellion"[76]; these contradictions are balanced in such a way as to provide both basis and summary for reforming efforts.

Through roughly a century of successes and failures on given issues, the reform party seemed to have been in a favorable position prior to the time of the Cromwellian Protectorate (1653–1658). However, history unfolded otherwise thereafter. In the turmoil of the mid-seventeenth century, the established church felt the necessity to reconsider its overall position on all forms of Dissent. That is to say, the argument that a movement toward greater religious pluralism produces only chaos gained persuasive force. Consequently, the Post-Cromwell milieu provided a fitting opportunity for such measures as the Act of Supremacy (1660) and the Act of Uniformity

(1662). By these acts many found themselves forced out of the church. Since the Act of Uniformity required that all clergy in the Church of England accept all contained and prescribed in the revised *Book of Common Prayer*, reestablishing a single standard of belief and worship within the church, the Puritans were forced "to choose between conformity," especially of liturgy, "and Dissent."[77] In some sense the eventual separatism of the Puritans was not chosen, but was thrust upon them. The party of John Pearson (1612–1686) had carried the day in the established church over both the Puritans and the Latitudinarians, inaugurating a difficult period for the Puritans—now Separatists—which was only partially relieved by the Toleration Act of 1689 and which yet prevailed into the next century as Wesley began his studies for ministry.

While several issues central to our concerns in regard to the separation of the Puritans were involved, two especially need to be noted. The first of these issues has to do with the nature of the Church as an identifiable institution. The Puritans believed that the Bible provides the indispensable guide to life and that the church should reflect the express teaching of Scripture. Further, for the Puritans, in every age the church, as the earthly institution representing Christ, symbolizes and expresses the gospel itself; therefore, its outward form represents its spiritual and inward character. The church's spiritual nature is, consequently, inexorably related to its outward expressions of governance, patterns of teaching, forms of worship, and social countenance. In the Puritans' eyes, the Church of England needed the further reform in order to be a true, spiritual Church. Now when they were forced to follow the established church without enough reform, many felt forced to separate from the Church.

The opposition to this view of Puritans was clearly given by John Pearson's *An Exposition of the Creed* (1659).[78] While much of what Pearson writes in the early portions of the treatise seems sufficiently inclusive, there is a clear rejection of any "new churches." He denied the legitimacy of the "churches" of the Separatists. There was to be no distinction between the visible and the invisible church in any way as to argue for two churches, for Christ founded only one Church: "Not that there are two Churches of Christ: one, in which good and bad are mingled together; another, in which they are good alone: one, in which the saints are imperfectly holy; another, in which they are perfectly such: but one and the same Church, in relation to different times, admitteth or not admitteth the permixtion of the wicked, or the imperfection of the godly."[79] Therefore, within the one Church are contained "persons truly good and sanctified, and hereafter to be saved, and together with them other persons void of all saving grace, and hereafter to be damned: and that Church containing these of both kinds may well be called *holy*."[80] The entire discussion leads to the conclusion that

> whosoever is not of the catholick Church, cannot be of the true Church. That Church alone which first began at Jerusalem on earth, will bring us to the Jerusalem in heaven; and that alone began there, which always embraceth 'the faith once delivered unto the saints.' . . . Whatsoever Church pretendeth to a new beginning, pretendeth at the same time to a new Churchdom, and whatsoever is so new is none. So necessary it is to believe in the *holy catholick Church*.[81]

For Pearson and the Church of England, there is one Church—and it worships and conducts itself in one particular way. It is this spirit which effectively shut the Puritan presence out of the established church and forced them, whether they would or not, into another ecclesiological model.

In *An Exposition of the Creed* Pearson did not attack just the Puritans but countered concessions by the Latitudinarian wing on issues such as apostolic succession, the role and nature of the episcopacy, the status of ordained clergy vis-à-vis the hierarchy, and the accommodation of variant styles of worship by imposing stringent requirements of uniformity. Latitudinarianism, however, covers a wide range of theological positions. Although in its worst expression it became associated with Deism and its rationalist and moralist cousins, some of those associated with Latitudinarianism remained closer to orthodox theology (that is, consistent with the *Book of Common Prayer* and Thirty-Nine Articles). As Roger L. Emerson puts it, one must distinguish the fundamental differences between the Latitudinarians and the deists.[82] The leading Latitudinarian John Tillotson and his friends preached a doctrine based upon belief in the Bible as revealed religion and rooted in the liturgy and *Book of Common Prayer* of the Church of England. This group included Edward Stillingfleet, whose *Irenicum* would become influential in Wesley's thoughts on the nature of church order.

The second issue that we must note in relation to the separation of the Puritans has to do with continuity. The Church of England argued for its continuity with the apostolic church through its bishop. The disagreement on the part of the Puritans was not with the idea of continuity with the apostolic church, or even with an order of bishops; it was with the tracing of that continuity through those bishops and, perhaps more importantly, through the structures of authority and forms of practice they erected. For the Puritans the outward patterns they found in the Church of England represented centuries of human additions. In their attempts to purge the Church of these additions, they sought to reestablish the pure, early church patterns revealed, as they understood it, in the Scriptures.[83] To put it differently, the struggle between the Puritans and the Church of England was that between those who advocated only those practices with direct scriptural precedent and those who, like Jewel and others who followed the *via media* with him, found in tradition a legitimating function in its own right.

The Puritan dissatisfaction with the established church led most of its leaders to a tireless but ultimately unsuccessful effort at reshaping that national Church. With the 1662 Act of Uniformity came to an end the Puritan effort to reform the Church of England from within. While hope remained among some supporters that there would be an eventual reconciliation on agreeable terms, the new situation served as a catalyst for rethinking the concept of the Church. The institutional model, while modified in some details by the established viewpoint, had not been replaced.

The Puritan dissatisfaction with a Church only partially reformed led to different ecclesiologies with an emphasis on discipline. The models of church which the Puritans moved toward were various. For example, some, mostly in England, contended for a Presbyterian state-church organization. Others, especially in Massachusetts and Connecticut, supported a congregational organization in league with the state. And others such as English Independents and Baptists as well as Roger Williams in New England believed that the Bible mandated congregational churches separate from the state. But for all of them the concept of the church as a disciplined community was predominant.

Among the qualities that made Methodism a distinct religious movement in eighteenth century England was Wesley's emphasis on establishing a disciplined Christian community. Wesley saw discipline as an essential element in the Christian life. In January 1787 Wesley wrote to Adam Clarke: "Discipline is the great want in Guernsey; without which, the work of God cannot prosper. You did well to set upon it without delay, and to be as exact as possible. It is a true saying, 'The soul and the body make the man; and the spirit and discipline make a Christian.'"[84] This stress on discipline was a consistent theme in Wesley's Christian experience and teaching from his days as an Oxford Methodist to the end of his life.

Wesley wanted his Methodist societies to be a disciplined Christian community within the Church of England. Wesley's form of the disciplined Christian community within the larger church was influenced by his, though not exclusively, Puritan heritage.[85] Wesley thought that a discipline could be maintained within the larger ecclesial structure without the necessity of separation. In this regard the Puritan who came closest to Wesley was Richard Baxter (1615–1691).[86] One of the outstanding Puritan scholars, Baxter was committed to church and civil discipline without arguing for separation from the Church. He, however, was critical of the lax episcopal system in England. This opposition to episcopal government led him to collegiality with Presbyterians and Congregationalists, while it also led him to support the Restoration of Charles II, which in turn gave the offer of a bishopric that he refused. Because of his refusal of the Act of Uniformity (1662), especially with regard to the episcopacy and reform of the Prayer Book, he was ejected from his living and persecuted until his later years. He died two years after the enactment of the Act of Toleration, which offered a measure of freedom to nonconformist ministers. Baxter is one of the key Puritan thinkers whose insights and works influenced Wesley.[87]

The family of Wesley's roots in seventeenth century English Puritanism are well known; his maternal grandfather (Samuel Annesley, "the Patriarch of Dissent"), his paternal great-grandfather (Bartholomew Wesley) and grandfather (John Westley) were all dissenting Puritan ministers. It is uncertain how much was made of his ancestor's nonconformity while Wesley was growing up in Epworth. However it is certain that Wesley read many Puritan writers, respected them, and included many extracts of their works in his *A Christian Library*. We will further discuss this matter later in this section. The important point here is the possibility of Puritan ecclesiology having helped shape Wesley's understanding of the disciplined community or society.

The possibility is illustrated in David Lowes Watson's *The Early Methodist Class Meeting: Its Origin and Significance*. Of the two traditions of English Protestantism (the Church of England and the Puritans) "[f]undamental to the whole of Wesley's theology and churchmanship," argues Watson, Wesley inherited from the Puritans the "concept of the gathered church . . . an ecclesiology which rejected the traditional authority of the church, and based its tenets on scripture alone."[88] Then, Watson traces a link between the Puritan emphasis on "ecclesal discipline" and the disciplined societies of early Methodism.[89] Howard A. Snyder in *The Radical Wesley and Patterns for Church Renewal* also sees as a feature of early Methodism "[a] community or brotherhood of discipline, edification, correction and mutual aid . . . as the primary visible expression of the church,"[90] which was an ideal of church for the Puritans.

Wesley certainly wanted the Methodist societies and class meetings to be a disciplined community. It is evident in the design of the class meetings. Wesley says: "I called together all the *Leaders* of the *Classes* (so we used to term them and their companies), and desired that each would make a particular inquiry into the behaviour of those whom he saw weekly. They did so. Many disorderly walkers were detected. Some turned from the evil of their ways. Some were put away from us. Many saw it with fear, and rejoiced unto God with reverence."[91] The class meeting, the basic unit of Methodism, was a means of weekly examination and correction for members of the societies. Therefore, discipline was a key element in the Wesley's Methodist societies.

At this point, one needs to clarify what Wesley means when he speaks of discipline in connection to the Methodist societies. Perhaps discipline is classified into two areas: the personal discipline of the religious life and the ecclesiastical discipline that maintains church order. One is concerned with certain spiritual exercises such as prayer, fasting, and meditation, while the other is associated with the ecclesiastical actions such as excommunication taken in response to gross immorality committed by a member of a congregation. The most consistent connotation of discipline in Wesley's writings, as shown above in the design of the class meetings, is the ongoing stress on moral accountability and an openness to the correction of the community in the life of the individual by members of Wesley's societies.[92] The continuous application of discipline is the practical manifestation of Wesley's doctrine of the ongoing process of the sanctification of believers.

Wesley's stress on discipline clearly reflects an influence, though not exclusively, by the Puritans. In addition to the emphasis on discipline, in many aspects, the Puritans exerted a substantial influence upon Wesley as a number of studies attempted to demonstrate it.

There have been many studies relating Wesley to Puritanism. The historical and specialized studies in the relationship between Wesley and Puritanism date from the nineteenth century. The early studies paid particular attention to the similarities between Wesley's Methodism and Puritanism, focusing on their ascetic ethic. Leslie Stephen, finding the connection in their moral and ascetic austerities, saw Methodism as a "new Puritanism." With somewhat critical tone, he stated, "The new Puritanism, excluding all the most powerful intellectual elements, was . . . of necessity a faint reflection of the grander Puritanism of the seventeenth century. The morality founded upon it showed the old narrowness without the old intensity."[93] John H. Overton, noting some of the theological interests common to the eighteenth-century Methodism and the seventeenth-century Puritanism, also recognized the resemblance of the two traditions for their strict asceticism: "METHODISM . . . resembled the Puritanism of the seventeenth century in that they contended for the immediate and particular influence of the Holy Spirit, for the total degeneracy of man, for the vicarious nature of the Atonement, for the absolute unlawfulness of certain kinds of amusement, for the strict observance of the Lord's Day or Sabbath."[94] This approach got so widespread recognition among scholars that Wesleyan scholars by the middle period of twentieth century have attempted to connect the two traditions in their moral and ascetic life. For instance, George C. Cell saw Wesley's ethic of life as Puritan in its ascetic temper.[95] Albert C. Outler also recognized that Wesley borrowed his "doctrine of the Christian life" from the Puritans.[96]

The recognition of Wesley's connection to certain aspects of the Puritan ethos was more prominent with the work of Élie Halévy, "La Naissance du Méthodisme en Angleterre."[97] In this work Halévy saw Wesley as an eighteenth-century High-Church nonconformist that attempted "to re-awaken or to revive, in a form more suitable to contemporary circumstances, the old Puritan faith."[98] According to Halévy, Wesley, through his Evangelical revival, "revived what was left of the Puritan religious sense in the national consciousness" that, with its accompanying practice, formed part of the very character of the English people.[99] Halévy's work has been more often investigated for the so-called Halévy's thesis that Methodism helped to prevent a political and social revolution like French Revolution in England.

Besides Halévy, there were a group of scholars who suggested Wesley's connection to Puritanism. Of them Sydney G. Dimond, in his psychological study of the Methodist movement, offered evidence for his view that "the Puritan strain in Methodist character was manifest from the first."[100] Maldwyn Edwards also argued that in Wesley's Methodist revival, Puritanism came to "a full flowering within the Church" of England.[101] Horton Davies, stressing the motivation, or spirit, of the movement, also credited Wesley and Methodism with reviving the "evangelical passion and experiential religion" of Puritanism, "without the latter's austerities and asperities."[102]

Some attempted to investigate the specific areas of contact between Wesley and the Puritans. George Eayrs, in "Links between the Ejected Clergy of 1662, the Wesleys, and Methodism," attempted to demonstrate Wesley's appreciation for the Puritan tradition and interpreted Wesley's church policy in relation to the Puritan ideas.[103] Duncan Coomer, in "The Influence of Puritanism and Dissent on Methodism," traced such several areas of direct connection as teachings regarding the Christian life, Wesley's use of Puritan authors in *A Christian Library*, his borrowing from this tradition of the covenant service that became a popular Methodist service, and the early Methodists' adoption of sabbatarianism (or the strict observance of Sunday) and discipline from the Puritans.[104]

Perhaps the first comprehensive monograph of Wesley's Puritan connections is John A. Newton's *Methodism and the Puritans*. In this work, Newton briefly examines the Puritan authors in Wesley's *A Christian Library* and suggests that "[i]t was . . . symbolic of a comprehensive debt which the Methodists owed to the Puritans, a debt which may be summarised under the heads of Theology, Liturgy, Pastoralia, Family Piety, and Ethics."[105] In theology, holds Newton, Wesley and the Puritans shared emphases on the supreme authority of Scripture, the Christocentric nature of faith, the importance of both justification and the consequent growth in grace in terms of sanctification or practical godliness, and assurance, or the witness of the Holy Spirit. Also, according to Newton, in liturgy and worship Wesley drew from the Puritans extemporaneous prayer and preaching, and covenant service; in Pastoralia he used in part Baxter's *Gildas Salvianus, the Reformed Pastor* (1656–1657) as a manual of pastoral practice for his own preachers and encouraged them to visit from house to house after Baxter's pattern; the homeliness and family spirit of Wesley's Methodist societies came from the Puritan's ideal of family piety; finally, he drew from the Puritans "ethical rigorism," and therefore an "active, self-disciplined life, lived within a framework of rule or 'method' characterised both Puritan and Methodist."[106] Newton further suggests that many of Wesley's preachers were also substantially influenced by the writings of the Puritans.[107]

In investigating Wesley's Puritan connections, Newton, furthermore, sees Susanna Wesley as the key figure that exercised a decisive Puritan influence on her son John. In *Methodism and the Puritans* Newton notes that Susanna created an "essentially Puritan home" and her Puritan piety conditioned the upbringing of John, which contributed to John's early appreciation of the disciplined life and, perhaps, an unconscious respect for the Puritan ethos.[108] Wesley's relationship to Puritanism through Susanna is further investigated in Newton's *Susanna Wesley and the Puritan Tradition in Methodism*. Here Newton, describing Susanna as one "who found it no inconsistency to be a Puritan, an Anglican, and a Methodist, and who embodies all three types of churchmanship," concludes that she was the central figure in the transmission of the Puritan tradition to Wesley and Methodism.[109] In doing so, Newton reads continuities within two traditions of Puritanism and Methodism.

A more comprehensive, thorough monograph of Wesley's indebtedness to Puritanism is given by Robert C. Monk's *John Wesley: His Puritan Heritage*,[110] in which he brings together an impressive amount of evidence to show how much Wesley inherited from the Puritans in constructing his own theology. Monk suggests that many theological and devotional statements in Wesley's own writings show direct dependence on the Puritan theological literature. For example, Puritan authors are one of the largest groups in his *A Christian Library*, and their materials make up its largest proportion. Wesley's heavy use of the Puritans, according to Monk, reveals that he must have received some of his views from the Puritan tradition. Furthermore, Monk investigates the nature and extent of Wesley's inheritance from Puritanism through a study of doctrinal affinities in experience, justification, assurance, covenant, sanctification, perfection, and the Christian life, especially as applied to the individual, the family, the church, and the world.

The specific connection between Wesley and the Puritans was also attempted by several studies in the liturgical practices Wesley drew from the Puritan tradition. In *Methodist Worship in Relation to Free Church Worship*, John Bishop, tracing the Methodist heritage in the free church tradition, saw the Methodist movement as "inevitably influenced by the practice of the older Puritan Dissenting bodies."[111] In doing so, Bishop offers together information on how Wesley adopted for Methodists the Puritan forms and modes of worship. The foundation on which Bishop investigates Methodist worship in relation to free church worship is "The Ordering of Methodist Worship," an appendix of *The Message and Mission of Methodism*,[112] which was the report of the committee appointed by the 1943 Methodist Conference "to re-consider and re-state the message and mission of Methodism in modern society" and was published by authority of the 1946 Conference. The section "Experiment in Public Worship" of this appendix reads:

> The time is ripe for making experimental changes in the ordering of public worship. Methodism is a Free Church and in the spirit of the Reformation and of John Wesley, we have an opportunity of creating forms of worship through which the Eternal Gospel in all its richness and relevance may reach the men and women of our time. Because we are a Free Church, we are not bound by the past. For that reason also, the inheritance of the Church Universal is ours to be used for the glory of God. . . .[113]

While Bishop gives his attention to the influence of Puritan tradition upon Methodist worship, Horton Davies emphasizes "the Methodist union of formal and free worship." According to Davies,

> THE ESSENCE of Methodist worship as it germinated in the fertile mind of its founder was the combination of the advantages of liturgical forms and of free prayers. John Wesley was unique in this century in being the bridge that crossed the chasm between the worship of Anglicanism and Dissent. In this respect he might be regarded with equal justice as the precursor of the Oxford Movement or as the last of the Puritan divines.[114]

Davies' view is more appealing than that of Bishop in that it recognizes the importance of the Anglican tradition in relation to Methodist worship while it does not overlook the Puritan influence.

Frederick Hunter, in "The Origins of Wesley's Covenant Service," asserts that Wesley's covenant service derived from such Puritan theologians as Joseph Alleine and Richard Alleine, and that it became "one of the distinctive features of Methodism."[115] Hunter shows that the covenant service is a direct incorporation into Methodism of a Puritan form, though used in a special way by Wesley. In his essay "Sources of Wesley's Revision of the Prayer Book in 1784–8," Hunter further argues that Wesley's revision of the *Book of Common Prayer* for American Methodists was based on the suggestions for revision offered by the Presbyterians at the Savoy Conference in 1661, and that Wesley consciously followed the summary of these suggestions as found in Edmund Calamy's *Abridgment of Mr. Baxter's History of His Life and Times*.[116] Hunter's suggestion that Wesley drew the covenant service from the Puritan tradition is affirmed in Frank Baker's "The Beginnings of the Methodist Covenant Service."[117] Baker saw one of the most important contributions of Methodism to religious liturgy as "the order 'For Such as would Enter into or Renew their Covenant with God.'"[118]

Certainly, these studies confirm Wesley's familiarity with and appreciation for many Puritan emphases and practices. Puritanism was obviously an important and immediate influence on Wesley's thought and practice. Much of Wesley's criticism of the established church echoes Puritan concerns. It is represented in the statement of his opinion of the Act of Uniformity. In "Thoughts upon Liberty" Wesley clearly said:

> So, by this glorious Act, thousands of men, guilty of no crime, nothing contrary either to justice, mercy, or truth, were stripped of all they had, of their houses, lands, revenues, and driven to seek where they could, or beg, their bread. For what? Because they did not dare to worship God according to other men's consciences! So they and their families were, at one stroke, turned out of house and home, and reduced to little less than beggary, for on other fault, real or pretended, but because they could not assent and consent to that manner of worship which their worthy governors prescribed![119]

He also acknowledged the unfairness of the treatment of Puritans. In April 1754, after reading Edmund Calamy (1671–1732)'s *Abridgment of Mr. Baxter's Life*,[120] he wrote: "In spite of all the prejudice of education, I could not but see that the poor nonconformists had been used without either justice or mercy, and that many of the Protestant bishops of King Charles had neither more religion, nor humanity, than the popish bishops of Queen Mary."[121] Wesley's respect for the Puritans and their suffering is more prominent in the following statement:

> AFTER an Account of the Lives, Sufferings and Deaths of those Holy Men, who sealed the Ancient Religion with their Blood, I believe nothing would either be more agreeable or more profitable to the serious Reader, than some Extracts from the Writings of those, who sprung up, as it were, out of their Ashes. These breathe the same Spirit, and were, in a lower De-gree, Partakers of the same Sufferings. Many of them took joyfully the Spoiling of their Goods, and all had their Names cast out as Evil; being branded with the Nick-name of Puritans, and thereby made a By-Word and a Proverb of Reproach.[122]

Some Methodist practices, like strict sabbatarian practice, had the same source as the Puritan ones. Indeed, in the eyes of many of his contemporaries, Wesley revived the spirit and practice of Puritanism while he ordinarily rejected such comments as irrelevant. For example, Wesley's use of extemporaneous preaching and free prayers, which were two principal Puritan practices, obviously made his contemporaries identified him with the Puritan tradition.

In fact, accusations that Methodism was another form of Nonconformity were often heard during Wesley's ministry. For example, Wesley's contemporaries such as Horace Walpole, Bishop Warburton, and Archdeacon Balguy suspected that Methodism was reviving the Puritanism of the seventeenth century.[123] Indeed one of the most persistent of the early Anglican attacks on Methodism was that its breaches of ecclesiastical order would result in the same sectarian avalanche as did the Puritans. It is obviously represented in John Smith's letter written to Wesley on February 26, 1746:

> [Thomas] Cartwright and the old Puritans, I believe, meant no harm, yet what a scene of disorder did their lectures produce! Strict order once broken, confusion rushes in like a torrent at a trifling breech. You find yourself every day going further and further from the orderly paths; you are now come to approve of lay preachers. Well, if they preach the gospel of peace, where is the harm? But what if, order once broke, unsent persons take upon them to preach all sorts of error, discord, and confusion?[124]

Wesley himself was aware that his Connexionalism might easily become Congregationalism. Wesley's response to such an attack was to draw a distinction between the Anabaptist enthusiasts and the learned and pious Puritans whom he greatly admired:

That 'the irregularities of Mr. Cartwright did more harm in the course of a
century than all the labours of his life did good' is by no means plain to
me. And the less so because I cannot learn from Mr. Strype or any other
impartial writer (whatever his mistakes in judgment were) that he fell into
any irregularities at all. I look upon him and the body of Puritans in that
age (to whom the German Anabaptists bore small resemblance) to have
been both the most learned and most pious men who were then in the English nation. Nor did they separate from the Church, but were driven out,
whether they would or no.[125]

However, Wesley's desire to follow his own version of authentic Christianity overrode his scruples about church order. As long as the Methodists
continued to attend Anglican worship and sacraments, and as long as the
bishops declined to enforce ecclesiastical disciplines in order to prohibit the
Methodists from preaching in the fields, practicing extemporaneous prayer,
employing lay preachers, forming and regulating United Societies, and
holding annual Conferences, Wesley's affection for the Church of England
remained unaltered.[126] But, in reality, similarly to the case of the Puritans,
the separation could not be avoided. Wesley's tenacious refusal to separate
from the Church of England could only retard but not stop Methodism from
moving toward a closer identity with Nonconformity.

It is certain that despite some obvious differences, there are clear re-
semblances between the seventeenth-century Puritanism and Wesley's
Methodism. Both stood in a dialectical relation to the Church of England,
originating within it, and yet standing over against it. Both made their fundamental appeal to Scripture, looking to reason and experience to corrobo-
rate its deliverances. The Puritans and Wesley were both greatly interested
in the Christian gospel's practical application to a believer's daily life. Both
embodied a conception of the Christian life in terms of disciplined living
("method" is a keyword for each of them), moral rigorism, and Christianity
in earnest. Both stood for warm popular piety and lay religion, genuinely of
and for the people. Both were intensely concerned for evangelical mission
and pastoral care, and were ready to adapt and supplement the system of the
Church in obedience to these primary needs. Both were concerned with the
sovereignty of grace, and eager to translate into human terms an understanding of the Christian life as "faith working by love." For many of
Wesley's commentators as well as his contemporaries, therefore, these
similarities were sufficient to recognize a significant relationship between
Wesley and the Puritans though not necessarily his direct dependence upon
them.

The evidence of Wesley's relationship to and direct dependence on the
Puritans is more clearly found in his use, abridgment, and recommendation

of Puritan literature. Puritanism is a multifaceted tradition. Wesley's *A Christian Library* contains works of various Puritans. Of them six were leaders in the Puritan movement during its earlier days, including John Foxe, Robert Bolton, Joseph Hall, John Preston, Richard Sibbes, and William Whateley. Five are such Independents or Congregationalists as Francis Rous (1579–1659), Thomas Goodwin (1600–1680), John Owen (1616–1683), Lewis Stuckley (1621–1687), and John Flavel (c.1630–1691). And representing the more radical wing of Puritanism, John Bunyan (1628–1688), a Baptist, is included in *A Christian Library*. Wesley also included such Presbyterians as Samuel Clarke (1599–1683), Herbert Palmer (1601–1647), John Kitchin (c.d.1662), Isaac Ambrose (1604–1663), William Dell (d.1664), Matthew Hale (1609–1676), Richard Alleine (1611–1681), Richard Baxter, Thomas Manton (1620–1677), Samuel Annesley (Wesley's own grandfather, c.1620–1696), Matthew Pool (1624–1679), Stephen Charnock (1628–1680), Joseph Alleine (1634–1668), Samuel Shaw (1635–1696), John Howe (1630–1705) and Thomas Crane (1631–1714), with three Scottish Presbyterians including Samuel Rutherford (1600–1661), John Brown (1610–1679) and Hugh Binning (1627–1653).[127] Of these nonconformist authors, only two, John Howe and Thomas Crane, lived in Wesley's century. In all, the *A Christian Library* contains works of seventy-one authors,[128] the largest groups of which are Church of England and Puritans. Of the writings of various authors, Puritan materials, in terms of its quantity, make up a largest proportion of the *A Christian Library*, and even larger than Anglican ones. This fact obviously shows that he was very sympathetic to certain Puritan teachings and valued them highly though it does not mean that Wesley considered the Puritan tradition to be of greater value than the Church of England.

In including the Puritans' works in *A Christian Library*, Wesley's primary concern was on their practical divinity and accounts of exemplary Christian living. Wesley's editing *A Christian Library*, as its title reveals, purposed to publish the "Choicest Pieces of Practical Divinity." In the age of Wesley, Christian literature normally fell into three main categories: 1) doctrinal and speculative works, 2) theological controversies, and 3) practical writings designed to help plain believers to understand and apply the truths of the gospel to their daily lives.[129] Wesley's *A Christian Library* falls into the category of the practical works. It is obviously demonstrated in the statement that "I believed nothing could be more acceptable to the serious Reader, than to see this Christianity reduced to *Practice*."[130] In the preface to the Puritan materials, Wesley described his reason for selecting them: "*I have therefore selected what I conceived would be of most general Use, and most proper to form a compleat Body of Practical Divinity.*"[131]

Robert C. Monk is right in asserting that "Puritan authors were the major source for Wesley's choice of 'practical divinity' included in the *Library*," and "Puritan lives illustrating the application of those teachings in daily living predominate in Wesley's selections."[132] The accounts of the Puritans' exemplary Christian living became a model for Wesley's "accounts" of his followers' lives.

Besides *A Christian Library*, Wesley published many other abridgments during his ministry, and a substantial portion of these publications was also made up of works of Puritan divines.[133] Wesley's comprehensive use of Puritan literature demonstrates his thorough acquaintance with the wide range of Puritan divines. He was not only acquainted with the well known leaders of the Puritan tradition but some of its lesser known divines. Interestingly, one finds that while Wesley's appreciation of the Puritans and their teachings and practices continued from his early period, it became more conspicuous after he had started field preaching.

In conclusion, there is clear evidence that Wesley read and used many Puritans and was to a substantial extent influenced by them. The Puritans had an important and immediate impact on Wesley's theology and practices. Wesley's image of the Christian life and his instructions in its practice reflect strong affinities with the Puritan ethos. Also, one clearly sees not only affinity but affiliation between Wesley and the Puritans in many aspects such as experimental theology, ethics, pastoral ideals, and the concept of the church as a disciplined Christian community.

However, despite many obvious similarities and parallels between some teachings and practices of Wesley and those of the seventeenth-century English Puritans, there are some issues to be discussed concerning Wesley's relationship to the Puritanism. First of all, Puritanism is a multifaceted tradition, not all of which was congenial or acceptable to Wesley as he worked out his own theological stance and packaged it as a resource for his Methodists. Although the Puritans' emphasis on a serious, circumspect, and disciplined daily life certainly attracted Wesley's attention, such an emphasis also came from his High-Church asceticism and from the influence of French Catholic mystics in his early phase. In addition, while the resemblance between Wesley and the Puritans are striking, all the similarities and parallels are not necessarily evidence of Wesley's direct dependence upon the Puritans except some cases in which one can prove the Puritans' direct impact upon Wesley. Wesley, in fact, rejected the accusation that he had reinstated Puritanism as he formed the Methodist societies. Therefore, it would be an overstatement to suggest that Wesley was a Puritan. No claim can be made that Wesley was a reinvigorated seventeenth-century Puritan, nor that Methodism was an eighteenth-century form of English Puritanism.

At this point, Monk's suggestion is helpful: "Only a truly unique combination of intense dedication to the Church of England and affinity with and sympathy for some aspects of Puritanism could produce one who so vigorously held the two together and lived with the resultant tensions."[134]

This chapter explored the influence of the reformation tradition upon Wesley's ecclesiology. In fact, it is difficult to prove the direct influence of the reformers upon Wesley's ecclesiology. Wesley does not seem to have had any distinct and functioning conception of "the Reformation" in the way that he had a distinct and functioning conception of "primitive Christianity." Of course, he did have a conception of "the Protestant," as opposed to "the Catholic"; and his stress on primitive Christianity is precisely one element of what it means for him to be Protestant. But he did not dwell or draw on the theologies of the so-called magisterial reformers in the way that the Lutheran and Calvinist traditions do. When he encountered their theology—as when he read Luther on Galatians—he often did not like it. But the reformers had an influence on Wesley's ecclesiology on the sense that they introduced certain themes—particularly sanctification and discipline—into ecclesiology which were to have an impact on Wesley not through any encounter with the works of the reformers themselves, but primarily through the way in which those themes played themselves out in the Anglican and Puritan traditions. The influence of the Church of England upon Wesley continued through his life but was in relationship of tension with his sympathy for some aspects of Puritanism. It is true that many of Wesley's views on the church were close to those of Anglicanism of the seventeenth and eighteenth centuries. However, Wesley's ecclesiology, as further investigated in Part Two, was not static but throughout his entire life developed in reaction to changing circumstances. In particular, after he became a field preacher in 1739, Puritanism was a main contributor to Wesley's unorthodox churchmanship. Another reformation tradition, Pietism to substantial extent influenced Wesley's doctrine of salvation, which was most important in understanding his ecclesiology, and Wesley's Methodist organization, as we will see in the next chapter.

Notes

1. Jaroslav Pelikan, *The Riddle of Roman Catholicism* (Nashville: Abingdon Press, 1959), 49.

2. In "The Babylonian Captivity of the Church," attacking the sacramental system of the Roman Catholic Church, Luther argues that there are only three sacraments: baptism, the eucharist, and penance. However, Luther, later, does not accept

penance as a sacrament, "because it lacks a visible sign appointed by God." Martin
Luther, *Luther's Works*. ed. Abdel Ross Wentz (Philadelphia: Muhlenberg Press,
1959), vol. xxxvi, intro. 7–8.

3. In *On the Councils and the Church*, Luther describes as the external marks
of the true church not just these three but all seven—which include a distinct office
or ordained ministry (divinely instituted, Luther insists), the authority of this ministry publicly to bind and loose sins (which involves the power of excommunication),
etc.—but here this study focuses on the first three marks where one may trace Luther's influence on Wesley through the Confession of Augsburg and the Thirty-
Nine Articles of Religion of the Church of England.

4. Martin Luther, "On the Councils and the Church," in *Luther's Works*, ed.
Eric W. Gritsch (Philadelphia: Fortress Press, 1966), vol. xli, 148–152.

5. *Luther's Works*, xli, 150.

6. Cited by Paul D. L. Avis, "'The True Church' in Reformation Theology,"
323. Here the author translates and cites *D. Martin Luthers Werke; kritische Gesamtausgabe* (Weimar: H. Böhlau, 1883–), vol. ii, 208.

7. Cited by Paul D. L. Avis, "'The True Church' in Reformation Theology,"
324; *D. Martin Luthers Werke*, vii, 721f.

8. Luther, "On the Councils and the Church," in *Luther's Works*, xli, 149–150.

9. Martin Luther, "The Ninety-Five Theses," 62th thesis, in *The Prince by Niccolo Machiavelli. Utopia by Sir Thomas More. Ninety-Five Theses, Address to the
German Nobility, Concerning Christian Liberty by Martin Luther. With Introductions, Notes and Illustrations*. Harvard Classics: The Five Foot Shelf of Books. ed.
Charles W. Eliot. vol. 36 (New York: P.F. Collier & Son, 1910), 270.

10. Luther, "Against Hanswurst," in *Luther's Works*, xli, 211. This ecclesiology, as Hans Küng points out, has a problem which it can't solve: How can one
distinguish the true church from the false? Küng states,

> these two characteristics of the true Church [word and sacrament] are not
> truly distinguishing features. They are not visible and serve to show where
> the church is hidden, rather than what it truly is . . . it cannot be denied
> that on the basis of these two criteria alone, it became more and more dif-
> ficult to distinguish the Protestant Church from the Catholic Church or
> from enthusiastic sects (Hans Küng, *The Church*, trans. Ray and Rosaleen
> Ockenden [London: Sheed and Ward, 1967], 267).

11. *Works*, xviii, 249–250.

12. Leo G. Cox, "John Wesley's View of Martin Luther," *Journal of the Evangelical Theological Society* 7, no. 3 (1964): 84.

13. Wesley, Sermon "Salvation by Faith," *Works*, i, 129.

14. *Works*, xix, 47.

15. *Works*, xix, 200–201.

16. Wesley "finished the translation of Martin Luther's life" on July 19, 1749.
Works, xx, 285.

17. "The Life of Martin Luther, Written Originally in German, by John Daniel
Hernnschmid," in *The Arminian Magazine: Consisting of Extracts and Original*

Treatises on Universal Redemption, vol. i, February-June (London: R. Hawes, 1778), 68–77, 116–127, 165–175, 210–218, 264–272.

18. *Works*, iii, 505.

19. *Works*, i, 450–451.

20. *Works*, i, 451. Cf. Peter Anstadt, *Luther, Zinzendorf, Wesley: An Account of John Wesley's Conversion through Hearing Luther's Preface to the Epistle to the Romans Read in a Moravian Prayer Meeting in London, England: To Which is Added a New Translation of Luther's Preface* (York, Pa.: P. Anstadt, [18--?]), 40.

21. Wesley's Twenty-Five Articles omitted of the Thirty-Nine Articles fourteen Articles, modified seven, while adopting eighteen unchanged. In regard to the Articles concerning the Church, Wesley omitted the closing part of Article XIX, Article XX (Of the Authority of the Church), Article XXI (Of the Authority of General Councils), Article XXIII (Of Ministering in the Congregation), Article XXVI (Of the Unworthiness of the Ministers Which Hinders Not the Effect of the Sacraments), Article XXXIII (Of Excommunicate Persons), and Article XXXVI (Of Consecration of Bishops and Ministers). Article XXXIV (Of the Traditions of the Church) was modified. Franz Hilderbrandt says that this omission or modification was done chiefly because it "savors too much of Catholic tradition and practice to be adapted to an American Church" (Franz Hilderbrandt, *From Luther to Wesley* [London: Lutterworth Press, 1951], 70). Hilderbrandt's interpretation may be supported by the fact that Wesley adopted from the Thirty-Nine Articles all of the anti-Catholic Articles such as the rejection of the doctrine of purgatory, the rejection of services in Latin, the rejection of the concept of the Mass, and the rejection of a celibate clergy. These Articles were aimed directly at distinguishing the beliefs held by the Church of England from Roman Catholicism. At this point, Wesley followed the Church of England.

22. Arthur W. Nagler, *The Church in History* (Nashville: Abingdon-Cokesbury Press, 1929), 353.

23. "The Augsburg Confession," in Philip Schaff, *The Creeds of Christendom with a History and Critical Notes*, 3 vols. (Grand Rapids: Baker Book House, 1966), vol. iii, 11–12. Brackets enclose additions made with the translation from the Latin text into German.

24. Gilbert Burnet, *An Exposition of the Thirty-Nine Articles of the Church of England by Gilbert, Bishop of Sarum*, ed. James R. Page (New York: D. Appleton and Company, 1866), 233.

25. Gordon E. Rupp, *John Wesley und Martin Luther: Ein Beitrag zum Lutherischen-Methodistischen Dialog* (Stuttgart: Christliches Verlagshaus, 1983), 5. "Die Frage, die im 16. Jahrhundert gestellt worden ist: 'Wo war eure Kirche vor Luther?' und im 18. Jahrhundert: 'Wo was eure Kirche vor Wesley?' hat ihre angemessene Antwort im Augsburger Bekenntnis bekommen: 'Wir existierten in der einen heiligen christlichen Kirche, die am Anfang war.'"

26. Luther, "On the Councils and the Church," in *Luther's Works*, xli, 150.

27. Hilderbrandt, *From Luther to Wesley*, 73.

28. Gordon E. Rupp, *The Righteousness of God: Luther studies,* (New York: Philosophical Library, 1953), 310.

29. Rupp, *The Righteousness of God*, 310.

30. Cf. see P. D. L. Avis, "'The True Church' in Reformation Theology," 319–345.

31. Cited by D. F. Wright, trans. and ed., *Common Places of Martin Bucer*, intro. 31. The discipline necessary for a pure, restored church took on a significant dimension in Bucer's thought, which profoundly influenced the English Reformation. For Bucer's impact on the English Reformation, see Wright, *Common Places of Martin Bucer*, intro. 24–29.

32. Wright, *Common Places of Martin Bucer*, 206.

33. Wright, *Common Places of Martin Bucer*, 439.

34. Wright, *Common Places of Martin Bucer*, 205ff.

35. Wright, *Common Places of Martin Bucer*, 211.

36. Wright, *Common Places of Martin Bucer*, 206.

37. For example, tracing the development from Bucer through Pietism to Methodism, August Lang describes Bucer as a precursor of Methodism. August Lang, *Puritanismus und Pietismus. Studien zu ihrer Entwicklung von M. Butzer bis zum Methodismus* (*Beiträge zur Geschichte und Lehre der Reformierten Kirche*, 6; Neukirchen, 1941). Also see E. G. Rupp, *Protestant Catholicity; Two lectures* (London: Epworth Press, 1960), 23; Wright, *Common Places of Martin Bucer*, intro. 32.

38. For example, in both the *Commentary on a Harmony of the Evangelists, Matthew, Mark, and Luke* and the *Institutes*, Calvin upholds the great value of discipline as great treasures entrusted to Christian pastors. See the comments on Matt. 16:19–20 and 23:13–14 in John Calvin, *Commentary on a Harmony of the Evangelists, Matthew, Mark, and Luke*, Translated from the original Latin and collated with the author's French version by William Pringle (Grand Rapids: Erdmans, 1949), vol. ii, 292–300 and vol. iii, 83–85; Also see John Calvin, *Institutes of the Christian Religion*, vol. xxi of The Library of Christian Classics, ed. John T. McNeill, trans. Ford Lewis Battles (Philadelphia: The Westminster Press, 1960), Book iv, chapters 8–12. Especially he assigned one chapter of the *Institutes* (iv, chapter 12) to "the Discipline of the Church," dealing with the nature, necessity, purpose, and stages of church discipline.

39. Paul M. Bassett, "A Survey of Western Ecclesiology to about 1700," in *The Church: An Inquiry into Ecclesiology from a Biblical Theological Perspective*, 210ff.

40. For Calvin's ecclesiology, see Benjamin. C. Milner, *Calvin's Doctrine of the Church* (Leiden: Brill, 1970); Kilian McDonnell, *John Calvin, the Church, and the Eucharist* (Princeton: Princeton University Press, 1967); Wilhelm Niesel, *The Theology of Calvin*, trans. Harold Knight (Philadelphia: Westminster Press, 1956); F. Wendel, *Calvin; the Origins and Development of his Religious Thought*, trans. Philip Mairet (London: Collins, 1963).

Calvin is well known to have held a strict doctrine of predestination. Perhaps his doctrine of predestination would seem to leave little room for a doctrine of the visible church. It is because, if, by God's eternal decree, some are elected to salvation and others are not, there would seem to be only a little place for the church as an historical institution. In other words, the provision of ministry and discipline would appear to be unnecessary for the elect, and useless for the reprobate. But Calvin does not see the question in this way. On the contrary, for him the existence of the church belongs to the mysterious eternal decrees of God. The visible church is "the divine institution to assemble and minister to the elect in the earthly condition in which they are" (*Institutes* IV, i, 1, footnote 2). The visible church is by God's provision the means by which, through the ministry of Word, sacraments, and discipline, He brings the elect to their salvation. Thus, paradoxically, one may say that Calvin's ecclesiology is closely linked to his doctrine of predestination. This understanding of predestination and church was more clearly developed later in Puritanism. For example, see William Perkins, *An Exposition of the Symbole or Creede of the Apostles: According to the Tenour of the Scriptures, and the Consent of Orthodoxe Fathers of the Church* (Cambridge: Printed by Iohn Legat printer to the Vniuersitie of Cambridge, 1596). In this work, which was first published in 1595, Perkins argued that predestination, in fact, is the "ground and cause" of the church.

41. *Works*, iii, 53–55.

42. Horton Davies, *Worship and Theology in England*, 5 vols. (Princeton, N.J.: Princeton University Press, 1961–1975), vol. i (*From Cranmer to Hooker, 1534–1603*), 3.

43. Eamon Duffy, *The Stripping of the Altars: Traditional Religion in England, c.1400 – c.1580* (New Haven: Yale University Press, 1992), 479. In this book Duffy's thesis is that Catholic piety continued in the midst of all the political changes during the English Reformation. By the 1570s, argues Duffy, the body politic, under Elizabeth, had the capacity of enforcing uniformity, but even then much of the Catholic piety continued underground.

44. Thomas Cranmer, "A Confutation of Unwritten Verities," in *The Works of Thomas Cranmer*, Edited for The Parker Society by Rev. John Edmund Cox (Cambridge: The University Press, 1840–), vol. ii, 13.

45. John Hooper, *Early Writings of John Hooper*, Edited for The Parker Society by Rev. Samuel Carr (Cambridge: The University Press, 1840–), 81.

46. Nicholas Ridley, *The Works of Nicholas Ridley*, Edited for The Parker Society by Rev. Henry Christmas (Cambridge: The University Press, 1988), 122–123. One of the interesting issues involved here is the possible influence of Martin Bucer in the emerging system of discipline. Initially coming to England at Cranmer's request, Bucer spent the last two years of his life there. He supported the official, cautious reform program of Cranmer and the scholarly Ridley. He is also known to have influenced both Edmund Grindal and Matthew Parker, successive holders of the Archbishopric of Canterbury. The latter was the more successful at following Bucer's ideas of discipline. See Mark E. Vanderschaaf, "Archbishop Parker's Efforts Toward a Bucerian Discipline in the Church of England," *Sixteenth Century Journal* 8 (1977): 85–103.

47. *The Two Liturgies, A. D. 1549, and A. D. 1552: with other documents set forth by authority in the reign of King Edward VI*, Edited for The Parker Society by Rev. Joseph Ketley (Cambridge: The University Press, 1844), 513 (561).

48. John Jewel, *An Apology of the Church of England*, ed. John E. Booty (Ithaca, N.Y.: Cornell University Press, 1963), part iv, 68.

49. On the Scriptural argument, see especially part iv of the *Apology* (Booty edition, 51–82).

50. On the support of Fathers, see part v, 83–102.

51. Jewel, *An Apology of the Church of England*, 26.

52. Booty, Preface to Jewel, *An Apology of the Church of England*, xliv.

53. Booty, Preface to Jewel, *An Apology of the Church of England*, xxxi.

54. Outler, "Do Methodists Have a Doctrine of the Church?" in *The Wesleyan Theological Heritage: Essays of Albert C. Outler*, 215.

55. This description is from John Pearson's *An Exposition of the Creed*. John Pearson (1612–1686) was Bishop of Chester when this commentary on the Apostles' Creed was published in 1659. See John Pearson, *An Exposition of the Creed: With an Appendix, Containing the Principal Greek and Latin Creeds*. Revised by the Rev. W.S. Dobson (New York: D. Appleton & Company, 1851), 499–524.

56. Eric G. Jay, *The Church: Its Changing Image through Twenty Centuries* (Atlanta: John Knox Press, 1980), 184.

57. Burnet, *An Exposition of the Thirty-Nine Articles of the Church of England by Gilbert, Bishop of Sarum*, 233.

58. Burnet, *An Exposition of the Thirty-Nine Articles of the Church of England by Gilbert, Bishop of Sarum*, 233.

59. The *sola scriptura* principle is more clearly expounded in Burnet's *An Exposition of the Thirty-Nine Articles*, 93:

> We . . . affirm, that the scriptures are a complete rule of faith, and that the whole Christian religion is contained in them, and no where else; and although we make great use of tradition, especially that which is most ancient and nearest the source, to help us to a clear understanding of the scriptures; yet as to matters of faith, we reject all oral tradition . . . and we refuse to receive any doctrine, that is not either expressly contained in scripture, or clearly proved from it.

60. The structure of the *Laws* indicates the shift. After a general introduction (Book I), Hooker moves immediately to the countering of Puritan positions on *sola Scriptura* (Book II), the source of church polity (Book III), the rejection of all things Roman (Book IV), the role of lay elders (Book V), the power of ecclesiastical jurisdiction (Book VI), the nature of the office of bishop (Book VII), and the role of the civil authorities in ecclesiastical matters (Book VIII). Whereas Jewel's *Apology* was structured for the opposition to Roman Catholics and stated in such a way as to simultaneously address Puritan concerns, Hooker's *Laws* does just the opposite. This may be seen as a clear indication that the Catholic moment in England had passed for good—or, at least, that Hooker thought so.

To offer the brief synopsis of the *Laws*, Books I–IV deal with laws in general: the divine law of God himself; the immutable natural law implanted by God in creation; and the positive law of human societies. Yet human reason, impaired by the Fall but assisted by divine revelation and grace, can understand the natural law and be guided in positive law according to times, circumstances, and experience. No positive law is perfect, but it is always reformable. Against the radical Puritans, Hooker argued that the scriptures were not self-authenticating. Their authority had been determined by the church. Nor did the scriptures contain a detailed ordering of the governance and worship of the church, but only its basic principles. These principles were different from the unchanging and essential revelation for faith and salvation. On the basis of scriptural principle, Hooker defended in book V the rites and customs of *The Book of Common Prayer* and in book VI its mode of penitential discipline. In book VII he based episcopacy not on any divine institution but on the universal practice of the church since apostolic times. Book VIII on the royal supremacy is cautiously ambivalent. Hooker defended on scriptural grounds the necessity of obedience to constituted civil authority by the consent of the people. In his England, as in ancient Israel, civil and ecclesiastical societies were coextensive. He was aware, however, that the Crown had used its prerogatives to limit the church's freedom in ordering its own internal life.

61. For Hooker, these three "Scripture," "Tradition," and "Reason" are the ultimate authorities for ecclesiastical matters. "John Wesley's own framework for authority owes an obvious debt to the Hookerian perspective that had become pervasive by his day" (Richard P. Heitzenrater, *Wesley and the People Called Methodists* [Nashville: Abingdon Press, 1995], 10).

62. Richard Hooker, "Of the Laws of Ecclesiastical Polity," in *The Folger Library Edition of the Works of Richard Hooker*, ed. P. G. Stanwood (Cambridge: The Belknap Press of Harvard University Press, 1981), vol. iii, 3.

63. Notably, Stanley Archer urges caution in reading Hooker's views on apostolic succession. According to Archer, although some of Hooker's comments indicate a close affinity to the Catholic view, and represent a view defended elsewhere in the early Church of England, other passages suggest a tendency which led to the Latitudinarian position of abandoning the necessity of physical succession. See Stanley Archer, "Hooker on Apostolic Succession: The Two Voices," *Sixteenth Century Journal* 24 (1993): 67–74.

64. Hooker, "Of the Laws of Ecclesiastical Polity," in *Works of Richard Hooker*, vol. iii, 14–15.

65. Wesley's interest in Stillingfleet's view of church government and episcopacy is well revealed in the letters to brother Charles, "To James Clark," and "To the Earl of Dartmouth (?)." *Letters*, iii, 136 and vii, 21; iii, 182; iv, 150. For Lord Peter King's impact upon Wesley, see the letter "To Our Brethren in America." *Letters*, vii, 238–239; *Works*, xiii, 211.

66. Baker, *John Wesley and the Church of England*, 2.

67. Wesley's love for the Church of England was his deepest human loyalty. It may be best shown by a couplet in his elegy on his friend, Robert Jones, in which he says somewhat extravagantly:

Like royal Charles and pious Jones, may I
A martyr for the Church of England die
(Rattenbury, *The Evangelical Doctrines of Charles Wesley's Hymns*, 228).

68. *Letters*, vii, 28.

69. *Letters*, vii, 163.

70. *Journal*, ii, 274–275.

71. *Letters*, vi, 28.

72. See the third chapter "The Beginning of a Party" of Patrick Collinson's *The Elizabethan Puritan Movement* (Berkeley: University of California Press, 1967), 45–55.

73. Patrick Collinson's analysis of the incompleteness of the English Reformation is presented in his second chapter "But Halfly Reformed." Patrick Collinson's *The Elizabethan Puritan Movement*, 29–44. Here he particularly notes the Puritan dissatisfaction with the role of the monarchy as head of the Church, citing Theodore Beza(1519–1605)'s observation that in England "the papacy was never abolished . . . but rather transferred to the sovereign" (43).

74. John Geree, *The Character of an old English Puritane, or Non-Conformist* (London: Printed by W. Wilson for Christopher Meredith at the Crane in Pauls Church-yard, 1646), in *Images of English Puritanism: A Collection of Contemporary Sources, 1589–1646*, ed. Lawrence A. Sasek (Baton Rouge: Louisiana State University Press, 1989), 209–211.

75. Many of the names of these Puritans we find in Wesley's *A Christian Library*.

76. Michael R. Watts, *The Dissenters*, 2 vols. (Oxford, England: Clarendon Press, 1978), vol. i, 16.

77. Watts, *The Dissenters*, vol. i, 220.

78. Pearson's *An Exposition of the Creed* was published just prior to the restrictive acts mentioned above. It went through four editions and multiple printings. Jay, *The Church*, 190.

79. Pearson, *An Exposition of the Creed*, 516.

80. Pearson, *An Exposition of the Creed*, 515.

81. Pearson, *An Exposition of the Creed*, 524.

82. See Roger L. Emerson's essay, "Latitudinarianism and the English Deists," in *Deism, Masonry, and the Enlightenment: Essays Honoring Alfred Owen Aldridge*, ed. J. A. Leo Lemay (Newark: University of Delaware Press, 1987), 19–48.

83. It must be noted that the Puritans differed among themselves about which biblical interpretations were best and that among them considerable differences eventually appeared over what Scripture revealed in questions relating to the church. This disagreement came to the fore after the success of the Puritan Revolution, and it led to the disintegration of Puritanism in England.

84. *The Works* (Jackson), xiii, 101.

85. In addition to Puritans, the antecedents of a disciplined Christian community are founded in the monastic communities in the Medieval Ages, Anglican religious societies in the seventeenth century, Pietist movements, etc. Also, as shown in the previous section, there was the emphasis on discipline from the side of the Church of England through the influence of reformers including Martin Bucer. Accordingly, one must note that the Puritans were not exclusive influence upon Wesley for this matter.

86. See David Lowes Watson, *The Early Methodist Class Meeting: Its Origin and Significance* (Nashville: Discipleship Resources, 1985), 32–34.

87. Wesley owned and read in 1730 Baxter's *The Saints' Everlasting Rest; or, A Treatise of the Blessed State of the Saints in their Enjoyment of God in Glory* (1650), and he later abridged and published it in his *Christian Library* in 1754. Heitzenrater, *John Wesley and the Oxford Methodists*, 496. For the study of Wesley's dependence upon Baxter's thought and work, also see Robert C. Monk, *John Wesley: His Puritan Heritage*, 2d ed. (Lanham, Maryland: The Scarecrow Press, Inc., 1999).

88. Watson, *The Early Methodist Class Meeting*, 6.

89. See Watson, *The Early Methodist Class Meeting*, especially 21–38.

90. Snyder, *The Radical Wesley and Patterns for Church Renewal*, 114. Here Snyder describes the disciplined Christian community as an element of the radical Protestant model in which he includes early Methodism.

91. Wesley, "A Plain Account of the People called Methodists in a Letter to the Rev. Mr. Perronet, Vicar of Shoreham in Kent, II, 3" in *Works*, ix, 261.

92. For Wesley's best summary of Methodist discipline, see Sermon "On God's Vineyard," III, 1–3, in *Works*, iii, 511–512.

93. Leslie Stephen, *History of English Thought in the Eighteenth Century*, 2 vols. (New York: Harcourt, Brace & World, Inc., 1962), vol. ii, 368. The first edition was published in New York in 1876.

94. John H. Overton, *The Evangelical Revival in the Eighteenth Century* (London: Longmans, Green, and Co., 1907), 44–45. The first edition was published in New York in 1886.

95. George C. Cell, *The Rediscovery of John Wesley* (New York: Henry Holt and Company, 1935), vii.

96. Albert C. Outler, "Towards a Re-Appraisal of John Wesley as a Theologian," *The Perkins School of Theology Journal* 14, no. 2 (Winter 1961): 7. In addition to the Puritans, according to Outler, Wesley borrowed the emphasis upon liturgy as the main factor in Christian continuity from the nonjurors, some theology and piety from such Caroline divines as Taylor, Beveridge, Tillotson, Horneck, etc, and the preference for comprehension over toleration from the Latitudinarians.

97. Halévy's "La Naissance du Méthodisme en Angleterre" was originally published as two articles in *La Revue De Paris* 4, 519–539 and 841–867 on August 1 and 15, 1906. It was translated into English by Bernard Semmel in 1971, entitled *The Birth of Methodism in England*. This work is using the translation edition of Semmel.

98. Élie Halévy, *The Birth of Methodism in England*, Translated and edited by Bernard Semmel (Chicago: University of Chicago Press, 1971), 38.

99. Halévy, *The Birth of Methodism in England*, 76–77.

100. Sydney G. Dimond, *The Psychology of the Methodist Revival: An Empirical and Descriptive Study* (Nashville: Whitmore & Smith, 1926), 136.

101. Maldwyn Edwards, *This Methodism: Eight Studies* (London: Epworth Press, 1939), 52.

102. Horton Davies, *The English Free Churches* (London: Oxford University Press, 1952), 141.

103. George Eayrs, "Links between the Ejected Clergy of 1662, the Wesleys, and Methodism," in *The Ejectment of 1662 and the Free Churches*, ed. Alexander Maclaren (London: National Council of Evangelical Free Churches, n.d.), 99–119.

104. Duncan Coomer, "The Influence of Puritanism and Dissent on Methodism," *London Quarterly and Holborn Review* 175 (1950): 346–350.

105. Newton, *Methodism and the Puritans*, 9.

106. Newton, *Methodism and the Puritans*, 14–17.

107. Newton, *Methodism and the Puritans*, 18.

108. Newton, *Methodism and the Puritans*, 4–7.

109. John A. Newton, *Susanna Wesley and the Puritan Tradition in Methodism* (London: Epworth Press, 2002), 17.

110. Robert C. Monk, *John Wesley: His Puritan Heritage* (Nashville: Abingdon Press, 1966). Monk published the second edition in 1999, giving an additional, greater attention to Wesley's dependence upon the insights and work of key Puritan thinkers, such as Richard Baxter and John Goodwin, as well as a more intensive analysis of the ways in which Wesley's ministry to the poor displayed continuities with his Puritan heritage.

111. Bishop, *Methodist Worship in Relation to Free Church Worship*, 8.

112. Bishop, *Methodist Worship in Relation to Free Church Worship*, 99–100.

113. *The Message and Mission of Methodism: The Report of the Committee Appointed by the Methodist Conference, 1943, 'to Re-consider and Re-state the Message and Mission of Methodism in Modern Society'* (London: Epworth Press, 1946), 54.

114. Horton Davies, *Worship and Theology in England*, vol. iii (*From Watts and Wesley to Maurice, 1690–1850*), 184.

115. Frederick Hunter, "The Origins of Wesley's Covenant Service," *Proceedings of the Wesley Historical Society* xxii (1939–1940): 126–131.

116. Frederick Hunter, "Sources of Wesley's Revision of the Prayer Book in 1784–8," *Proceedings of the Wesley Historical Society* xxiii (1941–1942), 123–133.

117. Frank Baker, "The Beginnings of the Methodist Covenant Service," *The London Quarterly and Holborn Review* 180 (1955): 215–220.

118. Baker, "The Beginnings of the Methodist Covenant Service," 215.

119. *The Works* (Jackson), xi, 39.

120. Its original title is *An Abridgment of Mr. Baxter's History of his Life and Times; With an Account of the Ministers, Etc., who were Ejected after the Restoration of King Charles II* (London, 1702).

121. *Works*, xx, 485.

122. "The Preface" to *Meditations and Vows, Divine and Moral. By Bishop Hall*, in *Christian Library*, vol. vii, 1. Throughout the *Christian Library* Wesley added the sections of "The Preface" or "To the Reader" to the sources of each author. Of them, some was written by Wesley, but some not by Wesley. In the cases that he did not write them, Wesley borrowed them from the sources he extracted

from. The Preface to the writings of Bishop Hall was most possibly written by Wesley. Thus, it is quite safe to say that the statement above is Wesley's.

123. Overton, *The Evangelical Revival in the Eighteenth Century*, 173.

124. *Works*, xxvi, 189.

125. Wesley, Letter "To 'John Smith,'" on March 25, 1747, in *Works*, xxvi, 235.

126. See *Works*, xxiv, 104.

127. For the list of the Puritan authors included in *A Christian Library*, see Robert C. Monk, *John Wesley: His Puritan Heritage*, 2d ed. (1999), 20–23.

128. Twenty-seven of the seventy-one authors Wesley "had noted reading while he was at Oxford as a student and tutor, 1725–35, when he 'collected' or abridged many of them." Richard P. Heitzenrater, "John Wesley's *A Christian Library*, Then and Now," *American Theological Library Association Summary of Proceedings* 55 (2001): 136. During the years 1749–1755 Wesley edited the *A Christian Library*. As Heitzenrater puts it, "[i]t is particularly interesting to note that these twenty-seven (and perhaps others) were read long before his evangelical experience at Aldersgate in 1738, yet he still considered them as significant enough to include in this collection a decade later" (Heitzenrater, "John Wesley's *A Christian Library*, Then and Now," 144, note 17).

129. Monk, *John Wesley: His Puritan Heritage*, 2d ed., 18.

130. "To the Reader" within *Acts and Monuments of the Christian Martyrs. Extracted from Mr. John Fox. To Which is prefix'd some Account of his Life*, in *Christian Library*, vol. ii, 209. It is evident that this "To the Reader" is Wesley's statement.

131. *Christian Library*, vol. vii, 1–2.

132. Monk, *John Wesley: His Puritan Heritage*, 2d ed., 23–24.

133. For the information of Wesley's other publications in relation to the Puritans' works, see Frank Baker, *A Union Catalogue of the Publications of John and Charles Wesley*, 2d ed. (Stone Mountain, Ga.: George Zimmermann, 1991); also Monk, *John Wesley: His Puritan Heritage*, 2d ed., 24–25.

134. Monk, *John Wesley: His Puritan Heritage*, 2d ed., 196.

Chapter 3

Pietism

It is generally acknowledged that the Pietists' influence upon Wesley was substantial. However, before the exploration of the Pietists' influence upon Wesley, we must briefly discuss the problem of definition and scope of Pietism, for understandings of Pietism vary widely among scholars and our explication of the impact of Pietism upon Wesley is made dependent upon how we define and interpret Pietism.

The origin and history of Pietism has been controversial. Pietism has come to be seen as a complex, often heterogeneous movement. Church historians like Kurt Aland say that a fixed Pietism has never existed but that Pietism has always existed in the very variety.[1]

The debate on the temporal and geographical boundaries of Pietism in recent scholarship has been led by Martin Brecht and Johannes Wallmann. Brecht emphasizes the origins of Pietism in a post-Reformation crisis of piety that resulted from the difficulties the Reformation churches experienced in realizing Christian life and activity and extends the temporal and geographical boundaries of Pietism to English Puritanism, *nadere Reformatie* in the Netherlands, the devotional movements in Germany (including Radical Pietism, Nicholas Ludwig von Zinzendorf [1700–1760] and the Moravians), Methodism, and the Awakening movements.[2]

This interpretation is quite close to that of the American F. Ernest Stoeffler. In his book *The Rise of Evangelical Pietism*, Stoeffler saw Pietism as a major Protestant movement which has its roots in mystical and sectarian streams and in Bucer's mediating position between Luther and

Calvin. According to him, Pietism was manifested first in English Puritanism and Dutch Reformed circles and appeared in Lutheranism through figures such as Johann Arndt (1555–1621), Philipp Jakob Spener (1635–1705),
August Hermann Francke (1663–1727), Johann Albrecht Bengel (1687–
1752), and Zinzendorf. And it was radicalized by people like Johanna
Eleonora Petersen (1644–1724), Gottfried Arnold (1666–1714), Ernst
Christoph Hochmann (1670–1721) and Johann K. Dippel (1673–1734), and
romanticized by Johann Heinrich Jung-Stilling (1740–1817). It was also
appropriated by Moravians, the Church of the Brethren, Swedish Mission
Friends, the Wesleyan movement and the evangelical revivals, and by the
end of the nineteenth century turned into a world-wide phenomenon. Pietism, furthermore, continues as the basic religious ethos of a host of organizations, societies, and denominations today.[3]

Stoeffler's and Brecht's understandings of Pietism have the advantage
of encompassing a wide range of renewal movements within Protestantism
that undoubtedly influenced each other. However, this inclusive and
chronologically broad interpretation of Pietism, as points out Wallmann,
has the disadvantage of blurring the contours of church history so that Pietism as a movement is no longer definable and distinguishable from other
movements.[4]

In contrast to Brecht's broad conception of Pietism, Wallmann distin-
guishes Pietism in a narrow sense from the broader piety movements. Asserting that Pietism in the proper sense of the term begins with Phillip Ja-
kop Spener, Wallmann presents the specific characteristics that distinguish
Spener's Pietism from the pervious piety movements: the development of
the conventicle movement (the *ecclesiola in ecclesia*), the universal priesthood of believers, the hope for better times before the end of the world, and
the pronounced emphasis upon lay reading and study of the Bible.[5] In
Wallmann's definition, most of the Dutch *nadere Reformatie* or English
Puritanism would not qualify as Pietism in the narrow sense, though one
could incorporate them under Pietism broadly conceived. Wallmann's interpretation of Pietism has the advantage of allowing us to distinguish
neatly between Pietism in its proper sense and broader piety movements.

Pietism cannot be treated solely as a German movement, nor may it be
reduced simply to its first sudden rise in the Protestant world of the seventeenth and early eighteenth centuries. But since the movements which historians call "Pietism"[6] apparently developed after the struggles within German Lutheranism, there is a certain logic in beginning with the German
movement initiated by Spener and Francke. In this chapter, this study focuses on the ecclesiologies of the German Pietism. But it does not offer any
survey account of the ecclesiologies of the German Pietists. It concerns cer-

tain elements in the ecclesiologies of the Pietists such as Spener, Francke, and Zinzendorf and Moravians because their connection with Wesley can be traced.

Spener-Francke Pietism and Wesley

Luther had placed the seat of faith in the heart, but following Luther's death, emphasis shifted to the intellect. Perhaps it was a rather natural shift from *kerygma* to *didache* as happened in every religious reform movement. "Both Lutherans and Calvinists developed a precise theological methodology and a vocabulary that characterized an academic theology known as Protestant Orthodoxy or Scholasticism."[7] Protestant Scholasticism, with its emphasis on creeds (for instance, the Formula of Concord, 1577) and precise doctrinal formulation, led to a clear redefining of the Christian believer. The ideal Christian believer was now thought to be "a person who interprets the Bible in terms of the Lutheran symbols as the truth of these symbols is expressed in an orthodox system of theology."[8] Such a scholasticism or creedalism soon resulted in the tendency "to overstress the objective aspects of God's promised salvation, such as the written Word, justification as a forensic act," and the sacraments as *opera operata*.[9] Accordingly, faith as trust in the living God, which was so prominent in the writings of Martin Luther, had now begun to develop into mere assent, into a simple subscription to the formulations of orthodoxy. "*Fiducia* had become *assensus*."[10]

Protestant Orthodoxy, however, does not seem to have separated theology and piety in an obsessive drive to right belief. It must be noted that beneath Orthodoxy there existed a rich and heartfelt spiritual life.[11] For instance, the period of Orthodoxy was the classical period of devotional literature and music.[12]

In Orthodoxy there were also the efforts for reform. In particular the mystics such as Valentine Weigel (1533–1588), Stephan Praetorius (1536–1603), Philipp Nicolai (1556–1608), Jakob Boehme (1575–1624) and Johann Arndt, and those who followed their tradition believed that the renewal of doctrine and ecclesiastical practice which had begun during the Reformation must be supplemented by a renewal of life. These pious mystics underscored the interior life, Christian devotion to God, and the love of neighbor. It is those who concentrated on the renewal of Christian life that are seen as sources for later Pietism.

F. Ernest Stoeffler designates Johann Arndt the father of German Pietism. "Lutheran Pietism in the seventeenth century," according to Stoeffler, "took its rise with Arndt and ended with Spener."[13] In contrast to Stoeffler's contention Johannes Wallmann sees German Pietism in the proper sense as beginning with Spener and classifies Arndt as a figure in the broader piety movements. However, Wallmann also admits that Arndt prepared the way for Spener. "From him [Arndt] has come the characteristic piety of Pietism, the priority of the godly life over doctrine, the insistence upon true, living and active faith, upon sanctification as the re-establishment of the image of God planted in the soul."[14]

Certainly the German Pietism was incredibly influenced by Arndt. Arndt's writings were so popular that their hundreds of editions overshadowed Luther's influence in the seventeenth and eighteenth centuries. We cannot discuss German Pietism without giving a proper attention to Arndt. In many senses Arndt was the trailblazer of German Pietism. In his *Bücher vom wahren Christentum*,[15] he emphasized the Christian's life which was not merely a product of orthodox doctrines, but involved an inner relationship based on the justified believer's union with God. He found in pre-Reformation mysticism the necessary inspiration and power for religious renewal for his time.

In the *Bücher vom wahren Christentum* Arndt stressed a godly life and religious renewal as well as justification by faith alone. Once to Duke August the Junior of Braunschweig-Wolfenbüttel, his patron and friend, Arndt spoke of two aims he was addressing in his work: "First of all I have desired to draw the souls of students and preachers back from their far too characteristic disputatious and quarrelsome theology that has again become nearly a *Theologia scholastica*. For the other I have intended to lead the believers in Christ from dead faith to a faith that brings forth fruits."[16] Such an effort to pair justification and sanctification became the words of Arndt's followers in Protestant Christianity including Spener and Wesley.

In England, Arndt's *Bücher vom wahren Christentum* (*True Christianity*) was read as early as 1648.[17] Judging from the fact that he included an extract of Arndt's *True Christianity* in his *Christian Library*, Wesley must have been acquainted with *True Christianity*. Wesley read the *True Christianity* in Georgia in March 1736, and for some time previous to this he must have been aware of Arndt.[18] He valued the *True Christianity* so highly that he included it in the first volume of his *Christian Library*.[19]

Philipp Jakob Spener followed Arndt's example. Against a prevailing scholastic theology, Spener tried to apply Christian theology to Christian living. For Spener "*it is by no means enough to have knowledge of the Christian faith, for Christianity consists rather of practice. . . .* Just because theology is a practical discipline and does not consist only of knowledge, study alone is not enough, nor is the mere accumulation and imparting of information."[20] This strong emphasis on *practice* was the core of Spener's thought, and actually Pietism. Although he did theology in the shadow of Martin Luther,[21] Spener knew that the reformer and he worked in quite different theological contexts: Luther served in an age when merit earned by good works was unduly stressed; Spener lived in a period when the doing of good works needed to be encouraged. Spener's life and thought constituted the efflorescence of German Pietism.[22]

There is no direct evidence that Wesley ever read Spener's works. Spener's name does not appear in Wesley's Journal, diaries, letters, or theological treatises. However, although he probably never read Spener himself, Wesley certainly read Arndt to whom Spener owed much, and he certainly read Francke who owed much to Spener. These points suggest that although we cannot prove his direct reading of Spener, Spener's theology had a significant, if indirect, influence on the theology of Wesley. Spener and Wesley clearly held some elements in common such as soteriology (e.g., pairing of justification and sanctification), the emphasis on inward religion and on practicality, Biblical theology, the avoidance of needless doctrinal disputation, the development of small groups (e.g., Spener's *collegia pietatis* [colleges of piety] and Wesley's class meetings, bands, or societies), the role of laity in developing spiritual life, and so on.

As a Lutheran, Spener thought that the church exists "where the Word of God is taught genuinely and purely, and the sacraments are rightly administered according to the divine institution."[23] At this point Spener stood firmly aligned with the doctrine of the church found in classical Protestantism. For Spener the Word and the sacraments are the marks of the visible church. And he believed that the Lutheran Church is the true visible church in his day.[24] The "Lutheran Church is a true church and is pure in its teaching," though "it is in such a condition, unfortunately, that we behold its outward form with sorrowful eyes."[25]

By the word "church," Spener didn't mean the building as meeting houses for worship but "the gatherings of Christians, in general as well as in certain special groups. The former is the universal; the latter are the singular churches."[26] Accordingly, the church is *organically* understood as a society or assembly of people who are bound together with one another, like a body.[27] Spener de-emphasizes the church's institutional side and stresses her essential character as a people, community, and body.

Spener maintained a clear distinction between the visible and invisible church. He says,

Here we call the visible church all those people who hold themselves externally to the word of God and confess that they stand in an external,

visible fellowship with other pious Christians, although many among them
are not pious from the heart; the invisible church, however, means only
the number of true children of God who are, as we have heard, nowhere
alone and separated from all others but rather live mixed with the wicked,
and who are known to God who recognizes only them as His own.[28]

This distinction became more clarified in Spener's *Einflätige Erklärung*,
where the visible church is depicted as consisting of all those who confess
with their mouths and external service, while the invisible church is "the
true spiritual body of Christ," whose members alone are "the true believers."[29] The invisible church consists of "the righteous believers who have
the true, divine, living faith, and therefore find themselves not only in the
outer assembly, and confess themselves to Christ, but who through such
faith in Him, abide in the true head, and out of Him, as the branches out of
the vine . . . receive living sap and spirit, and bring forth fruit out of the
same."[30] The purity of the visible church is made dependent upon the relative number of the invisible-church members it contains,[31] and membership
in the latter rather than in the former regarded as essential to salvation.

Spener's ecclesiology, like that of Luther, is Christological in the sense
that the church comes from Christ and is founded upon Him; the church is
"born out of Christ, for she is the seed which He is supposed to have and
which was promised to Him."[32] As all human beings are derived from the
first Adam, "so all believers, who are therefore the church, come from the
second Adam in spiritual fashion through the New Birth." And "through the
New Birth we enter the fellowship of the true church."[33]

Howard A. Snyder sees as three key themes of Spener's ecclesiology
the stress on the New Birth (*Wiedergeburt*), the universal and spiritual
priesthood of believers, and the importance of *ecclesiolae* or *collegia pietatis*.[34] In addition to these three, we should list his stress on the church reform which was partly based upon his eschatological hope for better times
for the church on earth.

Spener's emphasis on the New Birth is clearly revealed in the first of
the sixty-six sermons on the New Birth, *Der Hochwichtige Articul von der
Wiedergeburt*: "If one matter of our Christianity is necessary, it is certainly
the one of the New Birth, in which our conversion, justification, and the
beginning of our sanctification likewise come to us together, and it is also
the ground of all remaining sanctification or the fountain out of which all
that in our entire lives is good or happens concerning us or to us must necessarily flow."[35] When faith is created in the heart as a gift of God and justification is given to the believer, an entirely other and new nature is created in the believer and the New Birth provides for a restoration of the
Image of God.[36] Then, renewal (*Erneuerung*) follows the New Birth. The

renewal is the Holy Spirit's working through the Word and sacraments to hold believers steadfast in the new nature.[37] It involves putting off the old self and putting on the new one (Eph. 4:22–24). Spener often equated renewal with sanctification.[38] The significance of this understanding for ecclesiology is that it emphasizes the restorative and therapeutic "concern with the present life and fellowship of the church, not only with one's theological-juridical standing before God or one's eternal destiny." Furthermore, "Spener's rebirth theology was closely linked with his overall hope for a general church renewal."[39]

Spener reinforced his vision for church renewal by emphasizing the universal, spiritual priesthood of believers. With the establishment and practice of the universal, spiritual priesthood, in fact we come to the most distinctive phase of Spener's ecclesiology. Luther's idea of the priesthood of all believers signified that the individual had free access to God without priestly or church mediation. Spener placed more emphasis on the privilege of each Christian to help, serve, and edify his or her neighbor,[40] than did Luther. "Every Christian is bound . . . with the grace that is given him to teach others, especially those under his own roof, to chastise, exhort, convert, and to edify them, to observe their life, pray for all, and insofar as possible be concerned about their salvation."[41] Although a special call to the ministry was not disputed, this doctrine gave lay-people an opportunity to assert their spiritual independence from clergy and their right to all spiritual functions. Spener says, "all spiritual functions are open to all Christians without exception. Although the regular and public performance of them is entrusted to ministers appointed for this purpose, the functions may be performed by others in case of emergency. Especially should those things which are unrelated to public acts be done continually by all at home and in everyday life."[42] Spener further says that "teachers and preachers are the ordained workers and master-builders on whom the church is built" and who are prepared for the work of ministry.[43] But "other Christians," continues he,

> on the whole out of their universal priesthood . . . may and should strive to build the church . . . not only with prayer and good example, but according to each person's measure of grace, with instruction, admonition, warning, punishment and consolation. . . . All you Christians, not only the preachers, *are a chosen race, a royal priesthood, a holy people, a people belonging to God, that you may proclaim the virtues of him who called you out of darkness into his marvelous light*: through which they are supposed always to encourage their brethren and all others to enlist themselves so much more diligently at such a heavenly supper.[44]

Where there was no regular ministry the call of love and service might take the place of the call of the church. In cases of necessity a layperson might even baptize and declare absolution. In harmony with the spirit of his age, however, Spener refused women the right of active participation in church affairs.[45]

The universal priesthood became for Spener a fundamental category for understanding the church herself. The church, including all members, is a priesthood under the High Priesthood of Jesus Christ.

The universal, spiritual priesthood found its best expression in the famous *collegia pietatis*. Spener thought that the much-needed reform of the Lutheran Church could not issue from those in authority, that the great majority in the Church were unconverted while the converted easily went astray, and that conditions in general were so bad that something radical had to be done. Accordingly, he recommended that the clergy form *ecclesiolae* (little churches) of those who were in earnest about their souls' salvation.

Spener proposed such gatherings in the *Pia Desideria*:

> it would perhaps not be inexpedient . . . to reintroduce the ancient and apostolic kind of church meetings. In addition to our customary services with preaching, other assemblies would also be held in the manner in which Paul describes them in I Corinthians 14:26–40. One person would not rise to preach . . . but others who have been blessed with gifts and knowledge would also speak and present their pious opinions on the proposed subject to the judgment of the rest, doing all this in such a way as to avoid disorder and strife. This might conveniently be done by having several ministers . . . meet together or by having several members of a congregation who have a fair knowledge of God or desire to increase their knowledge meet under the leadership of a minister, take up the Holy Scriptures, read aloud from them, and fraternally discuss each verse in order to discover its simple meaning and whatever may be useful for the edification of all.[46]

The private meetings for mutual edification and spiritual communication were to avoid all appearance of false teaching and extravagance. They were to be instituted to supplement, not to supplant, the regular Church service. Spener opposed the celebration of the Lord's Supper in these meetings. The main exercises consisted of discussions on Scripture passages.[47] Because this was done under the direction of the pastor, it was hoped that he would be brought into closer touch with his members and learn to understand and appreciate their needs better.

These pious meetings were to be established wherever possible, and from the more spiritual fields Spener hoped the good leaven would gradually spread throughout the Church.[48] Actually, through the *Pia Desideria*, such meetings (or conventicles) became known far and wide and seem partly to have accomplished the immediate result for which they were instituted. Spener sought the salvation of the Church by means of the *ecclesiolae in ecclesia* (little churches within the Church) which is the righteous nucleus within the Church.

However, Spener was aware of the separatist tendencies promoted by these conventicles. He publicly deplored separation as a misfortune, claiming that it acted like a medicine which was more dangerous than the disease it was supposed to cure.[49] Spener's fear of separation is clearly revealed in the following statement: "I willingly confess that with all my heart I have a horror of separation and it is better to be in a very corrupted church than in none at all."[50]

Despite his fear of separation from the Church, Spener frequently criticized the Church of his day for parting from the primitive church model. Spener used many biblical images of the church, which showed the primitivist motif of his ecclesiology. He saw himself as attempting to reinstitute New Testament church patterns, and was accused of a "ridiculous aping" of the primitive church.[51] Spener saw the period of church history before Constantine as "the brilliant age of Christendom, when the church had not yet fallen into secularization," as Wesley later did. Spener saw himself as a reformer in his day striving to complete the Reformation, which had been begun by Luther's efforts to restore the Scriptural church, but not carried out sufficiently in the areas of life, morality, and the corporate experience of the church, with too much emphasis upon doctrine.[52]

Spener did not think that the Lutheran Church was the only Church in which salvation could be found while it was a true visible Church.[53] People could be saved in the Roman Catholic, Reformed, and other communions. Although he knew of no Church whose doctrine and confessions of faith was purer than his Lutheran Church, Spener said that Christ would indeed be a poor king if the only people in his kingdom of grace were Lutherans.[54] God is the housefather and the Church the housemother. However, Christians believe not in the Church but in God. The Church teaches its people God's Word genuinely and with most articulate explanations according to the measure of received grace, but the object of Christian faith is always God alone, and not the Church.[55]

Spener anticipated and believed that his visible church can be reformed. He said, "If we consult the Holy Scriptures we can have no doubt that God promised his church here on earth a better state than this. . . . I do not see how anybody can doubt that the whole true church would be in a more glorious and blessed condition than it is now."[56] His hope for better times for the church on earth in some degree derived from his optimistic eschatology. Spener believed that through the church's ministry of Word and sacraments, Christ will come to earth spiritually to reign with his saints on earth a thousand years before the Second Coming and Last Judgment. This post-millennialism fueled his belief in and hope for reform.[57]

In the view of sacraments Spener followed his Lutheran Church. He saw baptism and the Lord's Supper as the genuine sacraments of Christ. Baptism and the Lord's Supper are both essential.[58] Spener further noted the close link between the Word and the sacraments. The Word is the divine letter of grace in which the heavenly Father announces His will to give us salvation. The sacraments are the seal on this letter, confirming this grace. Baptism is the actual means of New Birth, and the Lord's Supper the means of renewal. God reveals His power and wisdom by doing mighty things through humble and despised means.[59] For Spener the sacraments were not only means by which to strengthen faith, but also to enable the participants to make Christ their own. With regard to II Peter 1:4, he says that the divine nature first begins in baptism and is further strengthened and increased in the Lord's Supper.[60]

Spener accepted the Lutheran doctrine of baptismal regeneration. Baptism is the actual means of the New Birth. In baptism faith is ignited in one's soul. The baptizand likewise receives forgiveness of sins and the new nature.[61] Spener also accepted the Lutheran doctrine of the Real Presence of Christ's body and blood in the bread and wine of the Lord's Supper. At the Lord's Supper, believers receive sacramentally the very body and blood of Christ. There is a spiritual eating of Christ by faith, but there is also a sacramental eating in which they actually receive Christ's body and blood as refreshing and medicinal food.[62]

However, Spener frequently complained against the *opus operatum* or "automatic efficacy."[63] On occasion he sharply argued that persons who do not belong to Christ cannot be saved. It would not matter whether they had been baptized a thousand times and had listened to ten thousand sermons, been absolved, and received the Lord's Supper.[64] Despite the fact that they are born again in baptism, said Spener, virtually all people lose this salvation and need it to be replaced with a second New Birth that comes through belief in the Word.[65]

Moreover, Spener aimed to stimulate the general church services. The confessional was retained, in spite of abuse, to be used as a means of teaching, disciplining, and comforting.[66] As edification was the main purpose of the church service, a change in the ceremony was occasionally permissible to retain its flexibility and to meet changing demands.[67] Because of its social character, Spener regarded congregational singing as helpful.[68] He was one of the first to emphasize extemporaneous prayer.[69] The aesthetic in worship and the artistic in decoration received scant notice, because they did not seem to be in harmony with true simplicity.[70]

If it can be said that Spener launched the German Pietist movement, it may also be said that August Francke institutionalized it. It was Francke who translated the German Pietist movement into a vast network of influence and outreach. From Halle, Francke gave the movement the prestige associated with academic theologians and invested an outstanding gift for organization in establishing numerous enterprises.

Wesley read August Hermann Francke more than Arndt or Spener. Wesley was twenty-four years old when Francke died, and the two never met. Although there was no direct contact between Francke and Wesley, Wesley was familiar with the writings and the work of Francke and the Pietist leaders in Halle knew the earliest activities of the Oxford Methodists through private report by Friedrich Michael Ziegenhagen (1694–1777).[71] Wesley read Francke's *Christus sacrae scripturae nucleus* in September 1732 and *Manductio ad lectionem scripturae sacrae* in July 1733, and the two were studied by the Oxford Methodists.[72] Francke's *Segensvolle Fuszstapfen* was translated into English and given the title *Pietas Hallensis*, published in the second edition in 1707. Wesley was acquainted with this *Pietas Hallensis*, but just how early in life is unknown. It is known that he read the *Pietas Hallensis* on his way to Georgia in 1735. He also read Francke's *Nicodemus* (or *A Treatise on the Fear of Man*),[73] which A. W. Boehm had translated into English in 1706.[74] Wesley's decision to include this work in his *Christian Library* would say that he valued it highly.

Nourished, like Spener, on the Lutheran-Arndtian tradition, Francke clearly was a Spenerian Pietist. He followed Spener in stressing spiritual experience, the new birth, the importance of Scripture as the source of life as well as of doctrine, and in a generally more organic and less institutional understanding of the church and the Christian life and an optimism as to the possibilities of reform. He, like Spener, saw the Lutheran Church as lacking "any kind of effective discipline," and felt that this visible church is "in need of a through-going renewal. Hence the responsible and earnest pastor must concentrate his efforts upon establishing within it the 'invisible church,' which is constituted of truly converted people."[75]

Yet, Francke was different from Spener in some respects. First, he believed that church renewal can come through educational reform while Spener strove to attain the renewal through church reform. Francke was a life-long educator, though also pastor at Glaucha. His initial and formative experience of *ecclesiola* was in the form of a *collegium philobiblicum* (college of bible-lovers) of students and professors at the University of Leipzig, rather than in a *collegium pietatis* in a parish setting. Francke's *collegium philobiblicum* studied the Bible in its original languages as Wesley and Oxford Methodists did some forty-three years later. As Halle became increasingly a Pietist center and Pietism gained ground, he became more a propagandist and educational reformer and less a church reformer and builder. For Francke, everything turned on education and discipline, which he thought are enabled by the New Birth, and his reform efforts were primarily in terms of training and education.[76]

Secondly, while Spener put stress on *corporate* life, Francke placed more emphasis, in theory and practice, on *individual* Christian experience, reflecting seemingly his own experience. The way to Francke's conversion reminds us of Wesley's Aldersgate. Francke's parents offered him a thorough religious education and the reception of Arndtian and Lutheran piety determined the formation of the young Francke. However, the young Francke was unable to believe with ultimate certainty, and hence could not stand security for the gospel he had to preach even after entering a pastoral or preaching position. In analogy to Wesley's Aldersgate experience, Francke's Lüneburg experience relieved his doubt.

> In such great fear I fell once more upon my knees on the aforesaid Sunday evening, and I cried to God, whom I did not yet know nor believe in, for salvation from such a miserable state, if indeed there would be truly a God.
>
> Then the Lord, the living God, heard me from his holy throne while I was still on my knees. So great was his fatherly love that he did not want to remove such doubt and unrest from my heart gradually, which could have been sufficient for me, but instead he all at once heard my prayer in order that I might be all the more assured and that my errant reason might be curbed not to make no objection to his power and faithfulness. Then all my doubt disappeared as suddenly as man turns his hand, I was assured in my heart of the grace of God in Christ Jesus, I could call God not only God but also my Father, all the sadness and unrest in my heart was taken away at once, and I was suddenly overwhelmed by a stream of joy so that from full heart I glorified and praised God who had shown me such great grace. . . .
>
> It is therefore the time which I can actually reckon as my true conversion. Then from that time on my Christianity has lasted. . . .[77]

As Dale W. Brown comments, Francke's "dramatic conversion experience and his introspective analyses of feelings of guilt, anxiety, sorrow, and joy resulted in a greater emotionalization and subjectivism in his theology of experience than in the theology of Spener."[78] This emotionalization and subjectivism were fostered by his "psychologizing tendencies."[79]

The key theme in Francke's theology was conversion (*Bekehrung*) and particularly the penitential struggle (*Busskampf*) that frequently accompanies it.[80] Other than Spener, Francke saw conversion or (second) rebirth as inaugurating a lasting new condition. The conversion is an enduring change of the will. And the experience of conversion is primarily bound to repentance. At this point, Francke refers to the Lutheran Confessional writings with their emphasis of "despairing repentance" (*contritio*), which, similarly to the traditional sacrament of penance, is the presupposition for the encounter with the forgiving gospel. Francke therefore placed a particular emphasis upon the penitential struggle. Because most people have fallen from their baptismal covenant, believed Francke, conversion through penitential struggle is necessary for most. As Gary R. Sattler notes, "self-examination plays a large role in the psychological life of the Halle Pietist. The heart, mind, and conscience are constantly plowed up and pored over, dissected under the light of Scripture and the Pietist understanding of the Christian life."[81] The significance of this stress on individual conversion experience ecclesiologically is that it seems to mark a shift away from the stress on *koinonia* and corporate life and discipleship in Spener toward individualism and greater subjectivism, and that there is an emphasis upon religious discipline with the penitential struggle.

Thirdly, Francke seems to have had less profound concept of the priesthood of believers than Spener. By comparison with Spener, Francke seems to have had a less existential apprehension of the priesthood of believers in the *corporate* Christian life which was developed with new accents in Spener's program and thinking, perhaps because "[h]is main concern was the Christian life of the individual believer."[82]

However, Francke's passion for Pietist reformation was no less than that of Spener. His reform program was to carry through and extend the reformation, especially from his significant power base in the university and Pietist institutions in Halle.

Wesley visited the Moravians in the summer of 1736, and on his way to Herrnhut, Wesley stopped over at Halle on 26–27 July. On the return to England from Herrnhut, he again visited Halle for two days, 18 and 19 August, and he conversed with Francke's son, Professor Gotthilf August Francke (1696–1769). Wesley was so impressed by Halle that he said, "Surely such a thing neither we nor our fathers have known, as this great thing which God hath done here!"[83] Furthermore, with great respect, Wesley wished to follow Francke: "August Herman Francke whose name is indeed as precious ointment. O may I follow him, as he did Christ!"[84]

Moravians and Wesley

While the influence of Arndt and the Spener-Francke Pietist movement
upon Wesley[85] has received relatively little attention, the Moravian sources
of Methodist piety and practice have been widely investigated,[86] both from
the Methodist and from the Moravian side. Through the Moravians, Pietism
entered into intimate relationship with Wesley and was instrumental in
permanently influencing Wesley's soteriology and some of the institutions
of early Methodism. Moravians' emphasis on the availability and necessity
of assurance of salvation had a deep impact on John Wesley's spiritual development. One can also trace the particular influence of Moravian customs
on the creation and development of Methodist Church organization and
practice. Wesley's admiration for Moravian organization led in some ways
to imitation, and the similarity of Moravian and Methodist church-order,
and even of terminology, is too close to be coincidental.

Wesley had generously admitted the influence of Peter Böhler (1712–
1775), August Gottlieb Spangenberg (1704–1792), and other Moravians
upon the shaping of his thought and spirit, and he was generous, both before and after the Methodists' separation from the Moravians, in acknowl-
edging his admiration of Moravian customs, while he with equal candor
declared his detestation of certain individual interpretations. In his *Journal*
and *Letters* he frequently commends their "discipline." After his visit to
Herrnhut in 1738, for example, in the letter which he began but did not send,
he says that "I greatly approve of your conferences and bands, of your
method of instructing children, and in general of your great care of the
souls committed to your charge."[87] Again, in the famous letter "To the Moravian Church" on June 24, 1744, he writes:

> I love and esteem you for your excellent discipline, scarce inferior to that
> of the apostolic age; for your due subordination of officers, every one
> knowing and keeping his proper rank; for your exact division of the peo-
> ple under your charge . . . for your care that all who are employed in the
> service of the church should frequently and freely confer together; and, in
> consequence thereof, your exact and seasonable knowledge of the state of
> every member, and your ready distribution either of spiritual or temporal
> relief as every man hath need.[88]

Later, in the letter to the Rev. Thomas Church, he quotes and approves his
letter of September 1738 and adds: "*in part* I esteem them still. Because I
verily believe, they have a sincere desire to serve God . . . because their
discipline is, *in most respects*, so truly excellent."[89]

The Moravians were refugees from the old Unitas Fratrum, a religious society which emerged as a withdrawn and rural community gathered to live with full intention the Sermon on the Mount, influenced by pacifist principles, in the Kunwald valley, Bohemia, in 1457. A revival of the society took place when a remnant from this old Hussite group found refuge on Herrnhut, the estate of Count Nicolaus Zinzendorf, a godson of Spener and student of Francke. Under the leadership of Zinzendorf, Herrnhut grew into an influential Pietist colony, attracting spiritual seekers from all over Germany.

Like Spener and Francke, Zinzendorf accepted the orthodox Lutheran creeds. Expounding the Articles concerning the church of the Augsburg Confession in the Moravian seminary at Marienborn on March 2, 1748, Zinzendorf showed his classical Protestantism, saying that

> what is....the Character of such a Church? "Therein *the Gospel is preached purely*, and the *Sacraments dispensed according to the Direction of the same Gospel*" *Item* "that the Gospel be proclaimed according to its purest Aim and Sense, (no more is required, than that a Man be sure of what he is speaking about, and speak it as he feels and apprehends it,) and each Sacrament administered according to the true Intent of God's Word."[90]

The most prominent feature of Zinzendorf's ecclesiology is Christocentrism. He saw the church as "a Congregation of Jesus Christ from Time to Time."[91] The word "Christian Church" means just "the general *Assembly of such Men, who are true Believers, and Saints*" (Article VIII of the Augsburg Confession), but for Zinzendorf, it was "synonymous" with saying that the church consists "of such who are poor Sinners, and thro' the Blood of Jesus Christ have obtained Forgiveness of their Sin."[92] This Christological interpretation of the church is clearly represented in the following quotation stressing Christ's Passion: "Has there been *at all Times* a holy Christian-Church? then she must needs have always kept to the *Doctrine* of the *SUFFERINGS of JESUS*: there must at all Times have been a Society, laying for their Foundation, the Lord's Passion, the Martyrology of Jesus Christ, the Doctrine $\tau\eta\varsigma$ $\upsilon\pi o\mu o\nu\eta\varsigma$ $\alpha\upsilon\tau\omega$ (*Rev.* iii. 10.) the Bonds and cruel Scourging which he sustained for the Sin of our Soul."[93] Christ is "the Chief Elder, the Bishop . . . and the Head" of the church. In his Moravian brotherhood, therefore, Zinzendorf tried to ensure the subordination of all human authority under the rule of Christ. "We promise on our part that we would love and honour Him as our Elder, and through His grace keep up an uninterrupted and confidential heart's intercourse with Him; that we would childlikely obey His will and direction, choosing no man as our head in spiritual matters, but cleave to Him with full purpose of heart, though all others should forsake Him."[94]

Zinzendorf's ecclesiology, like that of Spener, placed a great stress on *corporate* life. For Zinzendorf there is "no Christianity without community."[95] Christian faith aims at community.[96] Although each believer stands in a personal relation to Christ, Christ has not called his disciples to a solitary life but to fellowship and brotherly love: "He has created us for community and given us fellowship; it is His will that we may be recognized as His disciples when we love one another."[97] The church as community is revealed in the Holy Trinity, the "*Ur-Gemeine*" (Original-Church).[98]

Zinzendorf, like other German Pietists, stressed the living, organic nature of the church rather than its institutional side. One of the most characteristic and remarkable features of Zinzendorf's ecclesiology was the way in which he combined a persistent emphasis on the church as a close-knit community (the "little flock") with a strong stress on the universal church.[99] In general, Zinzendorf saw the local congregation as the little flock of the wounded Lamb, Christ, while on a more universal scale the church was the "Congregation of God in the Spirit."[100] And as the "Congregation of God in the Spirit," the church is united. Zinzendorf says, "For the rest, in order to true Unity in Christendom, it need not be insisted on, that Ceremonies framed by Men should be the same in all Places: What *Paul* enjoins, is *one Body, and one Spirit, even as we are called in one Hope of our Calling; one Lord, one Baptism*, &c."[101]

Like Spener and Francke, Zinzendorf distinguished the invisible church from the visible. He saw the invisible church as consisting of the "People of God in every Nation," even among "erroneous Sects and in the darkest Ages," where "Souls belonging to the Saviour are still preserv'd right in what is essential to Salvation," despite, perhaps, some false doctrines.[102] Zinzendorf recognized both wheat and tares in the visible church, even among the Moravians. "Tho' there are not many in our Congregation who do not believe," said he, "yet we are never quite without such...thus there is a Mixture of Faith and Unbelief," even as was true with Jesus' disciples.[103]

Zinzendorf further distinguished between three levels of ecclesial communion, expressed by the German terms *Kirche*, *Religion*, and *Gemeine*.[104] *Kirche* refers to the church in the fullest sense, which is the invisible communion of all true believers. Zinzendorf used *Kirche* primarily for the invisible church and not for congregations or denominational bodies. *Kirche* consists of the heavenly church triumphant and the earthly church militant. Zinzendorf's understanding of *Kirche* was Christocentric. Because the first human manifestation of the church created in Adam was imperfect, Christ came to earth and constituted the new church under the cross. This church is the Bride of Christ. As long as Christ is hidden, the church exists only in a concealed form, but it will become visible when Christ returns. Although the church is one, its members are scattered among the visible institutional churches.

The visible institutional churches Zinzendorf called *Religionen* (plural of *Religion*). *Religionen* refer to what we would call denominations or confessional traditions today. Zinzendorf employed *Religion* for a historically and culturally conditioned tradition and institution. *Religion* is organized community that teaches and practices the Christian faith according to a prescribed form. Some people can not believe without having Christianity in the particular form of their *Religion*. Although not all members of such *Religionen* are necessarily true children of God and none of these *Religionen* is without errors and imperfections, the *Religionen* are still necessary to lead people to Christ, and in their diversity they preserve the wealth of divine truths. Thus one should respect each *Religion* and leave people within it who belong within, not trying to proselytize. Each *Religion* represents the way in which God works historically and contextually, thus it is partially the result of human historical and cultural perspectives, but also especially the result of God's intention.

Finally, *Gemeine* refers to the spiritual brotherhood of all true believers across all confessional and denominational lines. *Gemeine* was the term Zinzendorf most frequently used for the church. Distinct from *Religion*, *Gemeine* was used for the church which lived with and from Christ and expressed the reality from which it lived.

> I always make a great difference between a *Gemeine* and a *Religion in genere* [in kind] . . . with respect to a *Gemeine* I am of the opinion that she stands in need of no new system because she is herself a daily system of God, a system which the Angels themselves study: so on the other hand in the *Religionen* from whence the *Gemeine* (here not congregation but universal church) is made up, from which it issues, where it has its old knowledge and in which it would also like to remain in order to set forth certain points freely, one must point out people who have spiritual eyes and ears, with whom *metanoia* [repentance] is going on.[105]

Gemeine is a community which is a living organism, universal as well as local. This invisible body of universal *Gemeine* can become partially visible in a local *Gemeine* when true believers unite in fellowship. Zinzendorf believed that all who belong to Christ, even if they come from different churches, yearn for such fellowship. According to Zinzendorf, throughout church history there have always been particular communities that for a limited time embodied a visible *Gemeine*. The Moravian brotherhood

(*Brüdergemeine*) is such a fellowship of believers in his own time. Thus, in Zinzendorf's view, the Moravians do not represent a *Religion* but rather a trans-denominational network within and beyond the structures of the institutional churches.[106]

In order to maintain such trans-denominational diversity within the *Brüdergemeine*, Zinzendorf implemented specific confessional groups with separate membership lists and ministerial oversight. These groups were called *Tropoi*. The term *Tropoi* is derived from the Greek *tropoi paideias* ("paths of training"). According to J. Taylor Hamilton, Zinzendorf developed his concept of *Tropus* (singular of *Tropoi*) during the Synod of Marienborn, from May 12 to June 15, 1744. Zinzendorf, notes Hamilton,

> believed that the evangelical churches were one in essentials but that each possessed its own special talent for training souls in accordance with its own traditions. Hence there should properly be a Lutheran, a Reformed, and a Moravian "trope"—later even a Methodist—within the Unity of Brethren, so that souls would be educated for eternity in conformity with the peculiar emphasis of each. For no one church alone has the exclusively correct method in the church of souls.[107]

For Zinzendorf each *Religion* of Christendom was a *Tropus*, one distinct "path of training" or "a school of wisdom," with its own particular jewel of truth, ritual or order, to contribute to the whole body of Christ in setting forth the full glory and mission of the Lamb.[108]

Zinzendorf would none of these *Tropoi* destroyed, although none of them was an end in itself. As Ronald A. Knox puts it, Zinzendorf meant the *Brüdergemeine* "to be a kind of religious order within the framework of Protestant Christendom, acting as a liaison between the rival sects by confusing its own outlines, and remaining always on terms with the religion of the country. Lutheranism in Germany, Anglicanism in England, should be united in spite of themselves because each had a concordat with Moravianism."[109] Zinzendorf was delighted when the *Brüdergemeine* was described as "a net cast over all Christendom, to enclose all denominations of Christians."[110] Within the *Brüdergemeine* at least until the last decade of the eighteenth century there were separate membership lists for Lutheran, Reformed, and Moravian *Tropoi*.

For Zinzendorf, the *Brüdergemeine* served two distinct goals: to further Christ's mission in the world and to preserve the souls entrusted to its spiritual care. Based on the model of the primitive church, the Herrnhut community developed distinct structures of ministry and social organization geared toward these goals. For example, in 1727 Zinzendorf began the use of "bands," voluntary associations of a small group of persons, to deal with the spiritual and interpersonal life of the community. Each band was led by a *Bandhalter* (band leader) who assumed primary responsibility for the pastoral care of persons in the band. Later another form of organization called "classes" came into being, which assigned persons according to age, status, and sex. By 1731 the organization "small classes," distinct from the "great classes," was used to refer to the groups which were arranged according to stages of spiritual development. Later the small classes gradually took the place of the bands, and the great classes were replaced by the organization "choirs." The division of men and women according to age and status provided for an interesting approach to spiritual life, for Jesus in His life paralleled the stages of human development and life experience. The life of Jesus and Mary then became a model for the classes and choirs. Each group, in its circumstances and with its gifts, modeled itself on Jesus in relationship to that stage of His life which was related to theirs. Multiple administrative and ministerial offices complemented the division of the congregation into multiple "choirs." Although Zinzendorf and the Moravians retained the concept of an ordained pastorate, they sought to recover the early Christian diversity of pastoral and administrative functions. In order to provide for the temporal and spiritual needs of each group within the community, a sophisticated system of lay-offices evolved, including that of elder, deacon, teacher, admonisher, caretaker of the sick, and almoner. In addition, each choir had an administrator, as well as a "choir-helper" in charge of pastoral care within the choir.

From childhood, especially through the influence of Spener and his circle, Zinzendorf was exposed to the idea of *ecclesiolae in ecclesia*.[111] In the period 1710–1716, "at Gross-Hennersdorf and at Halle, Zinzendorf was captivated by two cognate conceptions of Pietism which, after he had quickened them himself, were to irradiate his work for Christian unity: the conception of missions, and the conception of *ecclesiola in Ecclesia*."[112] Zinzendorf's idea, once Herrnhut began to develop, was that the Unitas Fratrum would be an *ecclesiola* within Lutheranism in Germany.

Zinzendorf, like Francke, put little stress *theoretically* on the priesthood of believers. His conception of the Brethren as a missionary community and of all Moravians as "soldiers of the Lamb," the many leadership and service functions within the Moravian communities, and the broad opportunities for missionary service, however, provided great openness to various kinds of "lay" leadership and ministry. Virtually every Moravian was given some ministry or service assignment, so that the priesthood of believers (in the form of ministry and of mutual edification) was probably *practiced* much more extensively among the Moravians than among Lutheran Pietists generally. Many young Lutherans, spiritually awakened through Pietism, were in fact attracted to the Moravians precisely because of the ministry and missionary opportunities the Brethren provided. Peter Böhler and August Gottlieb Spangenberg, who greatly influenced Wesley, are outstanding examples of the move from Lutheran Pietism to Moravianism.

Zinzendorf's stress on training and discipline finds parallels in Spener and especially Francke. Zinzendorf saw the various Christian traditions as training schools for God's people. But whereas Spener saw discipline and training happening primarily in local parishes through *collegia*, Francke promoted the same through educational and philanthropic institutions and agencies, Zinzendorf's more comprehensive (and perhaps less realistic) vision was of God's working freely through the various *Tropoi* to nurture a renewed, united Church of God. Within Moravianism, of course, Zinzendorf relied heavily also on small-group structures and educational agencies.

In comparing the ecclesiologies of the Pietists and Wesley, their similarities are very impressive in many respects. First, they both embodied a primitivism. To restore the Church to a condition approaching the model found in the early church and to spiritualize her members was the ideal to the realization of which the Pietists and Wesley devoted all their talents and energies. They were pleased when they felt their movement resembled early Christian practices. The Pietists had "a powerful appeal to Wesley in their regard for the order and spirit of the primitive Church."[113] Although the Church of England was a main source of Wesley's primitivism, the Pietists, especially the Moravians, "reminded Wesley of some elements of primitive worship of which the Church of England had lost sight."[114] Wesley aimed "to spread Scriptural holiness over the land," through the Methodist movement. He, like the Pietists, claimed that he was teaching nothing new, but merely emphasizing those fundamental truths which were found in the Scriptures.

Secondly, they challenged and were opposed by status quo religion. Pietism and Methodism both embodied evangelical orders within the church catholic. Their aim was not to set up a new church establishment in opposition to the Church, not to teach a new set of doctrines, but to promote the power of godliness in the Church. Spener and Wesley believed that the Lutheran Church or the Church of England was nearer the Scriptural plan than any of the other Churches,[115] and they tried to keep their allegiance to the Church despite the fact that they deplored the introduction of conditions similar to those existing in the time of Constantine.[116] But with all of their love for the Church, they could not close their eyes to the evils bound up with the establishment. Wesley mourned that there were few real Christians in the Church, that she was in a fallen state, that discipline was neglected, that the "parishioners are a rope of sand....so they have no connexion with each other."[117] Wesley believed that the majority of the clergy did not preach pure doctrine, that they were in a fallen state, and that they fell far short of performing the duties of Christian pastors.[118] Though he maintained membership for himself in the Church of England and advocated the same for others, he stated that Methodists would separate from the church, as they later did, rather than give up extemporaneous prayer, lay preachers or open air gatherings.[119]

Wesley, particularly after Aldersgate, was like Spener, Francke, and Zinzendorf in stressing that the essence of the church is persons in direct relationship with God and each other, rather than primarily an institutional reality. Wesley saw the church as the community or fellowship of the Spirit in which the key dynamic was "faith working by love." Though his terminology was not that of Spener, he had a similar organic-charismatic understanding of the church. However, Wesley on other hand admitted the validity of the church's institutional dimension. In this respect, Wesley was closer to Spener and Francke than to Moravians. While he admired the model of primitive agape-community in the Moravians and was attracted to the Moravian experiments in community, Wesley pursued in the established churchly settings the possibility of the reform through his community as did Spener and Francke. He was Spenerian in the way he saw community worked out in practice.

Wesley seems to have put less stress on the priesthood of believers but more on the gifts of the Spirit than did Spener. In this respect he is closer to Zinzendorf. One may say that the priesthood of believers simply was not a theme of Wesley's theology, though his ecclesiology is inherently compatible with the emphasis. Wesley didn't discuss the priesthood of believers as such, and I Peter 2:5–9 is not a prominent text in Wesley's writings as it is in Spener's. In commenting on the text, he applies it to holiness rather than to ministry.[120] In his "Farther Appeal to Men of Reason and Religion" he justified "layman" taking spiritual leadership (precisely of the kind Spener advocated) not on the basis of the universal priesthood, but on the basis that "these plain men" were not priests but simply believers helping one another, consistent with New Testament principles. He says, "I know no Scripture which forbids making use of such help in a case of necessity . . . [these people] no more take upon them to administer the sacraments, an honour peculiar to the priests of God. Only according to their power they exhort their brethren to continue in the grace of God."[121] Wesley could have given a stronger logical and theological grounding for his practice by combining the theme of the priesthood of believers with his stress on gifts.

Though Wesley did not use the *ecclesiola* terminology or explicitly draw on the Pietist *ecclesiola* model, he in fact viewed Methodism as an *ecclesiola* and his view of "extraordinary" ministers and gifts appears to presuppose some kind of *ecclesiola* conception. F. Ernest Stoeffler argues that Wesley's view of ministry is best explained against the background of his contacts with Moravianism and the *collegia pietatis* of Continental Pietism. Though Wesley's view might appear ambiguous, according to Stoeffler, the "ambiguities recede into the background if it is remembered that his view of the ministry is related to a conscious adaptation on his part of the *collegia pietatis* arrangement of the church-related Pietists on the Continent, especially as it was observed among the Moravians."[122] It is not certain that Wesley was consciously imitating or adapting Moravian and Pietist ideas, but he did see Methodism and its ministry as an evangelical order within the Church of England somewhat akin to Pietism within the Lutheran Church. And he was undoubtedly influenced in some measure by what he saw of Moravian and Pietist models on the Continent.

The Pietists and Wesley both believed in an invisible church, to which all true believers belonged, in all ages and among all nations.[123] They thought that membership in the invisible rather than in the visible church was regarded as essential to salvation, because without membership in the invisible church, external adherence to any special visible form availed nothing and the *"outside religion"* was insignificant.[124] Each identified the purest expression of that invisible church with his own group. Wesley, especially the later Wesley, feared that the Nineteenth Article on the Church in the Thirty-Nine Articles of Religion was too inclusive and proposed that the phrase "congregation of faithful men" be interpreted as congregation of "men endued with 'living faith.'"[125] True members of the Anglican Church would, therefore, include those inhabitants of England only who were members of the invisible church. It is easily seen how this Donatist view of Wesley's would tend to lead him away from institutionalism. However, eschatological considerations did not seem to make much impression upon Wesley. Though he felt that the current evils in the Church would be overcome, he did not consider her glorious era as imminent.[126]

In both movements there was a shifting of the center of gravity from the clergy and the established Church to the laity and the congregation. Although deliberate separation was repudiated, there were strong tendencies in that direction, for which the leaders were partly responsible. A glance at the two movements from the standpoint of organization will show that the well-developed, though intricate, Methodist organization was better adapted to a separate posture than that of Pietism. However, the sectarian posture was joined with an ecumenical spirit. German Pietism was responsible for the first mergers of Lutheran and Reformed congregations. Spener and Wesley espoused greater tolerance for Roman Catholics and defined unity primarily in terms of love, witness and mission.

Of course, there were some disagreements between the German Pietists and Wesley concerning the doctrine of the church. The means of grace and the baptismal regeneration were interpreted similarly. However, while the Pietists adhered to Luther's position in regarding the Eucharist as a real participation of the body and blood of Christ, Wesley agreed with Calvin's idea of a spiritual reception.[127] More precisely speaking, as will be seen in Chapter 5, Wesley's position was close to a combination of the Calvinistic doctrine of the spiritual presence and the Zwinglian "memorial" view.

For the Pietists and Wesley the Holy Scriptures were raised to a high position of authority. For example, Spener and Wesley both believed that the Scriptures obtain their authority not from the Church but from God Himself. Of each of the leaders it could be said that he was a man of one book. Spener and Wesley believed that the Holy Spirit inspired the Scriptures. However, Spener affirmed that the Holy Spirit took into account the natural gifts of the authors.[128] That is why the Holy Spirit sometimes spoke good Greek and other times not-so-good Greek.[129] Spener thought that the Scriptures are clear enough for all to see, but because of our human nature, we need the light and grace of the Holy Spirit to render the Scriptures understandable.[130] Wesley's position is close to a dictation theory of inspiration.[131] Wesley maintained that the authors of the scriptural texts and the texts themselves were inspired.[132] He further said that the readers of the Scriptures are inspired.[133] Spener's position was in greater harmony with the modern historical attitude in its recognition of the different values of diverse portions of Scripture. Wesley's doctrine of inspiration forced him to accept the Bible as being of about equal value in all its parts. But he on other hand allowed room for man's rational faculties in the interpretation of Scripture.

The Pietists and Wesley both pursued a reformation of religion within, and by means of, the Church, not through separation. Because the Established Churches failed to bring their members into a close bond of religious union, the *collegia pietatis* in Germany (Spener) and the class meeting in England (Wesley) sought to remedy this deficiency. Spener's attempt had its origin in the doctrine of the priesthood of all believers and in a feeling of despair of making any impression upon the masses or of reforming the Church by simply training the young. The same doctrine influenced Wesley, who nonetheless differed from Spener by asserting and demonstrating that the masses could be reached. Spener placed his hope in the leavening power of the *collegia*, believing that they would gradually spiritualize the Church through the influence of Christian example; while Wesley had bolder and larger hopes, trusting not so much in the power of example as in the active, aggressive proclamation of the gospel to all who would and to some who would not hear. This fact partially explains the difference in the development of the two movements. While the Methodist "society" gradually became more inclusive, the Pietist conventicle developed an esoteric character. The latter soon came to be regarded as the special congregation of the saints and in this respect resembled the "select societies" of Methodism.

In conclusion, the Pietists' impact upon Wesley was certainly significant. The Pietists exerted a powerful influence upon Wesley in their regard for the order and spirit of the primitive Church while the Church of England was a main source of Wesley's primitivism. Wesley seems to have derived the themes of religion of heart or inward religion and holy living from the Pietists, and possibly also from the mystics. He further learned from the Pietists the importance of the role and training of laity. He was also impressed by their discipline and enthusiasm for mission. Pietism was instrumental in permanently influencing Wesley's soteriology on which his theology including ecclesiology was centered. One can also see the particular influence of the Pietists' customs on the creation and development of Methodist Church organization. Wesley admired the Pietists' organization and in some ways imitated it. A good example of this is Wesley's import of "band" and "class" systems from the Moravian Pietists.[134] The similarity of Pietists' and Methodists' church-order is striking. Wesley's Methodist structure, however, was more *connectional* than that of the Pietists. Wesley's bands and classes were grouped into societies which were in turn grouped into circuits served by both local and itinerant preachers.

Finally, one needs to point out that the roots of Wesley's ecclesiology cannot be confined to one religious tradition. While the German Pietists significantly influenced Wesley in constituting his ecclesiology, attempts to make Wesley only a disciple of the Lutheran tradition may be misleading. Wesley was a product of his age. Wesley was not German, but English. He was an ordained priest of the Church of England, an Oxford graduate with an M.A., a rational intellect which he had inherited along with his deep primitivism, the Anglican piety, and a Puritan sense of moral responsibility. Wesley's theological heritage runs back into the primitive and Anglican as well as the Pietistic traditions.[135] The religious maturation of the young Wesley was governed by a mixture of primitivism, Puritan legalism, High-Church sacramental Anglicanism, and the piety, or holy living, found in the contemporary religious societies.[136] Also, from Roman Catholicism he drew examples of holy living and a literature on mysticism. He was also influenced by the Romantic spirituality appreciated on the Continent at that time. Wesley's indebtedness was remarkably broad, and he recombined many divergent Christian emphases and traditions.

Wesley did not simply incorporate the views or positions of any other group, even when the contributions of one tradition to Wesley are significant enough to merit close and careful study. Rather Wesley was quite eclectic in his appropriation of traditional sources and apparently owed no allegiance to any particular school, Pietist or other, with the possible exception of Anglicanism. This eclectic approach probably has made it possible for many to claim Wesley as their own. Wesley is a helpful and astute theologian because of the catholicity of his sources, which were bequeathed to him from a variety of traditions. His ecclesiology was in a sense an amalgam of various traditions. The traditions, together with his appeal to Scripture and reason (or common sense), and with his experience from the ministry in the developing Methodist revival, tempered his ecclesiology.

Notes

1. Kurt Aland, *Kirchengeschichtliche Entwürfe: Alte Kirche. Reformation und Luthertum. Pietismus und Erweckungsbewegung* (Gütersloh: Gerd Mohn, 1960), 545. "Pietismus . . . hat vielmehr immer nur in verschiedenen Ausprägungen existiert, die zwar in bestimmten Beziehungen zueinander standen und denen auch gewisse Züge gemeinsam sind . . . der Pietismus ist eben keine Einheit, sondern eine komplexe Größe."

2. See Martin Brecht, "Die Umstrittenheit des Gegenstandes und die Begründung der vorliegenden Konzeption" and "Das Aufkommen der neuen Frömmigkeitsbewegung in Deutschland,"in *Geschichte des Pietismus*, ed. Martin Brecht (Göttingen: Vandenhoeck & Ruprecht, 1993), Band i, 3–10, 113–203; "Pietismus," *Theologische Realenzyklopädie*, ed. Gerhard Krause and Gerhard Müller (Berlin: de Gruyter, 1977–), Band 26 (1996), 606–631; "Probleme der Pietismusforschung," *Nederlandsch archief voor Kerkgeschiedenis* 76 (1996): 227–237.

3. See F. Ernest Stoeffler, *The Rise of Evangelical Pietism*, Studies in the History of Religion 9 (Leiden: E. J. Brill, 1965).

4. Johannes Wallmann, "Eine alternative Geschichte des Pietismus. Zur gegenwärtigen Diskussion um den Pietismusbegriff," *Pietismus und Neuzeit* 28 (2002): 30–71.

5. Johannes Wallmann, *Philipp Jakob Spener und die Anfänger des Pietismus*, 2d ed. (Tübingen: Mohr, 1986); *Der Pietismus. In Die Kirche in ihrer Geschichte*, Band 4, Lieferung O1 (Göttingen: Vandenhoeck & Ruprecht, 1990); "Was ist Pietismus?" *Pietismus und Neuzeit* 20 (1994): 11–27; "Pietas contra Pietismus. Zum

Frömmigkeitsverständnis der Lutherischen Orthodoxie," in *Pietas in der Lutherischen Orthodoxie*, ed. Udo Sträter (Wittenberg: Hans Luft, 1998), 6–18.

6. Like the term "Methodist," "Pietism" was originally bestowed in contempt. See Mary Fulbrook, *Piety and Politic: Religion and the Rise of Absolutism in England, Württemberg and Prussia* (Cambridge: Cambridge University Press, 1983), 27; Peter C. Erb, *Pietists: Selected Writings* (New York: Paulist Press, 1983), 7 and xiii. Fulbrook says that the term "Pietist" appeared for the first time in a 1680 letter by Philipp Jakob Spener in which he referred to its use as a term of "mockery and abuse," and Erb suggests that the idea for the name might have come from Spener's *Pia Desideria*, a preface to Johann Arndt's postills which set forth Spener's pious desires for the reformation of the church.

7. Erb, *Pietists: Selected Writings*, 3.

8. Stoeffler, *The Rise of Evangelical Pietism*, 183.

9. Stoeffler, *The Rise of Evangelical Pietism*, 202.

10. Stoeffler, *The Rise of Evangelical Pietism*, 183.

11. See Udo Sträter, ed., *Pietas in der Lutherischen Orthodoxie*; Markus Matthias, "Lutherischen Orthodoxie," in *Theologische Realenzyklopädie*, Band 25, 464–485; Olivier Fatio, "Reformierte Orthodoxie," in *Theologische Realenzyklopädie*, Band 25, 485–497.

12. See Richard van Dülmen, *Kultur und Alltag in der Frühen Neuzeit*, Dritter Band: *Religion, Magie, Aufklärung: 16.–18. Jahrhundert*, (München: Beck, 1994), 65–66; Hartmut Lehmann, "The Cultural Importance of the Pious Middle Classes in Seventeenth-Century Protestant Society," in *Religion and Society in Early Modern Europe 1500–1800*, ed. Kaspar von Greyertz (London: George Allen & Unwin, 1984), 34. In particular Lehmann's description is notable:

> The amount of devotional literature increased sharply after about 1580 and reached its first peak during the first decades of the seventeenth century. Production only began to ebb in the second third of the eighteenth century. Almost a quarter of the total books printed between the Reformation and the Enlightenment belong in this category of devotional literature. Moreover, their influence was not restricted to the printed word: funeral sermons were given in front of congregations; hymns were sung by congregations. We can, therefore, scarcely overestimate the importance of devotional literature in the period ranging from the late sixteenth to the early eighteenth century.

In the period of Orthodoxy church music also flowered with the likes of Heinrich Schütz (1585–1672) and Johann Sebastian Bach (1685–1750) to name but the most famous.

13. Stoeffler, *The Rise of Evangelical Pietism*, 203.

14. Johannes Wallmann, "John Arndt (1555–1621)," in *The Pietist Theologians*, 36.

15. Johann Arndt's *Bücher vom wahren Christentum* (*True Christianity*) emerged as a work of progress. *Erstes Buch vom wahren Christentum* was published in 1605, and *Vier Bücher vom wahren Christentum* in 1610. After Arndt's

death, a fifth and a sixth book derived from his smaller writings and letters were added, so that the title now read *Sechs Bücher vom wahren Christentum.*

16. Cited from Johannes Wallmann, "John Arndt (1555–1621)," 28–29.

17. Nagler, *Pietism and Methodism,* 143.

18. Snyder, *Pietism, Moravianism, and Methodism as Renewal Movements,* 111. As early as 1734, Wesley already read Anton Wilhelm Boehm's *Several Discourses and Tracts for Promoting the Common Interest of True Christianity* (Heitzenrater, *John Wesley and the Oxford Methodists,* 497).

19. Kenneth Collins suggests that Wesley probably was attracted to *True Christianity* by three major themes found there: "first, its soteriological thrust; second, its emphasis on genuine Christianity as embracing inward, as opposed to formal or external religion; and third, its irenic aim and tone." Kenneth Collins, "John Wesley's Critical Appropriation of Early German Pietism," *Wesleyan Theological Journal 27* (Spring-Fall, 1992): 62.

20. Philipp Jakob Spener, *Pia Desideria,* trans. Theodore G. Tappert (Philadelphia: Fortress Press, 1964), 95, 112.

21. Spener himself once said, "next to the Holy Scriptures I owe....my theology to the dear Luther." Cited from Martin Schmidt, "Philipp Jakob Spener und die Bibel," in *Pietismus und Bibel,* ed. Kurt Aland, Arbeiten zur Geschichte des Pietismus 9 (Witten-Ruhr: Luther Verlag, 1970), 57, note 197.

22. Stoeffler, *The Rise of Evangelical Pietism,* 230.

23. Philipp Jakob Spener, "Die Evangelische Glaubens-Lehre 1688," in *Philipp Jakob Spener Schriften,* ed. Erich Beyreuther (Hildesheim: Georg Olms Verlag, 1986), Band III.1, Teilband 2, 1257.

24. Spener, "Die Evangelische Glaubens-Lehre 1688," in *Philipp Jakob Spener Schriften,* Band III.1, Teilband 2, 1267.

25. Spener, *Pia Desideria,* 67. The Spener's view of Lutheran church is analogous with the Wesley's view of the Anglican church which he saw as a true church and "the most scriptural national church in the world," though she has many iniquities (John Wesley, *Works,* ix, 538).

26. Spener, "Die Evangelische Glaubens-Lehre 1688," in *Philipp Jakob Spener Schriften,* Band III.1, Teilband 2, 1251.

27. Spener, "Die Evangelische Glaubens-Lehre 1688," in *Philipp Jakob Spener Schriften,* Band III.1, Teilband 2, 1261.

28. Spener, "Die Evangelische Glaubens-Lehre 1688," in *Philipp Jakob Spener Schriften,* Band III.1, Teilband 2, 1261.

Da nennen wir die sichtbare kirche all diejenige leute/ die sich äusserlich zu dem wort Gottes halten und bekennen/ daher in einer äusserlichen sichtbaren gemeinschafft mit andern frommen Christen stehen/ obschon viel unter ihnen von herzen nicht fromm sind; die unsichtbare kirche aber heisset die anzahl der wahren kinder Gottes allein/ die zwar wie wir gehört haben/ nirgend allein und von allen andern abgesondert/ sondern vielmehr mit den bösen vermischet leben/ indessen Gott bekant sind/ der sie allein vor die seinige erkennt.

29. Philipp Jakob Spener, "Einflätige Erklärung der Christlichen Lehr nach der Ordnung des Kleinen Catechismi deß theuren Manns Gottes Lutheri 1677," in *Philipp Jakob Spener Schriften*, Band II.1, 542.

30. Spener, "Die Evangelische Glaubens-Lehre 1688," in *Philipp Jakob Spener Schriften*, Band III.1, Teilband 2, 1260. "die rechtschaffene glaubige/ die den wahren Göttl. lebendigen glauben haben/ und also sich nicht nur in der äusserlichen versamlung finden/ und sich zu Christo bekennen/ sondern die durch solchen glauben an ihm/ als an dem wahren haupt hangen/ und aus ihm als die reben an dem einstock . . . lebendigen safft und geist empfangen/ und aus demselben frucht bringen. "

31. Spener, "Theologische Bedenken," in *Philipp Jakob Spener Schriften*, Band XIV.2, 688ff; Spener, "Die Evangelische Glaubens-Lehre 1688," 1261.

32. Spener, "Die Evangelische Glaubens-Lehre 1688," in *Philipp Jakob Spener Schriften*, Band III.1, Teilband 2, 1253.

33. Spener, "Die Evangelische Glaubens-Lehre 1688," in *Philipp Jakob Spener Schriften*, Band III.1, Teilband 2, 1253ff.

34. See Snyder, *Pietism, Moravianism, and Methodism as Renewal Movements*, 163–174.

35. Philipp Jakob Spener, "Der Hochwichtige Articul von der Wiedergeburt," in *Philipp Jakob Spener Schriften*, Band VII, Teilband 1, 1. "eine materie unsers Christenthums nöthig ist/ so ist es gewiß die jenige von der wiedergeburt/ als in welche unsere bekehrung/ rechtfertigung/ und der anfang unserer heiligung mit einlaufft/ und sie auch der grund ist/ aller übriger heiligung/ oder der bronnen/ aus dem alles/ was in unsrem ganzen leben von uns oder an uns gutes ist oder geschihet/ nohtwendig herfliessen muß."

36. K. James Stein, "Philipp Jakob Spener (1635–1705)," in *The Pietist Theologians*, 90–91.

37. Spener, "Der Hochwichtige Articul von der Wiedergeburt," in *Philipp Jakob Spener Schriften*, Band VII, Teilband 1, 142–150.

38. See Emanuel Hirsch, *Geschichte der Neuern Evangelischen Theologie im Zusammenhang mit den Allgemeinen Bewegungen des Europäischen Denkens*, 5 Bände (Gütersloh: Bertelsmann Velag, 1951), Band ii, 140–141; K. James Stein, "Renewal: Philipp Jakob Spener's Parallel Word for Sanctification," *The Asbury Theological Journal* 51/2 (1996): 5–13.

39. Snyder, *Pietism, Moravianism, and Methodism as Renewal Movements*, 164–165.

40. Spener, *Pia Desideria*, 92ff.

41. Spener, *Pia Desideria*, 94.

42. Spener, *Pia Desideria*, 93.

43. Spener, "Die Evangelische Glaubens-Lehre 1688," in *Philipp Jakob Spener Schriften*, Band III.1, Teilband 2, 1256.

44. Spener, "Die Evangelische Glaubens-Lehre 1688," in *Philipp Jakob Spener Schriften*, Band III.1, Teilband 2, 1256.

insgesamt aus ihrem allgemeinen priesterthum . . . mögen und sollen ander kirchen . . . nicht nur mit gebet und gutem exempel/ sondern sobiel als eines jeglichen maaß der gnaden noch mit sich bringet/ mit unterrichten/ vermachnen/ warnen/ straffen/ trösten trachten zu bauen. . . . Ihr/ alle Christen/ nicht nur die prediger/ seyd das außerwehlte geschlecht/ das königliche priesterthum/ das...volk/ das volk des eigenthums/ daß ihr verkündigen sollet die tugend des/ der euch berufsen hat von der finsternüss zu seinem wunderbaren liecht: durch welche verkündigung sie ihre brüder und alle andere stäts auffmuntern müssen/ so viel fleissiger beh solcher himmlischen mahlzeit sich einzustellen.

45. Philipp Jakob Spener, "Letzte Theologische Bedenken," in *Philipp Jakob Spener Schriften*, Band XV, Teilband 2, 147.

46. Spener, *Pia Desideria*, 89.

47. Spener, *Pia Desideria*, 87ff.

48. Spener, "Theologische Bedenken," in *Philipp Jakob Spener Schriften*, Band XIII.1, 514f.

49. Spener, "Theologische Bedenken," in *Philipp Jakob Spener Schriften*, Band XII.1, 46f.

50. Spener, "Theologische Bedenken," in *Philipp Jakob Spener Schriften*, Band XIII.1, 293.

51. Allen C. Deeter, *An Historical and Theological Introduction to Philipp Jakob Spener's Pia Desideria: A study in Early German Pietism*, Ph. D. dissertation (Princeton University, 1963), xii.

52. Nagler, *Pietism and Methodism*, 18.

53. Philipp Jakob Spener, "Auffrichtige Ubereinstimmung mit der Augsp. Confession, zu Nöthiger Vertheidigung Seiner Reinen Lehr 1695," 223, in *Philipp Jakob Spener Schriften*, Band V, 747.

54. Spener, "Theologische Bedenken," in *Philipp Jakob Spener Schriften*, Band XI.1, 254.

55. Spener, "Auffrichtige Ubereinstimmung mit der Augsp. Confession, zu Nöthiger Vertheidigung Seiner Reinen Lehr 1695," 74, in *Philipp Jakob Spener Schriften*, Band V, 598.

56. Spener, *Pia Desideria*, 76–77.

57. Cf. Johannes Wallmann, "Pietismus und Chiliasmus. Zur Kontroverse um Philipp Jakob Speners 'Hoffnung besserer Zeiten,'" *Zeitschrift für Theologie und Kirche* 78 (1981): 254–257; Martin H. Jung, "1836—Wiederkunft Christi oder Beginn des Tausendjährigen Reichs? Zur Eschatologie Johann Albrecht Bengels und seiner Schüler," *Pietismus und Neuzeit* 23 (1997): 137.

58. Spener, "Die Evangelische Glaubens-Lehre 1688," in *Philipp Jakob Spener Schriften*, Band III.1, Teilband 1, 437; Spener, "Theologische Bedenken," in *Philipp Jakob Spener Schriften*, Band XI.2, 601.

59. Spener, "Der Hochwichtige Articul von der Wiedergeburt," in *Philipp Jakob Spener Schriften*, Band VII, Teilband 1, 107–108.

60. Spener, "Auffrichtige Ubereinstimmung mit der Augsp. Confession, zu Nöthiger Vertheidigung Seiner Reinen Lehr 1695," 245, in *Philipp Jakob Spener Schriften*, Band V, 769. As mentioned in Chapter 1, Wesley interpreted II Peter 1:4 in the early Eastern understanding of the gradual restoration of humanity to God-

likeness. II Peter 1:4 in Wesley's version, that is *Explanatory Notes upon the New Testament*, reads, "Through which he hath given us precious and exceeding great promises: that by these, having escaped the corruption which is in the world through desire, ye may become partakers of the divine nature." Wesley's version was a limited revision of the King James version, done with reference to the 1734 Greek text of Johann Albrecht Bengel, a German Pietist, and with selected renderings and annotations drawn from the *Gnomon* which was Bengel's New Testament exegesis published in 1742 and from other sources. Like the *Gnomon*, Wesley's annotations were aimed toward the Christian life, in agreement with Spener's orientation.

61. Spener, "Der Hochwichtige Articul von der Wiedergeburt," in *Philipp Jakob Spener Schriften*, Band VII, Teilband 1, 121.

62. Spener, "Die Evangelische Glaubens-Lehre 1688," in *Philipp Jakob Spener Schriften*, Band III.1, Teilband 1, 423–431.

63. Dale W. Brown, *Understanding Pietism* (Grand Rapids: Eerdmans, 1978), 108.

64. Spener, "Der Hochwichtige Articul von der Wiedergeburt," in *Philipp Jakob Spener Schriften*, Band VII, Teilband 1, 121–123.

65. This position actually minimizes the doctrine of baptismal regeneration. Martin Schmidt criticizes Spener for making the sacraments "dispensable in principle." Martin Schmidt, "Spener und Luther," *Luther Jahrbuch* 24 (1957): 116.

66. Spener, "Theologische Bedenken," in *Philipp Jakob Spener Schriften*, Band XII.1, 161ff. He asserts that the confessional was unknown to the primitive Church.

67. Spener, "Theologische Bedenken," in *Philipp Jakob Spener Schriften*, Band XI.2, 654ff.

68. Spener, "Theologische Bedenken," in *Philipp Jakob Spener Schriften*, Band XIV.1, 320.

69. Spener, "Die Evangelische Glaubens-Lehre 1688," in *Philipp Jakob Spener Schriften*, Band III.1, Teilband 1, 610.

70. Spener, "Theologische Bedenken," in *Philipp Jakob Spener Schriften*, Band XI.1, 109. In "Theologische Bedenken," Spener states that a private house, a cave, the forest might be as useful for worship as a Church edifice (Spener, "Theologische Bedenken," in *Philipp Jakob Spener Schriften*, Band XI.1, 178ff).

71. See W. R. Ward, *The Protestant Evangelical Awakening* (Cambridge: Cambridge University Press, 1992), 3–4, 310. Here Ward holds that "Wesley's early career contributed to the enlightenment of Halle" and at least "[b]y 1740 Wesley was personally commending himself to Halle through German third parties."

72. Heitzenrater, *John Wesley and the Oxford Methodists*, 504. These two works are Francke's exegetical writings on Scriptures. Francke is one of the most important figures for Pietistic hermeneutics. His works exerted a remarkable influence upon later biblical hermeneutics. His hermeneutics promoted historical-critical exegesis and simultaneously unhistorical-kerygmatic interpretation. The study of Francke's influence upon Wesley's hermeneutics would be an interesting work but

require separate and special research. For the study of Francke's hermeneutics see Ulrich Barth, "Hallesche Hermeneutik im 18. Jahrhundert. Stationen des Übergangs zwischen Pietismus und Aufklärung," in *Die Hermeneutik im Zeitalter der Aufklärung*, eds. Manfred Beetz and Giuseppe Cac, Collegium Hermeneuticum 3 (Cologne: Böhlau, 2000), 69–98; Markus Matthias, "August Hermann Francke (1663–1727)," in *The Pietist Theologians*, 104–106.

73. The central theme of *Nicodemus* was the necessity of overcoming fear of humanity through the power of faith, which was not surprisingly one very congenial to Wesley.

74. Martin Schmidt, *John Wesley: A Theological Biography*, vol. i, 140.

75. F. Ernest Stoeffler, *German Pietism during the Eighteenth Century* (Leiden: E. J.Brill, 1973), 22.

76. For Francke's emphasis upon education and discipline, see August Hermann Francke, "Scriptural Rules of Life," in Gary R. Sattler, *God's Glory, Neighbor's Good: A Brief Introduction to the Life and Writings of August Hermann Francke* (Chicago: Covenant Press, 1982), 199–237. Cf. Snyder, *Pietism, Moravianism, and Methodism as Renewal Movements*, 178–180.

77. Markus Matthias, *Lebensläufe August Hermann Franckes*, Kleine Texte des Pietismus 2 (Leipzig: Evangelische Verlagsanstalt, 1999), 29 and 31.

In solcher großen angst legte ich mich nochmals an erwehntem Sontag abend nieder auff meine knie, und rieffe an den Gott, den ich noch nicht kante, noch Glaubte, un Rettung aus solchem Elenden zustande, wenn anders warhafftig ein Gott wäre.

Da erhörete mich der Herr, der lebendige Gott, von seinem h. Thron, da ich noch auff meinen knien lag. So groß war seine Vater=Liebe, daß er mir nicht nach und nach solchen zweiffel und unruhe des hertzens wieder benehmen wolte, daran mir wol hätte genügen können, sondern damit ich desto mehr überzeuget würde und meiner verirreten vernunfft ein zaum angeleget würde, gegen seine Krafft und Treue nichts einzuwenden, so erhörete er mich plötzlich. Denn wie man eine hand umwendet, so war alle mein zweiffel hinweg, ich war versichert in meinem hertzen der Gnade Gottes in Christo Jesu, ich kunte Gott nicht allein Gott sondern meinen vater nennen, alle Traurigkeit und unruhe des hertzens ward auff einmahl weggenommen, hingegen ward ich als mit einem Strom der Freuden plötzlich überschüttet, daß ich aus vollem Muth Gott lobete und preisete, der mir solche große Gnade erzeiget hatte. . . .

Und daß ist also die zeit, dahin ich eigentlich meine warhafftige bekehrung rechnen kan. Denn von der zeit her hat es mit meinen Christenthum einen bestand gehabt. . . .

78. Brown, *Understanding Pietism*, 118.

79. Sattler, *God's Glory, Neighbor's Good*, 102.

80. Stoeffler, *German Pietism during the Eighteenth Century*, 14–15.

81. Sattler, *God's Glory, Neighbor's Good*, 103.

82. Sattler, *God's Glory, Neighbor's Good*, 108.

83. *Works*, xviii, 264.

84. *Works*, xviii, 263–264.

85. There are some notable reference books in studying the influence of Early German Pietism upon Wesley. Martin Schmidt's *John Wesley: A Theological Biography* offers detailed information about Wesley's encounter with German Pietism. Arthur W. Nagler's *Pietism and Methodism*, notes the broad similarity in the concerns of the German Pietists and Wesley's Methodism to claim that "most of the principles at the basis of Methodism had their analogies in Pietism; and . . . many of Methodism's institutions and practices found a precedent in the German revival" (141).

86. Cf. Clifford W. Towlson, *Moravian and Methodist: Relationships and Influences in the Eighteenth Century*; Frederick Dryer, "John Wesley: Ein Englisher Pietist," *Methodist History* 40 (January, 2002): 71–84; Howard A. Snyder, *Pietism, Moravianism, and Methodism as Renewal Movements: A Comparative and Thematic Study*.

87. *Works*, xix, 221.

88. *Works*, xxvi, 111.

89. *Works*, ix, 88.

90. Nicolaus Zinzendorf, *Twenty One Discourses or Dissertations upon the Augsburg Confession, Which is Also the Brethren's Confession of Faith: Deliver'd by the Ordinary of the Brethren's Churches before the Seminary. To Which is Prefixed, A Synodal Writing Relating to the Same Subject*, translated from the High Dutch, by F. Okeley (London: W. Bowyer, 1753), 241–242.

91. Zinzendorf, *Twenty One Discourses or Dissertations upon the Augsburg Confession*, 240.

92. Zinzendorf, *Twenty One Discourses or Dissertations upon the Augsburg Confession*, 246.

93. Zinzendorf, *Twenty One Discourses or Dissertations upon the Augsburg Confession*, 237–238.

94. Cited from A. J. Lewis, *Zinzendorf the Ecumenical Pioneer: A Study in the Moravian Contribution to Christian Mission and Unity* (Philadelphia: Westminster Press, 1962), 139.

95. Hans-Christoph Hahn and Hellmut Reichel, eds. *Zinzendorf und die Herrnhuter Brüder: Quellen zur Geschichte der Brüder-Unität von 1722 bis 1760* (Hamburg: Wittig, 1977), 265. Zinzendorf indeed said, "ich statuiere kein Christentum ohne Gemeinschaft."

96. See Hahn and Reichel, *Zinzendorf und die Herrnhuter Brüder*, 202.

97. Erich Beyreuther and Gerhard Meyer, eds. *Nikolaus Ludwig von Zinzendorf, Hauptschriften in Sechs Bänden* (Hildesheim: Georg Olms, 1962–1963), Band v, 182. "Er hat uns zur gemeinschaft geschaffen, und uns gesellschaft gegeben; Er will daß wir daran erkant werden sollen als seine Jünger, wenn wir uns untereinander lieben."

98. For example, Zinzendorf in a public speech of 1747 said,

Die einige wahre Gemeinde, die einige Grund-Gemeine, die einige eigentliche Original-Kirche ist die heilige Dreyeinigkeit. Ihr GOttes-dienst besteht darinnen, daß sie sich unter ehren. . . . Das ist nun also die erstaunliche sache, . . . daß es dem Dreyeinigen GOtt gefallen hat, einen menschen zu machen, in der person des Adams, und demselben menschen die gnade zu thun, daß er der abdruk, daß er das modell, daß er das nachgemachte erste modell, von dieser GOttes-kirche auf erden seyn soll. . . . Denn er (= Christus) hat die Kirche, die der heiligen Dreyeinigkeit nachgeformte Kirche, die der satan nicht hat leiden können . . . die Kirche, sage ich hat der Heiland zu stande gebracht, wider des teufels dank . . . es ist wahr, daß die heilige Dreyeinigkeit die Ur-Gemeine ist. Und wenn ich von der Ersten Kirche rede, so meyne ich nicht des apostels Pauli seine, nicht die zu Ephesus oder zu Jerusalem, sondern ich meyne die heilige Dreyeinigkeit. Das ist die Erste Gemeine, das ist die Erste Kirche, das ist die Kirche ohne fehl (Cited from Theodor Wettach, *Kirche bei Zinzendorf* [Wuppertal: Theologischer Verlag Rolf Brockhaus, 1971], 12).

99. On this point, as at several others, Zinzendorf's ecclesiology shows some affinity with the Anabaptist or Radical Protestant tradition.

100. Lewis, *Zinzendorf the Ecumenical Pioneer*, 138–160.

101. Zinzendorf, *Twenty One Discourses or Dissertations upon the Augsburg Confession*, 242. This ecumenical perspective is in agreement with Wesley's "Catholic Spirit" in which Wesley accepted liturgical deviations in the visible institutional churches or denominations while he thought the universal church to be one Body, united by one Spirit, having one faith, one hope, and one baptism. See Wesley, Sermon "Catholic Spirit" (1750), in *Works*, ii, 81–95; also Wesley, Sermon "Of the Church" (1785), in *Works*, iii, 46–57.

102. Cited form Snyder, *Pietism, Moravianism, and Methodism as Renewal Movements*, 195.

103. Cited from Snyder, *Pietism, Moravianism, and Methodism as Renewal Movements*, 195–196.

104. Cf. Wettach, *Kirche bei Zinzendorf*; Arthur Freeman, "Gemeine: Count Nicholas von Zinzendorf's Understanding of the Church," *Brethren Life and Thought* 47, no. 1–2 (Winter-Spring 2002): 1–25; Peter Vogt, "Nicholas Ludwig von Zinzendorf (1700–1760), in *The Pietist Theologians*, 215–216.

105. Cited from Freeman, "Gemeine: Count Nicholas von Zinzendorf's Understanding of the Church," 6.

106. Zinzendorf considered himself a member of the Lutheran confession and did not wish to establish a new church. While the episcopal consecration of Davis Nitschmann (1735) and the British recognition of the Moravians as an ancient Protestant church (1749) were steps toward the restitution of the old Unitas Fratrum, Zinzendorf insisted that the *Brüdergemeine* formed an inter-confessional brotherhood rather than a church. Its specific purpose was to gather believers from various confessional backgrounds without abrogating their confessional identity.

107. J. Taylor Hamilton and Kenneth G. Hamilton, *History of the Moravian Church* (Bethlehem, Pa.: Interprovincial Board of Christian Education, Moravian Church in America, 1967), 101–102.

108. Lewis, *Zinzendorf the Ecumenical Pioneer*, 139.

109. Ronald A. Knox, *Enthusiasm: A Chapter in the History of Religion, with Special Reference to the XVII and XVIII Centuries* (London: Collins, 1987), 419.

110. Knox, *Enthusiasm*, 419.

111. Towlson, *Moravian and Methodist*, 18.

112. Lewis, *Zinzendorf the Ecumenical Pioneer*, 24.

113. Towlson, *Moravian and Methodist*, 174.

114. Towlson, *Moravian and Methodist*, 175.

115. Cf. Spener, *Pia Desideria*, 67; Wesley, *Works*, ix, 538.

116. Wesley, Sermon "Mysteries of Iniquity," in *Works*, ii, 462–463.

117. Wesley, "A Farther Appeal to Men of Reason and Religion," in *Works*, xi, 213f, 272ff, 301; Wesley, "A letter to the Right Reverend the Lord Bishop of Gloucester" (1763), in *Works*, xi, 518.

118. Wesley, "A Letter to the Rev. Dr. Rutherforth" (March 28, 1768), in *Works*, ix, 378ff; Wesley, "A Farther Appeal to Men of Reason and Religion," in *Works*, xi, 242ff.

119. In 1775 Wesley told the Cornish evangelical, Samuel Walker that

[i]t is from a full conviction of this that we have, (1), preached abroad; (2), prayed extempore; (3), formed societies; and (4), permitted preachers who were not episcopally ordained. And were we pushed on this side, were there no alternative allowed, we should judge it our bounden duty rather wholly to separate from the Church than to give up any one of these points. Therefore it we cannot stop a reformation without stopping lay preachers, the case is clear—we cannot stop it at all (*Works*, vol. xxvi, 595).

120. *Explanatory Notes upon the New Testament*, 877–878.

121. *Works*, xi, 300.

122. Stoeffler, "Tradition and Renewal in the Ecclesiology of John Wesley," 310.

123. Cf. Spener, "Die Evangelische Glaubens-Lehre 1688," in *Philipp Jakob Spener Schriften*, Band. III.1, Teilband 2, 1260ff; Spener, "Einfältige Erklärung der Christlichen Lehr nach der Ordnung des Kleinen Catechismi deß theuren Manns Gottes Lutheri 1677," in *Philipp Jakob Spener Schriften*, Band. II.1, 542; Wesley, Sermon "Of the Church," in *Works*, iii, 46ff.

124. Spener, "Die Evangelische Glaubens-Lehre 1688," in *Philipp Jakob Spener Schriften*, Band III.1, Teilband 2, 1261; Wesley, *Works*, iii, 56. "How clear is this! . . . the church, as to the very essence of it, is a body of believers. . . . If this whole body be animated by one spirit, and endued with one faith and one hope of their calling; then he who has not that spirit, and faith, and hope, is no member of this body."; *Works*, xi, 274.

125. *Works*, iii, 51.

126. Wesley, Sermon "The General Spread of the Gospel," in *Works*, ii, 498–499. "At that time will be accomplished all those glorious promises made to the Christian church . . . the work he hath begun he will carry on unto the day of his Lord Jesus; that he will never intermit this blessed work of his Spirit until he has

fulfilled all his promises; until he hath put a period to sin and misery, and infirmity, and death; and re-established universal holiness and happiness."

127. Wesley, "To William Law" (January 6, 1756), in *Letters*, iii, 357. "I . . . believe that our 'spiritually receiving the body and blood of Christ,' which is most eminently done in the Lord's Supper, is necessary to 'strengthen and refresh our souls, as our bodies are by the bread and wine.'"

128. Zinzendorf also held that the Holy Spirit was working through human agents whose writings were inevitably shaped by their individual abilities and particular historical circumstances. He rejected the concept of the literal inerrancy of Scriptures and acknowledged that the biblical text contains imperfections and errors.

129. Spener, "Auffrichtige Ubereinstimmung mit der Augsp. Confession, zu Nöthiger Vertheidigung Seiner Reinen Lehr 1695," 48–52, in *Philipp Jakob Spener Schriften*, Band V, 572–576.

130. Cf. Hirsch, *Geschichte der Neuern Evangelischen Theologie im Zusammenhang mit den Allgemeinen Bewegungen des Europäischen Denkens*, Band ii, 114. For Spener's use of the Bible, also see Schmidt, "Philipp Jakob Spener und die Bibel," 9–58.

131. In the Preface to the *Explanatory Notes upon the New Testament*, Wesley says,

Concerning the Scriptures in general, it may be observed, the word of the living God, which directed the first patriarchs also, was, in the time of Moses, committed to writing. To this were added, in several succeeding generations, the inspired writings of the other prophets. Afterwards, what the Son of God preached, and the Holy Ghost spake by the apostles, the apostles and evangelists wrote. This is what we now style the Holy Scripture: this is that 'word of God which remaineth for ever'; of which, though 'heaven and earth pass away, one jot or tittle shall not pass away.' The Scripture, therefore, of the Old and New Testament is a most solid and precious system of divine truth. Every part thereof is worthy of God; and all together are one entire body, wherein is no defect, no excess. It is the fountain of heavenly wisdom, which they who are able to taste prefer to all writings of men, however wise or learned or holy (Preface, 10, in *Explanatory Notes upon the New Testament*, 8).

132. See Wesley, Sermon "The Witness of Our Own Spirit," 6, in *Works*, i, 302–303.

133. II Tim. 3:16, in *Explanatory Notes upon the New Testament*, 794. "The Spirit of God not only once inspired those who wrote it, but continually inspires, supernaturally assists, those that read it with earnest prayer."

134. Wesley in "Directions Given to the Bands Societies" (1744) made provision for smaller groups of more serious believers divided by gender and marital status to pursue a rigorous holiness agenda. The bands were made up of five to ten Methodists who met frequently to "confess their faults one to another, and pray one for another, that they may be healed" (*Works*, xviii, 292; *Works*, ix, 77). For

Wesley's import of band and class systems from the Moravians, see Towlson, *Moravian and Methodist*, 184ff.

135. It must be remembered that in the first volume of his *Christian Library*, Wesley placed immediately ahead of Arndt's *True Christianity*, in good Anglican fashion, the *Apostolic Fathers* and the *Homilies of Macarius*.

136. John Wesley was well aware of the religious society movement in England which goes back to Anthony Horneck. He and his father, Samuel Wesley, were members of the Society for Promoting Christian Knowledge (SPCK), and the young John was greatly interested in the religious societies that encouraged holy living and their charitable causes.

Part Two

The Development of Wesley's Ecclesiology

In Part One this work traced the major traditions that influenced Wesley's ecclesiology. Then, the question is how Wesley developed his ecclesiology under the influences of the traditions. Wesley's ecclesiology was not static. Throughout his entire life Wesley developed his ecclesiology in reaction to changing circumstances. One finds in Wesley a progressive change, if not in theological substance, then at least in the placing of accents and the making of emphases. Since his ecclesiology was not just something he developed after the Aldersgate experience, but the work of his whole life, it will be useful to investigate his ecclesiology according to the chronological distinctions: "early Wesley (1703–1738)," "middle Wesley (1738–1765)," and "late Wesley (1766–1791)." These distinctions were first suggested by Albert C. Outler.

Wesley's conversion experience at Aldersgate has long been considered as an event of paradigm shift in his life and thought. In doing so, the thought of the so-called "late Wesley" has been often left out as a sort of blind spot. Even Martin Schmidt's monumental "theological biography" (1962) reaches only to 1765 and maintains a too simplistic thesis that "John Wesley's course remained constant after his conversion on 24th May 1738."[1] However, there have been a group of scholars who have paid attention to the later Wesley. For instance, Wesleyan scholars like Albert Outler and Robert Tuttle suggest that Wesley underwent a significant theological development in the dynamism of the second generation of Revival, after 1765.[2] These scholars mainly focus on Wesley's soteriology with respect to the emphasis on "later Wesley." But examining the development of his ecclesiology in those last two decades is also of great importance. During the period, Wesley approved some female preaching and ordained Methodist clergy. Particularly the action that he ordained two preachers and ordained Thomas Coke as a superintendent in 1784 was an event that transformed Methodism from an ancillary movement within the Church of England to an autonomous ecclesiastical body, at least in the United States.

Although through his life Wesley suffered changes of emphasis in his ecclesiology and periods of recasting basic motifs, there is continuity in the development of his ecclesiology. Wesley established his ecclesiology (both nature and function of the church) in relation to the saving work of Christ. The most striking and ever-relevant feature of Wesley's theology is its soteriological focus, an emphasis that shaped almost every aspect of his thought and actions. Accordingly, his doctrine of church must be examined in relation to soteriology as a whole.

Then, how did Wesley shape and develop his salvation-centered ecclesiology? To answer the question, particular attention must be given to several questions: What were the various elements and shifts in Wesley's understanding of the church throughout his lifetime? How did Wesley maintain the tension between institutional church and evangelical church? How was such tension maintained in his understanding of the crucial concepts, such as church, ministry, sacraments, and order? How did the concepts change through his life and ministry? What were the theological bases and reasons for his persistent concern for the church? And, overall, how did he express his theology of church in his pastoral oversight? The questions shape the framework of our investigation in this part.

Notes

1. Schmidt, *John Wesley: A Theological Biography*, vol. ii, part 1, 7.
2. Albert C. Outler, *Theology in the Wesleyan Spirit* (Nashville: Tidings, 1975), 50; Tuttle, *John Wesley: His Life and Theology*, 334–337.

Chapter 4

Ecclesiology of the Early Wesley

Wesley's concern for the church was the work of his whole life. The early Wesley can be understood by exploring the family background and literary influences he received, and by examining the way theological traditions shaped his thought.

Wesley's Formal Ecclesiology and Primitivism

Wesley's childhood years in the parsonage at Epworth provide the first pictures of his understanding of church. Both of his parents had left dissenting congregations to join the established church and they remained faithful communicants in the Church of England until their deaths. The case of Susanna Wesley is somewhat complex since she inherited a strong Puritan heritage from her parents and continued to practice and taught Puritan piety at her home in Epworth. It is most likely that the young John Wesley learned from his mother a respect for the Puritan disciplined life. However, Susanna, like her husband, obviously remained in the Church of England after joining the established church until her death. One has evidence that something of the zealousness of these converts was imparted to their son, considering Wesley's remembrance: "In my youth, I was not only a member of the Church of England, but a bigot to it, believing none but the members of it to be in a state of salvation."[1] This view, reflecting St. Cyprian's assertion that "outside the church there is no salvation,"[2] closely associates salvation with adherence to the rituals and rules of an institution rather than an inward experience of regeneration through faith.

This sacramental view of salvation persisted during Wesley's years at Oxford as he sought to attain holiness by rigorous devotion to various spiritual practices of the primitive church. Wesley had been taught by his father to revere the patristic age as containing the best commentaries upon the apostolic writings and schooled at Charterhouse in the classics. When he arrived at Oxford University, Oxford was favorable for the patristic studies. The patristic revival of the previous century at both Oxford and Cambridge had made numerous writings of the early church available to the serious student. The record of Wesley's reading at Oxford shows that he availed himself of this privilege and read many of the Fathers.[3]

Two additional influences played key roles in Wesley's developing primitivism during his Oxford years. First, the activities of Oxford Methodists were an experiment in early Christianity in many respects. The Oxford Methodists' charities were in imitation of the earthly ministry of Christ to the needy. The more serious members were instant in prayer and the study of the Scriptures. They made virtues of fasting and frequent attendance at the Lord's Supper. Through the disciplines of fasting, frequent partaking of the Lord's Supper, and observing the Christian holy days, Wesley tried to commit to primitivism and to the Church he belonged to. The persecution the group suffered for being righteous over much was reconciled in terms of the eighth beatitude, "Blessed are those who are persecuted because of righteousness." Wesley thought that the disciple ought to be like his Lord in all things.

Secondly, in his last years at Oxford, Wesley was in debt to such High Church nonjurors of the Church of England as John Clayton, John Byrom, and Thomas Deacon for his primitivism. John Clayton joined the Oxford Methodists in 1731 or 1732, subsequent to which he became a close friend of John Wesley. According to V. H. H. Green, Clayton joined the Oxford Methodists largely "because it seemed to him like a return to apostolic tradition."[4] But he, in turn, had opportunity through the new society to further the Wesleys' interests in the church of antiquity. In the summer of 1733 Wesley accompanied Clayton to Manchester, where he was introduced to several of Clayton's nonjuror friends, including John Byrom and Thomas Deacon. Through the early acquaintance with them, Wesley was exposed to the primitivistic emphases of the High Church nonjurors and strengthened his desire for restitution of the primitive church. A section written by Wesley was actually included in the Appendix to Thomas Deacon's *A Compleat Collection of Devotions*.[5] The nonjurors turned Wesley's interests to the liturgical and sacramental features of the early ecclesiastical tradition.

Wesley adopted the nonjurors' assessment of the so-called *Apostolic Constitutions* and the *Apostolic Canons*,[6] for they held them to be the authentic collection of apostolic teaching concerning proper church order.

Wesley went out to Georgia as a missionary inspired with the vision of primitivism. In a letter "To the Revd. John Burton" on October 10, 1735, Wesley wrote,

> They [the heathens in Georgia] have no comments to construe away the text, no vain philosophy to corrupt it, no luxurious, sensual, covetous, ambitious expounders to soften its unpleasing truths, to reconcile earthly-mindedness and faith, the Spirit of Christ and the spirit of the world. They have no party, no interest to serve, and are therefore fit to receive the gospel in its simplicity. They are as little children, humble, willing to learn, and eager to do the will of God. And consequently they shall know of every doctrine I preach, whether it be of God. From these, therefore, I hope to learn the purity of that faith which was once delivered to the saints.[7]

Wesley went as a missionary to Georgia to convert the heathen Indian and do "more good in America."[8] And Wesley's letter to Dr. Burton above quoted shows that his chief motive in going to Georgia was to save his own soul.[9] He felt the need to be converted himself before he could preach salvation. However, these are not the whole answer, by any means. Wesley's pursuit for primitivism led "eventually to his decision to undertake mission work in Georgia."[10] The chance to return to what he felt would be primitive church conditions appealed to him. Wesley had a desire to put his ideas of primitivism into practice, and he believed that "Georgia would provide him with the opportunity to speak and live as a primitive Christian."[11] Wesley, as Green suggests, "visualized the Church in Georgia as in some sense a return to pristine apostolic standards."[12]

However, the Georgia colonists showed little concern to their pastor's ecclesiastical primitivism so carefully selected and used from the *Apostolic Constitutions* and other treatises on the primitive church. His insistence upon the immersion of infants, early morning worship services, water mixed with the communion wine, and other ancient practices had them mystified. Some colonists suspected that Wesley was a Roman Catholic in disguise.[13]

During his Georgia years, Wesley still maintained a formal ecclesiology. On the way to Georgia, when Wesley met Ambrosius Tackner who taught him German on the ship, he rebaptized Tackner because "he had received only lay baptism before."[14] According to A. B. Lawson, this action reveals the influence of Thomas Deacon and the High Church nonjurors, who argued that the "sacrament of baptism had to rank on an equality with that of the Lord's Supper, insomuch that it was only valid when administered by an ordained minister."[15] Reflecting on his rigid formalism in Georgia, Wesley later wrote, "Can anyone carry *High Church* zeal higher than this? And how well have I been since beaten with my own staff!"[16] But, the formal ecclesiology did not suit the needs or tastes of his rough parishioners in Savannah. Accordingly, his attempt to restore primitive Christianity in Georgia was a failure.

However, the Georgia period is not only unproductive. Wesley's brief pastoral experience in Georgia was to have a great influence later on the formation of Methodist practices. For example, later with the growth of Methodist movement, Wesley organized a system where he appointed women as visitors to the sick, which was reminiscent of his ministry in Georgia.

The Georgia period also changed Wesley's vision and views of primitivism. His reading of Bishop Beveridge's *Pandectae canonum conciliorum* during the period corrected his views of the primitive church imbibed from the nonjurors. After reading this book, Wesley wrote in his journal, "Nothing could so effectually have convinced us that both particular and 'general councils may err, and have erred'; and that 'things ordained by them as necessary to salvation have neither strength nor authority unless they be taken out of Holy Scripture.'"[17] After a week, he continued:

> We ended (of which also I must confess I once thought more highly than I ought to think) the Apostolical Canons; so called, as Bishop Beveridge observes, 'because partly grounded upon, partly agreeing with, the traditions delivered down from the apostles.' But he observes farther (in the 159th page of his *Codex canonum ecclesiae primitivae* . . .), 'They contain the discipline used in the church at the time when they were collected, not when the Council of Nicaea met; for then many parts of it were useless and obsolete.'[18]

Now his faith in the Apostolical Canons was weakening somewhat, while his strictness in observing both them and the rubrics was by no means relaxed. He discovered that he had extended the primitive era too late into Christian history, and that he had accorded too much weight to the ecclesiastical decisions of the early councils, giving them a universal authority that should pertain to Scripture alone. Henceforth, he would date the end of the primitive church with Constantine's rise to power, and would consider the *Apostolic Constitutions* and *Canons* to be sub-apostolic, allowing no authority to approach that of Scripture. In the process Wesley had moved to a new understanding of the early church.

During Wesley's Georgia mission period, one event that attracts our attention is that Wesley was interested in the evangelical primitivism of the Moravians. It was the piety of the Moravians that first caught his eye, but it was not long before he was probing them with questions about their doctrine and discipline. Wesley was favorably impressed by the primitive character of their movement in these areas. Observing their election and consecration of Bishop Anton Seifart, he imagined himself carried back through the centuries to the primitive Christian assembly, where leaders were called to their task with true simplicity:

> They met to consult concerning the affairs of their church . . . After several hours spent in conference and prayer, they proceeded to the election and ordination of a bishop. The great simplicity as well as solemnity of the whole almost made me forget the seventeen hundred years between, and imagine myself in one of those assemblies where form and state were not, but Paul the tent-maker or Peter the fisherman presided; yet with the demonstration of the Spirit and of power.[19]

The Moravian revival of the primitive agape-community also captivated his spirit. In short, Wesley saw the Moravians as those who had recovered more of the primitive Christian religion than those like himself who had devoted themselves to ancient ecclesiastical practices. Undoubtedly Wesley was prepared by the Moravians' demonstration of genuine Christian primitivism to be instructed by them concerning justifying faith.

In sum, the early Wesley in Epworth, Oxford, and Georgia was a High Churchman in the Church of England equipped with a formal ecclesiology. At the same time, he committed to primitivism, showing his serious attempts at holy living. The encounter with the Moravians in Georgia invigorated his primitivism with evangelical features. These features of early Wesley will further be investigated in the next section in relation to his view of ministry.

Ministry

Wesley's early childhood environment and his relationship with parents were crucial and formative in his view of ministry. In his childhood, Wesley grew up in a context of hardship and poverty, experiencing his father's frequent absences on church business, the poverty of a rector's family, and the harassment of hostile parishioners. The memory of the misery of his childhood remained so long that later on December 10, 1734 when he received pressing letter from his father to take Epworth, John replied, "If

you say, 'The love of the people of Epworth' to me 'may balance these ad-
vantages,' I ask, How long will it last? Only till I come to tell them plainly
that their deeds are evil, and particularly to apply that general sentence, to
say to each, Thou art the man! Alas, sir, do I not know what love they had
to you once? And how have many of them used you since?"[20] Although
Wesley was already ordained and preaching at Oxford, he did not accept his
father's suggestion.

However, the childhood experiences at Epworth contributed to John
Wesley's understanding of the nature of church, especially ministry.
Wesley inherited from his parents their theology and models of ministry.
The inheritance from Samuel Wesley is dominated by biblical scholarship
and critical learning. From Susanna Wesley, John acquired the commitment
to saving souls through practical divinity. From both parents, John inherited
courage rooted in trust in the providence of God when faced with hardship.

Parents' theology was a formative influence on the early Wesley's view
of ministry. Sondra H. Matthaei suggests that Wesley drew from his parents
three themes: 1) trust in God's providence, 2) primary concern on saving
the souls, and 3) principle of loving God and loving neighbor.[21] Samuel and
Susanna Wesley had ongoing dependence on the providence of God and
taught their son to trust it. It is evidenced in their letters to John Wesley. In
a letter to John on October 19, 1725, Samuel Wesley wrote: "I've done
what I could; do you the same, and rest the whole with Providence."[22]
Susanna also wrote to his son on March 30, 1726: "Dear Jacky, I hope you
are a good Christian, and as such do firmly believe that no events happen
but by the commission, or rather at least permission of divine Providence.
Therefore do not much afflict yourself, let what will befall. God hath promised, "All things shall work together for good to those that love him."[23] This
theme is often repeated throughout Susanna's writings.[24]

Saving the souls was the senior Wesleys' primary concern. In particular
Susanna's primary concern as a parent had been saving the souls of her
children. For her concern on salvation of the souls, Susanna later would
encourage his son's ministry: "let us speak boldly without fear; these truths
ought to be frequently inculcated, and pressed home upon the consciences
of men."[25] And "save all the souls you can" was what John often admonished his preachers.[26]

Furthermore, the principle of loving God and loving neighbor, frequently repeated by the parents, left an indelible impression on the young
John. For Samuel and Susanna Wesley, *loving God and loving neighbor* is
"the principle and rule of all our thoughts, words, and actions, with respect
to either."[27] Whatever one does that does not flow "from this principle is
wrong, as wanting a good foundation, and a right conduct."[28] The only way

to evidence the sincerity of our love to God, says Susanna, is to obey all His commandments and "we express our love to God by being friendly and beneficent to all that bear his image."[29] From the love to God we perform "all those virtuous actions and religious duties" and "we endeavour to perfect our natures by recovering that image of God."[30] Thus, loving God and loving neighbor are the springs of our holy life.

In addition to these themes, Samuel and Susanna Wesley offered advices and models for ministry to John in different ways during his formative years. John Wesley was greatly indebted to his father for ministerial model that had much to do with molding his ministerial character. Samuel Wesley was an active clergyman, taking a deep interest in everything connected with the church and embracing every opportunity to show his devotion to the work of the church. Susanna once said about her husband: "I should think it a thousand pities that a man of his brightness and rare endowments of learning and useful knowledge in relation to the church of God should be confined to an obscure corner of this country, where his talents are buried, and he is determined to a way of life for which he is not so well qualified as I could wish."[31] Indeed Samuel was a literary man and was always studying and writing when he was not engaged in active parish duties, and he taught John and other children foreign languages and a knowledge of the classics, among other things. The power of his example in reading good books and in mastering the languages made a great impression on John. Samuel's writings were often used by John later. When he was only eight years old, John was admitted by his father to partake of the Lord's Supper in Epworth Church and to help in the Communion service. Samuel's theology of sacraments influenced John Wesley as investigated in the next section. Also, as a child, John had seen his father's dedication to parish ministry in spite of the parishioners' hostility. John, especially during the early period of his ministry, and Samuel were very close in many aspects. John sought to emulate his father in his studies, writings, and preaching.

Moreover, Samuel sometimes gave ministerial advice to John. For example, while John was studying at Lincoln College, he had an opportunity to draw on his father's experience during a controversy over the Oxford Methodists' involvement in prison ministry. Samuel shared advice from his own prison ministry and encouraged his son's continued involvement: "what if they will not accept of one who will be welcome to the poor prisoners? Go on, then, in God's name, in the path to which your Saviour has directed you, and that track wherein your father has gone before you. For when I was an undergraduate at Oxford, I visited those in the castle there, and reflect on it with great satisfaction to this day."[32] Samuel himself volunteered to be chaplain to the prisoners when he was imprisoned for debt in Lincoln Castle.[33]

Susanna also offered advice and model for ministry to John. Susanna started a daily school for her children. Her purpose was the saving of their souls, so the rigorous academics never took priority over instruction in God's Word. Each day before class, she set aside an hour to herself for Scripture reading and prayer, and then led them all in singing Psalms. Susanna also designated one evening a week for each child's spiritual guidance. Her sons, even when at the University, found the utility of her wise and parental advices. John often proposed to her his doubts, and consulted her in difficulties. Later, Susanna would advise John as he guided the spiritual growth of others.[34]

Samuel was often absent on church business. During his absence, Susanna made a special effort in the continuing process of providing spiritual formation for her children. She adopted the practice of family prayers on Sunday evening, which involved reading prayers and a sermon and discussing devotional topics. Soon neighbors began attending in considerable numbers and congregations increased till the parsonage could not contain all that came. She read to them "the best and most awakening sermons" she could find in the library[35] and talked to the people "with more warmth of affection."[36] Inman, the Curate, contacted Samuel in London complaining that she had turned the parsonage into a conventicle; that the Church was likely to be scandalized by such irregular proceedings; and that they ought to be tolerated no longer. When Samuel wrote his wayward wife implying that she desist from holding her public meetings, Susanna answered him by telling what good the meetings had done, and that none were opposed to them but Mr. Inman. She then concludes, "[i]f you do after all think fit to dissolve this assembly, do not tell me any more that you desire me to do it, for that will not satisfy my conscience; but send your positive command in such full and express terms as may absolve me from all guilt and punishment for neglecting this opportunity for doing good to souls, when you and I shall appear before the great and awful tribunal of our Lord Jesus Christ."[37] This event is especially notable because of its presumed impact on the nine-year-old John Wesley. Although he may not have sensed the controversy, John was surely present at the Sunday evening services, and later his Methodist societies and class meetings, innovations that like the meetings of his mother were not intended to rival the official church worship, may have had an unconscious model in his mother's earlier experiment. The effectiveness of his mother presiding at a public gathering may also have made John Wesley more receptive to the work of women in his own societies. Summing up his mother's life at the time of her death, John stated, "I cannot but farther observe that even she (as well as her father and grandfather, her husband, and her three sons) had been, in her measure and degree, a preacher of righteousness."[38] This image of Susanna as a preacher may have influenced Wesley's view of women preachers.

Moreover, John Wesley's childhood experiences of poverty gave him insight into a life of deprivation and may have led him to an innovative ministry in relation to human need. Financially, his father, Samuel Wesley, was a poor manager. The Wesley family was not among the most impoverished of their time but was often in financial straits and did not have enough to meet their needs. When in a letter to his mother, John asked why he was "little and weak,"[39] Susanna replied: "I believe the true cause of your being so is want of sufficiency of food for ten or twelve years when you were growing, and required more nourishment."[40] This awareness of what it meant to be poor and hungry influenced John Wesley's developing ministry and its emphasis on response to the need of his neighbor.

These formative experiences in theology, models of ministry, and a poor life at Epworth nurtured the beginnings of John Wesley's concept of ministry. To Wesley the lives of his parents were witness to and model of ministry based on the providence of God and the command to love God and one's neighbor. Also, his parents as advisors for his ministry helped and influenced the shape of his early view of ministry.

However, Samuel and Susanna Wesley were two strong-minded individuals who often disagreed and who appeared to have had very different ideas about the nature of ministry. The disagreement between them in the view of ministry particularly appeared as John Wesley declared his intention to seek holy orders. Samuel urged his son "to enter into holy orders" when John "was about twenty-two."[41] Once John decided to seek holy orders, a major conflict between his parents developed about the best way to prepare him for ministry. When Susanna voiced the hope that John would be his father's curate, Samuel offered reasons for why John should pursue holy orders:

[E]ntering into Holy Orders, 'tis indeed a great work. . . . (1), It's no *harm* to desire getting into that office, even as Eli's sons, 'to eat a piece of bread'; 'for the labourer is worthy of his hire'. Though, (2), a desire and intention to lead a stricter life, and a belief one should do so, is a better reason. . . . (3), If a man *unwilling* and *undesirous* to enter into Orders, 'tis easy to guess whether he can say . . . that he believes he's 'moved by the Holy Spirit' to do it. But, (4), the principal spring and motive . . . must certainly be the glory of God, and the service of his church, in the edification and salvation of our neighbour. . . . For which, (5), he should take all the care he possibly can, with the advice of wiser and elder men . . . with

fasting and prayer, the direction and assistance of Almighty God, and his
Holy Spirit, to qualify and prepare him for it.[42]

However, Samuel, for all the reasons for pursuing holy orders, advised John
to wait and prepare for ministry. Samuel recommended classical learning,
especially in biblical languages and scholarship, as the preparation for ministry: "The knowledge of the languages is a very considerable help in this
matter . . . then this must be prosecuted to the thorough understanding the
original text of the Scriptures, by constant and long conversing with
them."[43]

Susanna disagreed with her husband. She encouraged her son to prepare
for holy orders immediately, not because he had the spiritual preparation,
but because, in pursuing holy orders, he might become more spiritually
minded. In a letter written to John within a month after Samuel's advice,
Susanna said,

> I approve the disposition of your mind, I think this season of Lent the
> most proper for your preparation for Orders, and I think the sooner you
> are a deacon the better, because it may be an inducement to greater appli-
> cation in the study of practical divinity, which of all other I humbly con-
> ceive is the best study for candidates for Orders. Mr. Wesley differs from
> me, and would engage you, I believe, in critical learning (though I'm not
> sure), which, though of use accidentally, and by way of concomitance, yet
> is in no wise preferable to the other. Therefore I earnestly pray God to
> avert that great evil from you, of engaging in trifling studies to the neglect
> of such as are absolutely necessary.[44]

Here two points are notable. First, Susanna thought that the ministerial
office came first and fitness for it after. Underlying this thought was the
sacerdotal concept of the priesthood in the Church of England. Great emphasis was placed upon the power of the priest, made manifest by the Holy
Spirit said to be working through his every action. Richard Hooker asserted
that "when wee take ordination wee also receive the presence of the holy
Ghost partlie to guide direct and strengthen us in all our waies, and partlie
to assume unto it selfe for the more authoritie those actions that apperteine
to our place and calling."[45] The danger in this concept is the possibility that
a minister, believing that the Holy Spirit was received at ordination, might
neglect his own personal religious life. If the Spirit of God works through
this instrument set aside by the rites of the Church, what need was there for
a man to be concerned with his relation to God? "[O]nce consecrated unto
God they are made his peculiar inheritance for ever," declared Hooker.[46]
According to this thinking, ordination, and not personal religious experi-

ence, gives the man an increase of grace which enables him to minister in the discharge of his office. The priestly acts are valid, irrespective of the character of the person who performs them. Article XXVI of Thirty-Nine Articles of Religion says:

> Although, in the Visible Church, the Evil be ever mingled with the Good, and sometimes the Evil have chief Authority in the Ministration of the Word and Sacraments; yet for as much as they do not the same in their own Name, but in Christ's, and do minister by his Commission and Authority, we may use their Ministry both in hearing the Word of God, and in receiving the Sacraments. Neither is the Effect of Christ's Ordinance taken away by their Wickedness: Nor the Grace of God's Gifts diminished from such as by faith and rightly do receive the Sacraments ministered unto them, which be Effectual because of Christ's Institution and Promise, although they be ministered by Evil Men.[47]

Secondly, Susanna recommended a study of practical divinity as the best preparation for holy orders. What Susanna Wesley meant by practical divinity is stated much earlier in a letter to daughter Sukey: "it is not learning these things by heart, nor your saying a few prayers morning and night . . . you must understand what you say, and you must practice what you know . . . knowledge is requisite in order to practice." [48] For Susanna the primary educational task in preparation for ministry was to have knowledge requisite to the practice of faith.

Accordingly, the lines between Samuel as advocator of critical learning and Susanna as advocator of practical divinity were drawn over the best preparation for John's ministry. The father wanted his son to focus on the knowledge of faith; the mother on the practice of faith.

The debate over preparation for ministry seems to have been resolved when John Wesley, the next year after receiving the holy order of deacon, wrote to his mother: "I am perfectly come over to your opinion, that there are many truths it is not worth while to know."[49] Yet, the issue was a difficult one and John continued to confront the tension between critical learning and practical divinity at Oxford: "Shall I quite break off my pursuit of all learning but what immediately tends to practice? I once desired to make a fair show in languages and philosophy."[50] John's life at Oxford kept this issue constantly before him. His conclusion for this matter was to combine the two parental models of biblical scholar and practical theologian in his ministry. Reflecting on his early life, John Wesley later said: "The strongest impression I had till I was three or four and twenty was, *Inter sylvas Academi quaerere verum* [to seek for truth in the groves of Academe], and afterwards (while I was my father's curate), to save my own soul and those that heard me."[51]

Meanwhile, Samuel Wesley also changed his point of view. The change was clearly perceived during a conflict over who was to succeed him at Epworth. When John refused to leave the academy in Oxford for the Epworth parish, Samuel wrote to his son: "God made us for a social life; we are not to bury our talent. . . . And to this academical studies are only preparatory."[52] This statement rings of earlier admonitions by Susanna to avoid "trifling studies."

Therefore, the disagreement between the parents about the preparation for ministry had disappeared. Samuel and Susanna now were both intensely interested in practical divinity. Samuel, not knowing the ultimate direction of his son John's ministry, died at the age of 72 years on April 25, 1735, shortly after the controversy over the Epworth living. John went to Epworth before his father died, unsuccessfully seeking the succession in his father's living.

In conclusion, biblical scholarship and practical divinity are the parental models inherited by John Wesley, but with the passing of time, practical divinity appears to become the primary vision underlying John Wesley's understanding of ministry. While adhering to an Anglican view of ministry and committing to the rubrics and disciplines of the Church, Wesley was gradually developing his practical divinity.

What, then, was Wesley's practical divinity? For Wesley practical divinity was "the study of sin, repentance, faith, works, assurance, sanctification, and their links with Christian living."[53] Such a practical divinity was based on trust in the grace of God. Wesley's belief in grace available for all persons combined his father's emphasis on the providence of God with his mother's view that persons must work out their own salvation. Wesley believed that God's grace is at work in us and without it, we cannot be saved. But he also believed that we must respond the grace by faith. Without our response or participation, God's grace will not save us. In turn, for our response, grace does empower, but not coerce, us. Furthermore, for Wesley grace is taken to include not merely our free acceptance by God, but the "power of God which worketh in us both to will and to do of his good pleasure."[54] And faith is understood to be "not only an unshaken assent to all that God hath revealed in Scripture" but a disposition wrought in the heart that is "productive of all good works and all holiness."[55] In short, God's grace is at work in us and we must accept it by faith in response and live a faithful life with the assistance of grace.

For Wesley the goal of practical divinity was a life of holiness. By holiness, Wesley meant "not fasting, or bodily austerity, or any other external means of improvement, but that inward temper to which all these are subservient, a renewal of soul in the image of God . . . a complex habit of lowliness, meekness, purity, faith, hope, and love of God and man."[56] Here notable point is that adopting the soteriology of the Eastern patristic tradition, Wesley emphasized the renewal of soul in the image of God. Salvation is the renewal of soul after the image of God, and salvation can't be separated from a life of holiness. And Wesley's primary question "What must I do to be saved?"[57] extended to his ministry with others. In a letter to his father, Wesley said,

> That course of life tends most to the glory of God wherein we can most promote holiness in ourselves and others. I say in ourselves and others, as being fully persuaded that these can never be put asunder. For how is it possible that the good God should make our interest inconsistent with our neighbour's? That he should make our being in one state best for ourselves, and our being in another best for his church? . . . If it be best for others, then it is so for us; if for us, then for them."[58]

Accordingly, for Wesley a life of holiness addressed both the physical and spiritual needs of the neighbor, as well as one's own inward piety. Holiness means doing all the good you can for the love of God and neighbor. We choose to do God's will and do good in response to God's grace at work in us. John Wesley asked himself, "Can you do the good God would have you do?"[59] Samuel had repeatedly instructed John that "God fit you for your great work" with "the direction and assistance of . . . his Holy Spirit."[60]

Moreover, for Wesley, there was "no holiness but social holiness."[61] And for him social holiness meant Christian fellowship. Christianity is no solitary religion but social religion. From his own experience, John Wesley knew persons could not live a Christian life alone. For that reason he withdrew from the mystics. Susanna Wesley's educational method was foundational for much of John's work. Her instruction to "enter upon serious examination of yourself, that you may know whether you have a reasonable hope of salvation by Jesus Christ, that is, whether you are in a state of faith and repentance or not"[62] was later formalized into a series of questions for members of Methodist class meetings. Answering these questions weekly provided an avenue of accountability for class members in a community setting. The class meetings "were intended to accomplish . . . points of accountability for faithful Christian living in the world" and were a distinctive feature of early Methodism.[63] In that sense, Wesley's practical divinity was accountability in community.

This developing practical divinity of the early period became an important element to characterize Wesley's later ministry. To provide his Methodist preachers with a collection of the best practical divinity, Wesley published *A Christian Library* (1749–1755). He also employed his sermons as handbooks of experimental divinity and published *A Collection of Hymns, for the Use of the People Called Methodists* (1780) as "a little body of experimental and practical divinity."[64] And, on the basis of the practical divinity, he later after Aldersgate developed a practical view of ministry, as investigated in the later chapters of this work.

John Wesley's vision of ministry was not formed only from early childhood experience and parental influence, but from his desire to recreate the primitive faith community. In Wesley's day existed there a considerable concern on the part of many High-Church Anglicans for primitivism.

William Talbot, Bishop of Oxford, (1658–1730) summarized the basic assumptions of a high church as "'the independency of the Church upon the State', 'A Proper Sacrifice in the Sacrament of the Lord's Supper', 'the necessity of sacerdotal absolution' and 'the invalidity of baptism administered by persons not episcopally ordained.'"[65] As V. H. H. Green points out, "[t]his attitude was founded on what its advocates held to be the practice and principle of the primitive and apostolic Church."[66]

The early Wesley, especially of Oxford and Savannah, was a rigid High Churchman with a high view of ministry. He believed bishops, priests and deacons to be of divine appointment. The basic requisite for priesthood in the Church of England at the time of Wesley is described in Article XXIII "Of Ministering in the Congregation" of Thirty-Nine Articles of Religion:

> It is not lawful for any Man to take upon him the Office of public Preaching or Ministering the Sacraments in the Congregation, before he be lawfully called and sent to execute the same. And those we ought to judge lawfully called and sent, which be chosen and called to this Work by Men, who have public Authority given unto them, in the Congregation, to call and send Ministers into the Lord's Vineyard.[67]

Here it is obviously expressed that the basic requisite was ordination, the laying on of hands, by a bishop who stood in the line of apostolic succession. The Church held the doctrine of apostolic succession to be a continuous "transmission of office." The early Wesley followed the teaching of the Church.

Wesley had been ordained a deacon of the Church of England by Dr. John Potter, then Bishop of Oxford, on September 19, 1725. He was his father's curate at Epworth from August 1727 to July 1728. On September 22, 1728, he was ordained a priest, and was curate at Wroote and Epworth until November of 1729. Then he was called back to Oxford.

While in Oxford, Wesley was the leader of the Methodist group. The Oxford Methodists were eager to follow and practice the principle of the primitive and apostolic church. V. H. H. Green says that Wesley at Oxford "wished to refashion the English Church according to the apostolic ideal, restoring the sacrament of Holy Communion to the place that it had occupied in the life of the early Christians."[68] Over forty young persons from eight colleges of the University including John Clayton that furthered Wesley's interests in the practices of primitive church were associated with the Oxford Methodism under Wesley's leadership. These early Methodists met for prayer, fasting, discussion, and active sharing of the gospel of Christ, and formed rules for the regulation of their time and for their studies and self-examination. They also visited the sick and the prisoners, and received the Lord's Supper as often as possible. In Oxford days Wesley was a rigid High Churchman, pursuing the ideal of primitive church.

In 1735, with his controversy with his father and older brother (Samuel Jr.) as to undertaking a curacy, Wesley developed an idea that holy orders do not necessitate parochial ties. This idea came from Bishop Potter who had ordained him. When Wesley consulted the Bishop to close the debate, Bishop Potter replied, "[i]t doth not seem to me that at your ordination you engaged yourself to undertake the cure of any parish, provided you can as a clergyman better serve God and his Church in your present or some other station."[69] Now Wesley felt he had "all reasonable evidence" that he can "better serve God and his Church" in his present station.[70] He no longer thought that "the exercise of one's ministry was necessarily confined within parish boundaries."[71]

Wesley was profoundly impressed during these early days by George Herbert (1593–1633). Herbert was an early seventeenth-century Anglican priest and religious poet. Early in August 1725, Wesley already read Herbert's poems.[72] Herbert was the favorite poet of Wesley's mother, and there are frequent quotations from him in their correspondence. Particularly from George Herbert's *The Temple*, Wesley, from the early period of his life, began and continued the selection and adaptation of hymns.[73] In Georgia Wesley felt the need of a hymn-book something like that of the Germans, and in 1737 published *A Collection of Psalms and Hymns*, which was possibly "the first hymn-book printed for use in the Church of England" as well as the first Methodist hymn-book.[74] The *Collection* contained seventy hymns from various sources, including six of Herbert's poems adapted from *Temple*. Later on till his later years, Wesley adapted poems from Herbert for his collections of hymns.

Wesley was so attracted and influenced by Herbert that his *Hymns and Sacred Poems* (1739) included adaptations of Herbert's poems, that forty-eight pages of his anthology, *A Collection of Moral and Sacred Poems from the Most Celebrated English Authors* (1744), were taken up with poems of Herbert, that his *A Christian Library* included Izaak Walton's *Life of George Herbert*, and that he issued a separate book, *Select Parts of Mr. Herbert's Sacred Poems* (1773).[75] Also, in his *Collection of Hymns for the Use of the People called Methodists* (1780), he adapted or remodeled Herbert' poems. "As a Christian poet" Wesley was popularizing Herbert "in the early eighteenth century and for all future time."[76] William Jerdan said in 1853, "Had there not been a Herbert, it is probable there might never have been a Wesley; for in the founder of the Methodists, it is impossible not to recognize almost every impulse and emotion he expressed, every doctrine he preached, and every duty he practiced."[77] Jerdan's judgment is extreme and requires critical assessment. However, it is certain that Wesley set a high value on Herbert's poems. Writing to the *Monthly Review* in 1756 complaining of what he considered to be a slighting reference to Herbert, Wesley said that Herbert's poems were "scarce inferior either in sense or language to most compositions of the present age."[78]

The early Wesley's view of ministry was strongly influenced by Herbert's *A Priest to the Temple*.[79] While writing a good part of *A Priest to the Temple*, Herbert was an active Anglican priest who had a high view of ministry.[80] In *A Priest to the Temple*, Herbert depicted a priest as the one who is "in God's stead to his Parish"[81] and has an authority of Christ's deputy.

> A PASTOR is the Deputy of Christ for the reducing of Man to the Obedience of God. . . . Christ being not to continue on earth, but after he had fulfilled the work of Reconciliation, to be received up into heaven, he constituted Deputies in his place, and these are Priests. . . . St. Paul . . . fills up that which is behind of the afflictions of Christ in his flesh, for his Body's sake, which is the church, wherein is contained the complete definition of a Minister. Out of this Charter of the Priesthood may be plainly gathered both the Dignity thereof, and the Duty: The Dignity, in that a Priest may do that which Christ did, and by his authority, and as his Vicegerent. The Duty, in that a Priest is to do that which Christ did, and after his manner, both for Doctrine and Life.[82]

This high view of ministry is most clearly represented in Wesley in Georgia. Charles Wesley believed that "he was raised up by God to supply His place and to be a representation of Himself,"[83] and John in Georgia was not so much different from his brother in his high view of clergyman's office. In fact, reflecting on his ministry in Georgia, Wesley later recorded that he had carried High-Church zeal higher than anyone in Georgia.[84] In accordance with the high-church view, while in Georgia he "refused Holy

Communion to all those who had not received baptism at the hands of an episcopally ordained clergyman and only such were to receive Christian burial."[85] This action presupposes not only a high view of the sacraments but of apostolic succession as well.

Wesley in Georgia had the so-called "sacerdotal concept of the priesthood in the Church of England."[86] This concept is based on the assumption that the Holy Spirit is transmitted in the laying on of hands, thus enabling the minister to exercise his office. The Roman Catholic Church held this view, making of orders a sacrament, and the Anglican Church followed suit.[87]

While Wesley's views on the absolute necessity of apostolic succession appeared to change in time, as will be seen in later chapters, he was firmly against not only lay baptism, but more especially lay administration of the Lord's Supper, right up to his death. Why? The Church of England in Wesley's days distinguished the ordination for the priests to administer the sacraments from that for the deacons to preach and teach. Wesley followed this dichotomy of the Church, and he knew that if his lay-preachers were to have administered the sacraments without ordination, he would have been open to charges of schism. This matter will be further discussed later in Chapter 6.

Even though the Council of Nicea, A.D. 325, recognized lay baptism as valid, the early Wesley felt that "[t]he sacrament of baptism had to rank on an equality with that of the Lord's Supper, insomuch that it was only valid when administered by an ordained minister."[88] And valid ordination came only through true apostolic succession, which the Church of England claimed to have. In July of 1737 a man named John Martin Bolzius, a Salzburger,[89] known to be of pious and exemplary character, was refused communion by Wesley because of invalid baptism.[90] In those days, the assumption on the part of the Moravians that Christ has done all, and so good works, such as holy communion, were not necessary, caused Wesley to cast a suspicious eye on their theological doctrines. "He expressed anxiety when he heard that they regarded baptism by Lutheran ministers not episcopally ordained as fully valid."[91]

Wesley seems to have two minds and an ambiguous attitude toward the Moravians during his stay in Georgia. On the one hand he greatly admired and envied their courage, assurance of faith, and primitivism, but on the other hand he was uneasy about their credentials. It is well known that Wesley showed interest and respect toward Moravians on board ship on the way to America. His close association with them in the colony at Georgia occasioned many discussions between them on doctrine—most especially concerning "the validity of the consecrations of their bishops and baptism."[92] It is ironical that Wesley did not think that the ordination of Bishop Anton Seifart by the Moravians was invalid, for he still held to the validity and necessity of apostolic succession.[93]

While returning to England from Georgia, Wesley read the works of St. Cyprian.[94] His reading of Cyprian at this time is notable because probably Cyprian's views on Church government and episcopacy would appeal to him, and because it implies that until then Wesley still maintained the high view of the ministry.

Cyprian, in the face of divisions within the Church, saw the bishops as the center of the visible unity of the Church. Cyprian found the substance of the answer for the unity of the Church in Matt. 16:18–19 and John 20:20–23.

> The Lord speaks to Peter . . . ". . . thou art Peter; and upon the rock I will build my Church . . . " And although to all the apostles, after His resurrection, He gives an equal power . . . yet, that He might set forth unity, He arranged by His authority the origin of that unity, as beginning from one. Assuredly the rest of the apostles were also the same as was Peter, endowed with a like partnership both of honour and power; but the beginning proceeds from unity. . . . Does he who does not hold this unity of the Church think that he holds the faith? Does he who strives against and resists the Church trust that he is in the Church . . . ?[95]

Here Cyprian exalts the primacy of Peter among the apostles. The other apostles had the same honor and authority as Peter, but Peter was the first who received this authority, and thus he is the source of apostolic unity. This statement raises the questions of whether the Roman church, arguing that Peter was her first bishop, is the chief church whence the unity of church takes its source and whether the church of Rome and its bishop have a certain priority among Christian churches.

But Cyprian does not seem to grant the superiority of the bishop of Rome. Instead he emphasizes on the unity and collegiality of the whole body of bishops of the Church. Cyprian mentions Paul's witness to the oneness of the Church in Eph. 4:4–6, and claims that this unity, first given to the Church in Peter and the apostles, is now manifested in the episcopate. As the apostles formed a college or corporate body, so also does the episcopate: "The episcopate is one, each part of which is held by each one for the whole."[96] Cyprian's concept is of a corporation or college of bishops, with each within his own sphere of jurisdiction exercising the whole authority of the episcopate. He goes on to assert that whoever separates himself from the Church whose unity is thus constituted in the episcopal college, separates himself from the promises of Christ to the Church.[97] Thus, for Cyprian the schismatic groups which, for whatever reason, separate themselves from the Church which coheres in the corporate episcopate, are not parts of the Church. They are outside the Church altogether and probably outside the possibility of salvation. In short, for Cyprian the principle of unity is the episcopate. He clearly enunciates the principle of "No bishop, no Church."[98]

Cyprian's ecclesiology facilitated the hierarchical and sacerdotal view of the Church which was to dominate Western Christianity for centuries. According to Cyprian, episcopacy is represented as sacerdotal. It is the channel through which grace is conveyed to the Church. The Holy Spirit was given by Christ to his apostles. And by the apostles to bishops whom they ordained, and by these bishops to their successors. An unbroken episcopal succession is thus necessary to give efficacy to all religious exercises.

Wesley's reading of Cyprian and his response during the reading indicate that till then he still maintained his sacerdotal and high view of the ministry. A. B. Lawson was right in pointing out that, "[i]f Wesley had read the foregoing and retained his admiration of Cyprian, it is hard to believe that he was throwing overboard his high view of the Christian ministry. Rather he cries out during his reading, 'Stand thou in the good old paths!'"[99]

In sum, Wesley's initial view of ministry was formed from his childhood experience and parental influence. Samuel and Susanna Wesley's theology and their models of ministry all were bequeathed to their son John, and shaped John's formative experiences in ministry. And the poor life at Epworth led John Wesley to pursue an innovative ministry in relation to human need. During the early period of his ministry Wesley drew from High-Church Anglican divines and the Pietists an ideal to recreate the primitive faith community. He seems to have maintained his sacerdotal and high view of ministry at least up till his return to England from Georgia.

Sacraments

Wesley's sacramentalism is well known. One of the reasons that Wesley at Oxford was called Precisian and Methodist was his methodical observance of the Lord's Supper at frequent and regular seasons. At this point he seems most Anglican precisely.

The sacraments were one of the main topics of controversy at the English Reformation. It was chiefly for their teaching on the Lord's Supper that the martyred Anglican bishops (Cranmer, Hooper, Ridley, Robert Ferrar, and Hugh Latimer) were put to death. Most of the brief summary statements on the sacraments which are included in the *Book of Common Prayer* of 1549 and 1552 and the Thirty-Nine Articles of Religion are from Cranmer.

Cranmer had a radical view of the Lord's Supper. Along with many Protestant reformers, he no longer accepted Roman Catholic doctrine that by and at the consecration of the elements in the eucharist, the substance of the bread and wine changes into the body and blood of Christ, only the appearances of the bread and wine remaining (transubstantiation). He also rejected Luther's position of the actual substantial presence and combination of the body of Christ with the bread and wine (consubstantiation). Cranmer accepted Calvin's view that Christ is spiritually present in the Lord's Supper. Diarmaid MacCulloch well summarizes Cranmer's view of the Lord's Supper:

> He no longer believed that bread and wine could turn physically into the body and blood of Christ on every Eucharistic table in Christendom. Christ's body was in heaven at the right hand of God, and it was blasphemous to suppose that he could be elsewhere. Accordingly, for Cranmer, what happened in the eucharist was that Christ called believers up to him in heaven, rather than coming down to them himself in bodily form into bread and wine. If he was present in the service, it was in spiritual form, a gift provided only for those faithful whom God had chosen. People who were damned would have no experience of his presence, even if they were attending communion.[100]

This "spiritual presence" view of the eucharist underpinned the *Book of Common Prayer*.

The sacraments are the last main doctrinal topic in the Articles, occupying the seven Articles XXV–XXXI and being touched on in four others (XVI, XIX, XXIII, and XXIV). Article XXV draws a sharp distinction between the two sacraments of the Gospel and other practices which have been commonly called sacraments such as the rest of the seven Sacraments of the Roman Catholic Church. "There are two Sacraments ordained of Christ our Lord in the Gospel: that is to say, Baptism, and the Supper of the Lord. Those five commonly called Sacraments, that is to say, Confirmation, Penance, Orders, Matrimony, and extreme Unction, are not to be counted for Sacraments of the Gospel."[101] This distinction is made on the basis of two arguments: first, baptism and Lord's Supper are based on a New Testament command ("*ordained* of Christ our Lord in the Gospel"), whereas the other five have at most a New Testament example; secondly, this command includes a "*visible Sign or Ceremony* ordained of God," whereas in some of the other five cases the visible sign is uncertain or variable.

"A Catechism" in the *Book of Common Prayer* adds the further distinction that the two great sacraments are directly concerned with the salvation of those who receive them:

> Question. How many Sacraments hath Christ ordained in his Church?
> Answer. Two only, as generally necessary to salvation; that is to say, Baptism, and the Supper of the Lord.
> Question. What meanest thou by this word Sacrament?
> Answer. I mean an outward and visible sign of an inward and spiritual grace given unto us, ordained by Christ himself, as a means whereby we receive the same, and a pledge to assure us thereof.[102]

The other five, though they may be helpful, are not divinely commanded, and therefore not strictly necessary. The gospel promise of salvation is not attached to them in the same definite way.

An Homily "Of Common Prayer and Sacraments," in the Second Book of Homilies written by Bishop Jewel under Queen Elizabeth, deals with this matter at a little greater length:

> Now with like or rather more brevity you shall hear how many Sacraments there be that were instituted by our Saviour Christ, and are to be continued and received of every Christian in due time and order, and for such purpose as our Saviour Christ willed them to be received. And as for the number of them, if they should be considered according to the exact signification of a Sacrament, namely, for visible signs expressly commanded in the New Testament, whereunto is annexed the promise of free forgiveness of our sin and of our holiness and joining in Christ, there be but two, namely, Baptism, and the Supper of the Lord. For, although Absolution hath the promise of forgiveness of sin, yet by the express word of the New Testament it hath not this promise annexed and tied to the visible sign, which is imposition of hands. For this visible sign, I mean laying on of hands, is not expressly commanded in the New Testament to be used in Absolution, as the visible signs in Baptism and the Lord's Supper are; and therefore Absolution is no such Sacrament as Baptism and the Communion are. And, though the Ordering of Ministers hath his visible sign and promise, yet it lacks the promise of remission of sin, as all other Sacraments besides do. Therefore neither it or any other Sacrament else be such Sacraments as Baptism and the Communion are.[103]

The Homily "Of Common Prayer and Sacraments" acknowledges that in a broad sense "the name of a Sacrament may be attributed to any thing whereby an holy thing is signified" and that in such an understanding, "the ancient writers have given this name, not only to the other five commonly of late years taken and used for supplying the number of the seven Sacraments, but also to divers and sundry other ceremonies, as to oil, washing of feet, and such like."[104] But it doesn't mean that the practices are sacraments in such signification as baptism and Lord's Supper are. The Homily continues,

> although there are retained by the order of the Church of England, besides these two, certain other rites and ceremonies about the Institution of Ministers in the Church, Matrimony, Confirmation of children by examining them of their knowledge in the Articles of the Faith and joining thereto the prayers of the Church for them, and likewise for the Visitation of the Sick; yet no man ought to take these for Sacraments in such signification and meaning as the Sacrament of Baptism and the Lord's Supper are, but either for godly states of life, necessary in Christ's Church, and therefore worthy to be set forth by public action and solemnity by the ministry of the Church, or else judged to be such ordinances as may make for the instruction, comfort, and edification of Christ's Church.[105]

The Thirty-Nine Articles of Religion clearly places great weight on the sacraments. The reason for singling out two is because of their importance. Three of the sacramental Articles (Articles XXV, XXVII and XXVIII) each begin with a "not only": "Sacraments . . . be not only Badges or Tokens of Christian Men's Profession"; "Baptism is not only a Sign of Profession and Mark of Difference"; "The Supper of the Lord is not only a Sign of the Love that Christians ought to have among themselves one to another." Rather, they are "certain sure Witnesses, and effectual Signs of Grace" (Articles XXV), and "Effectual because of Christ's Institution and Promise" (Article XXVI). The unworthiness of the ministers doesn't hinder the effect of the sacraments. By baptism we are "grafted into the Church" (Article XXVII); and the holy communion is "a partaking of the Body of Christ, and . . . a partaking of the Blood of Christ" (Article XXVIII). One will recall many parallels to the latter statements in the sacramental services of the Prayer Book, and also in the Catechism.

The way in which the sacraments bring about these beneficial effects is noteworthy. It comes about, say the Articles, through their character as signs or symbols. Article XXV says that they are "witnesses" and "signs" of God's grace, by which He does "work" invisibly in us, and "quicken," and "strengthen and confirm" our faith in him.[106] Through the sign of baptism he awakens our faith and through the sign of the holy communion he strengthens our faith, since baptism marks the beginning of the Christian life and holy communion its continuance.

The Anglican Church previous to Wesley's birth emphasized the sacraments, with regular observance enforced among her members. The sacraments were the means of grace necessary to fulfill the conditions of justification.

> The sacraments . . . must be understood, not in the sense of supernatural
> operations which in themselves confer on man the right to be justified by
> God regardless of his moral achievements, but rather as supernatural op-
> erations which enable man to perform moral acts and to achieve a quality
> of moral goodness which cause God to appropriate unto him the merits of
> his Son and to pronounce him justified.[107]

The sacraments were the means for the release of supernatural power or grace into natural channels and instruments for the achievement of moral goodness.

Reflecting on his family heritage, Wesley later wrote that he was reared "to love and reverence . . . the Bible, the primitive Church, and the Church of England." "Next after the primitive Church," says Wesley, "I esteemed our own, the Church of England, as the most scriptural national church in the world."[108] This statement was true despite the fact that his great-grandfather and grandfather, and once parents, were nonconformists and dissenters. His parents eventually returned to the established church.[109] They saw the sacraments as "divine instruments appointed by God as the means of aiding man to work out his salvation."[110] The parents' view of sacraments, faithful to the teachings of the Church of England, was bequeathed to Wesley. Wesley saw baptism and the Lord's Supper as divinely ordained means of grace.

When Wesley entered Charterhouse in 1714, he entered "in a state of grace," and there he observed the Lord's Supper regularly, which he had learned from his church and family. From 1713 to1720, Wesley was a faithful adherent to the church which he attended regularly, including the sacrament.[111] Following his ordination in 1725 he began to take communion every week. The formation of the Oxford Methodism in 1729 included the rule of taking communion as often as possible.[112] Wesley urged members to frequent the sacrament; Converts from the Oxford Methodists were called "proselytes from the sacrament."[113] From 1729 to 1732, Wesley communicated at least once per week.[114] Umphrey Lee says, "The club [the Oxford Methodists] was High Church in principles. The members spoke of the Communion as a 'sacrifice,' were convinced that baptism regenerated the subject, and talked of 'confession.'"[115] Wesley declined the offer of his father's parish for it would not permit him to "have the opportunity of . . . weekly communicating" which he thought would help his religious life.[116] Perhaps this excuse was not persuasive to his father who had weekly penitential services with the Lord's Supper. Wesley in Oxford struggled greatly with sin "before and after the Holy Communion," which he "was obliged to receive thrice a year."[117] In this Oxford period, however, Wesley was a faithful, punctilious observer of communicant worship in the Church of England, believing that the more the sacraments were used the more grace they would confer.

On October 14, 1735 John Wesley, in company with his brother Charles, Benjamin Ingham, who was one of the most active Oxford Methodists, and Charles Delamotte, left for Georgia as a missionary in order to save his own soul, "to live wholly to the glory of God." [118] Before leaving for Georgia, he and Oxford Methodists still were, as they had done, "communicating as often as [they] have opportunity."[119] From three days after embarking, John Wesley administered communion and began to carefully instruct candidates for baptism and the Lord' Supper.[120]

Several storms at sea revealed his lack of assurance of salvation. Wesley realized and was much ashamed that he "was unwilling to die."[121] He could not but say to himself, "'How is it that thou hast no faith?' being still unwilling to die."[122] Later his conversation with Spangenberg, one of the pastors of the Moravians, intensified his spiritual anxiety about salvation. Wesley wrote on the event of the day:

> He said . . . Does the Spirit of God bear witness with your spirit that you are a child of God? I was surprised, and knew not what to answer. He observed it, and asked, 'Do you know Jesus Christ?' I paused, and said, 'I know he is the Saviour of the world.' 'True', replied he, 'but do you know he has saved you?' I answered, 'I hope he has died to save me.' He added, 'Do you know yourself?' I said, 'I do.' But I fear they were vain words.[123]

Probably he came to more depend on his sacramentarian and legalistic approach. Upon arriving in Georgia, Wesley "arranged weekly Communion"[124] and emphasized the rules of the Church of England which must be followed for administering and receiving baptism and the Holy Communion.[125] The climax of his legalistic approach was reached in his repulsion of Miss Sophia Hopkey from the communion for her failure to obey communion law, and perhaps because of Wesley's unrequited love. The charges brought against him by the Grand Jury, and Wesley's response, show him to be a fastidious priestly administrator of the sacrament and a churchman rigidly faithful to ecclesiastical laws.[126]

In 1737, he left Georgia for England, and was still unsure of his salvation. Reflecting on his past days, Wesley lamented: "that vain desire which had pursued me for so many years, of being in solitude in order to be a Christian. I have now, thought I, solitude enough. But am I . . . the nearer being a Christian? Not if Jesus Christ be the model of Christianity. I doubt indeed I am much nearer that mystery of Satan."[127] Wesley before Aldersgate had zealously practiced the sacraments expecting divine grace, but without assurance. A greater deliverance was necessary.

In sum, the early Wesley was a faithful member of the Church of England and was enthusiastic to practice the sacraments following the teachings of the Church. He endeavored to pursue holiness through strict adherence to the rubrics and disciplines of the Church. To the young Wesley his religious self-understanding was tied up with the Church of England and his religious responsibility was centered in the Church of England. To be a good Christian was essentially to be loyal to that Church and its teaching, to share in its sacramental life, and to induce others to do the same. The early Wesley's heavy attachment to the Church of England is represented in his often-cited statement: "I therefore not only assented to all the doctrines, but observed all the rubric[s] in the Liturgy, and that with all possible exactness, even at the peril of my life."[128]

The early Wesley also vigorously attempted to restore the primitive church. Wesley, in Oxford, devoted himself to the spiritual practices of the primitive church. He went to Georgia with the vision of primitivism and attempted to put his ideas of primitivism into practice by rigidly following the teachings of the *Apostolic Constitutions* and *Canons*, though it was a failure. On the whole, pursuing the ideal of primitive church, the early Wesley adhered to the concept of the church as an institution while he was developing his practical divinity which he got from his parents.

Notes

1. *The Works* (Jackson), xiii, 268–269.
2. Using an image of the Church as the indispensable ark of salvation, St. Cyprian, Bishop of Carthage (martyred A. D. 258), said, "[i]f any one could escape who was outside the ark of Noah, then he also may escape who shall be outside of the Church," but just as in the time of Noah no one who was outside the ark could be saved, "there is no salvation out of the Church." Cyprian, Treatise "On the Unity of the Church," I:6 and Epistle "To Jubaianus, Concerning the Baptism of Heretics," LXXII:21 in *The Ante-Nicene Fathers: Translations of the Writings of the Fathers down to A.D. 325*, Alexander Roberts and James Donaldson, Editors. American Reprint of the Edinburgh Edition. Revised and Chronologically Arranged, with Brief Prefaces and Occasional Notes, by A. Cleveland Coxe (New York: Charles Scribner's Sons, 1899), vol. v, 423 and 384. Cyprian was "a great upholder of church discipline and order", and Wesley's correspondence shows "his continued respect for Cyprian...in these matters." *Works*, xviii, 209–210, note 79.

3. Cf. Heitzenrater, *John Wesley and the Oxford Methodists*, 493–526. Wesley especially read much of writings of the early church after his decision to become a clergyman.

4. V. H. H. Green, *The Young Mr. Wesley: A Study of John Wesley and Oxford* (New York: St Martin's Press, 1961), 173.

5. The full title is *A Compleat Collection of Devotions, both Publick and Private, Taken from the Apostolical Constitutions, the Ancient Liturgies and the Common Prayer Book of the Church of England* (London, 1734).

6. Wesley read the *Apostolic Constitutions* in June 1732 and the *Apostolic Canons* in August 1732, and used them in the Methodist group study at Oxford. Heitzenrater, *John Wesley and the Oxford Methodists*, 494–495.

7. *Works*, xxv, 439.

8. *Works*, xxv, 441.

9. *Works*, xxv, 439.

10. V. H. H. Green, *John Wesley* (London: Thomas Nelson Ltd, 1964), 7.

11. Green, *John Wesley*, 39–40.

12. Green, *John Wesley*, 39.

13. The charge that Wesley was a Papist in disguise was made against him throughout his life from the Georgia period to his later years. For example, see the charges by Thomas Causton in Georgia in 1737, by Bishop George Lavington in 1749, and by a Calvinist in 1773 in Richard P. Heitzenrater, *The Elusive Mr. Wesley*, 2d ed. (Nashville: Abingdon Press, 2003), 86, 289–293; George Lavington, *The Enthusiasm of Methodists and Papists Compar'd*. It must be noted that in the case of Causton, the legal guardian of Sophia Hopkey hated Wesley in many reasons and deceitfully charged Wesley. The other two charged Wesley for theological reasons.

14. Journal on October 18, 1735, in *Works*, xviii, 313.

15. A. B. Lawson, *John Wesley and the Christian Ministry: The Sources and Development of His Opinions and Practice* (London: SPCK, 1963), 12.

16. Journal on September 29, 1749, in *Works*, xx, 305.

17. Journal on September 13, 1736, in *Works*, xviii, 171.

18. *Works*, xviii, 171–172.

19. Journal on February 28, 1736, in *Works*, xviii, 151.

20. *Works*, xix, 43. Here this letter is given in an edited and abridged form in Journal on March 28, 1739. For the original form see the letter "To the Revd. Samuel Wesley, Sen." *Works*, xxv, 405.

21. Sondra Higgins Matthaei, "Practical Divinity: Ministry in the Wesleyan Tradition," *Quarterly Review: A Journal of Theological Resources for Ministry* 12, no. 4 (Winter 1992): 59.

22. *Works*, xxv, 182.

23. Wallace Jr., *Susanna Wesley: The Complete Writings*, 123. Susanna continues to encourage her son to have the trust in God's providence in her latter letters to John. For example, see Susanna's letters to John on 31 January 1726/27, 26 July 1727, 30 March 1734, in Wallace Jr., *Susanna Wesley: The Complete Writings*, 131–132, 137, 166.

24. Cf. Wallace Jr., *Susanna Wesley: The Complete Writings*, 67–68, 178 (Susanna's letters), 206, 208–209, 218–219, 229, 236–240, 257, 263, 273, 290, 294–295, 309, 322, 326, 332 (journals), 414–415 (a brief exposition on the Ten Commandments), 440 (a religious conference between mother and Emilia), 468 (some remarks on a letter from Whitefield).

25. Letter "From Mrs. Susanna Wesley," Feb. 14, 1734, in Wallace Jr., *Susanna Wesley: The Complete Writings*, 378.

26. For example, see *The Works* (Jackson), viii, 310 and xiii, 134.

27. Letter "From the Revd. Samuel Wesley," Oct. 19, 1725, in *Works*, xxv, 185; Susanna's letter "To John Wesley," Nov. 10, 1725, in Wallace Jr., *Susanna Wesley: The Complete Writings*, 121.

28. *Works*, xxv, 185; Wallace Jr., *Susanna Wesley: The Complete Writings*, 121.

29. Wallace Jr., *Susanna Wesley: The Complete Writings*, 47.

30. Wallace Jr., *Susanna Wesley: The Complete Writings*, 47.

31. Wallace Jr., *Susanna Wesley: The Complete Writings*, 99.

32. Sept. 28, 1730, in Adam Clarke, *Memoirs of the Wesley Family* (New York: Lane and Tippett, 1976), 249.

33. J. B. Wakeley, *Anecdotes of the Wesleys: Illustrative of Their Character and Personal History*. With an Introduction by Rev. J. M'Clintock (New York, Carlton & Lanahan, 1870), 26–27.

34. Cf. See Letter "From Mrs. Susanna Wesley," Nov. 10th, 1725, in *Works*, xxv, 183–185.

35. Wallace Jr., *Susanna Wesley: The Complete Writings*, 80.

36. Letter from Susanna on Feb. 6, 1711/12, in *Works*, xix, 285.

37. Wallace Jr., *Susanna Wesley: The Complete Writings*, 82–83.

38. Journal August 1, 1742, in *Works*, xix, 284.

39. Letter "To Mrs. Susanna Wesley," March 19th, 1726/7, in *Works*, xxv, 212–215.

40. Letter "From Mrs. Susanna Wesley," April 22, 1727, in *Works*, xxv, p. 216.

41. Journal of May 24, 1738, in *Works*, xviii, 243.

42. Letter "From the Revd. Samuel Wesley," Janry. 26, 1724/5, in *Works*, xxv, 157–158.

43. *Works*, xxv, 158.

44. Letter "From Mrs. Susanna Wesley," Feb. 23, 1724/5, in *Works*, xxv, 160.

45. Hooker, "Of the Laws of Ecclesiastical Polity," in *The Folger Library Edition of the Works of Richard Hooker*, vol. ii, 430.

46. Hooker, "Of the Laws of Ecclesiastical Polity," in *The Folger Library Edition of the Works of Richard Hooker*, vol. ii, 426.

47. Burnet, *An Exposition of the Thirty-Nine Articles of the Church of England by Gilbert, Bishop of Sarum*, 386. Wesley omitted this Article in his Twenty-Five Articles of Religion.

48. Jan. 13, 1710, in Adam Clarke, *Memoirs of the Wesley Family*, 347–348.

49. Letter "To Mrs. Susanna Wesley," Jan. 24, 1726/7, in *Works*, xxv, 208. Earlier, in the letter to John on Aug. 18, 1725, Susanna said that "there are some

truths which are comparatively of so small value, because of little or no use, that 'tis no matter whether ever we know them or not . . . in some instances 'tis better never to know them." *Works*, xxv, 178.

50. Letter "To Mrs. Susanna Wesley," Feb. 28, 1731/2, in *Works*, xxv, 328.

51. Heitzenrater, *The Elusive Mr. Wesley*, 45.

52. Letter "From the Revd. Samuel Wesley, Sen." Nov. 20, 1734, in *Works*, xxv, 396.

53. Frank Baker, "Practical Divinity—John Wesley's Doctrinal Agenda for Methodism," *Wesleyan Theological Journal* 22, no. 1 (Spring 1987): 11.

54. *The Works* (Jackson), ix, 103.

55. Wesley, Sermon "The Circumcision of the Heart," I, 7, in *Works*, i, 405; Wesley, Sermon "Salvation by Faith," III, 1, in *Works*, i, 125.

56. *Works*, xxv, 399.

57. Heitzenrater, *The Elusive Mr. Wesley*, 91.

58. Letter "To the Revd. Samuel Wesley, Sen." Dec. 10, 1734, in *Works*, xxv, 398–399.

59. Letter "To the Revd. Samuel Wesley, Sen." June 13, 1733, in *Works*, xxv, 351.

60. Cf. Letters "From the Revd. Samuel Wesley" (Janry. 26, 1724/5; Sept. 7, 1725), in *Works*, xxv, 157–159, 182.

61. *The Works* (Jackson), xiv, 321.

62. Letter "From Mrs. Susanna Wesley," Feb. 23, 1724[/5], in *Works*, xxv, 160.

63. Watson, *The Early Methodist Class Meeting*, xi.

64. Wesley, *A Collection of Hymns, for the Use of the People Called Methodists*, The Preface, 4, in *Works*, vii, 74.

65. Green, *The Young Mr. Wesley*, 272–273.

66. Green, *The Young Mr. Wesley*, 273.

67. Burnet, *An Exposition of the Thirty-Nine Articles of the Church of England by Gilbert, Bishop of Sarum*, 333.

68. Green, *John Wesley*, 30.

69. Letter "To the Revd. Samuel Wesley, Jun." on March 4, 1735, in *Works*, xxv, 421.

70. *Works*, xxv, 421. In a letter to his father on December 10, 1734, Wesley offers the reasons why he wants to stay in Oxford, with the conclusive statement that "where I was most holy myself, there I could most promote holiness in others; and consequently that I could more promote it here than in any place under heaven." *Works*, xxv, 404.

71. Lawson, *John Wesley and the Christian Ministry*, 11.

72. Heitzenrater, *John Wesley and the Oxford Methodists*, 507.

73. *Journal*, i, 242, note 1. Wesley frequently refers to Herbert's *Temple* throughout his *Letters* during his whole life. Cf. Letters "To Mrs. Mary Granville" on December 12, 1730, in *Works*, xxv, 260; "To the Revd. Samuel Wesley, Sen." on December 10, 1734, in *Works*, xxv, 400; "To Thomas Church" on February 2, 1745, in *Letters*, ii, 205; "To Mrs. Judith Madan" on November 9, 1750, in *Works*, xxvi,

441; "To Robert Carr Brackenbury" on January 10, 1783, in *Letters*, vii, 163; "To Mrs. Bradburn" February 26, 1783, in *Letters*, vii, 170.

74. T. B. Shepherd, *Methodism and the Literature of the Eighteenth Century* (London: Epworth Press, 1947), 100–101; *Works*, vii, "Introduction," 22–23. In 1623 George Wither published possibly the first Anglican hymn-book, *Hymns and Songs of the Church*, but it was not intended for public worship and restricted to private use.

75. For Herbert's impact on Wesley, see F. E. Hutchinson, "John Wesley and George Herbert," *London Quarterly and Holborn Review* 161 (1936): 439–455; Thomas W. Herbert, *John Wesley as Editor and Author* (Princeton, NJ: Oxford University Press, 1940), 54–58, 82–84; Martha W. England and John Sparrow, "The First Wesley Hymn Book," in *Hymns Unbidden: Donne, Herbert, Blake, Emily Dickinson and the Hymnographers* (New York: New York Public Library, 1966), 31–42; and Elsie A. Leach, "John Wesley's Use of George Herbert," *Huntington Library Quarterly* 16 (1952–1953): 183–202.

76. *Journal*, i, 242, note 1.

77. Cited from C. A. Patrides, ed., *George Herbert: The Critical Heritage* (Boston: Routledge & Kegan Paul, 1983), 16.

78. Cited from Shepherd, *Methodism and the Literature of the Eighteenth Century*, 100.

79. Wesley read *A Priest to the Temple* in July 1730. Heitzenrater, *John Wesley and the Oxford Methodists*, 507.

80. Stanley Stewart, *George Herbert* (Boston: Twayne Publishers, 1986), 25.

81. George Herbert, *The Works of George Herbert in Prose and Verse*, ed. Robert A. Willmott (London: George Routledge and Co., 1854), 255.

82. Herbert, *The Works of George Herbert in Prose and Verse*, 217–218.

83. Lawson, *John Wesley and the Christian Ministry*, 13.

84. *Works*, xx, 305.

85. Lawson, *John Wesley and the Christian Ministry*, 13.

86. Nygren, "John Wesley's Changing Concept of the Ministry," 266.

87. William R. Cannon, "The Holy Spirit in Vatican II and in the Writings of Wesley," *Religion in Life* 37 (Autumn 1968): 440–453.

88. Lawson, *John Wesley and the Christian Ministry*, 12.

89. One needs to distinguish the Salzburgers from the Moravians. Although they are both German Pietists, their views were not entirely in agreement. The Salzburgers, who grounded in the Spener-Francke tradition and settled at New Ebenezer, were "a bit less solifidian in their maintenance of a basically German Lutheran tradition" than the Moravians, who settled at Herrnhut in central Germany and later also at Savannah following the teachings of August Spangenberg and Nicholas Ludwig von Zinzendorf. The "tension between the groups seems to have been caused primarily by peculiar differences in polity, practice, and personality." Heitzenrater, *Wesley and the People Called Methodists*, 60.

90. This event happened on July 17, 1737. Later Wesley said in his *Journal* for September 29, 1749 after he had received a letter from Bolzius: "What a truly Christian piety and simplicity breathe in these lines! And yet this very man, when I

was at Savannah, did I refuse to admit to the Lord's Table, because he was *not baptized*; that is, not baptized by a minister who had been *episcopally ordained*." *Works*, xx, 305.

91. Green, *John Wesley*, 43.

92. Green, *John Wesley*, 43.

93. Lawson, *John Wesley and the Christian Ministry*, 12–13. The Moravians then were to be organized into a Church by ordination of Seifart, who Wesley described as a "far-seeing and humble-minded man."

94. Journal on January 9, 1738, in *Works*, xviii, 209.

95. Cyprian, Treatise "On the Unity of the Church," 1:4, in *The Ante-Nicene Fathers: Translations of the Writings of the Fathers down to A.D. 325*, vol. v, 422.

96. Cyprian, Treatise "On the Unity of the Church," 1:5, in *The Ante-Nicene Fathers: Translations of the Writings of the Fathers down to A.D. 325*, vol. v, 423.

97. Cyprian, Treatise "On the Unity of the Church," 1:6, in *The Ante-Nicene Fathers: Translations of the Writings of the Fathers down to A.D. 325*, vol. v, 423.

98. Cyprian's ecclesiology has a weakness. What is the Christian's duty if his bishop, properly elected and validly consecrated, lives a scandalous life which is tolerated by his brother bishops, and makes demands which are unreasonable and against conscience? In the course of the Church's existence many have felt that they must refuse obedience and form a separated Christian community. Christian disunity occurs not only when men depart from obedience to the college of bishops in the pride and obstinacy which was characteristic of the schismatics of Cyprian's day, but also when they do so for motives of high Christian principle. For example, the rise of Protestant churches, including the Methodist movement. The problem of the Church's unity is a more difficult one than Cyprian saw, or perhaps could possibly see in his day.

99. Lawson, *John Wesley and the Christian Ministry*, 19.

100. *The Book of Common Prayer, 1662 Version (includes Appendices from the 1549 Version and other Commemorations)*, with an Introduction by Diarmaid MacCulloch (London: David Campbell, 1999), xii.

101. Burnet, *An Exposition of the Thirty-Nine Articles of the Church of England by Gilbert, Bishop of Sarum*, 346.

102. *The Book of Common Prayer, 1662 Version*, 189.

103. *The Two Books of Homilies Appointed to Be Read in Churches* (Oxford: The University Press, 1859), 355.

104. *The Two Books of Homilies Appointed to Be Read in Churches*, 355.

105. *The Two Books of Homilies Appointed to Be Read in Churches*, 356.

106. Latin translation reads: "Sacramenta . . . sunt . . . testimonia, et efficacia signa gratiae . . . per quae invisibiliter ipse in nobis operatur, nostramque fidem in se, non solum excitat, verum etiam confirmat." Here *excitat* ("quicken") means "awaken." Edgar C. S. Gibson, *The Thirty-Nine Articles of the Church of England*, 2d ed. (London: Methuen, 1898), 585.

107. Cannon, *The Theology of John Wesley*, 42–43.

108. "Farther Thoughts on Separation from the Church" (1789), in *Works*, ix, 538.

109. It must, however, be noted that as for Wesley's parents, "there was an obscurity on several great points of evangelical religion which hung over their minds till towards the close of life." "The Life of the Rev. John Wesley," in *The Works* (Jackson), v, 505.

110. Cannon, *The Theology of John Wesley*, 47.

111. P.L. Higgins, *John Wesley, Spiritual Witness* (Minneapolis: T. Denison and Co., 1960), 13.

112. "The rule among the Oxford Methodists was to take the sacrament of Holy Communion once a week; hence their title 'Sacramentarians.'" *Journal*, i, 98, note 2.

113. *Works*, xxv, 341.

114. *Works*, xxv, 339.

115. Umphrey Lee, *The Lord's Horseman: John Wesley the Man* (Nashville: Abingdon Press, 1954), 36. Lee further suggests that "these opinions may have been influenced by men like William Law and Thomas Deacon" (36).

116. Letter "To the Revd. Samuel Wesley, Sen." on December 10, 1734, in *Works*, xxv, 401.

117. *Works*, xviii, 243.

118. Journal on October 14, 1735, in *Works*, xviii, 136–137.

119. *Works*, xviii, 131.

120. *Works*, xviii, 137ff.

121. *Works*, xviii, 140.

122. *Works*, xviii, 142.

123. Journal on February 7, 1736, in *Works*, xviii, 146.

124. John Telford, *The Life of John Wesley* (New York: Hunt & Eaton, 1888), 81.

125. See Journals on February 21, 1736 and March 14, 1736, in *Works*, xviii, 150, 154.

126. *Works*, xviii, 182–216.

127. *Works*, xviii, 209.

128. Wesley, "Farther Thoughts on Separation from the Church," in *Works*, ix, 538.

Chapter 5

Ecclesiology of the Middle Wesley

No man ever completely dispenses with his environment, and so it was with Wesley. The High-Church views inherited from his background were working beneath his conscious mind throughout his life. In particular the early Wesley was committed to the institutional concept of the church and had a High-Church churchmanship. These High-Church views, however, clashed with the evangelical conversion of 1738, and later, despite the supremacy of the evangelical thrust, insoluble tensions and difficulties remained in Wesley's theological development.

Pastoral failures in Georgia pushed Wesley to the brink of spiritual despair. However, the Georgia period is not entirely unproductive. Contact with Moravian Christians opened up new prospects for assurance of salvation, and upon his return to England those prospects became personally appropriated in his evangelical awakening.

Aldersgate and Wesley's Ecclesiology

As described in the previous chapter, Wesley's view of church before Aldersgate was a High-Church one with emphasis upon practical divinity. Did, then, Wesley's Aldersgate experience alter his conception of church? Regarding Wesley's change generally, there are two schools of thought. Scholars including Frederick Hockin, J. Ernest Rattenbury, John C. Bowmer and others, show that Wesley's earlier views, even after Aldersgate,

remained with him to the end of his days.[1] Other authorities such as James
H. Rigg, Julia Wedgwood, Luke Tyerman, John S. Simon, Luke L. Keefer
and others suggest that Wesley adopted a new sense of church as a result of
his evangelical conversion.

The position adopted by the second group is clearly illustrated in James
Rigg's words:

> we see evidences of the essential change in ecclesiastical bias which had
> passed upon Wesley. Henceforth his dominant tendency was altogether
> different from what it had been before. His face was now set in an oppo-
> site direction.
>
>   Wesleyan writers take their stand here. None have shown so distinctly
> and fully the rigid and excessive Churchmanship of Wesley up to the date
> of 1738. But they insist that, from that date, everything was essentially
> different, and that the essential difference very swiftly developed into
> striking results.[2]

Rigg's point is that Wesley in 1738 began to change from a High-Church
sacramentalist to an evangelical preacher.

In a similar tone, Julia Wedgwood notes, "Wesley's homeward voyage,
in 1738, marks the conclusion of his High-Church period . . . his journals
during this voyage chronicle for us that deep dissatisfaction which is felt
wherever an earnest nature wakes up to the incompleteness of a traditional
religion; and his after life . . . makes it evident that he passed at this time
into a new spiritual religion."[3] Wedgwood, and probably Rigg, are careful
to allow that Wesley did not give up all his High-Church principles immediately. They admit that Wesley, immediately after Aldersgate, didn't abate
"his attachment to the ordinances of the Church . . . and he did not so soon
reach that degree of independence of her hierarchy and some of her rules
which marks his furthest point of divergence."[4] Nevertheless, although he
didn't cast all his grave-clothes of High-Churchmanship off at once,
Wesley, according to this second group, began to get rid of them rapidly.

In the line of the second group, Luke Tyerman refers to Wesley's High-
Churchman extremes as "silly, popish practices, not only unauthorised and
useless, but too much resembling the pernicious nonsense of the high
church party of the present day to receive the approval of those who have
learned to be thankful for the inestimable blessings of the great Protestant
reformation."[5] While not so insistent as Rigg, he likes to demolish as much
as possible of Wesley's High Churchmanship when recording the post-
Aldersgate period.

John S. Simon, with an emphasis upon the change of Wesley's sense of
mission, further suggests:

If we compare the Wesley of the Holy Club and the Wesley of Georgia with the Wesley of 1739 we are almost startled at the contrast. The punctilious 'High Churchman' can scarcely be recognized . . . in his case the birthday of a Christian was shifted from his baptism to his conversion. . . .

John Wesley's conversion changed his view of the neglected doctrines of the Church and modified his ecclesiastical position. It did more. It made him an evangelist filled with an insatiable desire to save the souls of men.[6]

Following the line of Simon, Luke L. Keefer also argues that the Aldersgate experience brought about an "inevitable ecclesiological readjustment."[7] He proposes that the years 1738 (the Aldersgate experience) and 1739 (the field preaching in Bristol) were crucial in the understanding of development of Wesley's ecclesiology in that they "serve as significant code names for the soteriology and ecclesiology that marked the rest of his career."[8] Finding "his true link to the primitive faith at Aldersgate, namely, conversion as a conscious work of the Holy Spirit," argues Keefer, Wesley's primitivism continued but became primarily soteriological, rather than ecclesiological.[9]

It is true that after Aldersgate we find a shift from a more static to a more dynamic view of the church in Wesley. But the immediate effect of Wesley's conversion was not, as Simon and Keefer endeavored to prove, a change in doctrine. Although Aldersgate gave Wesley an overwhelming urge to proclaim gospel whenever and wherever the opportunity afforded itself, it did not cause a radical change in his ecclesiastical views. This assumption is demonstrated by the incident that Wesley was summoned before Dr. Edmund Gibson, Bishop of London, on 20 October 1738, almost five months after Aldersgate. Wesley had been insisting again on the re-baptism of Dissenters, which was a practice that the bishop condemned. This incident can hardly be regarded as indicative of a departure from his previous position, the High-Churchman one. Charles Wesley also found himself in trouble for the same reason.

However, although there is no indication of an immediate change in his conception of church, it must be noted that, after his conversion, Wesley indulged in notable irregularities of practice. For instance, unauthorized preaching was his first departure from orthodox practice during this period. The canons of 1603 didn't allow strangers to preach without showing their license: "Neither the minister, churchwardens, nor any other officers of the church shall suffer any man to preach within their churches or chapels, but such as, by showing their licence to preach, shall appear unto them to be sufficiently authorized thereunto."[10] Because of his unauthorized preaching since 1739, Wesley inevitably came into conflict both with the ecclesiastical authorities and secular officials.

Also, after Aldersgate, Wesley clearly advocated a new means for attaining spirituality. In addition to creedal assent to the truths of Scripture, now believed Wesley, a Christian must possess "a sure confidence in his [Christ's] pardoning mercy, wrought in us by the Holy Ghost."[11] Although the institutional concept of the church was not abandoned, no longer was salvation determined by one's relationship to the ecclesiastical institution. Salvation is more closely associated with an inward experience of regeneration through faith. Therefore, after Aldersgate, for Wesley, the priorities of life and ministry now began to be altered.

Furthermore, after Aldersgate, soteriology took a more central place in Wesley's theology, and all other doctrines, including ecclesiology, established their character and validity in relation to the saving work of Christ. Lawson is right in saying that "After his evangelical conversion, churchmanship seems to have taken a subordinate place in Wesley's thinking. It did not, as some have supposed, become unimportant. Rather it must be flexible enough to be adapted to changing circumstances and never be in opposition to his evangelical endeavors."[12]

As described above, after Aldersgate the center of Wesley's entire theology was on soteriology. He gradually began to speak of salvation with two branches: justification and sanctification. This balanced relationship between the two major branches of salvation is repeatedly found in Wesley's works from after 1745 to his later years. A statement from his sermon on "God's Vineyard" is representative:

> It is then a great blessing given to this people that, as they do not think or speak of justification so as to supersede sanctification, so neither do they think or speak of sanctification so as to supersede justification. They take care to keep each in its own place, laying equal stress on one and the other. They know God has joined these together, and it is not for man to put them asunder. Therefore they maintain with equal zeal and diligence the doctrine of free, full, present justification on the one hand, and of entire sanctification both of heart and life on the other—being as tenacious of inward holiness as any mystic, and of outward as any Pharisee.[13]

Creedal affirmations and conversion experiences were significant elements in Wesley's ecclesiology, but in themselves they did not suffice. Since salvation was "the whole work of God," embracing both his justifying and sanctifying work, true believers must manifest their salvation to the world through a daily ethic of faith and love. For that reason, Wesley wanted Methodists to be visible saints: "We look upon the Methodists in general, not as any particular party . . . but as living witnesses in and to every party of that Christianity which we preach, which is hereby demonstrated to be a real thing, and visibly held out to all the world."[14]

The pattern for this "proper Christian church" was to be found in the primitive community established by the disciples of Jesus; not only had Christ taught the truths of religion, but after Pentecost, he "effectually planted it in the earth" in the living witnesses of first-century Christians.[15] But that primitive model of an evangelized and evangelizing congregation soon deteriorated in the Constantinian age, not so much through political dominance and corruption as through the accumulation of material wealth and the consequent loss of spiritual zeal among its members. Wesley's vision was to restore the church to that original purity and he countenanced no compromise with nominal Christianity in the fellowship, any more than he tolerated some darling lust or residue of carnality in the individual who was pressing on to perfect love.

The Spirit's sanctifying work was crucial in the life of the church as well as in the life of the believer. In relation to the holiness of the church, Wesley wrote,

'The church is called holy because Christ the head of it is holy.' . . . 'It is so called because all its ordinances are designed to promote holiness;' and yet another, 'Because our Lord *intended* that all the members of the church should be holy.' . . . the church is called 'holy' because it is holy; because every member thereof is holy, though in different degrees, as he that called them is holy. How clear is this! If the church, as to the very essence of it, is a body of believers, no man that is not a Christian believer can be a member of it. If this whole body be animated by one spirit, and endued with one faith and one hope of their calling; then he who has not that spirit, and faith, and hope, is no member of this body.[16]

However, this demand for genuine Christianity in the church never degenerated into sectarian pride or exclusiveness. Wesley accepted any person with a "desire to flee the wrath to come" into the fellowship. When one's heart was right (i.e. one was pure in intention and open to the Spirit's direction), Wesley could disregard deviations in both doctrine and liturgical practice in order to further the task of the mission to the world.[17]

Therefore, the saving work of Christ was the heart of Wesley's understanding of church. Faith in that redemptive work was the primary prerequisite for membership in the body of Christ. At the same time, the ongoing process of "faith working by love" resulted in a holy people who proclaimed to the world the reality of the transformation wrought by the Spirit. In short, for Wesley the church is a *saved* and *saving* community.

It is true that for Wesley's ecclesiology, his religious renewal com-
mencing in 1738 and his trip to the Continent soon after Aldersgate are of
major importance. The one afforded him a new vision of the religious life
and the other afforded him a look at a new model, not found in his own tradition, by means of which his newly found religious experience could become an integral part of his inherited understanding of the church. The impact that Wesley's observations of the Moravians on the Continent had
upon him was mentioned in the previous chapters and later will be further
investigated.

In conclusion, Aldersgate did not mean a shift away from ecclesiology,
but a shift toward a more organic and functional view of the church. The
Aldersgate experience did not lead to a repudiation of the institutional
church, but forced Wesley to consider, more than before, the primacy of the
soteriological mandate. The result, according to Robert S. Paul, was an
"evangelical pragmatism," a functional understanding of ecclesiology controlled by the gospel message and justified by the mission of the church.[18]
After Aldersgate and his observations on the Continent, Wesley's interest in
the church as an institution continued, but it was now subordinated to the
sense of mission which grew out of his conversion and which was embodied in the purpose and activities of his Methodist societies.[19] Therefore, in
this period, Wesley's ecclesiology was dictated by his desire for the salvation of souls or his highly developed sense of mission.

Ministry: Toward a Practical View

Wesley's view of ministry after Aldersgate was changing to meet the pragmatic needs of a developing work. E. Herbert Nygren notes the change of
emphasis in Wesley after Aldersgate:

> Previously he had been concerned about spiritual fitness *after* receiving
> holy orders. Now he believed that a man must have some sort of personal
> religious experience and be converted in order to become a worthy minis-
> ter of the church.
>
> Though not in agreement with Luther's concept of the priesthood of
> all believers, that "we are all consecrated as priests by baptism," Wesley
> was in accord with Luther's teaching that, "The unction by a pope or a
> bishop, tonsure, ordination, consecration, clothes differing from that of
> laymen—all these may make a hypocrite or an annointed puppet, but
> never a Christian or a spiritual man . . . for, if we had not a higher conse-
> cration in us than pope or bishop can give, no priest could ever be made
> by the consecration of pope or bishop."

Wesley's new conception of the ministry was evolving. Heretofore he had considered it to be primarily a priestly function; now he began to emphasize the prophetic aspect. . . .

Wesley now believed that the call of God was of more importance than standing in the succession of the priesthood. . . . More and more his emphasis was upon evangelism rather than the sacerdotal aspect of the priesthood. His chief desire was to lead men to an experience of conversion like the one which he had undergone.[20]

Nygren's point is that the Aldersgate experience and the assurance of conversion it gave Wesley were instrumental in changing the direction of Wesley's thinking about the ministry.

While Wesley supported the authority of the Church of England in the ordination of persons to holy orders, it was clear to Wesley after Aldersgate that the power of the Spirit working within persons' lives could not be denied. Now Wesley recognized and supported a variety of ministries as legitimate responses to God's call. Because of his conviction that God's grace and justification by faith are available to all, Wesley accepted, although sometimes reluctantly, the responses by laypersons to the movement of the Spirit within their lives. Now the primary measure for Wesley was evidence of gifts, grace, and fruits of the Spirit in a person's living witness.

W. Stephen Gunter described this change as a move from "formal ecclesiology to a 'practical ecclesiology' that met the need of a specific situation."[21] After Aldersgate, notes Gunter, Wesley "exhibited a tendency to minister to the needs of his converts even at the expense of ecclesiastical protocol."[22] Certainly, Wesley's ministry in this period was in tune with the physical and spiritual needs of the persons. And during this period, more prominent for Wesley was the view that every believer should take spiritual leadership in the place he/she is given by the Spirit regardless of the dictates of formal ecclesiology. Wesley was eager to respond to God's saving grace and inward call with a social passion to care for one's neighbor. He accepted the forms of ministry shaped by the gifts that persons were given and the needs of the neighbor. What resulted was a variety of ministries to the outcast, the poor, the hungry, the ill, the imprisoned, the young, and so on.

The situation of early Methodism led Wesley to the practical ecclesiology. A notable example of this was the emergence of open-air preaching and lay preaching. Wesley accepted George Whitefield's request by preaching in the open air on the afternoon of April 2, 1739, when he preached in the brickyard at the farther end of St. Philip's Plain, Bristol, to about three thousand people. He described that day in his Journal: "At four in the afternoon I submitted to 'be more vile', and proclaimed in the highways the glad tidings of salvation."[23] Although he did it with reluctance, he was surprised at the work of the open-air preaching as a means of converting sinners, and he soon adopted the open-air preaching.

Likewise Wesley came to accept lay preaching in which he saw an effective means of converting sinners. He remembered, "the first lay preacher that assisted me in England" was Joseph Humphreys. It took place, according to him, "in the year 1738."[24] Wesley supplies this information fifty-two years after the event. Luke Tyerman, Wesley's biographer, claims that Wesley was mistaken and suggests that John Cennick, who began his work "as early as the month of June, 1739," was the first lay preacher.[25] The most famous instance of lay preacher is that of Thomas Maxfield whom at the Conference of 1766 Wesley remembered as "the first layman who 'desired to help him as a son in the gospel', which did not quite entitle him to be called the first lay preacher."[26] In 1742 Wesley gave Maxfield charge of the Foundery Society in London and "instructed him to pray with the people."[27] Soon Maxfield began reading and expounding the Scriptures, and finally moved to preaching without permission in Wesley's absence.[28] On his return, Wesley was quite angry, but his mother confronted him, saying, "My son, I charge you before God, beware what you do; for Thomas Maxfield is as much called to preach the gospel as ever you were!"[29] Susanna advised his son that he would hear Maxfield's preaching and examine its fruits.[30] Wesley took Susanna's advice, and the fruits of preaching as the primary measure of calling. The fruits of lay preaching surprised Wesley, and he began to use lay preachers more and more.

The lay preaching shows the peculiarity of Methodist ministry in that it is difficult to make proper distinction between clergy and laity in Methodism—except the administration of sacraments—or at least to provide a theological reason for such distinction even when the distinction is, in practice, observed in a Methodist church. And, in most historical instances, ministry is incapable of definition apart from the church to which it belongs and in compliance with the doctrines and disciplines of which it serves, but the ministry of Methodism as a matter of historical fact emerged before the Methodist Church. This peculiarity inhered in the very origin of the ministerial office in the eighteenth century Methodism under the leadership of John Wesley.

There is a point to be noted in relation to the lay preaching. The ministry of the lay preachers, though perhaps spiritually richer and morally more effective in some aspects, was regarded as far less complete than the ministry of the ordained clergy by the Churches of the time including the Church of England and the Roman Catholic Church. There was a very definite demarcation between the vocation of lay preachers and that of the ordained clergy. The former was designed to meet specific needs in the church; the latter was set apart to care for the total work of the church and to serve the members of the church from cradle to the grave. In particular the administration of the sacraments was the work of the ordained clergy. Wesley did not see his lay preachers as "chosen for the fulness of the priesthood"[31] or gifted with sacramental grace enabling them to exercise a perfect role of pastoral oversight in the church, as expected to the priests by the Church of England or the Roman Catholic Church.

Wesley is very explicit on this point. Answering the basic question as to the nature of the work and ministry of his lay preachers in the 1746 Conference, he considered the Methodist preachers as "extraordinary messengers, designed of God to provoke the others to jealousy."[32] The work of these extraordinary messengers was "wholly and solely to preach the gospel."[33] They were not allowed even to baptize children,[34] a privilege given to any Christian in emergencies. Wesley admonished his preachers: "'You are to do *that part* of the work which we appoint.' . . . Did we ever appoint you to administer the sacraments, to exercise the priestly office? Such a design never entered into our mind; it was the farthest from our thoughts. And if any preacher had taken such a step we should have looked upon it as a palpable breach of this rule, and consequently a recantation of our connexion."[35] Here, it is clear that the major distinction between the ordained priests and the lay preachers was whether they have the right to administer the sacraments. Wesley denied that an inextricable bond existed between the ministry of the Word and the ministry of sacrament: "And those who imagine these offices to be inseparably joined are totally ignorant of the constitution of the whole Jewish as well as Christian church. Neither the Romish, nor the English, nor the Presbyterian Churches ever accounted them so."[36] He clarified that he had received his lay preachers for the ministry of Word but not for the ministry of sacrament.

The reason that underlies this distinction is apparent. Wesley knew that to allow his preachers to perform the ministry of sacrament, he should ordain them,[37] and it would lead to the separation from the Church of England. Methodists did not at first constitute themselves into a sect, a party, or a church. Methodists, insists Wesley, "do not separate from the religious community to which they at first belonged. They are still members of the Church; such they desire to live and to die."[38]

However, it is particularly notable that the United Societies of the early Methodism which the lay preachers served were, in the intention of their founder Wesley, ecumenical.[39] Before the end of the year 1739, Wesley began the United Societies, groups of people who "united themselves 'in order to pray together, to receive the word of exhortation, and to watch over one another in love, that they might help each other to work out their salvation.'"[40] The United Societies were not designed as substitutes for the Church of England. They were primarily designed to deepen the spiritual life in the Church. Nevertheless, the United Societies were not confined in the Church. They welcomed into membership persons of any church. Wesley held, "in order to their union with us we require no unity in opinions, or in modes of worship, but barely that they 'fear God and work righteousness.'"[41] Wesley hoped that his lay preachers were evangelists serving the whole of Christendom while he wanted them to remain within the Church of England. In fact, he thought of what he and Methodists were doing as a unique development, different from anything else in the entire range of Christian history. "Point any such out, whoever can. I know none in Europe, Asia, Africa, or America! This is the glory of the Methodists, and of them alone! They are themselves no particular sect or party; but they receive those of all parties who 'endeavour to do justly, and love mercy, and walk humbly with their God'."[42]

To understand Wesley's ecclesiology, the United Societies of Methodism must be further investigated. The United Societies were neither churches nor any ecclesiastical organization or institution. They did not qualify for the designation "churches" or "ecclesial communities," since nothing about them approximated the meaning of church either in Anglican or in Roman Catholic usage or for that matter according to the broad and loose patterns of the free churches functioning in Wesley's day. In fact the Societies were not designed as substitutes for the Anglican or any other church. They were auxiliary to the church, supporting her mission by enriching and deepening the spiritual life of the members who used their services. In reality, they most clearly resembled "Tertiaries" or "Third Orders" of High Medieval Western Catholicism, though there was never an element of strict monasticism about them, since they did not provide for goods in common or encourage celibacy. The Societies were composed of men and women engaged in ordinary occupations.

It was in relationship to the United Societies that Wesley employed his lay preachers. The lay preachers were the itinerant men who were Wesley's full-time lieutenants in the work. They were used for what they could very well do. The requirements for their ministry was simply their gifts, grace, and fruits necessary for the work. The lay preachers were not merely preachers, but they also gradually came to function as pastors with due pastoral authority. It is true that while Wesley was alive, they were essentially preachers and he would not allow them to be styled "ministers." At the same time, however, under his general supervision, they exercised real pastoral authority. The admission and expulsion of members was entirely in their hands—subject, of course, to Wesley's final arbitration. They had all the authority of pastors, as defined by Wesley, and they were in no sense elected by, or the servants of, the local congregation. Therefore, Wesley's itinerant preachers were pastors as well as preachers, and it is not surprising that, at a very early stage, a conception of the pastoral office was taking shape in their minds.

Wesley had a high view of the ministry. John C. Bowmer was right in describing the two main elements which shows Wesley's high view of ministry: *separated order* and *divine call*.[43] Wesley required the Methodist preachers' separation from secular employment. For example, when in the Conference of 1768 Wesley asked, "Should Itinerant Preachers follow trades?" the answer was "No!" After considering the question thoroughly, Wesley decisively answered,

> The question is not, whether they may occasionally work with their hands, as St. Paul did; but whether it be proper for them to keep shop, and follow merchandise. . . . But this has already offended, not only many of the world, but many of our own brethren. . . . If one Preacher follows trade, so may twenty; so may every one. And if any of them trade a little, why not ever so much? Who can fix how far he should go? Therefore we advise our brethren who have been concerned herein, to give up all, and attend to the one business. And we doubt not but God will recompense them a hundred fold, even in this world, as well as in the world to come.[44]

Secondly, the ministry for Wesley requires a *divine call*. Wesley had his fill of enthusiastic young men who professed to be called of God to preach, but whose acceptance into the itinerancy would have been a disaster for the societies and a disillusionment to themselves. Thus, in 1746, the Conference laid down rules for the testing of "those who believe they are moved by the Holy Ghost, and called of God to preach."[45] The questions for the testing were

> 1. Do they know in whom they have believed? Have they the love of God in their hearts? Do they desire and seek nothing but God? And are they holy in all manner of conversation?
> 2. Have they gifts (as well as grace) for the work? Have they (in some tolerable degree) a clear, sound understanding? Have they a right judgment in the things of God? Have they a just conception of salvation by faith? And has God given them any degree of utterance? Do they speak justly, readily, clearly?
> 3. Have they success? Do they not only so speak as generally either to convince or affect the hearers? But have any received remission of sins by their preaching? A clear and lasting sense of the love of God?

As long as these three marks undeniably concur in any, we allow him
to be called of God to preach. [46]

These questions are significant in that they place the origin of the Christian
ministry in the divine call and gifts of God and not in popular election.

At John Wesley's first Conference (1744) the question was asked,
"What is the office of our Assistants?" and the answer was, "In the absence
of the Minister, to feed and guide, to teach and govern the flock."[47] The
terms, "feed," "guide," "teach," and "govern" are vital in understanding
Wesley's view of the ministry of the lay preachers. The simple but profound terms underlie the strict discipline which Wesley imposed on his
helpers; they form the basis of the oversight which is exercised at every
level of Methodist life and organization. Feeding, guiding, teaching, and
governing the souls are the office of ministers as well as that of the helpers.
At the same Conference the question was also asked, "What is the office of
a Minister?" and the answer given was, "To watch over the souls whom
God commits to his charge, as he that must give account."[48] Wesley saw a
minister as a man sent from God, to watch over, feed, guide, teach and govern the souls whom God commits to his charge.

Although his statement was made more than a century later, John
Beecham was consistent with the thought of Wesley. Methodist ministers,
said Beecham, are

> to both feed and regulate the flock over which they are appointed to watch
> . . . the Ministers of Christ . . . are to take the oversight of the flock *will-*
> *ingly, &c.* The word rendered "taking the oversight," is the present parti-
> ciple of ἐπισκοπέω, from which is derived ἐπίσκοπος, "Bishop;" . . . From
> hence it appears, that the Christian Bishop is to oversee the church, as a
> man oversees his own family: that as a man provides for his family, and
> authoritatively directs and controls it, so is the Bishop to take care of the
> church; providing for its spiritual wants, and directing and disciplining it
> for its good.[49]

Obviously an emphasis on nurture and discipline was prominent in the ministry of Wesley. Particularly in regard to the matter of discipline, Wesley
noted:

> *Whose soever sins ye remit*—According to the tenor of the gospel; that is,
> supposing them to repent and believe. *They are remitted*; *and whose so-*
> *ever sins ye retain* (supposing them to remain impenitent), *they are re-*
> *tained*—So far is plain. But here arises a difficult: Are not the sins of one
> who truly repents, and unfeignedly believes in Christ, *remitted* without
> sacerdotal absolution; and are not the sins of one who does not repent or

believe *retained* even with it? What, then, does this commission imply? Can it imply any more than (1) a power of declaring with authority the Christian terms of pardon? Whose sins are remitted, and whose retained? As in our daily form of absolution; and (2) a power of inflicting and remitting ecclesiastical censures? that is, of excluding from, and re-admitting into, a Christian congregation.[50]

This note clearly reflects Wesley the disciplinarian. The power of "excluding from, and re-admitting into a Christian congregation" (or Methodist societies for Wesley) was no more than the authority which Wesley himself exercised and delegated to his Assistants.

The authority of lay-preachers was not to lead to the extreme of their despotic power. Wesley avoided the two extremes of the ministry: the ministry as the despotic power on one hand and as the power "altogether dependent upon the people"[51] on the other hand. Those who argued for the latter believed that they "have a right to direct as well as to choose their ministers," but Wesley rejected it.[52]

The Wesley's conception of the ministry in general emphasizes responsibility with authority. The best model for such a ministry was Wesley himself. He believed that there were committed to his charge the souls of men for whom he was accountable before God. He knew that this belief imposed a terrible responsibility, but he realized that with it, to enable him to discharge it, there was given a certain power and authority.

This authority, in Wesley's case, had a dual origin. First of all, he had the authority of an Anglican clergyman. The authority counted for something at a time when the parson was a *persona* in the parish. But Wesley had another authority peculiar to himself. He was the head of "the People called Methodists," the leader of those who *voluntarily* placed themselves under his care. His relationship to the Methodist people was much more personal than that which existed between the Anglican clergyman and his parishioners. The sheep of the cure's flock were his just because they happened to live in his parish. Wesley's flock were his because they had freely chosen to place themselves under his direction.

His authority in Methodism was supreme, and once at least he had to defend it against his critics:

What is that power? It is a power of admitting into and excluding from the Societies under my care; of choosing and removing Stewards; of receiving or not receiving Helpers; of appointing them when, where, and how to help me; and of desiring any of them to confer with me, when I see good. And as it was merely in obedience to the Providence of God, and for the good of people, that I at first accepted this power, which I never sought,

nay, a hundred times laboured to throw off; so it is on the same considerations, not for profit, honour, or pleasure, that I use it at this day.[53]

His authority was supreme, but it was not Roman Catholic. Rather, as he
pointed out in his sermon "On Obedience to Pastors," it was really a happy
"medium between . . . two extremes,"[54] Rome and Geneva. The Romanists
demanded explicit obedience while "the generality of Protestants are apt to
run to the other extreme, allowing their pastors no authority at all, but making them both the creatures and the servants of their congregations."[55]
Wesley's position lay somewhere between these two. He believed that once
a person has found a pastor who will nourish his soul, he should submit to
him in all things, save those which offend conscience or are contrary to
what is prescribed in Scripture. This position is the foundation of Wesley's
doctrine of the ministry.

In conclusion, the middle Wesley's view of ministry is a result of the
developing Methodist movement. It was changing to meet the pragmatic
needs of a developing work, and the development of the Wesleyan doctrine
of the ministry was essentially a growing awareness of status. The idea of
pastoral responsibility and authority was inherent in Wesley's system from
the start, but it was formulated by the itinerants only as circumstances
called for it. Wesley's concern now was not with the nature of the doctrinal
entities in a nice theological structure, but rather with effective functioning
and satisfactory activity within an expanding ecclesiastical organism and
with what it has taken to be tangible results in the salvation of souls and the
improvement of the world.

Sacraments

Aldersgate and Wesley's View of the Sacraments

Wesley returned to England from Georgia with the resolution that he
would seek justifying faith by adding "continual prayer" to "'the constant
use of all the' other 'means of grace'" that he had fervently been practicing.[56] And, in the evening of May 24, 1738, he had the experience of conversion at Aldersgate. He wrote on the event of that day:

> I continued thus to seek it [justifying, saving faith] (though with strange
> indifference, dullness, and coldness, and unusually frequent relapses into
> sin) till Wednesday, May 24. . . . In the evening I went very unwillingly to
> a society in Aldersgate Street, where one was reading Luther's Preface to

the Epistle to the Romans. About a quarter before nine, while he was describing the change which God works in the heart through faith in Christ, I felt my heart strangely warmed. I felt I did trust in Christ, Christ alone for my salvation, and an assurance was given me . . . [57]

The interesting thing is that after the Aldersgate experience the sacraments took on deeper meaning for Wesley, and never less. Rather than trading off the sacramental means of grace for the direct intimacy of his new-found experience of God, he thrived on them as nourishment for the new life of God in his soul. Aldersgate, as F. Ernest Stoeffler notes, "had less of an impact on his understanding of the nature and meaning of the sacraments than on any other aspects of his theology."[58]

However, one finds a marked shift of emphasis after his heart-warming experience. Wesley basically elevated his evangelical experience above his sacramental heritage. After Aldersgate, Wesley, while remaining fond of the liturgy of the Church, was no longer bound by the formal ecclesiology. The Aldersgate event gave Wesley an experience never to be forgotten throughout his after life, which was one of the most significant developments in his spiritual pilgrimage. And the evangelical experience sometimes clashed with his Anglican background causing him to act and speak inconsistently at times.

After Aldersgate, Wesley did not abstain from the sacraments. Rather his understanding of the nature and meaning of the sacraments deepened. He still exhorted persons to use the sacraments as means of grace: "In September 1738, when I returned from Germany, I exhorted all I could to follow after that great salvation . . . waiting for it 'in all the ordinances of God.'"[59] However, salvation for Wesley no longer consisted "in using the ordinances of God."[60] God might work through the sacraments or apart from them; God was not limited. Nor was the grace of God irresistibly operative upon a person; a response was necessary. Wesley exhorted people neither to rest in the sacraments nor neglect them[61]; they were to use them as means, for God had so intended them.

The Lord's Supper and baptism must be appreciated and used as the means of grace God has ordained. Since baptism is a means of grace, however, it is not equated with the new birth as it was by many Anglican priests. Wesley says, "They speak of the *new birth* as an *outward* thing, as if it were no more than baptism. . . . I believe it to be an inward thing; a change from inward wickedness to inward goodness."[62] We will further investigate this matter in the next sections.

In June 1738, after Aldersgate, Wesley went via Holland to Germany, where he encountered among the Moravians the view that no one should receive the Lord's Supper until she/he had the full assurance of faith.[63] The same thinking he found in the Fetter Lane Society of London upon his return. Quietism and mysticism reared their heads when the Society asserted that Christ alone was the means of grace, hence one was not to take the sacrament if she/he had doubt or fear. Many in the Society left the sacraments. Wesley exhorted the Society "to keep close to the Church, and to all the ordinances of God."[64] Wesley disagreed with the Moravians and supported his view by a woman who had been found by grace in receiving the bread.

> I then indeed found one who, when many (according to their custom) laboured to persuade her she had no faith, replied, with a spirit they were not able to resist, 'I know that "the life which I now live, I live by faith in the Son of God, who loved *me*, and gave himself for *me*." And he has never left me one moment, since the hour he was made known to me *in the breaking of bread*.' . . . *one that had not faith received it in the Lord's Supper*.[65]

After Aldersgate, Wesley under the Moravian influence admitted that there is no virtue in keeping the sacraments alone, but he didn't drive himself into the Moravian extremism. Wesley concludes, "(1)that there are 'means of grace', i.e., outward ordinances, whereby the inward grace of God is ordinarily conveyed to man, whereby the faith that brings salvation is conveyed to them who before had it not; (2) that *one of these means is the Lord's Supper*; and (3) that *he who has not this faith ought to wait for it in the use both of this and of the other means which God hath ordained*."[66]

In 1739 and 1740, there was a further debate on this matter between Wesley and Philip Henry Molther, a Moravian leader of the Fetter Lane Society. As the Moravians of the Society argued for practicing 'stillness' and persecuted those who were using the sacraments, Wesley replied by asserting the inwardness of religion mediated through means. Wesley's points in the controversy were that a person needs only seeking faith to use the sacrament, that she/he should seek faith through the means, and that there are means of grace through which God gives grace to unbelievers. Against the Moravians, Wesley wrote in his journal on December 31, 1739,

> There are *degrees of faith*. . . . The way to attain faith is to *wait* for Christ and be *still*, In using 'all the means of grace'. Therefore I believe it right for him who knows he has not faith . . . To go to church; To communicate; To fast; To use as much private prayer as he can, and To read the Scripture. . . . Because I believe these are 'means of grace', i.e., do ordinarily convey God's grace to unbelievers; and That it is possible for a man to *use* them, without *trusting* in them.[67]

Molther during Wesley's visitation on April 25, 1740 replied

> that there are *no degrees* in faith; that none has any faith who has ever any
> doubt or fear, and that none is justified till he has a clean heart . . . that
> everyone who has not this ought, till he has it, to be *still*; that is . . . not to
> use the ordinances, or 'means of grace', so called . . . that to those who
> have a clean heart the ordinances are not *matter of duty*. They are not
> *commanded* to use them; they are *free*; they *may* use them, or they *may*
> *not*. . . . That those who have not a clean heart *ought not* to use them, par-
> ticularly not to communicate, because God neither *commands* nor *designs*
> they should (commanding them to none, designing them only for believ-
> ers) and because they are not 'means of grace', there being no such thing
> as means of grace, but Christ only.[68]

As the controversy moved to a climax, Wesley came to conclusions

> (1) that the Lord's Supper was ordained by God to be a *means of convey-*
> *ing* to men either *preventing* or *justifying*, or *sanctifying grace*, according
> to their several necessities; (2) that the persons for whom it was ordained
> are all those who know and feel that they *want* the *grace* of God, either to
> *restrain* them from sin, or to *show their sins forgiven*, or to *renew their*
> *souls* in the image of God; (3) that inasmuch as we come to his table, not
> to *give* him anything but to *receive* whatsoever he sees best for us, there is
> *no previous preparation* indispensably necessary, but *a desire* to receive
> whatsoever he pleases to give; and (4) that *no fitness* is required at the
> time of communicating but *a sense of our state*, of our utter sinfulness and
> helplessness; every one who knows he is *fit for hell* being just *fit to come*
> *to Christ*, in this as well as all other ways of his appointment.[69]

In the course of the controversy, Wesley argued not only against the Moravian Quietists (who he thought despised the means of grace) but at the same
time against Roman Catholics (who he thought abused the means of grace).

Wesley finally withdrew from the Society, but even as late as 1776,
again and again Wesley had to repute the Moravian position.[70] In the controversy he had established his instrumental view of the sacraments. The
sacraments as means of grace are divine ordinances parallel to inward religion.[71] Spiritual life then is Christ-centered and requires the objective means
of grace; the life of the visible church is also important.

In sum, the controversy with the Moravians after Aldersgate deepened
Wesley's understanding of the nature and meaning of the sacraments.
Wesley still exhorted persons to use the sacraments as means of grace. At
this point, he was precisely an Anglican. Since the sacraments are major
means of grace, they must be neither neglected nor abused. One must use
the sacraments for nourishing the new life of God in his/her soul.

Means of Grace

No doubt Wesley was theologically conscious of the two Protestant marks of the church: the gospel truly preached and the sacraments duly administered, which is stated in the Thirty-Nine Articles of Religion of the Church of England. However, he accepted and valued the gospel and the sacraments not as much as marks of the true church as means of grace. As Scott J. Jones notes, John Wesley believed "that God has ordained certain ways in which human beings can reliably receive God's grace," and that "the best way to experience God's mercy, forgiveness, and love is to use the normal ways God has established."[72] These ways Wesley called the means of grace, including not only baptism and Lord's Supper, but also prayer, Scripture, fasting, etc.

To call the sacraments "means of grace" suggests both the use and limitations of such ordinances. They must be respected and used, for they convey God's grace. Wesley believed that a due administration of the sacraments, particularly the Lord's Supper, was necessary "if not to the *being*, at least to the *well-being* of a Church," for they are "the ordinary means whereby God increaseth faith."[73] But they are only instruments; they are means, and not ends in themselves. As the primitive church lost its earlier purity, considered Wesley, the means became mistaken for ends. Therefore, you should "use all means *as means*; as ordained, not for their own sake, but in order to the renewal of your soul in righteousness and true holiness. If...they actually tend to this, well; but if not, they are dung and dross."[74] Wesley further asserts that "God is above all means" and that one must "seek God alone" in using the means.[75] He also points out that there is no automatic power in the means and that one must not use the means as a source of religious pride.[76]

His sermon, "The Means of Grace," well summarizes his views. The sermon's purpose was to prove the validity and the necessity of the sacraments, as taught and administered in the Church of England. In the sermon Wesley held that the sacraments are outward signs, words, or actions ordained of God as the usual means by which one experiences grace or God's power. For example, the Lord's Supper is an outward sign appointed by God "to be *ordinary* channels whereby he might convey to men preventing, justifying, or sanctifying grace."[77] The inclusion of "preventing" grace shows that they were to be used by the seeker after God as well as the man of great faith. "[T]he whole value of the means depends on their actual subservience to the end of religion,"[78] and the effect of the means is dependent upon the Holy Spirit since grace is the power of God working in us through the Spirit. Wesley says, "all outward means whatever, if separate from the

Spirit of God, cannot profit at all. . . . Whosoever therefore imagines there is any intrinsic *power* in any means whatsoever does greatly err."[79]

Scriptures are held to be the main means. Here we can see a Reformation view. Scriptures are "the great means God has ordained for conveying his manifold grace to man."[80] The presence of the Spirit, the Scripture, and the Sacrament point toward a real presence of Christ mediated through the means and received through faith.

As mentioned previously, Wesley's controversy with the Moravian Quietists at Fetter Lane made clear his view of the means of grace. Wesley attacked those who *despised* the means of grace and at the same time those who *abused* them. The issues were set by a question about the extent to which the means of grace are either salvific or symbolic.

The position of Roman Catholicism was that sacraments are the means of God's saving grace, so some benefit is conveyed by the sacraments even when not received in conscious faith, since the sacraments are, in some sense, converting ordinances and thus means of grace. Grace is conferred by the sacraments *ex opere operato*, i.e., from the ritual observance itself. Baptism cleanses away the guilt of original sin and the eucharist is celestial food or the medicine of immortality. Furthermore, the list of sacraments includes five other rites that provide grace necessary for the nurture and sustenance of the believer throughout life and at death. In Roman Catholic theology and practice, saving grace is mediated through the sacraments. The Word is incomplete apart from the sacraments.

As movements within Protestantism distanced themselves from their Roman Catholic roots, the sacraments were accorded lesser importance. Reformers charged that the Roman Catholics taught that the bare, ritual observance of the sacraments conferred saving grace, apart from faith. While Lutherans especially, but also Calvinists, managed to maintain a prominent and active place for the sacraments in their soteriologies, other Protestant groups, although they did not forsake sacramental teaching and practice, accorded the sacraments a symbolic meaning only. The Protestants' commitment to the doctrine of salvation by faith alone seemed to project a negative sense of "work righteousness" upon sacramental observance. Baptism and the Lord's Supper assumed more incidental roles and the additional five sacraments of Roman Catholicism were rejected altogether. For such Protestants the faith by which we are saved is not mediated by sacramental observance. Salvation is symbolized by the sacrament. But the faith that saves comes from hearing the Word of God (Rom. 10:17). The place of primacy and action in the salvation of the individual is filled completely by the proclamation of the Word of God. Sacraments are outward and visible symbols of an inward and spiritual act. Sacraments apart from the Word are incomplete. Accordingly, although the Protestant reformers generally appreciated the value of the sacraments together with the Word, they elevated the Word above the sacraments.

The temptation that follows from these two positions is to conclude that since one or the other mark of the church is accorded primacy as a means of saving grace, the remaining mark is incidental or purely formal. Wesley saw neither mark as only incidental or formal. For him Word and Sacrament as means of grace are essential to the church.

In his sermon "The Means of Grace" Wesley includes both preaching and the Lord's Supper when he defines his own position as separate from both "those who *abused* the ordinances of God . . . [and] those who *despised* them."[81] The error of the first group is reflected in Wesley's succinct treatment of the relationship between the ordinances and God's grace.

> Settle this in you own heart, that the *opus operatum* [i.e., the ritual observance itself],[82] the mere work done, profiteth nothing; that there is no *power* to save but in the Spirit of God, no *merit* but in the blood of Christ; that consequently even what God ordains conveys no grace to the soul if you trust not in him alone. On the other hand, he that does truly trust in him cannot fall short of the grace of God, even though he were cut off from every outward ordinance, though he were shut up in the centre of the earth.[83]

Those who abuse the ordinances "mistake the *means* for the *end*." They "imagine that though religion did not principally consist in these outward means, yet there was something in them wherewith God was well-pleased, something that would still make them [the worshipers] acceptable in this sight, though they were not exact in the weightier matters of the law, in justice, mercy, and the love of God."[84]

The opposite error was to *despise* the means of grace. Wesley had to deal with this error when he faced the issue of "stillness" in the Fetter Lane Society, and he, in the summer of 1740, withdrew from the Society. "Stillness" was the result of preaching the futility of good works, including among such works the ordinary means of grace. Those who would practice stillness were "pressed not to 'run about to church and sacrament', and to keep their religion to themselves; to be still, not to talk about what they had experienced."[85] The appeal of the doctrine was strong, and they insisted, "Christ has fulfilled the law for *you*. You are no longer a subject to ordinances. You are now to 'be still,' and 'wait' upon God."[86] Consequently, they didn't go to the sacraments. The phrase "means of grace," criticized the Quietists, is not the language of Scripture either. Wesley conceded the point but argued, "the sense of it [the term "means of grace"] is undeniably found in Scripture. For God hath in Scripture ordained prayer, reading or hearing, and receiving the Lord's Supper, as the ordinary means of conveying his grace to man."[87]

Here Wesley broadened his concept of the means of grace to include prayer, reading and hearing Scripture, and the Lord's Supper. Moreover, his list of means of grace is not limited to such "instituted means of grace" as prayer, searching Scripture, the sacraments, fasting, and religious conversation. By such instituted means or "works of piety" we experience grace, or the power or presence of God, but they are not all. We also experience grace by such "works of mercy" as doing good, visiting the sick and prisoners, and feeding and clothing people. Wesley referred to them as "prudential means" of grace. Such means are "merely prudential, not essential, not of divine institution,"[88] but through them we experience the presence of God. The prudential means of grace also include attending class and band meetings.[89] Moreover, the covenant with God, though "seldom used, either in Romish or Protestant churches" except the Methodists, also was regarded as a means of grace.[90] Wesley believed that Christians must live and grow in God's grace, which first prepares us for belief, then accepts us when we respond to God in faith, and sustains us as we do good works and participate in God's mission.

In conclusion, what Wesley gives us in his critique of those who abuse the means of grace and those who despise them is a critique of error in both Catholic and Protestant Quietist assumptions gone astray. While the first group values one mark (sacraments) of the two marks of the church, Word and sacraments, the latter group actually values neither. Wesley can be seen as calling the Protestant church to her own identity when he asserts the value of both. More importantly, for Wesley, the means of grace are established on their own merit. They are not primarily marks of the Church. They are channels of God's redeeming grace. Where the church is truly alive there will be neither abuse nor neglect of either the hearing of the Word or of the sacraments. Nor will one be displaced by the other as if there were a primacy of one over the other. Wesley called the Methodists to affirm in doctrine and practice both the hearing of the Word and the celebration of the sacraments. To do anything less is not so much to fall short of the status of the "true church" as it is to miss the gracious opportunities afforded to every church.

The Lord's Supper

Wesley's eucharist theology takes a very important place in his ecclesiology, for the Lord's Supper was, in Wesley's view and practice, central to the life of the faithful congregation. In line with his insistence that to grow in grace requires regular attendance on all the means of grace, Wesley placed great emphasis on this sacrament[91] and spoke of it as "the grand channel whereby the grace of His Spirit was conveyed to the souls of all the children of God."[92] Wesley was never tired of emphasizing the early church's daily use of communion.[93] He saw the constant communion as "the duty of every Christian."[94]

For Wesley, the Lord's Supper was a preventing, justifying, and sanctifying ordinance: "Lord's Supper was ordained by God to be a *means of conveying* to men either *preventing* or *justifying*, or *sanctifying grace*."[95] That is, it drew a person to God and was instrumental in his justification and sanctification. Thus it was useful and needed at every stage of one's life. The sacrament is for all who are seeking God, and not just for the truly converted. The only essential preparation or qualification is a sense of worthlessness, trusting in nothing but God's grace alone.

The Lord's Supper is "a Memorial of the Sufferings and Death of Christ."[96] Wesley says that the bread is a sign of Christ's body, broken for our iniquities and sins.[97] The wine is "a perpetual sign and memorial" of Christ's blood "as shed for establishing the new covenant."[98] When Jesus said "This is my body," He used it as a *figurative* language, and not ontological. Wesley notes on Luke 22:19,

> *And he took bread*—Namely, some time after, when supper was ended, wherein they had eaten the paschal lamb. *This is my body*—As He had just now celebrated the paschal supper, which was called the Passover, so, in the like figurative language. He calls this bread His body. And this circumstance of itself was sufficient to prevent any mistake, as if this bread was His real body, any more than the paschal lamb was really the Passover.[99]

Just as the paschal lamb was only figuratively the Passover, so the bread is a *figure* of Christ's body. Likewise, the cup of "the new testament in Christ's blood" is not Christ's real blood or "the new testament itself, but only the seal of it [the new testament] and sign of that blood which was shed to confirm it."[100]

Wesley holds that the custom of Scripture is "to call things of a sacramental nature, by the names of those things they are the figure of." Accordingly, "as circumcision was the covenant, and the lamb the passover, by signification and representation, by type and figure . . . so the elements are called by the Fathers, 'the images' . . . 'the symbols' . . . 'the figure' . . . of Christ's body and blood."[101] There is no change of substance in the elements, and the Lord's Supper is a memorial of Christ's sufferings and death. At this point, Wesley's view is very close to Zwingli's "memorial" view.

However, for Wesley the Lord's Supper doesn't have only the meaning of memorial. The effect of the Lord's Supper is to confirm the new covenant. The cup is the means of partaking of the blessing won by the blood of Christ. The bread is the means of partaking of the blessing purchased by Christ's body. The Lord's Supper is the grand channel whereby the grace of the Spirit is conveyed to the participants. Accordingly, as for the Lord's Supper, Wesley's view was very similar to Zwingli's "memorial" view, but he accepted the Calvinistic emphasis on spiritual reception[102] and remained evangelical and instrumental in his view of the sacrament.

As seen before, Wesley clearly expressed his view of sacraments, particularly the Lord's Supper, in his conflict with the advocates of "stillness" in the Fetter Lane Society. The Quietists interpreted the doctrine of justification by faith alone to mean that a believer should do literally nothing to receive God's grace but must wait in stillness on God's approach. Against this view, Wesley replied that God moves us by his grace to come to him through the instituted means, to receive the further grace that leads us along the road to salvation.[103] The Lord's Supper for Wesley is a sacrament in which Christ is truly present through the Spirit, conveying grace to the recipient. Some degree of faith is necessary, but this faith must not be interpreted as a work righteousness by which we make ourselves worthy to receive Christ. We come, bringing only a recognition of our unworthiness and a divinely wrought conviction of the trustworthiness of his promise to be present.

The Lord's Supper as a chief means for taking us along the road to salvation is well presented in Wesley's "The Christian Sacrament and Sacrifice," which he extracted from Daniel Brevint: "The Lord's Supper was chiefly ordained . . . (1) To *represent* the sufferings of Christ which are *past*, whereof it is a *memorial*. (2) To *convey* the first-fruits of these sufferings, in *present graces*, whereof it is a *means*. And (3) To *assure* us of *glory to come*, whereof it is an infallible *pledge*."[104] For Wesley, the importance of the Lord's Supper is that it directs our faith to the merits of the death of Christ by which alone we are saved. For this reason, the Lord's Supper is not simply a reminder of something that is past. God re-presents the Sacrifice of Christ in the Lord's Supper in order that our faith may be aroused by His present grace. The recipients in the Supper may receive the merits of Christ made available to us "by the one oblation of himself once offered" on the cross for "a full, perfect, and sufficient sacrifice, oblation, and satisfaction for the sins of the whole world."[105]

According to Dom Gregory Dix, the New Testament word for "memorial" or "remembrance" is ἀνάμνησις, which means "'re-calling' or 're-presenting' before God an event in the past, so that it becomes *here and now operative by its effects.*"[106] Wesley follows this interpretation. For Wesley, memorial has the sense of "re-calling" or "brought back," so that the Lord's Supper is "the extension of an act done in the past until its effects are a present power."[107]

The Christ's sacrifice in Calvary can be and is re-presented in the Lord's Supper. In his note on I Cor. 11:25 "Do this in remembrance of me," Wesley wrote: "The ancient sacrifices were in remembrance of sin: this sacrifice, once offered, is still represented in remembrance of the remission of sins."[108]

Then, did Wesley go beyond the reformers in his view of the Sacrifice, even to the point of common ground with the Roman Catholic or Eastern Orthodox concepts of the Mass? Did Wesley lead us into the danger of turning the sacrament from a gift of God into a meritorious work of man? One may sense this danger when she/he reads Wesley's "The Christian Sacrament and Sacrifice," which Wesley extracted from Brevint's work on the Lord's Supper:

> this sacrifice, which by a *real* oblation was not to be offered more than once, is, by a devout and thankful commemoration to be offered up every day. This is what the apostle calls, *to set forth the death of the Lord*: to set it forth as well before the eyes of God His Father as before the eyes of men: and what St. Austin *explained*, when he said the holy flesh of Jesus was offered in three manners; by *prefiguring sacrifices* under the Law before His coming into the world, in *real deed* upon His cross, and by a *commemorative Sacrament* after He ascended into heaven. All comes to this: (1) That the *sacrifice* itself can never be repeated; (2) That nevertheless this Sacrament, by our remembrance, becomes a kind of *sacrifice*, whereby we present before God the Father that precious oblation of His Son once offered. And thus do we every day offer unto God the meritorious sufferings of our Lord, as the only sure ground whereon God may give, and we obtain, the blessing we pray for. Now there is no ordinance or mystery, that is so blessed an instrument to reach this everlasting sacrifice, and to set it solemnly forth before the eyes of God, as the Holy Communion is. *To men* it is a *sacred table*, where God's minister is ordered to represent from God his Master the passion of His dear Son, as still fresh, and still powerful for their eternal salvation. And *to God* it is an *altar*, whereon men mystically present to Him the same sacrifice, as still bleeding and suing for mercy.[109]

This statement, though Brevint himself was an Anglican divine who held strongly the Reformed doctrines and even wrote books to oppose Roman superstitions, implies a danger of the sacrament being interpreted as a meritorious act by which we invoke the power of the once-for-all sacrifice of Christ by our re-presentation of it.

However, though adapting Brevint's work, Wesley in fact took care to prevent any such interpretation. He maintained that we are to re-present the sacrifice of Christ, not trusting in our own act, but in the promise of Christ that He will be present. Trusting in the Lord's Supper as the means of grace never means "seeking salvation by works." Rather it means expecting "that he will meet me there because he has promised so to do . . . that he will fulfil his Word, that he will meet and bless me in this way. Yet not for the sake of any works which I have done, nor for the merit of my righteousness; but merely through the merits and sufferings and love of His Son, in whom he is always well-pleased."[110]

The Council of Trent (1545–1563), in the twenty-second session, Canon 1, announced that "[i]f anyone says that in the mass a true and real sacrifice is not offered to God; or that to be offered is nothing else than that Christ is given us to eat, let him be anathema."[111] The Catholic Church at Wesley's days still saw the mass as a true and proper sacrifice, and this sacrifice was certainly not identical with the Anglican understanding of the eucharist. Wesley never agreed to the Roman doctrine that the Christ's sacrifice is repeated in the mass. For him Christ's sacrifice was offered once for all in Calvary. Wesley also denied the sacrifical power of the priest in the Lord's Supper. He specially stressed that the sacrifice, offered "once for all," can never be supplemented. Some of the Reformation divines, in extreme reaction from medieval Christianity, took an excessive care to prevent a danger of the eucharist's being abused, and as a result, minimized the ceremony. Their cause was the devotion to the Bible. Others, while objecting strongly to Roman accretions, maximized this great historical service and preserved its true Christian values. Wesley belonged to the second class. Wesley severely criticized the doctrine that masses could add anything to the sacrifice of Christ offered once for all, but he wanted to preserve the values of the Lord's Supper.

Wesley didn't interpret the nature of the presence of Christ in the Lord's Supper in terms of substance. Roman Catechism holds that upon consecration, there is a change of the whole substance of the bread and wine into the substance of Christ's body and blood while the accidents such as taste, color, and feeling remains the same. The change is usually called transubstantiation. Wesley replied against this doctrine:

(1.) No such change of substance of the bread into the substance of Christ's body, can be inferred from the Saviour's words, "This is my body," (Matt. xxvi. 26;) for it is not said "This is turned into my body," but, "This is my body;" which, if it be taken literally, would rather prove the substance of the bread to be his body . . . it is nowhere said in the Gospel that the bread is changed into the body of Christ. . . .

(2.) It is farther evident that the words are not to be taken in their proper sense; for it is called bread as well after consecration as before it. (1 Cor. x. 17; xi. 26–28.) So that what was called his body was also bread at the same time.[112]

The phrase "No local Deity" in one of Charles' Hymns in itself also shows that the Wesleys rejected the doctrine of transubstantiation.[113]

Yet, at the same time the Wesleys sang, "To every faithful soul appear, And show Thy real presence here!"[114] and believed that the Lord's Supper was "The great unbloody sacrifice, The deep tremendous mystery."[115] For the Wesleys the elements of the Lord's Supper were real channels of saving grace to those who humbly partook of them in faith.

John Wesley did not interpret Christ's presence in the Lord's Supper in corporal terms at all. He didn't accept the doctrine of the ubiquity of Christ's body and so didn't allow for His corporal presence along with the elements. Again, Wesley replied against the Roman teaching:

What honour is to be given to the consecrated host? . . . We freely own that Christ is to be adored in the Lord's Supper; but that the elements are to be adored, we deny. If Christ is not corporally present in the host, they grant their adoration to be idolatry. . . . And that he is not corporally present anywhere but in heaven, we are taught, Acts i. 11, iii. 21, whither he went, and where he is to continue till his second coming to judgment.[116]

Christ is present, not in any corporal way, but through the mediation of the Holy Spirit.

On the way to Georgia, Wesley read Jeremy Collier's *Reasons for Restoring Some Prayers and Directions*,[117] which advocated the restoration of the ancient *epiclesis*, or the prayer for the descent of the Holy Spirit. The epiclesis was contained in the First Prayer Book of Edward VI (1549), but was removed in the 1662 Prayer Book.[118] The epiclesis from the First Prayer Book reads: "Heare us (o merciful father) we besech thee; and with thy holy spirite and worde, vouchsafe to blesse and sanctifie these thy gyftes, and creatures of bread and wyne, that they maie be unto us the bodye and bloude of thy moste derely beloued sonne Jesus Christe."[119] Omitting the epiclesis, the 1662 Prayer Book reads: "Hear us, O merciful Father, we most humbly beseech thee; and grant that we receiving these thy creatures of bread and wine, according to thy Son our Saviour Jesus Christ's holy institution, in remembrance of his death and passion, may be partakers of his most blessed Body and Blood."[120] Restoring the epiclesis from 1549 Book, Charles and John Wesley sang:

> Come, Holy Ghost, Thine influence shed,
> And realize the sign;
> Thy life infuse into the bread,
> Thy power into the wine.
>
> Effectual let the tokens prove,
> And made, by heavenly art,
>
> Fit channels to convey Thy love
> To every faithful heart.[121]

Because of the active presence of the Holy Spirit bringing Christ's grace through the elements, John Wesley saw peculiar power in the Lord's Supper to arouse our faith response which must be given by the believer to the approach of God. In Wesley's view, however, there is no *ex opere operato* efficacy in the sacraments: "the *opus operatum*, the mere work done, profiteth nothing . . . there is no *power* to save but in the Spirit of God."[122] Faith is a living response to Christ leading to imitation of Him. Accordingly, the Lord's Supper must be a place where we not only represent the sacrifice of Christ but present ourselves as a sacrifice:

> Too many who are called Christians live as if under the gospel there were no sacrifice but that of Christ on the cross. And indeed there is no other that can atone for sins, or satisfy the justice of God. Though the whole church should offer up herself as a burnt-sacrifice to God, yet could she contribute no more towards bearing away the wrath to come, than those who stood near Christ when He gave up the ghost did toward the darkening of the sun or the shaking of the earth. But what is not necessary to this sacrifice, which alone redeemed mankind, is absolutely necessary to our having a share in that redemption. So that though the sacrifice of ourselves cannot *procure* salvation, yet it is altogether needful to our *receiving* it. . . . This *conformity* to Christ, which is the grand principle of the whole Christian religion, relates first to our duty about His *sufferings*; and then to our happiness about His *exaltation*, presupposing His *sufferings*.[123]

The grace of Christ brought through the Holy Spirit empowers a faith response by which the believer can die to the world and rise to a new transformed life in conformity with Christ. It is sanctifying grace.

The Lord's Supper for Wesley is also a main means for bringing that faith which prepares us for our final destiny. Not only does it convey that justifying and sanctifying grace which prepare us for heaven; it is also to "assure us of *glory to come*, whereof it is an infallible *pledge*."[124] For that reason the Lord's Supper is pre-eminently the place where the Church Militant and the Church Triumphant draw together. Bowmer says, "The early Methodists lived, communicated and died in the reality of the doctrine of the Communion of Saints. The Church militant and the Church Triumphant constitute 'one family' . . . divided by 'the narrow stream of death'. The Lord's Supper was celebrated against the background of 'angels and arch-angels' and with 'all the company of heaven'."[125]

Furthermore, for Wesley, the Lord's Supper is a "converting" as well as a "confirming" ordinance. Against the Quietists in the Fetter Lane Society, Wesley replied:

> In the ancient church everyone who was baptized communicated daily. So in the Acts we read, they 'all continued daily in the breaking of bread and in prayer'.
>
> But in latter times many have affirmed that the Lord's Supper is not a *converting*, but a *confirming* ordinance.
>
> And among us it has been diligently taught that none but those who are converted, who 'have received the Holy Ghost', who are believers in the full sense, ought to communicate.
>
> But experience shows the gross falsehood of that assertion that the Lord's Supper is not a *converting* ordinance. Ye are the witnesses. For many now present know, the very beginning of your *conversion* to God (perhaps, in some, the first deep *conviction*) was wrought at the Lord's Supper. Now one single instance of this kind overthrows the whole asser-tion.
>
> The falsehood of the other assertion appears both from Scripture pre-cept and example. Our Lord commanded those who were then *uncon-verted*, who had *not* yet 'received the Holy Ghost', who (in the full sense of the word) were not *believers*, to 'do this in remembrance of him'. Here the precept is clear. And to these He delivered the elements with his own hands. Here is example, equally indisputable.[126]

Wesley's view of the Lord's Supper as a converting ordinance must be understood on the basis of his belief as to the nature of the new birth. As we will see in his doctrine of baptism, there is a new birth given in baptism, especially of infants. But this new birth is meant to come to fulfillment in a conscious acceptance of Christ in mature years. The Lord's Supper is a powerful means of grace in the sense of bringing prevenient and justifying grace leading to this conscious acceptance of Christ. At the same time, it is also a means of grace which brings sanctifying grace for the nurture of the converted. Accordingly, the Lord's Supper should not be reserved for those who have reached the mature new birth of conversion. And, for that reason, Wesley was willing to admit baptized children to the Lord's Supper, provided they received instruction as to its meaning.[127]

In sum, Wesley still after Aldersgate maintained his sacramentalism. In fact the middle Wesley further deepened his understanding of the Lord's Supper in the controversy with the Quietists in the Fetter Lane Society. The Lord's Supper for Wesley was a chief means for taking persons along the road to salvation, conveying to them preventing, justifying, and sanctifying grace of God. Wesley rejected to interpret the Lord's Supper in terms of substance (transubstantiation or consubstantiation), and saw the Lord's Supper as a memorial of the sufferings and death of Christ of which effects become a present power. On one hand, Wesley's view of the Lord's Supper was close to Zwingli's "memorial" view, with a very different view of memorial. For Wesley, memorial has the sense of "re-calling" or "re-presenting" an act done in the past until its effects are a present power. On the other hand, Wesley did not interpret the Lord's Supper only in the terms of commemoration. He accepted the Calvinistic idea of the spiritual presence. Wesley believed that Christ is present through the mediation of the Holy Spirit in the Lord's Supper. The Lord's Supper, because of the Spirit's presence bringing Christ's grace in it, has a power to arouse the participants' faith and therefore is a converting ordinance. Ultimately, to Wesley, the Lord's Supper must be a place where the participants not only re-present the sacrifice of Christ but present themselves as a sacrifice.

Baptism

As James H. Rigg remarks, "It is remarkable, indeed, how very little is found on the subject of baptism . . . in Wesley's works."[128] Wesley said a little on the baptism in his *Explanatory Notes Upon the New Testament* and *A Farther Appeal to Men of Reason and Religion*. In 1756, Wesley revised the treatise "Of Baptism" which his father had published in 1700, and reissued it under his own name.[129] Besides them, Wesley said a little on the baptism in his sermons, journals and letters.

Henry Carter in his *The Methodist Heritage* comments that "[i]t cannot be said that an adequate account of Christian Baptism is a part of the heritage bequeathed by John Wesley."[130] William Cannon writes in the same vein, "simply because Wesley deliberately attempts to harmonize his conception with that of the Anglican Church, we receive at his hands no clear-cut and definitive statement in regard to baptism; and what he has written on the subject serves more to confuse than to clarify the issue."[131]

These estimates may be justified in some sense. However, an examination of Wesley's passages on baptism is important in that they reveal an inescapable tension between the institutional and the evangelical which runs through Wesley's theology and comes to its height in his doctrine of church.

Wesley regarded baptism as "a proper sacrament, a sign, seal, pledge, and means of grace, perpetually obligatory on all Christians," which Jesus himself showed by example.[132] Baptism, according to Wesley, is included in the whole design of Christ's great commission, and therefore, "should remain in his Church" until the end of the world.[133] Wesley believed that baptism is an "initiatory sacrament."[134] Just as Jews entered the covenant with God through circumcision, so Christians are admitted into the church by baptism. Wesley says, "By baptism, we enter into covenant with God; into that everlasting covenant . . . we are admitted into the Church, and consequently made members of Christ, its Head . . . we who were "by nature children of wrath" are made the children of God."[135] Baptism is, in the ordinary way, the only "means of entering into the Church or into heaven."[136]

Wesley believed that the free gift and merits of the atonement "are applied to us in baptism,"[137] through the work of the Holy Spirit. Through baptism we receive the gift of the Holy Spirit, through whom we begin a new life and grow throughout Christian life to maturity. If God's Spirit has not operated powerfully in our souls, our baptism has not reached its end.[138] Here one sees Wesley's evangelical, instrumental view of baptism. Baptism for Wesley is a means by which the work of the Spirit is accomplished.

Wesley published his *Explanatory Notes Upon the New Testament* in 1755. In this work, he interpreted and elaborated the vast biblical knowledge he had amassed and we can also read his view of baptism. Baptism is a dying and rising with Christ. In the commentary on Rom. 6:3–4 Wesley notes,

> *As many as have been baptized into Jesus Christ have been baptized into his death*—In baptism we, through faith, are ingrafted into Christ; and we draw new spiritual life from this new root, through His Spirit, who fashions us like unto Him, and particularly with regard to His death and resurrection.
> . . . *as Christ was raised from the dead by glory . . . Of the Father, so we also*, by the same power, should rise again; and as He lives a new life in heaven, so we *should walk in newness of life*. This, says the apostle, our very baptism represents to us.[139]

Believers are to be baptized in token of their faith in Christ and are to testify their faith in Christ by being baptized.[140] Baptism is a means by which God begins his work of regeneration in our heart when in baptism we repent and believe. Wesley here again shows his evangelical principle of the sacraments as instruments of divine grace when inward faith is present.

The matter of baptism is the water which has the natural power of cleansing and hence is fit for its spiritual use in cleansing. As to the mode of baptism, Wesley argued that while immersion was the "ancient manner of baptizing,"[141] any of washing, dipping, pouring, or sprinkling is recognized, for "it is not determined in Scripture in which of these ways it shall be done, neither by any express precept, nor by any such example as clearly proves it; nor by the force or meaning of the word *baptize*."[142] The word "baptize" does not imply necessarily washing, dipping, pouring, sprinkling, or any other way in and of itself. The word is used in other ways in other instances.[143]

Wesley believed that infant baptism is supported by Scripture. Children are to be baptized before they are taught as the Jews circumcised their children. In the note on Matt. 28:19, Wesley says,

> Baptizing and teaching are the two great branches of that general design. And these were to be determined by the circumstances of things; which made it necessary, in baptizing adult Jews or heathens, to teach them before they were baptized; in discipling their children, to baptize them before they were taught: as the Jewish children, in all ages, were first circumcised, and after taught to do all God had commanded them.[144]

Furthermore, Wesley listed the reasons that infants should be baptized in his "A Treatise on Baptism." Infants should be baptized because 1) they are guilty of original sin, and baptism washes away the original sin; 2) they are capable of making a covenant with God through their parents, and were and still are under the evangelical covenant; 3) they ought to come to Christ and can come to Him by no other means than baptism; 4) the apostolic church baptized infants; and 5) baptizing infants has been the general practice of the Christian Church, in all places and in all ages.[145]

It must be noted that Wesley's "A Treatise on Baptism" was the revision work of his father's treatise "Of Baptism," but Wesley followed his father's view by adopting the list in his revision work. This explanation of infant baptism is interesting in that it emphasizes the external, institutional, visible church as the means of the salvation of infants centering in baptism. "If outward baptism be generally, in an ordinary way, necessary to salvation, and infants may be saved as well as adults, nor ought we to neglect any means of saving them," said Wesley.[146] He again wrote, "it is certain by

God's word, that children who are baptized, dying before they commit actual sin, are saved."[147] This language is difficult to fit into an evangelical position of baptism as means of God's grace effected through faith.

How, then, can the external and institutional view and the evangelical and instrumental view of baptism coexist in Wesley? For this matter we need to note that he distinguished between infant baptism and adult baptism, coming close to affirming baptismal regeneration in infants but not in adults.[148] Concerning this matter Frank Baker comments:

> Baptism in infancy Wesley supported because it was instituted by Jesus and because it was the successor of the Old Testament rite of infant circumcision. He continued to believe that in some way objective grace was conferred upon the child by God, so that in a sense it was regenerated, or at least the process of regeneration was begun. At the same time he insisted that another form of regeneration was possible in adult experience quite apart from any sacramental rite. These two aspects of regeneration he never quite reconciled, but continued to insist on both.[149]

Wesley felt that children "who are baptized in their infancy are....born again" at that time and that this was presupposed in the *Book of Common Prayer* of the Church of England.[150] To support his view Wesley said of his own experience, "I believe, till I was about ten years old I had not sinned away that 'washing of the Holy Ghost' which was given me in baptism."[151]

But in the case of adults, not all who are baptized are necessarily regenerated. "A man may possibly be 'born of water', and yet not be 'born of the Spirit'. There may sometimes be the outward sign where there is not the inward grace . . . whatever be the case with infants, it is sure all of riper years who are baptized are not at the same time born again."[152] Wesley provides its example in his journal entry of January 25, 1739:

> I baptized John Smith . . . and four other adults at Islington. Of the adults I have known baptized lately, one only was at that time born again, in the higher sense of the word; that is, found a thorough, inward change, by the love of God shed abroad in her heart. Most of them were only born again in a lower sense, i.e., received the remission of their sins. And some (as it has since too plainly appeared) neither in one sense nor the other.[153]

For infants baptism is a justifying and regenerating sacrament, but in the case of adults, if they are to receive new birth simultaneously in baptism, they must repent and believe.[154]

This view is clarified in Wesley's interpretation of new birth. Wesley speaks of the new birth in two senses. First, the new birth is that God enters the dead life of the unregenerate, bringing the grace without which it is impossible to know God or to receive Him. Secondly, in a sense of fulfillment, the believer comes to conscious acceptance of Christ. It is in the sense of fulfillment that Wesley could say "baptism is not the new birth: they are not one and the same thing."[155] He believed that any denomination of Christians, whether the Church of England or the Dissenters, didn't claim that baptism and new birth are identical. That he affirmed baptismal regeneration in infants but not in adults can be understood in the light of this interpretation of new birth. Whereas infants are at the same time regenerated in baptism, in adults baptism only brings the new birth when there is also a conscious response or faith bringing with it a new life of holiness.[156]

Baptism is the God-given sign which declares the fact that it is God who begins the work of generation in our lives, but God's purpose is to bring us to conscious acceptance of the new birth. "[I]f we do not experience this [being risen with Christ], our baptism has not answered the end of its institution."[157] For that reason, Wesley could say: "Lean no more on the staff of that broken reed, that ye *were* born again in baptism. Who denies that you were then made 'children of God, and heirs of the kingdom of heaven'? But notwithstanding this, ye are now children of the devil; therefore ye must be born again."[158]

The effects of baptism also present to us an irresolvable tension and contradiction in Wesley's thought. On one hand, Wesley shows his high sacramentalism. He claims that there is one outward baptism which is the sign of the visible church. "'There is one baptism,' which is the outward sign our one Lord has been pleased to appoint of all that inward and spiritual grace which he is continually bestowing upon his church. It is likewise a precious means whereby this faith and hope are given to those that diligently seek him."[159] Through baptism we are engrafted into Christ the Word, that is, into the new covenant of God, being admitted into the Body of Christ.[160] Also, through baptism "the guilt of original sin" is washed away from us, "by the application of the merits of Christ's death."[161] Moreover, his high sacramentalism is evident when he proclaims that baptism is "the ordinary instrument of our justification," and that "in the ordinary ways, there is no other means of entering into the Church or into heaven."[162]

On the other hand, however, an evangelical note is sounded when he writes: "By water then, as a means, the water of baptism, we are regenerated and born again; whence it is called by the Apostles, 'the washing of regeneration.' Our Church therefore ascribes no greater virtue to baptism than Christ himself has done. Nor does she ascribe it to the outward washing, but to the inward grace, which added thereto, makes it a sacrament."[163] The outer baptism is a means of inner grace and *saves* only when a person

lives in correspondence thereto, and repents, believes and obeys the gospel.[164] That is, baptism must be an outward sign and means of "inward
change by the Spirit."[165] If in baptism, "'with the outward and visible sign,'
we received the 'inward and spiritual grace,'" the guilt and power of sin is
cleansed by the washing of water.[166] Here Wesley is the evangelically converted Churchman who has not yet cast off his sacramental background.

Wesley did believe that God ordinarily uses baptism as the means by
which God enters the life of the believer to bring new life. But it is at the
same time true that he did not believe that it was the exclusive means. He
wrote to Gilbert Boyce on May 22, 1750, "You think the mode of baptism
is 'necessary to salvation'. I deny that even baptism itself is so. If it were,
every Quaker must be damned, which I can in no wise believe. I hold nothing to be (strictly speaking) necessary to salvation but the mind which was
in Christ."[167]

God's sovereignty and freedom must be recognized. We cannot limit
God's operation only to the means which He has ordained as the ordinary
channels of His coming to us. Although baptism or the Lord's Supper is not
the exclusive means of God's work, nevertheless, because God's normal
way is to work through established means, the Christian is expected to observe them. On the basis of this belief, he wrote to William Law on January
6, 1756. "The plain meaning of the expression, 'Except a man be born of
water,' is neither more nor less than this, 'Except he be baptized.' And the
plain reason why he ought to be thus born of water is because God hath
appointed it. He hath appointed it as an outward and visible sign of an inward and spiritual grace; which grace is 'a death unto sin and a new birth
unto righteousness.'"[168]

It will perhaps help in understanding Wesley's view of baptism to recall his dynamic and experiential conception of conversion and the Christian life. Since his emphasis was on the present life of God in the soul,
Wesley could say that "[b]aptism doth now save us, if we live answerable
thereto."[169] Present evidence of the fruit of the Spirit in one's life proves
that the new birth earlier took place when the believer was baptized. Still, it
was not baptism itself, independently, that wrought the change, but the
grace of God appropriated by faith. Wesley, as John Chongnahm Cho concludes, perhaps held "both a Catholic element (baptismal regeneration in
infants) and an evangelical apprehension (emphasis on 'living faith' for
evangelical conversion in adults)," and disregarded neither of them.[170]

In sum, for Wesley baptism is an initiatory sacrament through which
we are engrafted into the new covenant of God and admitted into the Body
of Christ, the Church. Baptism is a means of grace in which free gift and
merits of the pardon are applied to us through the work of the Holy Spirit.

God begins his work of forgiveness and regeneration in our heart when in baptism we repent and believe. Through baptism we receive the gift of the Holy Spirit, through whom we begin a new life and grow throughout Christian life to maturity. Believers are to be baptized in token of their faith in Christ and are to testify their faith in Christ by being baptized. Infants should be baptized, but infant baptism is distinguished from adult baptism in that the one is a justifying and regenerating sacrament, but the other requires repentance and faith to receive new birth simultaneously in baptism. At this point Wesley's view of baptism shows a tension between the institutional and the evangelical.

In conclusion, the middle Wesley moved from formal ecclesiology to a more practical and functional understanding of ecclesiology that is controlled and justified by the need of a specific situation. During this period his interest in the church as an institution continued, but it was now in relationship of tension with the sense of mission which came to be more prominent from his conversion. Wesley, while on one hand showing his high sacramentalism, on the other developed his "evangelical pragmatism" which was embodied in the development of his Methodist societies.

The situation of England in Wesley's days and early Methodism led him to the practical ecclesiology. The lack of interest on the part of the clergy of that day in the preached gospel for saving souls led Wesley to preach to those willing to listen in any place, and to accept lay-helpers with no thought he was separating from the established church. John Whitehead, a Wesleyan biographer, says,

> Mr. Wesley was so fully convinced of the great design of a preached gospel, that if sinners were truly converted to God, and a decent order preserved in hearing the word, he thought it a matter of less consequence, whether the instrument of the good done, was a layman, or regularly ordained. And if a regularly ordained preacher did no good, and a layman by preaching did; it was easy to judge which was acting most agreeably to the design of the gospel, and most for the benefit of society. It is probable that such reflections as these had arisen in his mind on the fact before him: and his judgment was confirmed by repeated facts of the same kind which occurred. And thus he was induced to make use of the labors of laymen, on a more extensive scale than had hitherto been allowed.[171]

Then, given a man with High-Church views of the sacraments and of apostolic succession, what would cause Wesley to preach in the open air, which was not a manner of the Church of England? And what would cause such a man to begin to gather about him other men to similarly preach? Wesley's main cause for preaching in the open fields and employing unordained persons was necessity. He was first shocked at the lay-preaching of Thomas Maxfield, but he himself went for preaching in open fields and finally wound up beginning an ordination of ministers outside the established church for work in another country, as will investigated in the next chapter. The cause for these actions was necessity.

Notes

1. See Frederick Hockin, *John Wesley and Modern Methodism* (London: Rivingtons, 1887); J. Ernest Rattenbury, *The Conversion of the Wesleys: A Critical Study* (London: Epworth Press, 1938); Bowmer, *The Sacrament of the Lord's Supper in Early Methodism.*

2. James H. Rigg, *The Churchmanship of John Wesley, and the Relations of Wesleyan Methodism to the Church of England* (London: Wesleyan-Methodist Book-Room, 1886), 59.

3. Julia Wedgwood, *John Wesley and the Evangelical Reaction of the Eighteenth Century* (London: MacMillan and Co., 1870), 140.

4. Wedgwood, *John Wesley and the Evangelical Reaction of the Eighteenth Century*, 140.

5. Luke Tyerman, *Life and Times of the Rev. John Wesley, M.A., Founder of the Methodists*, 3 vols. (New York: Harper & brothers, 1872), vol. i, 95.

6. John S. Simon, *John Wesley and the Religious Societies* (London: Epworth Press, 1921), 333–334.

7. Keefer, "John Wesley: Disciple of Early Christianity," 26.

8. Keefer, "John Wesley: Disciple of Early Christianity," 25.

9. Keefer, "John Wesley: Disciple of Early Christianity," 25.

10. Gerald Bray, ed., *The Anglican Canons 1529–1947* (Woodbridge: Boydell Press, 1998), 339.

11. Wesley, Sermon "The Circumcision, of the Heart," I, 7, in *Works*, i, 405. This sermon was preached at Oxford University on January 1, 1733. After Aldersgate, Wesley realized the true meaning of the circumcision of the heart.

12. Lawson, *John Wesley and the Christian Ministry*, ix.

13. Wesley, Sermon "On God's Vineyard" (1787), I, 8, in *Works*, iii, 507.

14. Wesley, "Ought We to Separate from the Church of England?" V, 1, in *Works*, ix, 577.

15. Wesley, Sermon "The Mystery of Iniquity" (1783), 11, in *Works*, ii, 455.

16. Wesley, Sermon "Of the Church" (1785), 28, in *Works*, iii, 55–56.

17. See Wesley, Sermon "Catholic Spirit" (1750), in *Works*, ii, 81–95.

18. Robert S. Paul. *The Church in Search of Its Self* (Grand Rapids: Eerdmans Publishing Co., 1972), 123.

19. It becomes explicit in the following passage: "What is the end of all *ecclesiastical order*? Is it not to bring souls from the power of Satan to God? And to build them up in his fear and love?" See a letter to John Smith on June 25, 1746,

build them up in his fear and love?" See a letter to John Smith on June 25, 1746, in *Works*, xxvi, 206.

20. Nygren, "John Wesley's Changing Concept of the Ministry," 268–269.

21. W. Stephen Gunter, *The Limits of 'Love Divine': John Wesley's Response to Antinomianism and Enthusiasm* (Nashville: Kingswood Books, 1989), 157.

22. Gunter, *The Limits of 'Love Divine,'* 169.

23. *Works*, xix, 46.

24. Journal on Thursday, September 9, 1790, in *Works*, xxiv, 186.

25. Tyerman, *Life and Times of the Rev. John Wesley, M.A., Founder of the Methodists*, vol. i, 274–276.

26. *Works*, xix, 61, note 5.

27. *Works*, xix, 61, note 5.

28. Later Maxfield became a popular preacher and separated from Wesley in 1763 when he began to prophesy that the end of the world would fall on February 28. He then acted as an Independent minister in London. *Works*, xix, 61, note 5 and *Works*, xx, 406, note 2.

29. Clarke, *Memoirs of the Wesley Family,* 412.

30. *The Works* (Jackson), v, 516.

31. This expression is stated in the *Constitution on the Church* of the Second Vatican Council. Although it is of twentieth century, the ordained clergy in the Catholic Church, and also the Church of England, of Wesley's time was chosen to exercise the full priesthood. Cf. Article 41 of "Constitution on the Church" of Vatican II reads, "Those chosen for the fulness of the priesthood are granted the ability of exercising the perfect duty of pastoral charity by the grace of the sacrament of Orders. This perfect duty of pastoral charity is exercised in every form of episcopal care and service, prayer, sacrifice and preaching" (Floyd Anderson, ed., *Council Daybook: Vatican II, session 1–4* [Washington, D.C.: National Catholic Welfare Conference, 1965–1966], Session 3, 326).

32. *Minutes of the Methodist Conferences, from the First, Held in London by the Late Rev. John Wesley, A.M., in the Year 1744*, vol. i, 30.

In Thomas Jackson's edition, the answer is "as extraordinary messengers, (that is, out of ordinary way,) designed, (1.) To provoke the regular Ministers to jealousy. (2.) To supply their lack of service toward those who are perishing for want of knowledge" ["Minutes of Several Conversations between the Rev. Mr. Wesley and Others from the Year 1744, to the Year 1780," in *The Works* (Jackson), viii, 309].

In his sermon "Prophets and Priests" (1789), Wesley also remembers that when he held his very first conference with his preachers in 1744, "that question was proposed, 'In what light are we to consider ourselves?' it was answered, "As *extraordinary messengers*, raised up to provoke the *ordinary* ones to jealousy'" (*Works*, iv, 79).

33. Wesley, Sermon "Prophets and Priests," 12, in *Works*, iv, 80.

34. Wesley, Sermon "Prophets and Priests," 13, in *Works*, iv, 80.

35. Wesley, Sermon "Prophets and Priests," 11, in *Works*, iv, 79.

36. Wesley, Sermon "Prophets and Priests," 10, in *Works*, iv, 79.

37. In Wesley's days in England, sacramental leadership required ordination, and Wesley admitted and insisted on this condition till his last days.

38. Wesley, Sermon "Prophets and Priests," 14, in *Works*, iv, 80.

39. It is most likely that the term "ecumenical" was not used in the eighteenth century. Accordingly, here we deliberately use our own contemporary label to describe a unique eighteenth-century Methodist phenomenon.

40. *Works*, ix, 256. In "A plain Account of the People Called Methodists" (1749), Wesley spoke of the origin of the United Societies: "Above ten years ago my brother and I were desired to preach in many parts of London. . . . Thus arose . . . what was afterwards called a *Society*—a very innocent name, and very common in London for any number of people *associating* themselves together" (*Works*, ix, 254–256). December 27, 1739 is the most probable date for the beginning of the United Societies, though there is no entry under this date in Wesley's *Journal*. Prior to this date he had been a prominent member of Fetter Lane Society, London, founded May 1, 1738. The Society was dominated by the Moravians. When he withdrew from this Society, he organized a society of his own in London. Later he organized another at Bristol.

41. Wesley, Sermon "Prophets and Priests," 21, in *Works*, iv, 83.

42. Wesley, Sermon "Prophets and Priests," 21, in *Works*, iv, 84.

43. John C. Bowmer, *The Wesleyan Doctrine of the Ministry: A Lecture Delivered on April 15, 1970 at Perkins School of Theology* (Dallas: Southern Methodist University, 1970), 9–10.

44. *Minutes of the Methodist Conferences, from the First, Held in London by the Late Rev. John Wesley, A.M., in the Year 1744*, vol. i, 78–79.

45. *Minutes of the Methodist Conferences, from the First, Held in London by the Late Rev. John Wesley, A.M., in the Year 1744*, vol. i, 30.

46. *Minutes of the Methodist Conferences, from the First, Held in London by the Late Rev. John Wesley, A.M., in the Year 1744*, vol. i, 30–31.

47. *Minutes of the Methodist Conferences, from the First, Held in London by the Late Rev. John Wesley, A.M., in the Year 1744*, vol. i, 30–31.

48. *Minutes of the Methodist Conferences, from the First, Held in London by the Late Rev. John Wesley, A.M., in the Year 1744*, vol. i, 23.

49. John Beecham, *An Essay on the Constitution of Wesleyan Methodism, in Which Various Misrepresentations of Some of Its Leading Principles Are Exposed, and Its Present Form Is Vindicated* (London: John Mason, 1851), 85.

50. John 20:23, in *Explanatory Notes upon the New Testament*, 387.

51. Wesley, Sermon "On Obedience to Pastors," 1, in *Works*, iii, 374.

52. *Works*, iii, 374.

53. It was stated in the 1766 Conference at Leeds. *Minutes of the Methodist Conferences, from the First, Held in London by the Late Rev. John Wesley, A.M., in the Year 1744*, vol. i, 61.

54. *Works*, iii, 374.

55. *Works*, iii, 374.

56. *Works*, xviii, 248.

57. *Works*, xviii, 249–250.

58. Stoeffler, "Tradition and Renewal in the Ecclesiology of John Wesley," 312.

59. *Works*, xviii, 219.

60. Journal on October 14, 1738, in *Works*, xix, 17.

61. *Works*, xix, 122.

62. *Works*, xix, 97.

63. Cf. *Works*, xviii, 279–280.

64. *Works*, xix, 96.

65. Journal on November 10, 1739, in *Works*, xix, 120–121.

66. *Works*, xix, 121.

67. *Works*, xix, 132–133.

68. *Works*, xix, 147.

69. Journal on June 28, 1740, in *Works*, xix, 159.

70. See his journal on June 3, 1766, in *Works*, xxiii, 19–20.

71. *Works*, xix, 158.

72. Scott J. Jones, *United Methodist Doctrine: The Extreme Center* (Nashville: Abingdon Press, 2002), 242–243.

73. Wesley, "An Earnest Appeal to Men of Reason and Religion," in *Works*, xi, 78.

74. Wesley, Sermon "The Means of Grace," V, 4, in *Works*, i, 396–397.

75. *Works*, i, 395–396.

76. *Works*, i, 396–397.

77. *Works*, i, 381.

78. *Works*, i, 381.

79. *Works*, i, 382.

80. *Works*, i, 388.

81. *Works*, i, 379.

82. Canon VIII of the Trent Council (Seventh Session), against the Protestants who say that the sacraments don't confer grace on the recipients *ex opere operato* (i.e., by means of the work done), proclaimed that some benefit is conveyed by the sacraments even when not received in conscious faith. This canon represents the position of Roman Catholicism. See George D. Smith, ed., *The Teaching of the Catholic Church: A Summary of Catholic Doctrine*, 2 vols. (New York: Macmillan, 1949), vol., ii, 755–758; Richard P. McBrien, *Catholicism* (Minneapolis: Winston Press, 1981), 736–743.

83. Wesley, Sermon "The Means of Grace," V, 4, in *Works*, i, 396.

84. *Works*, i, 378.

85. Journal on May 25, 1742, in *Works*, xix, 267–268.

86. *Works*, xx, 101.

87. *Works*, xix, 157.

88. *Works*, ix, 263.

89. *The Works* (Jackson), viii, 323.

90. *Works*, xxii., 430 and *Works*, xxiv, 164.

91. For an analysis of Wesley's personal practice of the Lord's Supper, see Bowmer, *The Sacrament of the Lord's Supper in Early Methodism*, 49–61. Wesley

communicated, on average, once every four or five days throughout his ministerial life.

92. Wesley, Sermon "Upon our Lord's Sermon on the Mount, VI," II, 11, in *Works*, i, 585.

93. For instance, see his journal on June 27, 1740, in *Works*, xix, 158.

94. Wesley, Sermon "The Duty of Constant Communion," in *Works*, iii, 428–439.

95. *Works*, xix, 159.

96. *The Poetical Works of John and Charles Wesley: Reprinted from the Originals, with the Last Corrections of the Authors; Together with the Poems of Charles Wesley Not Before Published.* Collected and arranged by G. Osborn, 13 vols. (London: Wesleyan-Methodist Conference Office, 1869), vol. iii, 186. Hereafter *The Poetical Works*.

97. I Cor. 11:24, in *Explanatory Notes upon the New Testament*, 620.

98. Mark 14:24, in *Explanatory Notes upon the New Testament*, 187.

99. *Explanatory Notes upon the New Testament*, 286.

100. *Explanatory Notes upon the New Testament*, 286.

101. Wesley, "A Roman Catechism, Faithfully Drawn out of the Allowed Writings of the Church of Rome. With a Reply Thereto," in *The Works* (Jackson), x, 118–119.

102. In fact, Zwingli and Calvin had much in common in their view of the Lord's Supper. Zwingli did not deny that Christ is spiritually present in the Lord's Supper while he saw the sacrament as primarily an act of commemoration, a memorial to Christ's death with no supernatural change in the elements. But Calvin saw Christ's real, spiritual presence in the elements. For him the elements were not changed but Christ was present by "virtue," or through the power, of the Holy Spirit. In doing so, Calvin maintained a more emphasis on the spiritual reception in the Lord's Supper.

103. *Works*, xix, 159.

104. Wesley, "The Christian Sacrament and Sacrifice," in *The Poetical Works*, iii, 186.

105. Wesley, Sermons "Justification by Faith," I, 7, "The End of Christ's Coming," II, 6, and "Spiritual Worship," I, 7, in *Works*, i, 186, *Works*, ii, 480, and *Works*, iii, 93; also Wesley, "A Second Dialogue Between an Antinomian and His Friend," in *The Works* (Jackson), x, 277. This expression was Wesley's paraphrase from "The Communion" of *Book of Common Prayer*. In the *Book of Common Prayer* (1662) it was originally "by his one oblation of himself once offered...a full, perfect, and sufficient sacrifice, oblation, and satisfaction, for the sins of the whole world." See *The Book of Common Prayer: 1662 Version*, 156.

106. Dom Gregory Dix, *The Shape of the Liturgy* (London: Dacre Press, 1975), 161.

107. Bowmer, *The Sacrament of the Lord's Supper in Early Methodism*, 178–179.

108. *Explanatory Notes upon the New Testament*, 621.

109. *The Poetical Works*, iii, 203–204.

110. Wesley, Sermon "The Means of Grace," IV, 2, in *Works*, i, 391.

111. *Canons and Decrees of the Council of Trent; Original Text with English Translation by H. J. Schroeder* (St. Louis, Mo.: B. Herder Book Co., 1941), 149.

112. Wesley, "A Roman Catechism, Faithfully Drawn out of the Allowed Writings of the Church of Rome. With a Reply Thereto," in *The Works* (Jackson), x, 118.

113. John and Charles Wesley, "Hymns on the Lord's Supper," Hymn LXIII, in *The Poetical Works*, iii, 262; J. Ernest Rattenbury, *The Eucharistic Hymns of John and Charles Wesley: To Which Is Appended Wesley's Preface Extracted from Brevint's Christian Sacrament and Sacrifice Together with Hymns on the Lord's Supper*, ed. by Timothy J. Crouch (Cleveland, OH: OSL Publications, 1990), H-21.

114. John and Charles Wesley, "Hymns on the Lord's Supper," Hymn CXVI, in *The Poetical Works*, iii, 302; Rattenbury, *The Eucharistic Hymns of John and Charles Wesley*, H-38.

115. John and Charles Wesley, "Hymns for Our Lord's Resurrection," Hymn VI, in *The Poetical Works*, iv, 137.

116. Wesley, "A Roman Catechism, Faithfully Drawn out of the Allowed Writings of the Church of Rome. With a Reply Thereto," in *The Works* (Jackson), x, 121.

117. Bowmer, *The Sacrament of the Lord's Supper in Early Methodism*, 87.

118. The First Book of 1549 included the so-called "usages of the Non-Jurors." The nonjurors insisted on the sequence—Account of the Institution, Oblation, and then Invocation. Wesley publicly used the 1662 Book for a time, but restored the usages from 1549 Book, because of which he was accused of "inverting the order and method of the Liturgy" in August 1737. Wesley put them in the order taken by the nonjurors from the Apostolical Constitutions. See Frederick Hunter, *John Wesley and the Coming Comprehensive Church* (London: Epworth Press, 1968), 34.

119. *The First Prayer-Book of King Edward VI 1549, Reprinted from a Copy in the British Museum* (London: Griffith Farran Okeden & Welsh, 1888), 203.

120. *The Book of Common Prayer: 1662 Version*, 156.

121. John and Charles Wesley, "Hymns on the Lord's Supper," Hymn LXXII, in *The Poetical Works*, iii, 266; Rattenbury, *The Eucharistic Hymns of John and Charles Wesley*, H-23. The word "realize" in line 2 would be better to read "make real."

122. Wesley, Sermon "The Means of Grace," V, 4, in *Works*, i, 396.

123. Wesley, "The Christian Sacrament and Sacrifice," in *The Poetical Works*, iii, 205–206. Here Wesley rejects the so-called "cheap grace."

124. *The Poetical Works*, iii, 186.

125. Bowmer, *The Sacrament of the Lord's Supper in Early Methodism*, 185.

126. Journal on June 27, 1740, in *Works*, xix, 158.

127. For example, see journals on September 12, 1773 and on October 2, 1784, in *Works*, xxii, 389 and *Works*, xxiii, 333.

128. Rigg, *The Churchmanship of John Wesley, and the Relations of Wesleyan Methodism to the Church of England*, 42.

129. The treatise teaches "baptismal regeneration" after the mildest type of the doctrine, and much as it had been taught by the Puritan divines of the Church of England.

130. Henry Carter, *The Methodist Heritage* (Nashville: Abingdon-Cokesbury Press, 1951), 159.

131. Cannon, *The Theology of John Wesley, With Special Reference to the Doctrine of Justification*, 127.

132. Wesley, "A Treatise on Baptism," in *The Works* (Jackson), x, 188; Matt. 3:15–16, in *Explanatory Notes Upon the New Testament*, 24–25.

133. Wesley, "A Treatise on Baptism," in *The Works* (Jackson), x, 193.

134. *The Works* (Jackson), x, 188.

135. *The Works* (Jackson), x, 191.

136. *The Works* (Jackson), x, 191–192.

137. *The Works* (Jackson), x, 191.

138. Col. 2:12, in *Explanatory Notes Upon the New Testament*, 746.

139. *Explanatory Notes Upon the New Testament*, 540.

140. Gal. 3:27, in *Explanatory Notes Upon the New Testament*, 690.

141. Col. 2:12, in *Explanatory Notes Upon the New Testament*, 746.

142. Wesley, "A Treatise on Baptism," in *The Works* (Jackson), x, 188.

143. *The Works* (Jackson), x, 189f.

144. *Explanatory Notes Upon the New Testament*, 138.

145. Wesley, "A Treatise on Baptism," in *The Works* (Jackson), x, 193–198.

146. *The Works* (Jackson), x, 198.

147. *The Works* (Jackson), x, 191.

148. For this subject, see John Chongnahm, Cho, "John Wesley's View on Baptism," *Wesleyan Theological Journal* 7, no. 1 (Spring 1972): 60–73. For the classical summary of Wesley's teaching on baptismal regeneration see Wesley's "A Treatise on Baptism," and on non-baptismal regeneration his sermon "'The New Birth," which he first published in 1760 though probably preached much earlier.

149. Baker, *John Wesley and the Church of England*, 155–156.

150. Wesley, Sermon "The New Birth," IV, 2, in *Works*, ii, 197.

151. Journal on May 24, 1738, in *Works*, xviii, 242–243.

152. Wesley, Sermon "The New Birth," IV, 2, in *Works*, ii, 197.

153. *Works*, xix, 32.

154. Wesley, "A Farther Appeal to Men of Reason and Religion," part i, II, 4, in *Works*, xi, 111.

155. Wesley, Sermon "The New Birth," IV, 1, in *Works*, ii, 196.

156. *Works*, ii, 197–198.

157. Col. 2:12, in *Explanatory Notes Upon the New Testament*, 746.

158. Wesley, Sermon "The Marks of the New Birth," IV, 5, in *Works*, i, 430.

159. Wesley, Sermon "Of the Church," in *Works*, iii, 49; Eph. 4:5, in *Explanatory Notes Upon the New Testament*, 712.

160. Wesley, "A Treatise on Baptism," in *The Works* (Jackson), x, 191.

161. *The Works* (Jackson), x, 190.

162. *The Works* (Jackson), x, 190, 192.

163. *The Works* (Jackson), x, 192.

164. *The Works* (Jackson), x, 192.

165. John 3:5, in *Explanatory Notes Upon the New Testament*, 311; "A Farther Appeal to Men of Reason and Religion," part i, I, 5, in *Works*, xi, 107.

166. Eph. 5:26, in *Explanatory Notes Upon the New Testament*, 719.

167. *Works*, xxvi, 425.

168. *Letters*, iii, 357.

169. Wesley, "A Treatise on Baptism," in *The Works* (Jackson), x, 192.

170. John Chongnahm, Cho, "John Wesley's View on Baptism," 65.

171. John Whitehead, *The Life of the Rev. John Wesley, M. A.: Some Time Fellow of Lincoln College, Oxford. Collected from His Private Papers and Printed Works; and Written at the Request of His Executors. To Which is Prefixed Some Account of His Ancestors and Relations; with the Life of the Rev. Charles Wesley, M. A . Collected from His Private Journal, and Never before Published. The Whole Forming a History of Methodism, in Which the Principles and Economy of the Methodists are Unfolded* (Boston: Dow & Jackson, 1845), 371.

Chapter 6

Ecclesiology of the Later Wesley

Examining the development of ecclesiology in the later Wesley is of great importance. During this period, there were many crucial actions and steps for Wesley himself and Methodism. Wesley approved some female preaching though not generally, and became acutely aware of the need for ordained Methodist clergy to administer the sacraments, administrate the Methodist societies, and perpetuate the movement in America. "Not by choice, but necessity" he ordained two ministers for the ministry in America in 1784. This action transformed Methodism from an ancillary movement within the Church of England to an autonomous ecclesiastical body in the United States. Subsequently Wesley ordained Methodist ministers for Ireland, Scotland, and England, and after the ordinations, Methodism eventually needed to depend upon no other ministry than their own to satisfy the ecclesiastical needs of their people including the administration of the sacraments.

Principle of Necessity

Throughout his life, Wesley continued to hold to the Articles of the Church of England, and in particular to its definition of the church militant: "The visible church is a congregation of faithful men, in which the pure word of God is preached, and the sacraments be duly administered."[1] However, late in his life, the concept of "congregation of faithful men" was significantly redefined. No longer was this phrase understood in terms of sacramental rites or birthright privileges alone. Rather the church must be seen as the congregation of "men endued with 'living faith.'"[2]

In relation to the doctrine of church "professed, taught, and believed by the People called Methodists, in connection with the late Rev. Mr. John Wesley," William Hobrow wrote,

> Q. 36. *What, and where is the visible Church of Jesus Christ?*
> A. The visible Church of Christ is dispersed throughout the whole World, and is the different Congregations of justified Believers, where the pure Doctrines of Jesus Christ, according to the Scriptures are preached; either on a Mountain, (Mat. v.) Sea Shore, in the Street, Lane, Village, Ship, or House; and no other is the Church of Christ, either in Europe, Asia, Africa, or America.[3]

The church exists where there are congregations of justified believers regardless of place and time. This view is also reflected in Wesley's sermons. In the sermon "The Mystery of Iniquity" (1783), Wesley says,

> Here was the dawn of the proper gospel day. Here was a proper Christian church. . . . He [Christ] not only taught that religion which is the true 'healing of the soul', but effectually planted it in the earth; filling the souls of all that believed in him with *righteousness*, gratitude to God, and goodwill to man, attended with a *peace* that surpassed all understanding, and with *joy* unspeakable and full of glory.[4]

In the sermon "Of the Church" (1785), he continues,

> I dare not exclude from the church catholic all those congregations in which any unscriptural doctrines which cannot be affirmed to be 'the pure Word of God' are sometimes, yea, frequently preached. Neither all those congregations in which the sacraments are 'duly administered.' . . . Whoever they are that have 'one Spirit, one hope, one Lord, one faith, one God, and Father of all', I . . . include them within the pale of the catholic church.[5]

For the later Wesley, the true members of the true church are not found in terms of sacramental rites, modes of worship or doctrines but in those who have living faith and live holy lives.

The sermon "Of the Church" was written in response to critics who saw him as antagonistic to institutional Christianity. His emphasis throughout the sermon is on the spiritual character of the constituents of the church, and not its organizational structure. His premise is, "[t]he catholic or universal church is all the persons in the universe whom God hath so called out of the world . . . as to be 'one body', united by 'one spirit'; having 'one faith, one hope, one baptism; one God and Father of all, who is above all, and through all, and in them all.'"[6] Wesley further elaborates the evangelical aspect of each term, relating the Spirit to the work of regeneration, faith to personal trust in the gospel, and baptism to the inward assurance of the transforming work of grace in the believer. He concludes that all those whose character conforms to these evangelical criteria are members of the church of saints or the true church.

This evangelical view of church led Wesley to respond to the situations according to the needs of mission. For the understanding of the later Wesley's ecclesiology, one must take care to understand his principle of necessity. Edgar W. Thompson lists four principles guiding Wesley's spiritual life and theology:

(1) Acceptance of the Holy Scriptures as the Rule of Faith and Practice;
(2) Reverence for the usages of the Primitive Church;
(3) A warm and unquenchable love for the Church of England, and especially for her Doctrines and Liturgy, as these are to be found in the *Book of Common Prayer* and the *Homilies*;
(4) A constant and unshakable conviction that God had commanded him to proclaim the Good News of Salvation to all whom he could reach, and had appointed him to care for the souls of those who were converted under the preaching of himself and his 'Helpers.'"[7]

To these four, one may add the principle of necessity. In a letter to Nicholas Norton on September 3, 1756, Wesley clearly declares,

I act on one and the same principle. . . . My principle (frequently declared) is this: 'I submit to every ordinance of man wherever I do not conceive there is an absolute necessity for acting contrary to it.' Consistently with this I do tolerate lay-preaching, because I conceive there is an absolute necessity for it; inasmuch as, were it not, thousands of souls would perish everlastingly. Yet I do not tolerate lay-administering, because I do not conceive there is any such necessity for it; seeing it does not appear that, if this is not at all, one soul will perish for want of it.[8]

This statement shows that for Wesley, where the salvation of soul is demanded, there is a necessity. If there is an absolute necessity, he was ready to follow even irregularities.

At the end of his career Wesley wrote a summary of his relations with the Church of England: "we have in a course of years, out of necessity not choice, slowly and warily varied in some points of discipline by preaching in the fields, by extemporaneous prayer, by employing lay preachers, by forming and regulating societies, and by holding yearly Conferences. But we did none of these things till we were convinced we could no longer omit them but at the peril of our souls."[9] This passage is important not only because it points to Wesley's great sense of mission, but because it points to the fact that in the deepest sense ecclesiastical authority is now found in the needs of the mission, though the usages and ordinances, and the doctrine and the discipline of the Church of England continue to be respected.

The principle of necessity developed in Wesley in parallel to the development of the Methodist movement. Wesley tended to operate on the basis of priority of beliefs or a scale of doctrinal and ecclesiastical values, the more important taking precedence over and confirming or negating the less important. For him all the regulations concerning church-government, ordination, and the like were subservient to the effectiveness of mission. On June 25, 1746, Wesley wrote to John Smith:

> I would inquire, What is the end of all *ecclesiastical order*? Is it not to bring souls from the power of Satan to God? And to build them up in His fear and love? *Order*, then, is so far valuable as it answers these ends; and if it answers them not it is nothing worth. . . . And, indeed, wherever the knowledge and love of God are, *true order* will not be wanting. But the most *apostolic order* where these are not is less than nothing and vanity.[10]

Whatever facilitated saving souls seemed tight to Wesley.

For that reason, although he supported the episcopal form of church-government which he thought agrees with the practice and writings of the apostles, Wesley believed that "several who are not episcopally ordained are nevertheless called of God to preach the gospel."[11] In a letter to James Clark on September 18, 1756, he said,

> Concerning diocesan Episcopacy, there are several questions which I should be glad to have answered: as (1) Where is it prescribed in Scripture? (2) How does it appear that the Apostles settled it in all the Churches which they planted? (3) How does it appear they settled it in any so as to make it of perpetual obligation? It is allowed that Christ and His Apostles settled the Church under some form of government. But (i) Did they put all Churches under the same precise form? If they did, (ii) Can you prove this to be the precise form and the very same which now obtains in England?[12]

This statement indicates the pragmatic bent of Wesley's concern. He was preparing himself to take any action that he deemed wise and expedient in the furtherance of his mission and in the propagation of the gospel. For

Wesley, where mission is demanded, there is a necessity. And if the necessity requires an irregularity, he was willing to follow it: "I will not separate from the Church; yet . . . in cases of necessity I will vary from it."[13]

As Edgar Thompson describes, "his principle of *Necessity* had carried him beyond obedience to the rule of the Anglican Church, and . . . he had taken to himself a power of consecration which his Church did not allow."[14] Writing on the event where he had ordained Thomas Coke and other two lay preachers in 1784, Wesley himself said a year later, "These are the steps which, not of choice, but necessity, I have slowly and deliberately taken. If any one is pleased to call this separating from the Church, he may."[15]

The circumstances forced the Methodist movement to move toward becoming an autonomous ecclesiastical body. He wrote to a friend on September 20, 1788:

> Those ministers (so called) who neither live nor preach the gospel I dare not say are sent of God. Where one of these is settled, many of the Methodists dare not attend his ministry; so, if there be no other church in that neighborhood, they go to church no more. This is the case in a few places already, and it will be the case in more; and no one can justly blame me for this, neither is it contrary to any of my professions.[16]

What had been a partial and restricted ministry during the early and middle years of Wesley's career became a full and unrestricted ministry during his later years, for the Methodist movement itself, at least in one of its major geographical segments, became a church. The Methodist movement became an autonomous ecclesiastical body, as independent and as competitive for members as any other existing denomination. That which Wesley had earlier disallowed in regard both to his preachers and to his societies, disclaiming for the former sacramental rights and for the latter ecclesiastical status, he not only allowed and sanctioned but also he in some sense took the initiative in causing to happen. Wesley's rationale for it was necessity. Here circumstances dictated policy, and theology defined a situation which had already been brought about by a practical man's response to the pressure of events.

Wesley and Women Preachers

In his book *John Wesley and the Women Preachers of Early Methodism*, Paul Wesley Chilcote described the theological transformation of Wesley from an early strict position against female preaching to its most influential

defender.[17] Chilcote is correct to identify the evolution of Wesley's attitude
towards female preaching. Wesley's attitude towards the ministry of women
particularly on preaching was a result of a series of influence and evolution
of thought in parallel to the development of the Methodist movement within
his ministry through the years. And in such an evolution was working the
principle of necessity.

Certainly Wesley did more for women than what others did during his
time. From the early period of his ministry for the Methodist movement, he
had positive attitudes towards women's ministry. Wesley organized a system for visiting of the sick, which was reminiscent of his ministry in Georgia wherein he appointed women as visitors to the sick. This role found
prominence among Methodist women. The importance of the role of women
in performing such ministry is well reflected in Wesley's commentary on
Romans 16:1: "*I commend unto you Phoebe*—The bearer of this letter. *A
servant*—The Greek word is a *deaconess. Of the church in Cenchrea*—In
the apostolic age, some grave and pious women were appointed deacon-
esses in every church. It was their office, not to teach publicly, but to visit
the sick, the women in particular, and to minister to them both in their temporal and spiritual necessities."[18]

Aside from visiting chores, avenues that supplemented the spiritual
growth of women were bands and classes. To some women, leading prayers
within these meetings was their first exposure to public speaking. Women
proved to be "highly gifted" in the art of prayer. And to some women, praying was not just confined in the meetings. It evolved into some form of
ministry for them as they went out visiting people and praying for them.

As Methodism flourished, sometimes at their own initiative, women
have been at the forefront of pioneering societies. From the earliest years of
the Wesleyan revival, a motto of John Wesley's theology was "plain truth
for plain people." For Wesley an "ideal Methodist must speak plain English
so that . . . the dairymaid might be as much at home in hearing the word as
were the dons of Oxford . . . on such terms she could come to her class, and
give her experience with no shame for her rustic speech, and no embar-
rassment."[19] Unlike some other societies organized before Wesley's time in
England, from the beginning Wesley's societies admitted women. Women
actually outnumbered men. When Wesley formed the Foundery Society in
London after breaking-up with the Moravians of Fetter Lane Society, forty-
seven or forty-eight women from Fetter Lane, almost twice the number of
male followers, joined Wesley.[20] As Wesley broke down the society into
the more intimate "classes," women naturally became leaders. From as
early as 1742 female class leaders were appointed at the Foundery.

Women as well as men were encouraged to speak of their spiritual life in public worship and to exhort fellow Methodists to faith and repentance. Some popular women evangelists like Ann Cutler, Hester Ann Roe, and Sarah Crosby enjoyed such a reputation for holiness that their lives were made the subject of devotional works. Consequently, those women assumed leadership roles within the Methodist movement.

To understand Wesley's view of the women's leadership in Methodism, the role of Wesley's mother, Susanna, is particularly of importance. With the model of his mother as a "preacher of righteousness," Wesley seems to have appointed women as leaders of classes in Bristol as early as 1739. It is clear that Wesley did not consider class or gender to be appropriate criteria for leadership. Criteria for the role of women were also formed by Wesley's vision of "primitive Christianity." He used the authority of the New Testament to validate the role of women in ministry. Wesley addressed women in one of his sermons:

> Let all you that have [it] in your power assert the right which the God of nature has given you. Yield not to [that] vile bondage any longer! You, as well as men, are rational creatures. You, like them, were made in the image of God; you are equally candidates for immortality; you too are called of God, as you have time, to "do good unto all men [sic]" . . . It is well known, that, in the primitive Church, there were women particularly appointed for this work [visiting the sick]. Indeed there was one or more such in every Christian congregation under heaven. They were then termed Deaconesses, that is, servants; servants of the church and of its great Master.[21]

However, despite his positive attitudes towards women's ministry, up to the middle period of his ministry Wesley still maintained a strict stance against female preaching. As an example, when the female-friendly atmosphere brought Methodism into comparison with the Quakers as it was accused of harboring female preachers, Wesley was quick to deny such allegations. In an effort to dissociate the movement from such an accusation, in 1747–1748 Wesley published *A Letter to a Person Lately Joined with the People Called Quakers*. Here he made an argument against the Quaker's approval of female preaching based from the biblical texts which cites speaking and prophesying by women. Wesley asked, "Very good. But how do you prove that prophesying in any of these places means preaching?"[22] For Wesley, prophesying as mentioned in the Bible is different from preaching. He actually dispelled any possibility of using these texts in defense of female preaching.

Despite the innovations already accorded in favor of the female adherents of Methodism for the years, Wesley dismissed allegations that the Methodists have female preachers. It is clearly shown in his *A Second Letter to the Author of The Enthusiasm of Methodists and Papists Compar'd* (1751). Responding to the accusation that "*[w]omen and boys* are actually employed in this ministry of *public preaching*" among the Methodists, Wesley asked, "Please to tell me where? I know them not, nor ever heard of them before."[23] This response shows how uncomfortable Wesley was to see Methodism being branded as such.

Moreover, in his commentary on the often-referred text against female preaching, wherein the Apostle Paul commanded that "Let a woman learn in silence with all subjection" as he prohibited them to teach, Wesley affirmed that "public teaching" is not for women to do for it usurps the authority over men. Referring to Eve's persuasion of Adam to sin in Genesis 3, Wesley also said that the "preceding verse showed why a woman should not 'usurp authority over the man': this shows why she ought not 'to teach.' She is more easily deceived, and more easily deceives."[24]

However, these allegations are not to deny the importance of the role of women in Wesleyan revival. Even before women were permitted to preach, they clearly "gained the respect and admiration of Wesley's followers as the pioneers, the sustainers, and martyrs of the Methodist cause."[25]

Wesley's thought took some form of a shift during the third decade of the Wesleyan movement as sharing of experiences by both men and women developed within the meetings. Within the intimate bands and love-feasts, women would find themselves testifying the inner joy wrought by a personal experience of Christ. During one of his usual meetings with the bands at the Foundery, January 30, 1761, Wesley affirmed that God can also use women in touching people's hearts: "While a poor woman was speaking a few artless words out of the fullness of her heart, a fire kindled and ran as flame among the stubble, through the hearts of almost all that heard—so when God is pleased to work it matters not how weak or how mean the instrument!"[26] As such spiritual experiences of women developed, the sharing of their stories naturally led to the making of appeals. It was natural that testimonies would somehow expand. This expansion would eventually take the shape of something similar to exhortation or even preaching.

The problem of female preaching arose in the class meetings. In the class meetings, women leaders were constrained in certain degrees but they faced the situations that forced them to go beyond the set-forth boundaries. Highlighted in this kind of dilemma was Sarah Crosby. She came close to preaching on two occasions in February, 1761 when faced with a large audience. Crosby requested Wesley's advice and Wesley responded:

I think you have not gone too far. You could not well do less. I apprehend all you can do more is, when you meet again, to tell them simply, "You lay me under a great difficulty. The Methodists do not allow of women Preachers: Neither do I take upon me any such character. But I will just nakedly tell you what is in my heart." . . . I do not see that you have broken any law. Go on calmly and steadily. If you have time, you may read to them the Notes on any chapter before you speak a few words; or one of the most awakening sermons, as other women have done long ago.[27]

This response shows Wesley's understanding of how far should a female exhorter should go. Though he found nothing wrong with Mrs. Crosby's action, still he made it clear that the Methodists do not allow female preaching.

Eight years later, Wesley still held on with the same understanding as he cautioned Mrs. Crosby in a letter dated March 18, 1769.

I advise you, as I did Grace Walton formerly, 1. Pray in private or public, as much as you can. 2. Even in public, you may properly enough intermix short exhortations with prayer; but keep as far from what is called preaching as you can: Therefore never take a text; never speak in a continued discourse, without some break, above four or five minutes. Tell the people, "We shall have another prayer-meeting at such a time and place."[28]

At this point, nothing changed much with Wesley's view. However, he drew a clearer line by implying that to take a text from the Scriptures or to continually speak beyond four or five minutes without any break is already qualified as preaching. Thus, if situations necessitated the need to speak more, Wesley advised that it is better to schedule a next meeting instead of wandering into preaching.

Two years later, however, Wesley's thinking and attitude toward female preachers took a leap. In an often-quoted letter to Mary Bosanquet written in June 13, 1771, Wesley claimed that some women possess an "extraordinary call" from God that exempts them from "ordinary rules of discipline." Wesley says:

I think the strength of the cause rests there—on your having an *extraordinary* call. So I am persuaded has every one of our lay preachers; otherwise I could not countenance his preaching at all. It is plain to me that the whole work of God termed Methodism is an extraordinary dispensation of His providence. Therefore I do not wonder if several things occur therein which do not fall under the ordinary rules of discipline. St. Paul's ordinary rule was, 'I permit not a woman to speak in the congregation.' Yet in extraordinary cases he made a few exceptions; at Corinth in particular.[29]

This statement is monumental in that it showed Wesley's affirmation of the extraordinary call which is in Ms. Bosanquet. Likewise, it affirmed the possibility of the existence of the same extraordinary call among the other women leaders as well. The letter also served to remind Wesley that it was by this same reason that he appointed lay preachers in the first place.

Randy L. Maddox is right in suggesting that Wesley came to regard his revival as an "extraordinary" event, which would then account for his leniency in letting women preach.[30] In the note on I Corinthians 14:34 Wesley said that women may speak in the churches if "they are under an extraordinary impulse of the Spirit."[31] By this note Wesley already implied that women may preach in extraordinary cases.

As approaching the later period of his ministry, as Chilcote suggests, theologically Wesley seems to have formulated a more charismatic view of ministry, which emphasized inward inspiration over institutional authority. Wesley prized "the value of individual souls, the possibility of direct communion with God" over church hierarchy.[32] In this theological climate, women were allowed to take on public religious roles in praying bands, class meetings, and love-feasts. Many also served as informal "exhorters" who offered personal spiritual reflections after preachers finished their sermons. As Chilcote explains, the line between exhorting and preaching was thin, and by the 1760s, there were scores of women preaching in Methodist churches across the countryside. At last, in 1787, four years before Wesley's death, women's fate with regards to the right to preach was finally sealed when he gave an official authorization to Sarah Mallet. The Assistant of the Manchester Conference (1787), by order of Wesley and the Conference, wrote and delivered a permission slip to Mallet: "We give the right hand of fellowship to Sarah Mallet, and shall have no objection to her being a preacher in our connexion so long as she continues to preach the Methodist Doctrine and attends to our Discipline. . . . [N.B.] You receive this by order of Mr. Wesley and the Conference."[33] This permission was limited to one circuit under provision to allow "outside" preachers within one circuit for one year, but it was a landmark step for female preaching in the Methodist movement.

While Wesley did not approve of the formal ordination of women, he did name them to serve as class leaders, lay preachers, and evangelists. In conclusion, his attitude and thought of female preaching changed or developed with a series of progression through the years, and, ultimately, in the later period of his ministry, Wesley approved of female preaching by necessity and its fruits.

The Problem of Ordination

Perhaps we should have begun the discussion of the problem of ordination with the middle Wesley. Wesley wrestled with this issue at least as early as the 1740s. In his later period, however, we can more clearly see Wesley's theological transformation or evolution concerning the issue of ordination.

Influence of King and Stillingfleet

Like the case of female preaching, Wesley's view of ordination was a result of a series of influence and evolution of thought in parallel to the development of the Methodist movement within his ministry through the years. There is evidence that long before 1784, Wesley thought about the problem of ordination, particularly in relation to presbyterial ordination. For instance, on September 24, 1755 Wesley had written to Samuel Walker, "is it lawful for presbyters circumstanced as we are to appoint other ministers?" and answered his own question later in October of that year in a letter to Thomas Adam:

> It is not clear to us that presbyters, so circumstanced as we are, may *appoint* or *ordain* others; but it is, that we may *direct*, as well as *suffer*, them to do what we conceive they are 'moved to by the Holy Ghost'. It is true that in *ordinary* cases both an *inward* and an *outward* call are requisite. But we apprehend there is something far from 'ordinary' in the present case. And upon the calmest view of things, we think they who are only called of God, and not of man, have *more* right to preach than they who are only called of man, and not of God. Now that many of the clergy, though called of man, are not called of God to preach his Gospel, is undeniable: (1). Because they themselves utterly disclaim, nay, and ridicule the inward call. (2). Because they do not know what the gospel is; of consequence they *do not* and *cannot* preach it.[34]

By this statement Wesley probably was referring to the fact that he understood his own mission primarily as that of an extraordinary minister, called forth by God to help remedy the insufficiencies of the ordinary ministry of the established church.

With respect to the matter of the ordination, the middle Wesley was greatly influenced by Lord Peter King (1669–1734) and Bishop Edward Stillingfleet (1635–1699).[35] As early as January 20, 1746 Wesley read King's *An Enquiry into the Constitution, Discipline, Unity, and Worship of the Primitive Church*.[36] In his book King argued that although the presbyters were the bishops' curates and assistants, and so inferior to them in the actual exercise of their ecclesiastical commission . . . yet, notwithstanding, they had the same inherent right with the bishops, and so were not of a distinct specific order from them . . . the presbyters were different from the bishops *in gradu*, or in degree; but yet . . . They were equal to them *in ordine*, or in order.[37]

King's book became an instrument of breaking down some High-Church prejudices of Wesley. Just three weeks ago Wesley had defended a version of the apostolic succession to his brother-in-law, Westley Hall.[38] However, after his reading King, Wesley wrote, "I set out for Bristol. On the road I read over Lord King's Account of the Primitive Church. In spite of the vehement prejudice of my education, I was ready to believe that this was a fair and impartial draught. But if so, it would follow that bishops and presbyters are (essentially) of one order."[39] Hereafter, in fact, the view that bishops and presbyters were essentially of one order remained with Wesley for life. King's work convinced Wesley that in the early church there was no episcopal monarchy comparable to what is to be seen in the Middle Ages and in modern times. He came to the conclusion that "originally every Christian congregation was a church independent on all others!"[40]

King's work also led Wesley to the conclusion that the espiscopal form of the church government is described, but not prescribed in the New Testament. Revealing King's influence upon Wesley's view, the Conference *Minutes* of 1747 records:

Q. 8. Are the three orders of Bishops, Priests, and Deacons plainly described in the New Testament?
A. We think they are; and believe they generally obtained in the churches of the apostolic age.
Q. 9. But are you assured that God designed the same plan should obtain in all churches, throughout all ages?
A. We are not assured of this; because we do not know that it is asserted in Holy Writ.[41]

The *Minutes* continues,

Q. 12. Must there not be numberless accidental varieties in the government of various churches?
A. There must, in the nature of things. For, as God variously dispenses His gifts of nature, providence, and grace, both the offices themselves and the officers in each ought to be varied from time to time.
Q. 13. Why is it, that there is no determinate plan of church-government appointed in Scripture?

A. Without doubt, because the wisdom of God had a regard to this necessary variety.[42]

Wesley holds that till before the Queen Elizabeth's reign, the divine right of
episcopacy had not been asserted in England and "all the Bishops and
Clergy in England continually allowed and joined in the ministrations of
those who were not episcopally ordained."[43]

At the time of Wesley, in the Church of England the right administration of the sacraments rested on valid succession. A. B. Lawson argues that
at least till 1745 Wesley "still held to the Anglican principle of a threefold
ministry and the necessity for episcopal ordination for valid sacraments,"[44]
but after reading King, Wesley no longer insisted on the necessity of apostolic succession for valid sacraments, and the historic episcopate as the only
true line of ministry. Wesley in his note on Matt. 10:5 stated that "None but
God can give men authority to preach His word."[45] Lawson says, after
Wesley read King, "to Wesley, the conception of Apostolic Succession
seems to have meant a limitation of 'free grace'. To restrict the work of the
Holy Spirit by mechanical means did not appeal to him."[46]

John C. Bowmer also argues that "while Wesley once believed in the
traditional view of Episcopal ordination and Apostolic Succession, from
1746 onwards he ceased to hold it."[47] Wesley believed uninterrupted succession to be a fable in that "it is impossible to draw up a list of any see
with an uninterrupted succession from the Apostles' time to the present
day."[48]

However, even after he moved beyond a necessity of valid succession
from St. Peter, Wesley didn't completely discard a concept of episcopal
succession. Concerning this matter, Bowmer says,

> Wesley's idea of succession was still, in effect, episcopal; not, it is true,
> the traditional and usually accepted view of episcopal succession, but in
> accordance with his belief that presbyters, discharging their function as
> ἐπίσκοποι, have the right to ordain. When Wesley ordained, it was as a
> presbyter exercising the inherent right of a New Testament ἐπίσκοπος. In
> this respect, it was still episcopal succession; and when Dr. Coke or-
> dained, too, he did so as a Bishop, for the certificates he issues began, "I,
> Thomas Coke, a Bishop in the Church of God . . ." Furthermore, in the
> ordinal to be found in Wesley's *Sunday Service of the Methodists* the
> presence of the Superintendent (the counterpart of ἐπίσκοπος of which it
> is a translation) for the laying-on of hands is required at the ordination of
> all three orders of ministers—deacons, presbyters, and superintendents.[49]

Wesley, while not excluding other church-government forms, believed
that the episcopal form was the best one of church-government. Indeed, he

had begun his ministry with belief in the necessity of episcopal ordination and even in the validity of apostolic succession. In 1745, when the Methodist revival was quickly developing, Westley Hall, Wesley's brother-in-law, suggested that Wesley renounce the Church of England and his ways. Indignant, Wesley replied, "We believe it would not be right for us to *administer* either Baptism or the Lord's Supper unless we had a commission so to do from those bishops whom we apprehend to be in a *succession* from the apostles."[50] Furthermore, Wesley went to the extreme by asserting: "We believe that the threefold order of ministers (which you seem to mean by 'papal hierarchy' and 'prelacy') is not only authorized by its 'apostolical institution', but also by the 'written Word.'"[51]

John S. Simon has a different opinion from that of Lawson. Simon holds that Wesley read Lord King in 1746 but "he was not prepared to accept Lord King's assertion until he had given it full consideration."[52] To support his view, Simon provides as an example Wesley's letter to the Rev. James Clark on July 3, 1756, ten years after he read King. In the letter Wesley said that he still believed "the Episcopal form of church government to be scriptural and apostolical," though not prescribed in Scripture.[53] Certainly, there is no evidence that Wesley ever abandoned his preference for the episcopal form of church-government. However, preference is not the same as conviction that this form of government is essential and that any other form of government is therefore to be excluded.

Whatever the exact details of the situation, it is clear that King convinced Wesley that presbyter and bishop were of one order, but different in degree. Later Wesley went forward to a conviction that he *could* ordain, given unusual circumstances, and he told his brother Charles, "I verily believe I have as good a right to ordain as to administer the Lord's Supper."[54]

Wesley's opinion on 'the problem of ordination' was not solely derived from Lord King's book, while that book set him thinking on the subject. At the time of Wesley, there were some other persons who justified presbyterial ordination. For example, persons like Archbishop James Usher said, "I have ever declared my opinion to be that bishop and presbyter differ only in degree, and not in order; and, consequently, that in places where bishops cannot be had, the ordination by presbyters standeth valid."[55]

In particular Bishop Stillingfleet helped to establish Wesley's view of ordination. Well-known as a critic of John Locke's *Essay concerning Human Understanding*, Stillingfleet, in his *Irenicum*,[56] argued that the power to ordain is "radically and intrinsically" in every presbyter, but to prevent schisms in the church "the exercise of that power may be restrained" in the presbyters.[57] According to Stillingfleet, the superiority of bishops above presbyters was not founded "upon any *divine right*, but only upon their convenience of such an order for the peace and unity of the church of God."[58] Wesley wrote to his brother Charles on July 3, 1756:

> As to my own judgment, I still believe 'the Episcopal form of Church government to be both scriptural and apostolical': I mean, well agreeing with the practice and writings of the Apostles. But that it is prescribed in Scripture I do not believe. This opinion (which I once heartily espoused) I have been heartily ashamed of ever since I read Dr. Stillingfleet's *Irenicon*. I think he has unanswerably proved that neither Christ or His Apostles prescribed any particular form of Church government, and that the plea for the divine right of Episcopacy was never heard of in the primitive Church.[59]

King and Stillingfleet's works led Wesley to the conclusion that "bishops and presbyters are the same order" and consequently he has "a right to ordain."[60] For a long time Wesley was reluctant to exercise this right since it contradicted all that he had been taught to believe. On September 24, 1755 he wrote to the Reverend Samuel Walker, saying that he was still doubting the propriety of himself, as a presbyter, to appoint other ministers: "This is the very point wherein we desire advice, being afraid of learning to our own understanding."[61] Again, on June 8, 1780, he wrote to his brother Charles: "Read Bishop Stillingfleet's *Irenicon* or any impartial history of the Ancient Church, and I believe you will think as I do. I verily believe I have as good a right to ordain as to administer the Lord's Supper. But I see abundance of reasons why I should not use that right, unless I was turned out of the Church."[62] For many years Wesley had not exercised the right to ordain his itinerant preachers.

One reason why he behaved in this manner is that he himself was a conscientious, faithful and devout member of the Church of England. It was not his disposition to act contrary to the teachings and practices of his own church. He did himself what he instructed his preachers always to do: "And in general, do not mend our Rules, but keep them; not for wrath, but for conscience' sake."[63] In fact, therefore, Wesley didn't exercise the right to ordain "not only for peace' sake," but because he was determined "as little as possible to violate the established order" of the Church to which he belonged.[64]

Wesley did not also allow his lay preachers to administer the sacraments because he saw such a step as separation from the Church of England. The fact that the Methodists never did separate from the Church during his lifetime he called their particular glorying.[65] Wesley's followers were constantly urged to attend their parish churches for the sacraments.

However, circumstances made this impossible. Even though until then Wesley still held that the godliness of the minister did not affect the efficacy of the sacrament, many Methodists were staying away from the communion of ungodly men. And even though they wanted to accept the communion, the clergy in many places were actually resisting the approach of the Methodists to the Lord's Supper. Some of clergy even raised the mob against the Methodists and violently persecuted them. The Methodist people could not understand why they should run the risk of being repelled from the sacrament by such men, and why they could not receive the sacrament from the hands of their own preachers from whom they received the Word of life.

In fact, there were lay administrations of the sacraments among Methodists before Wesley took the step in ordaining. As early as 1754 a few of the preachers began to administer the Lord's Supper to the small groups in some of the Societies. Charles Wesley recorded regarding this scandal:

> 1754: October 17.—Sister Macdonald first, and then sister Clay, informed me that Charles Perronet gave the sacrament to the preachers, Walsh and Deaves, and then to twelve at sister Garder's, in the Minories . . .
> October 18.—Sister Meredith told me that her husband had sent her word that Walsh had administered the sacrament at Reading . . .
> October 19.—I was with my brother, who said nothing of Perronet, except, 'We have in effect ordained already.' He urged me to sign the preachers' certificates; was inclined to lay on hands; and to let the preachers administer.[66]

Later in March, 1760, in a letter to his brother John, Charles wrote again,

> The case stands thus. Three preachers, whom we thought we could have depended upon, have taken upon them to administer the sacrament, without any ordination, and without acquainting us (or even yourself) of it beforehand. Why may not all other preachers do the same, if each is to judge of his own right to do it? And every one is left to act as he pleases, if we take no notice of them that have so despised their brethren.
>
> That the rest will soon follow their example I believe; because: (1) They think they may do it with impunity. (2) Because a large majority imagine they have a right, as preachers, to administer the sacraments. So long ago as the Conference at Leeds [1755], I took down their names. (3) Because they have betrayed an impatience to separate. . . .
>
> Upon the whole, I am fully persuaded, almost all our preachers are corrupted already. More and more will give the sacrament, and set up for themselves, even before we die; and all, except the few that get orders, will turn Dissenters before or after our death.[67]

Just how correct these observations are cannot be ascertained, but John Wesley was sufficiently concerned about the numbers being denied the sacraments. For one reason or another, he decided to change what up to then he had been inflexibly against. He decided to hold services during the hour of regular Church Service. In his journal of October 7, 1770, Wesley says, "my brother and I complied with the desire of many of our friends and agreed to administer the Lord's Supper every other Sunday at Bristol. We judged it best to have the entire service and so begin at nine o'clock."[68]

The day was fast approaching when the decision would have to be made as to whether it was possible to remain in the Church of England. The situations forced Wesley to seriously consider the change of his position.

The circumstances in North America particularly accelerated the change, forcing Wesley to exercise the right to ordain. In 1784, he told the brethren in America that

> the case is widely different between England and North America. Here there are bishops who have a legal jurisdiction: in America there are none, neither any parish ministers. So that for some hundred miles together there is none either to baptize or to administer the Lord's supper. Here, therefore, my scruples are at an end; and I conceive myself at full liberty, as I violate no order and invade no man's right by appointing and sending labourers into the harvest.[69]

Up until 1784, when the first of his ordinations took place, Wesley, at least in his outward behavior and public utterances, seemed to subscribe to the age-old three-ordered ministry of bishop, priest and deacon, in which each order is received by the sole means of the episcopate through the laying on of hands. These orders had characterized the clerical character of the Greek, Latin and Anglican Churches. Now in 1784, however, he was well prepared to justify his ordinations, scripturally and theologically, at least to himself, and hopefully to others.

Wesley actually appointed Thomas Coke and Francis Asbury to be Joint Superintendents over the Methodists in North America, and Richard Whatcoat and Thomas Vasey to act as elders among them, by baptizing and administering the Lord's Supper.[70] He again wrote to the Methodists in America explaining what he had done in ordaining Whatcoat and Vasey as "elders" and setting apart Dr. Coke as a "superintendent":

> Lord King's *Account of the Primitive Church* convinced me many years ago that bishops and presbyters are the same order, and consequently have the same right to ordain. For many years I have been importuned from time to time to exercise the right by ordaining part of our traveling

preachers. But I have still refused, not only for peace' sake, but because I was determined as little as possible to violate the established order of the National Church to which I belonged.

. . . But the case is widely different between England and North America. Here . . . my scruples are at an end. . . .

. . . If anyone will point out a more rational and scriptural way of feeding and guiding those poor sheep in the wilderness, I will gladly embrace it. At present I cannot see any better method than that I have taken.

. . . As our American brethren are now totally disentangled both from the State and from the English hierarchy, we dare not entangle them again either with the one or the other. They are now at full liberty simply to follow the Scriptures and the Primitive Church. And we judge it best that they should stand fast in that liberty wherewith God has so strangely made them free.[71]

On Wesley's actions of the ordination, Samuel Drew, a biographer of Thomas Coke, stated:

That keeping his eye upon the conduct of the primitive churches in the ages of unadulterated Christianity, he had much admired the mode of ordaining bishops which the church of Alexandria had practised. That to preserve its purity, that church would never suffer the interference of a foreign bishop in any of their ordinations; but that the presbyters of that venerable apostolic church, on the death of a bishop, exercised the right of ordaining another from their own body, by the laying on of their own hands; and that this practice continued among them for two hundred years, till the days of Dionysius. And finally, that being himself a presbyter, he wished Dr. Coke to accept ordination from his hands, and to proceed in that character to the continent of America, to superintend the societies in the United States.[72]

Edgar W. Thompson follows Drew's suggestion by holding that Wesley consecrated Coke "by taking the case of North America out of the circumstances of the Primitive Church,"[73] as described in King's *Account of the Primitive Church* and Stillingfleet's *Irenicum*. Wesley in his ordinations, according to Thompson, followed the precedent of the Church of Alexandria in the first three centuries, where presbyters appointed and consecrated their own bishops without intervention from other sees.[74] Thompson also stresses that Wesley should have acknowledged that in this act he had moved "beyond obedience to the rule of the Anglican Church, and that he had taken to himself a power of consecration which his Church did not allow."[75] This is true, and it emphasizes Wesley's belief that God in his sovereignty is not bound by the given order of the Church.

However, it is needed to note that we miss the significance of Wesley's struggle unless we take account of his almost painful attempt, not only to maintain continuity with the threefold order by finding the precedent in Alexandria, but also to maintain unity with the Church of England. Wesley could allow no theory of the threefold order which sought to bind God to an uninterrupted succession through bishops by claiming that the church could not exist where that form of succession was absent. Yet he could and did allow the normality of the threefold order, and the importance of doing all that was possible to preserve continuity and unity in this ministry.

At any rate, following his principle of necessity, John Wesley ultimately exercised the right of ordaining others in 1784. From King and Stillingfleet Wesley learned that presbyters have inherently the right of ordination, and he thought that this right can be exercised in ordinary circumstances only by the bishop's authority and permission. Now in North America the circumstances were extraordinary, for there was no bishop. Perhaps Wesley felt that he had to exercise the right which was inherent in him for the benefit of those who were without minister or sacrament. Answering his brother's objections to his ordinations, he wrote on August 19, 1785: "It is the obedience to these laws that I have never exercised in England the power which I believe God has given me. I firmly believe I am a scriptural ἐπίσκοπος as much as any man in England or in Europe; for the *uninterrupted succession* I know to be a fable, which no man ever did or can prove."[76]

John Wesley had obviously come to believe that priest, or presbyter, and bishop did not differ in order, and that he had the authority to do what any bishop in any church was authorized to do. Therefore, he most likely intended his ministerial ordinations to carry with them all the rights and privileges appertaining to full priesthood in the church.

Moreover, Wesley must have believed that he had the power as well to set aside persons for the office of general government in the church. He constituted Thomas Coke a superintendent, and actually sent over to America the service for the third order of superintendents. Wesley avoided the word 'bishop' because of its connotation of pomp, prestige, and temporal privileges and power. When Asbury took the title 'bishop,' indignant, Wesley wrote to Asbury on September 20, 1788, "How can you, how dare you suffer yourself to be called Bishop? I shudder, I start at the very thought! Men may call me a knave or a fool, a rascal, a scoundrel, and I am content; but they shall never by my consent call me Bishop! For my sake, for God's sake, for Christ's sake put a full end to this!"[77] Nevertheless, Wesley conferred on his superintendents all the administrative authority that has traditionally been associated with the episcopacy. He did not in any way delimit the powers appertaining to that office which he himself had from the beginning exercised over both his preachers and his followers. Charles Wesley saw this and candidly admitted it in a letter to Dr. Chandler, an Episcopal clergyman: "I can scarcely yet believe it, that, in his eighty-second year, my brother, my old, intimate friend and companion, should have assumed the episcopal character, ordained elders, consecrated a bishop, and sent him to ordain our lay preachers in America!"[78]

John S. Simon offers a distinctive view concerning Wesley's ordinations. According to Simon, up until the time of 1788 Wesley had ordained his selected preachers for "deacons" and "elders" orders, and he had ordained the preachers only for the United States, Scotland, and the British Dominions in America. But from Alexander Mather's ordination of 1788, says Simon, Wesley ordained ministers not as elder but as "presbyter in the Church of God," without sending them out of England.[79] For the Methodist ministry in England, Wesley ordained Alexander Mather in August 1788 and Thomas Rankin and Henry Moore in February 1789. Simon suggests that Wesley was providing for the inevitable break with the Church of England by ordaining them for England, and in doing so the Methodist Societies took up "a distinct position as one of the Churches of England."[80]

Then, was Wesley providing for Presbyterian succession when ordaining Mather, Rankin and Moore as presbyter? Charles Wesley once made the charge that his brother John substituted Presbyterian succession for Episcopal succession. *"What foul slanderers those (enthusiasts?) are! How have they for three score years said (John Wesley was?)...a Papist: and lo he turns out at last a Presbyterian!"*[81] Yet to say that Wesley adopted Presbyterian succession for Episcopal succession is only partly true. It is true in the sense that he believed orders could be transmitted through presbyters. But he never held a view of ordination similar to that of the historic Presbyterian Churches. Wesley advocated nothing of ordination contingent upon the consent of, or requiring the approval of the Church or congregation within which the ordinand was to minister. In addition, his early ordinations were conducted in privacy and secrecy, a procedure which is alien to historic Presbyterianism. Wesley never thought that he followed the Presbyterians. He was much in favor of Episcopal, rather than Presbyterian, government. He once wrote, "Let the Presbyterians do what they please, but let the Methodists know their calling better."[82]

The ordination of Alexander Mather, Thomas Rankin and Henry Moore had the advantage of regularizing subsequent British practice, and Wesley's statement that the Reformed ministries were used by God as valid must here be kept in view. Nevertheless, we must be careful not to make too much of Wesley's use of presbyter here. He had often used it before as a synonym for elder, as he did in his ordination certificate of Coke. Wesley's use of presbyter is by no means a proof that he had decided that a single order is the best form of the ministry.

In sum, Wesley's view of ordination developed with a series of progression through the years, and in such a development the influence of King and Stillingfleet was vital. Their works convinced Wesley that in origin presbyter and bishop were of one order and accordingly orders could be transmitted through presbyters as well as through bishops. Wesley came to believe that he as a presbyter has a right to ordain, given extraordinary circumstances. And finally the day came when he had to exercise his right by necessity.

Wesley and American Methodism

American Methodism was a catalyst that caused Wesley to exercise the right to ordain that he had long reserved. In addition to its connection with the problem of ordination, American Methodism is particularly notable in that it pushed Wesley to take the action which in fact transformed Methodism from an ancillary movement within the Church of England to an autonomous ecclesiastical body in the United States.

The origin and development of American Methodism has an interesting history. As early as in 1766, Philip Embury, who had been a member of Wesley's United Societies in Ireland, began to preach in New York without Wesley's knowledge and permission and formed "a society of his own countrymen and the citizens."[83] In the same year Thomas Webb was preaching "in a hired room, near the barracks" in New York, and in 1767 Robert Strawbridge, a local preacher from Ireland, was preaching in Frederic county, Maryland, without Wesley's appointment.[84] However, rather than stopping Embury and the others' preaching, Wesley responded by sending in 1769 Richard Boardman and Joseph Pilmore as "the first regular Methodist preachers on the continent."[85] These preachers were sent by Wesley according to a request that had been made to him to supply the Americans with "able, experienced" preachers.[86] In latter end of the year 1771 Francis Asbury and Richard Wright, of the same order, came over to America. Later on Methodism spread rapidly in the New World. Concerning the rapid development of the early American Methodism, Thomas Coke and Francis Asbury described:

> The first Methodist church in New-York was built in 1768 or 1769. . . .
> And we humbly believe that God's design in raising up the preachers
> called Methodists in America, was to reform the continent, and spread

scriptural holiness over these lands. As a proof hereof, we have seen, in
the course of 22 years, a great and glorious work of God, from New-York
through the Jersies, Pennsylvania, Maryland, Virginia, North and South-
Carolina, and Georgia; as also the extremities of the Western Settle-
ments.[87]

The method of operation in America was, broadly speaking, the same
as it was in Britain. The primary organizational elements such as society,
circuit, and conference, were identical. Wesley's authority was unques-
tioned and on occasion was appealed to. In regard to Wesley's authority in
America, John J. Tigert says,

> from the beginning in both England and America, Methodism has been a
> "Connection". The term is technical, and characteristic of the denomina-
> tion. Connectionalism is of the essence of the system, equally opposed to
> congregationalism in the churches and to individualism in the preachers.
> Mr. Wesley, in America no less than in England, was at the first, the cen-
> ter of union. Connection with him was the living bond which held incipi-
> ent American Methodism together. He was the foundation of authority,
> acknowledged by all as rightful, original, and supreme.[88]

In October 1772 Asbury received a letter from Wesley, appointing him
to be the Assistant of the American Societies.[89] At this time, however, Asbury was not entirely effective as an administrator and he faced some difficulties. At the Quarterly meeting that year the question was raised if the
Methodist people would be contented without their administering the sacraments.[90] Robert Strawbridge was in favor of having them, even without
ordination, but Asbury would not agree to it. As a result, in 1773, the first
Conference in America was called by Rankin and the rules were made and
agreed to by the preachers. Two of the rules were:

> 1. Every preacher who acts in connection with Mr. Wesley and the
> brethren who labour in America is strictly to avoid administering the ordi-
> nances of baptism and the Lord's supper.
> 2. All the people among whom we labour are to be earnestly exhorted
> to attend the [Anglican] Church, and to receive the ordinances there; but
> in a particular manner to press the people in Maryland and Virginia to the
> observance of this minute.[91]

Although Strawbridge violated the rules by administering the sacraments of
baptism and the Lord's Supper in Maryland, his case was an exception.
Preachers were not to behave like priests by administering the sacraments,

and they were to follow the directions of the superintending preacher appointed by Wesley.

A drastic change came with the Revolutionary War, which forced the Methodist Societies in America to be transformed into a church. As the political tensions between the colonies and Great Britain grew during the 1760s and 1770s, the Methodists and the Anglican Church both found themselves in an awkward position. Methodists had "Wesley, a strong British Tory loyalist, as their leader."[92] The Anglican Church, the clergy of which were all ordained in England and which had no American bishop, became an anachronism in America when the subjects in the colonies repudiated the crown. During the American Revolutionary War, many of the Anglican priests in America returned to Great Britain. This left only those few priests who were loyal to the Methodist cause. Also, most of the British Methodist preachers returned to Great Britain. As a result, the American Methodists were like sheep without shepherds. In the thinking of many, what America now needed was an American church.

The only one of Wesley's British missionaries who had remained by his post of duty in America throughout the war was Francis Asbury. Asbury tried to remain neutral as a pacifist, but in revolutionary times, pacifism can be easily taken for disloyalty. For that reason Asbury was forced to hide for a while. He recorded on the difficult situation of that time: "I was under some heaviness of mind. But it was no wonder: three thousand miles from home—my friends have left me—I am considered by some as an enemy of the country—every day liable to be seized by violence, and abused. However, all this is but a trifle to suffer for Christ, and the salvation of souls. Lord, stand by me!"[93]

However, at least up till 1779 many Methodists were neither neutral nor sided with the American cause. They showed loyalty to the crown, and as a result they were objects of persecution to the patriots. They were doubted to keep in contact with Wesley, a Tory loyalist, still use the English *Book of Common Prayer*, and oppose the disestablishment of the Church of England in America. In fact, many American Methodists opposed the abolishment of establishment.[94]

During the Revolutionary War, American Methodists suffered a series of schismatic difficulties from inside as well as the persecution from outside. The sacramental issue arose right in the middle of the war. The growing lack of Anglican clergy, caused by their return, presented a sacramental crisis for the Methodists who depended upon their ministrations. As the war was drawing to a close, the preachers in America, especially the southern ones, were feeling in a measure independent of Wesley's direct rule. Jesse Lee (1758–1816), who was writing as a contemporary of Wesley, observed

it: "Many of our travelling preachers in *Virginia* and *North-Carolina*, seeing and feeling the want of the instituted means of grace among our societies . . . concluded, that if God had called them to preach, he had called
them also to administer the ordinances of baptism and the Lord's Supper."[95]
In fact a temporary schism occurred among the southern preachers in 1779.

Asbury, fearing the schism,[96] called a Conference in April 1779 to
Judge Thomas White's home in Delaware, which was then his place of
confinement.[97] During the Conference the following questions were central:

> Quest. 10. *Shall we guard against a separation from the Church, directly
> or indirectly?*
>   By all means. . . .
> Quest. 12. *Ought not brother Asbury to act as general assistant in Amer-
> ica?*
>   He ought; 1st, on account of his age; 2d, because originally appointed
> by Mr. Wesley; 3d, being joined with Messrs. Rankin and Shadford, by
> express order from Mr. Wesley.
> Quest. 13. *How far shall his power extend?*
>   On hearing every preacher for and against what is in debate, the right
> of determination shall rest with him, according to the Minutes.[98]

The southern preachers, feeling Asbury had gone behind their backs,
held their own conference at Brokenback Church, Fluvanna county in Virginia, in May of 1779. They proceeded to appoint some of the older preachers to ordain ministers for them, forming a presbytery. Jesse Lee himself
recorded his observation of this incident:

> the conference chose a committee for the purpose of ordaining ministers.
> The committee thus chosen, first ordained themselves, and then proceeded
> to ordain and set apart other preachers for the same purpose, that they
> might administer the holy ordinances to the church of Christ. The preach-
> ers thus ordained, went forth preaching the gospel in their circuits as for-
> merly, and administered the sacraments wherever they went.[99]

Now the situation became serious indeed. Lay preachers, albeit in America
and feeling separated from the direct rule of John Wesley, took it in their
own hands to ordain for the purpose of administration of the sacraments.
Frank Baker writes on this scandal:

> For the 1779 Conference a preparatory meeting was held at Judge Thomas
> White's in Delaware, mainly for the convenience of Asbury, whose head-
> quarters this was. William Watters came in the hope of persuading Asbury
> to attend the regular Conference planned to meet in Fluvanna, Virginia,
> but without success. Asbury and those of the northern circuits felt it un-

wise to court danger to their cause by going into Virginia, and Watters was deputed to carry their greetings and opinions. When the more numerous southern brethren met at the appointed time they were inclined to regard this preliminary gathering as a conspiracy to defeat their position on the sacramental issue, and accordingly refused to endorse the northern proposition that in succession to Rankin Asbury should be regarded as "General Assistant in America." Claiming that "the Episcopal Establishment is now dissolved, and therefore in almost all our circuits the members are without the ordinances," they appointed a presbytery of three preachers to ordain themselves and the others in order that they might duly administer the sacraments.[100]

Norman W. Spellmann notes, "The eighteen preachers present chose and empowered a committee of four to supervise them. Three of the same men were appointed to be 'the presbytery': Philip Gatch, Reuben Ellis, and James Foster. They were authorized 'to administer the ordinances themselves; and to authorize any other preacher or preachers, approved by them, by the form of laying on of hands.'"[101]

Asbury knew that Wesley would never allow such an action. He persuaded the southern brethren that those who had participated in the irregular ordination should stop exercising their new-found powers, and "for the sake of peace, and the union of the body of Methodists," they agree "to drop the ordinances for a season till Mr. Wesley could be consulted."[102] Finally, at Baltimore in April 1780 a conference was held, and "[a]ll but one agreed to return to the old plan, and give up the administration of the ordinances."[103] Also, Asbury was recognized as the leader of American Methodism. The rebellion of the southern preachers seemed to subside and the *status quo* prevailed. Then Asbury was able to reassure Wesley: "We are now united; all things go on well, considering the storms, and difficulties we have had to ride through."[104]

It took five years for the American Methodists to get Wesley's solution to the sacramental crisis. When the preachers in America began to beg Wesley to send over more men who could minister to them, and especially administer the sacraments, Wesley tried to appeal to Bishop Robert Lowth, then bishop of London, to ordain some men for America. However, it is natural that any bishop of the Church of England would show a reluctance to ordain the Methodist preachers as clergymen in the Church of England, if they remained Methodist preachers and especially if they planned to go to the rebellious colonies. Such a reluctance is well represented in Bishop Lowth's words,

I can easily believe, that many, if not most, of those who shall survive you, will separate from the Church . . . except . . . you get them fastened where they are by prevailing on one or more of the bishops to ordain them. But then, what Bishop, either in England or Ireland, will ever do this? will ordain a Methodist preacher, to be a Methodist preacher? For my part, as poor and worthless a wretch as I am, I could not submit to it on the terms on which most of my brethren have hitherto got it.[105]

By the late summer of 1784, Wesley determined to take the step of ordaining preachers himself for the American brethren, "convinced that under the exigent circumstances (the need for the sacraments being a 'case of necessity') . . . he was acting properly as a 'scriptural bishop.'"[106] Writing on this determination a year later, Wesley said,

> since the late revolution in North America, these have been in great distress. The Clergy, having no sustenance, either from England, or from the American States, have been obliged almost universally to leave the country, and seek their food elsewhere. Hence those who had been members of the Church, had none either to administer the Lord's supper, or to baptize their children. They applied to England over and over; but it was to no purpose. Judging this to be a case of real necessity, I took a step which, for peace and quietness, I had refrained from taking for many years. . . . These are the steps which, not of choice, but necessity, I have slowly and deliberately taken.[107]

In February 1784, Wesley suggested that by the imposition of his hands he would ordain Thomas Coke for leadership in America. But Coke at first would not agree to this. On Coke's response to Wesley's suggestion, Samuel Drew records, "Coke was at first startled at a measure so unprecedented in modern days; and he expressed some doubts, as to the validity of Mr. Wesley's authority to constitute so important an appointment. But the arguments of Lord King, which had proselyted Mr. Wesley, were recommended to his attention, and time was allowed him to deliberate on the result."[108] After the study of the biblical and patristic evidence for presbyterial ordination, Coke came to the same conclusions Wesley had, and he was ready to cooperate with Wesley. Coke suggested in a letter of August 9, 1784 that Wesley go ahead and ordain him, and ordain Richard Whatcoat and Thomas Vasey. Coke also suggested that for the ordination of Whatcoat and Vasey he could bring James Creighton, another minister of the Church of England of Methodist persuasion. This suggestion was intended to have three presbyters, including Wesley and Coke himself, for the ordinations in accordance with the practice of the primitive churches.[109]

Wesley finally acted. After 2 a.m. of September 1, 1784, in a private home, in Bristol, England, John Wesley, assisted by Thomas Coke and James Creighton, priests of the Church of England like himself, ordained

Richard Whatcoat and Thomas Vasey deacons. The next day he ordained these same men elders (or presbyters) and ordained Coke to set aside for the office of superintendent, being assisted by other ordained ministers (Creighton, and either Whatcoat or Vasey—or both Whatcoat and Vasey).[110] He issued certificates to the three men. Those of Richard What-coat and Thomas Vasey were alike. The copy of Whatcoat's certificate of ordination reads:

> Whereas many of the people in the southern provinces of North America, who desire to continue under my care, and still adhere to the doctrines and discipline of the Church of England, are greatly distressed for want of ministers, to administer the Sacraments of Baptism, and the Lord's Supper, according to the usage of the said Church: and whereas there does not appear to be any other way of supplying them with Ministers:
>
> Know all men, that I, John Wesley, think myself to be providentially called at this time, to set apart some persons for the work of the Ministry in America. And therefore, under the protection of Almighty God, and with a single eye to his glory, I have this day set apart for the said work, as an Elder, by the imposition of my hands and prayer, (being assisted by two other ordained Ministers) Richard Whatcoat, a man whom I judge to be well qualified for that great work. And I do hereby recommend him to all whom it may concern, as a fit person to feed the flock of Christ, and to administer Baptism and the Lord's Supper, according to the usage of the Church of England.[111]

Coke's, very similarly, reads:

> Know all men that I John Wesley think myself to be providentially called at this time to set apart some persons for the work of the ministry in America. And therefore under the Protection of Almighty God, and with a single eye to his glory, I have this day set apart as a superintendent, by the imposition of my hands and prayer (being assisted by other ordained ministers) Thomas Coke, Doctor of Civil Law a Presbyter of the Church of England, man whom I judge to be well qualified for that great work. And I do hereby recommend him to all whom it may concern as a fit person to preside over the Flock of Christ.[112]

It was his intention that those three brethren would do for Francis Asbury and the other qualified lay preachers in America what he had done for them.

On September 18, 1784, by Wesley's orders, the three brethren set sail for America, arriving there on November 3. The Christmas Conference of 1784 convened in Baltimore on December 24. The very next day Francis Asbury was ordained deacon and on the two succeeding days elder and su-perintendent respectively. Asbury then joined Thomas Coke, and the two, assisted by Vasey and Whatcoat, ordained a number of others as elders and deacons.[113]

E. Herbert Nygren says that when Wesley ordained his people, he was convinced that "God had given him the function of an *episcopos* in Methodism," and he saw himself as "a New Testament or 'missionary bishop,'" a presbyter uniquely required to exercise his inherent right to ordain.[114] This action was no extraordinary transaction. It was designed to set in motion a process that would be continuous. This assumption is supported by the fact that Wesley sent the American Methodists doctrinal standards, a hymnal, and a book of discipline along with Coke, Vasey, and Whatcoat. He in fact gave to his people in America all the forms of ritual, doctrinal confession, administration, and ministry which he deemed necessary for the maintenance of an independent and autonomous church.[115] Indeed, the fact that even the service for the ordination of deacons, elders, and superintendents was included in materials he sent reveals that he acted with premeditated care. Wesley did not intend that American Methodism would end with the deaths of Coke, Asbury, Whatcoat, and Vasey, but rather that the ordination he gave them would be conferred by them on others through all succeeding generations. Methodism in America continued to grow, and, despite its short history, at Wesley's death Methodists in the United States outnumbered British Methodists.[116]

Issues Associated with Wesley's Ordination

Now we need to discuss the issues associated with Wesley's ordination. First, was the ordination of Whatcoat and Vasey Methodism's first ordination? And was it an exceptional case? It was John Wesley's first ordination as a presbyter, but there had been some notable cases. We have seen that Charles Wesley wrote that as far as he was concerned they had ordained already, with the instances of lay administration. In addition, Methodist ministers, in fact, had already been ordained by the southern preachers in America in 1779.

Wesley himself finally did ordain in 1784. A year after the ordination of Coke, Whatcoat, and Vasey, Wesley ordained three "well-tried preachers, John Pawson, Thomas Hanby, and Joshep Taylor, to minister in Scotland."[117] In doing these ordinations, Wesley felt that he was entitled, by virtue of his own ordination, to ordain for areas outside the jurisdiction of the Church of England. In 1786 he added two more to the Scottish number and one for Antigua and another for Newfoundland. In 1787 five more received ordination at his hands, and the two following years he ordained two and seven respectively. One of the seven was set apart for the work of Superintendent in Scotland. Most of these were for the work in Scotland, where the Church of England was not involved and where no separation was effected with the Church of Scotland. Up until 1788 Wesley's ordinations were for foreign mission fields.

But, in 1788 and 1789, Wesley finally ordained Alexander Mather, Henry Moore and Thomas Rankin for the Methodist work in England. Concerning this incident, William Myles said,

> Mr. Wesley had hitherto ordained Ministers only for America and Scotland, but from this period, being assisted by the Rev. James Creighton and the Rev. Peard Dickenson, Presbyters of the Church of England, he set apart for the sacred office, by imposition of his hands, and prayer, Messrs. Alexander Mather, Thomas Rankin, and Henry Moore, without sending them out of England; strongly advising them at the same time, that, according to his example, they should continue united to the Established Church, so far as the blessed work in which they were engaged would permit.[118]

However, as Henry Moore himself suggested, Wesley in fact was providing for the inevitable break with the Church of England by ordaining his people though he did not allow them to exercise their ordination.

The second issue of Wesley's ordination is whether Wesley actually intended to separate from the Church of England with his ordinations. As early as 1747/8 Wesley was accused of assuming the apostolate of England. Denying the charge, he wrote to John Smith on March 22, 1747/8, "I no otherwise assume the apostolate of England . . . than I assume the apostolate of all Europe, or rather of all the world."[119] This argument, as V. H. H. Green points out, is in some sense tautologous.[120] Wesley had a rather distinctive view of the apostolate, that is, after he moved beyond a necessity of valid succession from St. Peter. Within the range of authority of the Church of England, Wesley felt he could not assume episcopal functions. But he clearly felt that once outside of that range of authority, necessity dictated his actions. On March 25, 1785 Wesley wrote to Barnabas Thomas, "I know myself to be as real as a Christian bishop as the Archbishop of Canterbury. Yet I was always resolved, am so still, never to act as such except in case of necessity. Such a case does not (perhaps never will) exist in England. In America it did exist."[121] This statement would indicate that he considered his authority to ordain, whether for America or for Scotland, to be localized to those areas. Wesley felt that England was a different case entirely from America and Scotland: "The alteration which has been made in America and Scotland has nothing to do with our kingdom. I believe I shall not separate from the Church of England till my soul separates from my body."[122]

However, we know that Wesley *did* ordain for England before his death. Why did he do it? Was Wesley worried over the future of Methodism after his death? When for the first time in history representatives of the Church of England met representatives of the Methodist Church, they stated,

> The ordinations for England, at the end of Wesley's life, sprang from his preoccupation with the future of Methodism after his death. Throughout his life . . . John Wesley was exercised as to how his societies should be saved from disintegration after his death. His thought of Fletcher of Madeley . . . as his successor; the Deed of Declaration which constituted a hundred of the preachers as the legal Conference . . . all are symptoms of his quandary.[123]

Whether this statement was the explanation or not, it is clear that Wesley had been faced for some time with the decision to separate in word, when he had already separated in fact. He only was putting off the decision until his death. Certainly he never wanted to separate—no one can deny that. But by ordaining for America, he must have known, as Charles Wesley seems to have, that he was in essence separating from the Established Church of England. And his ordinations for England clinched the matter.

The issues must be considered now which go deeper than whether Wesley separated or not: Were Wesley's ordinations valid? And how does one go about determining the validity? Wesley's ordinations were neither episcopal nor presbyterian. Concerning the ordinations of 1784 by Wesley, one of the Methodist preachers wrote, "this business of ordination . . . is neither *episcopal* nor *presbyterian*; but a mere hodge-podge of inconsistencies."[124] In relation to the validity of Wesley's ordinations, John Whitehead, though he was a local preacher with several axes to grind, makes some salient points, whether we agree with them all or not.

> His Episcopal authority, was a mere gratuitous assumption of power to himself, contrary to the usage of every church, ancient or modern, where the order of bishops has been admitted. There is no precedent either in the New Testament, or in church-history, that can justify his proceeding in this affair. And as Mr. Wesley had received no right to exercise Episcopal authority, either from any bishops, presbyters, or people, he certainly could not convey any right to others: his ordinations therefore, are spurious, and of no validity.
>
> Nor can Mr. Wesley's practice of ordaining be justified by those reasons which Presbyterians adduce in favor of their own method of ordaining to the ministry: for Mr. Wesley ordained, not as a presbyter, but as a

bishop! his ordinations therefore were not Presbyterian, nor will the arguments for Presbyterian ordination apply to them.

Let us review the arguments on this subject, reduced to a few propositions: 1. Mr. Wesley in ordaining or consecrating Dr. Coke a Bishop, acted in direct contradiction to the principle on which he attempts to defend his practice of ordaining at all. 2. As Mr. Wesley was never elected or chosen by any church to be a bishop, nor ever consecrated to the office, either by bishops or presbyters, he had not the shadow of right to exercise Episcopal authority in ordaining others, according to the rules of any church, ancient or modern. 3. Had he possessed the proper right to ordain, either as a bishop or presbyter (though he never did ordain as a presbyter) yet his ordinations being done in secret, were rendered thereby invalid and of no effect, according to the established order of the primitive church, and of all Protestant churches. 4. The consequence from the whole is, that the persons whom Mr. Wesley ordained, have no more right to exercise the ministerial functions than he had before he laid hands upon them."[125]

Wesley found the justification of his ordinations in the teachings of King and Stillingfleet. The cases both King and Stillingfleet were concerned primarily with were those where bishops were not available. The imposition of hands must come from bishops if it was to come from a prior source, that is, a human one. The ordination by presbyters stands valid where bishops are not available. When Wesley ordained, the Methodists had no bishop to lay on of hands in America, but had in England. Wesley appealed to King and Stillingfleet for authority for what was done for America. However, why then did he not move according to the pattern outlined in both King and Stillingfleet when he ordained for England? Probably a consent in the Church was necessary. This consent Wesley did not have. Nor does it seem he sought it.

Wesley stated repeatedly that he never wanted to separate from the Church of England—before and even *after* his ordinations. What then led him to take a step which he must have known meant separation? Wesley knew the charges from the Church of England that the Methodists "maintain it lawful for men to preach who are not episcopally ordained," that they "disclaim all right in the bishops to control them," and that they "say that, rather than be so controlled, they would renounce all communion with this Church." He answered as to the charge in the letter "To the Earl of Dartmouth (?)" on April 10, 1761: "In every point of an indifferent nature they obey the bishops for conscience' sake; but they think Episcopal authority cannot reverse what is fixed by divine authority."[126] Wesley's best argument for his ordaining Methodist preachers would seem to be the appeal to the commission and approval of God, via the fruits of their labor. This appeal would be in keeping with his emphasis on the divine call, whether the

human call was present or not. A person's true call is the call from God to
do His work among one's fellow-men. The act of ordination, the imposition
of hands of the bishops or presbyters, is human authorization, authorization
by men set apart to superintend the work of the ministers, of the call which
only God can give.

However, Wesley could not allow this same argument—"by their
fruits"—when it came from the lay preachers who felt it all right to administer the Lord's Supper without ordination. It is not because he felt himself
the only proper judge of such matters, but because, to give Wesley the
benefit of the doubt, he had a strong penchant for ongoing order rather than
chaos.

Furthermore, when Wesley ordained Coke as a superintendent by the
imposition of hands, Coke, in fact, was to function as bishop. If Wesley
meant only to delegate to Coke his own personal authority in America, for
he could not be there himself, then he must have known this did not require
the laying on of hands of a presbytery. Wesley himself was not a bishop in
the eyes of the Church of England, but a presbyter. It would seem impossible for a lower order to confer the powers of a higher. Coke obviously felt
he had received the power to ordain, a power reserved in the Church of
England to bishops in the apostolic succession. Coke being a Church of
England man as much as Wesley himself, surely Wesley knew he was making it possible for Coke to assume espiscopal powers, since this was their
experience of the way things were done. Therefore, in essence, Wesley was
in fact substituting Wesleyan succession for Apostolic succession.

Now let us go back to the question, "Were Wesley's ordinations valid?"
From the standpoint of an historical action, Wesley's ordinations might be
seen as invalid, since they did not correspond to the model to which he appealed as authority for his action. But when considered in the light of the
total picture, they can be seen as the only possible response, the necessary
one, and, under such circumstances, valid. Some may claim that Wesley's
allowing lay preachers was the first step toward ordination of Methodist
ministers, but if the Anglican Church had incorporated Wesley's movement
into itself, as the Roman Church did its various orders of monks, and as
Wesley had been in hopes she would, then there would have been no difficulty. The fact is she didn't, and one sees the events leading up to the ordinations of 1784.

The constitution of the Methodists into an independent and autonomous
church in England did not take place during John Wesley's lifetime. But
still, despite his protestations to the contrary, Wesley himself did all that it
was necessary to do to prepare the way for this event. In the light of what
he did, it would have taken almost a miracle to have reversed the process

and to have kept the United Societies as they had been during the early years of the revival. In regard to the Methodist ministry, just as much as the Methodist Church, Wesley was definitely and unmistakably its architect and its builder.

This argument holds true in the various fields of the service of the Methodist preachers, at home in rivalry with the clergy of the Church of England, as well as abroad in foreign lands. The Plan of Pacification, issued by the British Conference in 1795, only four years after Wesley's death, allowed each society to decide for itself whether or not it would hold service in church hours with the sacraments as well as preaching and other ministerial activities. If the society would do so, the Plan provided it with Wesley's abridgement of the sacraments and instructed it that only those persons authorized by the Conference could perform the sacraments. But by the Plan, the right to administer the sacraments and to hold service in church hours was established, and the Plan actually made possible the transformation of "the United Societies into a distinct church, with its own ministry and ordinances."[127] Thirty years after the adoption of this Plan, the traveling preachers began to call themselves ministers. They performed every ministerial function and depended upon no other ministry than their own to satisfy the ecclesiastical needs of their people.

Sacraments

As investigated before, the problem of sacraments played an important role in Wesley's ordinations. The need for administering sacraments to the Methodist people in America was the actual cause for which Wesley considered ordinations. However, Wesley's understanding of the nature and meaning of the sacraments didn't suffer any considerable change through his life. Late in his life, Wesley preached the sermon "The Duty of Constant Communion" (1787), which is based on a treatise he had written "above five and fifty years ago" at Oxford. In the preface to "The Duty of Constant Communion" he stated that his views have not in essence changed from those of fifty five years ago.[128] The content of "The Duty of Constant Communion" did not differ markedly from the nonjuror, Robert Nelson (1656–1715)'s *The Great Duty of Frequenting the Christian Sacrifice* (1707), which had helped shape John Wesley's theology of the sacraments. In the last years of his life Wesley was remaining with the sacramental picture of the early 1732–1733. F. Ernest Stoeffler was right in saying that "Generally speaking . . . it can be asserted that his religious renewal beginning in 1738 had less of an impact on his understanding of the nature and meaning of the sacraments than on any other aspects of his theology."[129]

When Wesley and his fellow preachers were not allowed the use of Anglican pulpits, they took to the fields to preach more and more, and began
meeting in homes for mutual help and encouragement. But according to the
Act of Uniformity of 1662, all English persons ought to belong to the
Church of England, and if any English person did not belong, then the person must be subjected to deprivations and penalties. The Act of Uniformity
was followed by the Conventicle Acts of 1664 and 1670 which made penal
all meetings of more than five persons beyond a household, if any, for worship other than that prescribed by the Liturgy. According to these Acts,
field preaching was what the law did not allow, and therefore a crime. Although a partial freedom of worship was given to nonconformists by the
Toleration Act of 1689,[130] since Wesley did not consider himself a Dissenter, nor regard what he was doing as separation in any way from the Established Church, the Toleration Act was not much help. Despite the legal
restriction, Wesley could not close his eyes to the need for a preaching and
a pastoral care which was not in sufficient evidence in the Established
Church of his day. He used his preachers to satisfy the need, and organized
class meetings and the United Societies.

However, Wesley never tolerated his preachers' lay administration of
the sacraments. In the Church of England, there was a dichotomy between
preaching and administering the sacraments. There are a separate ordination
for deacons to preach and teach, and one for the priests to administer the
sacraments, usually after a two-year probation.[131] Given the sequence of
ordination for the two functions, preaching in the Church of England seems
to have been given a slightly more inferior position. Following the dichotomy of the Anglican Church, Wesley distinguished the prophetic function
of preaching from the priestly one of administering the sacraments even
though he didn't think the former is inferior to the latter.[132] Wesley always
held the sacrament of the Lord's Supper in high esteem. He, even when he
left behind his insistence on apostolic succession, wasn't leaving behind the
sacerdotal aspect for the administration of the sacraments. His requiring
ordination for administration of sacraments would support the assumption.
Wesley always held to the belief that only duly ordained men should administer the sacraments.

The dichotomy apparent between the Word and the Sacraments was, in
part, why Wesley connected lay administration with separation from the
Church. At the Leeds Conference of 1755, "[t]he principal subjects discussed concerned the administration of the sacraments by the lay preachers,
and the formal separation of the Societies from the Established Church. The
two subjects were so closely related that it was inevitable that they should

be considered at the same time, and the Conference discussed them for nearly three days."[133] The decision was made "not to separate from the Church,"[134] and therefore lay administration could not continue. Later on May 19, 1783, in reply to a letter from Joseph Benson regarding lay baptism, Wesley wrote, "Dear Joseph,—I do not, and never did, consent that any of our preachers should baptize as long as we profess ourselves to be members of the Church of England."[135] Also, Wesley once announced that "Modern laziness has jumbled together the two distinct offices of preaching and administering the sacraments. But, be that as it may, I will rather lose twenty Societies than separate from the Church."[136] As Lawson says, "[t]he necessity of ordination for the administration of the sacraments was always a fixed principle with Wesley. . . . To Wesley preaching and administering the sacraments were two totally different acts, which could be, but were not necessarily, linked together."[137]

Wesley knew that if his lay-preachers were to have administered the sacraments without ordination, he would have been open to charges of schism. Earlier Bishop Stillingfleet in his *Irenicum* defined "schism" as below:

> The controversies . . . which tend to break the peace of a religious society, are either matter of different practice, or matter of different opinion. The former, if it comes from no just and necessary cause, and ends in a total separation from that society the person guilty of it was joined with, is justly called *schism*; which, (as one defines it,) is an ecclesiastical sedition, as sedition is a lay-schism; both being directly contrary to that communion and friendliness which should be preserved in all societies.[138]

In Wesley's view, at that time the sacraments were available in the Church, but preaching of salvation and the care of souls were not. Thus, in allowing lay preachers, Wesley could hold that his action was not schismatic in the light of the definition of Stillingfleet for it has necessary cause. He clearly declared that he received his first preachers "wholly and solely to preach, not to administer sacraments."[139]

When the preachers at Norwich like Paul Greenwood, Thomas Mitchell, and John Murlin began to administer the Lord's Supper to the society in 1760, they were forbidden on the grounds that they had not been ordained to the office. In 1787, Wesley applied this principle to the sacrament of baptism, "we have not yet made a precedent of any one that was not ordained administering baptism."[140]

Wesley never changed his views on the distinction between the call to preach and the authority to administer the sacraments. It is well demonstrated in his sermon "Prophets and Priests" which he published in his late

year (1789). This sermon was written after certain preachers in Ireland took
it upon themselves to administer the Lord's Supper. Wesley begins the sermon by showing that from the days of Aaron, "[i]n ancient times the office
of a priest and that of a preacher were known to be entirely distinct."[141] He
then points out that although, after Constantine, it is common for one person to discharge both the offices of priest and of prophet for a congregation,
all the historic Christian Churches, including the Presbyterians, the Church
of England, and even the Church of Rome, distinguish the office of prophet
or evangelist from that of priest or pastor "to whom peculiarly belongs the
administration of the sacraments."[142] Finally, describing the rise of Methodist lay-preaching, Wesley says:

> In 1744, all the Methodist preachers had their first Conference. But none
> of them dreamed that the being called to preach gave them any right to
> administer sacraments. And when that question was proposed, 'In what
> light are we to consider ourselves?' it was answered, 'As *extraordinary
> messengers*, raised up to provoke the *ordinary* ones to jealousy.' In order
> hereto one of our first rules was—given to each preacher—'You are to do
> *that part* of the work which we appoint.' But *what work* was this? Did we
> ever appoint you to administer sacraments, to exercise the priestly office?
> Such a design never entered into our mind; it was the farthest from our
> thoughts. And if any preacher had taken such a step we should have
> looked upon it as a palpable breach of this rule, and consequently as a re-
> cantation of our connexion.[143]

Here Wesley was not saying anything new, for he was repeating what he
had written in 1745: "They take not upon them to administer the sacraments, an honour peculiar to the priests of God."[144] Wesley, till his late
years, maintained the sacerdotal position of sacraments. The right to preach
was not the right to administer the sacraments. He was still in some degree
the man reared by the Church.

However, while requiring the priestly office for the administration of
the sacraments, Wesley never in the least minimized the vocation of a
preacher. Rather the office of preacher is more important for saving souls.
This Wesley clearly expressed in the letter to Nicholas Norton on September 3, 1756. "I do tolerate lay-preaching, because I conceive there is an absolute necessity for it; inasmuch as, were it not, thousands of souls would
perish everlastingly. Yet I do not tolerate lay-administering, because I do
not conceive there is any such necessity for it; seeing it does not appear
that, if this is not at all, one soul will perish for want of it."[145] Wesley
thought no less of preaching because he would not allow his preachers to
administer the sacraments. It is true that as Methodist revival developed,

Wesley, in his ever-increasing use of lay preachers, came to emphasize more and more the "extraordinary call" of his preachers. "[We] permit laymen whom we believe God has called to preach. . . . And upon the calmest view of things we think they who are only called of God and not of man have more right to preach than they who are only called of man and not of God."[146] In the sermon "Prophets and Priests," he highlights the importance of the preaching mission: "the first principle of Methodism . . . was wholly and solely to preach the gospel."[147]

But, however highly Wesley regarded the vocation of a preacher, and even when some form of ordination was observed in recognition thereof, it was clearly understood that this did not, of itself, constitute an authority to administer the sacraments. This sacerdotal position of sacraments is further represented in the fact that Wesley agreed with the Twenty-Eighth Article of Thirty-Nine Articles that "the unworthiness of the minister does not hinder the validity of the sacraments,"[148] while he took great care to see that his "Helpers" were as godly a group of men as possible. In the sermon "On Attending the Church Service" (1787) Wesley dealt with the question of whether God blesses the ministry of unholy men. His conclusion was that "the unworthiness of the minister doth not hinder the efficacy of God's ordinance"[149] and that God blesses even the ministry of unholy man: "[I]f God never did bless it, we ought to separate from the Church, at least where we have reason to believe that the minister is an unholy man; if he ever did bless it, and does so still, then we ought to continue therein."[150] Wesley uses Judas as an example to prove God sends whom He will send, holy or not. Of those who would separate from ungodly ministers and go off somewhere, Wesley said that salt "heaped in a corner" loses its savor. Perhaps Wesley feared the people were no longer "affected by the rites" in the Church of England, due to the poor state of the clergy. He hoped that if they could be brought back to a living faith, then the sacraments could again have their pre-eminent place in the Christian life, and be meaningful as a "means of grace."

In sum, Wesley maintained a sacerdotal position of sacraments up till his last days. Throughout his life he continued to emphasize the constant participation in the Lord's Supper and the effect of sacraments as means of grace. Wesley distinguished the call to preach from the authority to administer the sacraments and this dichotomy followed that of the Church of England. He never allowed his preachers to administer the sacraments without ordination, even after his eventual action toward an autonomous church by ordination. His ordination for the American Methodists is also associated with the issue of the sacraments.

In conclusion, Wesley continued to respect the usages and ordinances, and the doctrine and the discipline of the Church of England by his last days. However, what had been a partial and restricted ministry during the early and middle years of Wesley's career became a full and unrestricted ministry during his later years, for the Methodist movement itself was rapidly growing up and, at least in one of its major geographical segments, became a church. Circumstances required Wesley to respond to the pressure of events. Wesley was a practical theologian equipped with the evangelical view of church. He saw the needs of the mission as ecclesiastical authority in the deepest sense. He was prepared to take any action that he deemed wise and expedient in the furtherance of his mission and in the propagation of the gospel. For him, where the salvation of soul is demanded, there is a necessity. If there is such an absolute necessity of mission, he was willing to follow even irregularities, such as field preaching, lay-preaching, female preaching, and ordination by his hand.

Wesley's ecclesiology was basically conservative and the irregularities he approved or exercised came with a certain reluctance, departing from traditional patterns only when necessity or careful reflection indicated the need. Even when he attempted to practice irregularities or innovations, they were "first prepared for in the realm of thought, and were translated into ecclesiastical action later."[151] In Wesley's ecclesiology his inherited High-Church tradition remained intact with respect to many of its essential features. It would not right to assert that Methodism during the days of its incipiency discarded the Anglican understanding of the church and of related doctrines. Wesley's Anglican understanding of the church, however, was necessarily modified as a result of his highly developed sense of mission and his observation of the corporate religious experience, as well as the religious needs, of his Methodists. Wesley could never have simply been satisfied with the ecclesiology of the Church of England, since, without modification, it would not have worked enough for the soteriological dynamic of early Methodism. Wesley's evangelical, functional understanding of the church permitted him to develop his own ecclesiology, responding to the spiritual needs of the people he sought to serve.

Notes

1. Wesley, Sermon "Of the Church," 16, in *Works*, iii, 51.

2. *Works*, iii, 51.

3. *The Doctrines of the Methodists, Dedicated to the Preachers, in Connection with the Late Reverend Mr. John Wesley, M. A. By Way of Question and Answer;*

Designed as a Catechism for them, Fourth Edition (Liverpool, England: E. Johnson, 1793), 2 [preface] and 8–9.

4. Wesley, Sermon "The Mystery of Iniquity," 11, in *Works,* ii, 455.

5. Wesley, Sermon "Of the Church," 19, in *Works,* iii, 52.

6. *Works,* iii, 50.

7. Edgar W. Thompson, *Wesley: Apostolic Man, Some Reflections on Wesley's Consecration of Dr Thomas Coke* (London: Epworth Press, 1957), 14.

8. *Letters,* iii, 186.

9. Journal on August 4, 1788, in *Works,* xxiv, 104.

10. *Works,* xxvi, 206.

11. *Letters,* iii, 200.

12. *Letters,* iii, 201.

13. Wesley, Sermon "Prophets and Priests," 16, in *Works,* iv, 81.

14. Thompson, *Wesley: Apostolic Man, Some Reflections on Wesley's Consecration of Dr Thomas Coke,* 52.

15. *The Works* (Jackson), xiii, 256.

16. *Letters,* viii, 92.

17. Paul Wesley Chilcote, *John Wesley and the Women Preachers of Early Methodism* (Metuchen, N.J.: Scarecrow Press, 1991).

18. *Explanatory Notes Upon the New Testament,* 580.

19. Leslie F. Church, *The Early Methodist People* (London: Epworth Press, 1948), 13.

20. *Works,* xix, 163.

21. Wesley, Sermon "On Visiting the Sick," in *Works,* iii, 396.

22. *The Works* (Jackson), x, 180.

23. *Works,* xi, 406.

24. 1 Tim. 2:11–14, in *Explanatory Notes Upon the New Testament,* 776.

25. Chilcote, *John Wesley and the Women Preachers of Early Methodism,* 47.

26. *Works,* xxi, 301.

27. *The Works* (Jackson), xii, 353.

28. *The Works* (Jackson), xii, 355.

29. *Letters,* v, 257. The recipient of this letter has been often incorrectly identified as Sarah Crosby. As an example, in *The Works* (Jackson), xii, 356, it appears that this letter was addressed to Sarah Crosby. However, this letter is to Bosanquet, and the next letter of the same date is to Crosby.

30. Maddox, *Responsible Grace,* 135.

31. *Explanatory Notes Upon the New Testament,* 632.

32. Chilcote, *John Wesley and the Women Preachers of Early Methodism,* 238.

33. Recited from John S. Simon, *John Wesley, the Last Phase* (London: Epworth Press, 1934), 182; Cf. Chilcote, *John Wesley and the Women Preachers of Early Methodism,* 195.

34. *Works,* xxvi, 595, 609–610.

35. For an analysis of the impact on Wesley of King and Stillingfleet respectively, see Lawson, *John Wesley and the Christian Ministry,* 47–70.

36. *Works*, xx, 112. Lord Peter King, John Locke's nephew by his mother's side, was a figure who inherited not only one half of Locke's library but a large portion of the penetration and liberality of mind of the philosopher. As a Dissenter, King sought to pave the way for the comprehension of Dissenters into the national church. King's book, fully entitled *An Inquiry into the Constitution, Discipline, Unity and Worship of the Primitive Church, that Flourished within the First Three Hundred Years after Christ, Faithfully Collected out of the Fathers and Extant Writings of Those Ages*, was first published in London in 1691 when King was no more than twenty-two years of age. It was reprinted by G. Lane and P. P. Sandford in New York in 1841.

37. Peter King, *An Inquiry into the Constitution, Discipline, Unity and Worship of the Primitive Church, that Flourished within the First Three Hundred Years after Christ, Faithfully Collected out of the Fathers and Extant Writings of Those Ages* (New York: G. Lane and P. P. Sandford, 1841), 62.

38. Journal on December 27, 1745, in *Works*, xx, 109–111; also Wesley's letter to Westley Hall on December 30, 1745, in *Works*, xxvi, 173–175. A. B. Lawson calls it "his last statement in defence of uninterrupted Apostolic Succession." Lawson, *John Wesley and the Christian Ministry*, 80.

39. Journal on January 20, 1746, in *Works*, xx, 112.

40. *Works*, xx, 112.

41. *Minutes of the Methodist Conferences, from the First, Held in London by the Late Rev. John Wesley, A.M., in the Year 1744*, vol. i, 36.

42. *Minutes of the Methodist Conferences, from the First, Held in London by the Late Rev. John Wesley, A.M., in the Year 1744*, vol. i, 36.

43. *Minutes of the Methodist Conferences, from the First, Held in London by the Late Rev. John Wesley, A.M., in the Year 1744*, vol. i, 36.

44. Lawson, *John Wesley and the Christian Ministry*, 45.

45. Notes on Matt. 10:5, in *Explanatory Notes Upon the New Testament*, 53.

46. Lawson, *John Wesley and the Christian Ministry*, 82.

47. Bowmer, *The Sacrament of the Lord's Supper in Early Methodism*, 158.

48. Bowmer, *The Sacrament of the Lord's Supper in Early Methodism*, 158.

49. Bowmer, *The Sacrament of the Lord's Supper in Early Methodism*, 159.

50. Letter "To the Revd. Westley Hall," on December 30, 1745, in *Works*, xxvi, 173.

51. *Works*, xxvi, 174.

52. John S. Simon, *John Wesley, the Master-Builder* (London: Epworth Press, 1927), 303.

53. *The Works* (Jackson), xiii, 211.

54. *Letters*, vii, 21.

55. Nicholas Bernard, *Judgment of the Late Archbishop of Armagh*, etc. (1675), 125–127; recited from Gerald F. Moede, *The Office of Bishop in Methodism: Its History and Development* (Zurich, Switzerland: Publishing House of The Methodist Church, 1964), 39.

56. Stillingfleet's book, fully entitled *Irenicum; A Weapon Salve for the Churches Wounds; Or the Divine Right of Particular Forms of Church Govern-*

ment; Discussed and Examined According to the Principles of the Law of Nature, the Positive Laws of God, the Practice of the Apostles, and the Primitive Church, and the Judgment of Reformed Divines. Whereby a Foundation Is Laid for the Church's Peace, and the Accommodation of Our Present Differences. Humbly Tendered to Consideration, was first published in Bedfordshire in 1659. In the *Irenicum*, Stillingfleet sought to give expression to the prevailing weariness of the faction between Episcopacy and Presbyterianism, and to find some compromise in which all could conscientiously unite. He looked upon the form of church government as non-essential, but condemned Nonconformity. In 1662 (the year of the Act of Uniformity) he reprinted the *Irenicum* in London with an appendix "concerning the Power of Excommunication in a Christian Church," in which he sought to prove that the church is a distinct society from the state, and has diverse rights and privileges of its own. The first American edition of the *Irenicum*, with the change of subtitle, entitled *The Irenicum, or Pacificator: Being a Reconciler as to Church Differences*, was printed by M. Sorin in Philadelphia in 1842.

57. Edward Stillingfleet, *The Irenicum, or Pacificator: Being a Reconciler as to Church Differences* (Philadelphia: M. Sorin, 1842), 301.

58. Stillingfleet, *The Irenicum*, 302.

59. *Letters*, iii, 182.

60. See Wesley's letter to his brother Charles on June 8, 1780, in *Letters*, vii, 21; Letter "To 'Our Brethren in America,'" on September 10, 1784, in *Letters*, vii, 238.

61. *Works*, xxvi, 595.

62. *Letters*, vii, 21.

63. *The Works* (Jackson), viii, 310.

64. *The Works* (Jackson), v, 541.

65. "Now as long the Methodists keep to this plan they cannot separate from the Church. And this is our peculiar glory." Wesley, Sermon "Prophets and Priests," 14, in *Works*, iv, 80.

66. Recited from Tyerman, *The Life and Times of the Rev. John Wesley, M.A., Founder of the Methodists*, vol. ii, 202, note 1.

67. Recited from Simon, *John Wesley, The Master Builder*, 72–73.

68. *Works*, xxii, 255.

69. *Letters*, vii, 238.

70. *Letters*, vii, 238–239.

71. *Letters*, vii, 238–239.

72. Samuel Drew, *The Life of the Rev. Thomas Coke, LL.D.: Including in Detail His Various Travels and Extraordinary Missionary Exertions, in England, Ireland, America, and the West-Indies: With an Account of His Death, on the 3d of May, 1814, While on a Missionary Voyage to the Island of Ceylon, in the East-Indies.: Interspersed with Numerous Reflections; and Concluding with an Abstract of His Writings and Character* (New York: J. Soule and T. Mason, 1818), 64.

73. Thompson, *Wesley: Apostolic Man, Some Reflections on Wesley's Consecration of Dr Thomas Coke*, 30.

74. Thompson, *Wesley: Apostolic Man, Some Reflections on Wesley's Consecration of Dr Thomas Coke*, 31–32.

75. Thompson, *Wesley: Apostolic Man, Some Reflections on Wesley's Consecration of Dr Thomas Coke*, 52.

76. Letter "To his Brother Charles," in *Letters*, vii, 284.

77. *Letters*, viii, 91.

78. Recited from Tyerman, *The Life and Times of the Rev. John Wesley, M.A., Founder of the Methodists*, vol. iii, 439.

79. John S. Simon, "Wesley's Ordinations," *Proceedings of the Wesley Historical Society* 9 (1913–1914): 152–153.

80. Simon, "Wesley's Ordinations," 154.

81. Frank Baker, *Charles Wesley As Revealed by His Letters* (London: Epworth Press, 1948), 135.

82. *Letters*, viii, 91.

83. Thomas Coke and Francis Asbury, "To the Members of the Methodist Societies in the United States," in *A Form of Discipline: For the Ministers, Preachers, and Members (Now Comprehending the Principles and Doctrines) of the Methodist Episcopal Church in America, Considered and Approved at a Conference Held at Baltimore, in the State of Maryland, on Monday the 27th of December, 1784: In Which Thomas Coke, and Francis Asbury, Presided. Arranged under Proper Heads, and Methodised in a More Acceptable and Easy Manner* (Philadelphia: Printed by Joseph Crukshank, and Sold by John Dickins, 1791), iii.

84. Coke and Asbury, "To the Members of the Methodist Societies in the United States," iii.

85. Coke and Asbury, "To the Members of the Methodist Societies in the United States," iii.

86. Thomas Taylor wrote a letter to Wesley on April 11, 1768, appealing to Wesley for qualified preachers. See Frank Baker, *From Wesley to Asbury: Studies in Early American Methodism* (Durham, N.C.: Duke University Press, 1976), 70–83.

87. Coke and Asbury, "To the Members of the Methodist Societies in the United States," iii.

88. John J. Tigert, *A Constitutional History of American Episcopal Methodism*, Second Edition (Nashville: Publishing House of the Methodist Episcopal Church, South, 1904), 58–59.

89. Jesse Lee, *A Short History of the Methodists in the United States of America; Beginning in 1766, and Continued till 1808. To which is Prefixed, a Brief Account of Their Rise in England, in the Year 1729, &c* (Baltimore: Magill and Clime, 1810), 33; Moede, *The Office of Bishop in Methodism, Its History and Development*, 28. Wesley himself wrote to Miss Ann Bolton in October 1772, "Francis Asbury says in his *Journal* on October 10, 1772: 'I received a letter from Mr. Wesley, in which he required a strict attention to discipline; *and appointed me to act as Assistant.*' The letter is not known." *Letters*, v, 341.

90. Lee, *A Short History of the Methodists, in the United States of America*, 34.

91. "Minutes of Some Conversations between the Preachers in Connection with the Rev. Mr. John Wesley. Philadelphia, June, 1773," in *Minutes of the Annual*

Conferences of the Methodist Episcopal Church, for the Years of 1773–1828 (New York: T. Mason and G. Lane, 1840), 5; Cf. Moede, *The Office of Bishop in Methodism, Its History and Development*, 29; Arthur Bruce Moss, "Methodism in Colonial America," in *The History of American Methodism*, eds. Emory Stevens Bucke and others, 3 vols. (Nashville: Abingdon Press, 1964), vol. i, 124. In his note for the Rule 1, Moss, citing Asbury's words "No preacher in our connexion shall be permitted to administer the ordinances at this time; except Mr. Strawbridge, and he under the particular direction of the assistant," points out that "[t]he Minutes do not record this easement in favor of Strawbridge." Also, as for the Rule 2, Moss notes, "Asbury makes no reference to this action. It was directed to the Maryland societies that had developed under Strawbridge's leadership and to those in Virginia in the area where Devereux Jarratt was working hand in hand with Methodist preachers. There was no desire to strain the cordial ties with him and with many other Anglican clergymen."

92. *Wesley in America: An Exhibition Celebrating the 300th Anniversary of the Birth of John Wesley, February 3 – April 11, 2003*, Curated by Richard P. Heitzenrater & Peter S. Forsaith (Dallas, Tex.: Bridwell Library, Perkins School of Theology, Southern Methodist University, 2003), 31.

93. Asbury's journal on March 13, 1778, in *The Journal and Letters of Francis Asbury*, eds. by Elmer T. Clark, J. Manning Potts, and Jacob S. Payton, 3 vols. (London: Epworth Press; Nashville: Abingdon Press, 1958), vol. i, 263–264.

94. For example, see "Methodist Petition, Oct. 28, 1776," *The Virginia Magazine of History and Biography* 18, no. 2 (April 1910): 143–144. Here Methodists in Virginia set forth, "that we are not Dissenters, but a Religious Society in Communion with the Church of England,—that we do all in our power to strengthen and support the said Church—And as we Conceive that very bad Consequences would arise from the abolishment of the establishment—We therefore pray that as the Church of England ever hath been, so it may continue to be Established."

95. Lee, *A Short History of the Methodists, in the United States of America*, 63.

96. For Asbury's effort to prevent and cure the schism, see Asbury's journals on, April 28, 1779, July 26, 1779, April 23, 1780, and April 24, 1781, in *The Journal and Letters of Francis Asbury*, vol. i, 300, 307, 346, and 402.

97. Gerald F. Moede says that Asbury invited only those "in agreement with him on the sacramental question" at hand. Moede, *The Office of Bishop in Methodism, Its History and Development*, 32.

98. "Minutes of Some Conversations between the Preachers in Connection with the Rev. Mr. John Wesley. Kent County, Delaware, April 28, 1779," in *Minutes of the Annual Conferences of the Methodist Episcopal Church, for the Years of 1773–1828*, 10.

99. Lee, *A Short History of the Methodists, in the United States of America*, 63–64.

100. Frank Baker, "Wesley's Early Preachers in America," *The Duke Divinity School Review* 34, no. 3 (Autumn 1969): 160.

101. Norman W. Spellmann, "The Early Native Methodist Preachers," *The Duke Divinity School Review* 34, no. 3 (Autumn 1969): 174.

102. Lee, *A Short History of the Methodists, in the United States of America*, 64; *Wesley in America: An Exhibition Celebrating the 300th Anniversary of the Birth of John Wesley*, 37.

103. Asbury, Journal on April 24, 1781, in *The Journal and Letters of Francis Asbury*, vol. i, 402.

104. Asbury, Letter to John Wesley on September 20, 1783, in *The Journal and Letters of Francis Asbury*, vol. iii, 31–32.

105. Recited from Lawson, *John Wesley and the Christian Ministry*, 117.

106. *Wesley in America: An Exhibition Celebrating the 300th Anniversary of the Birth of John Wesley*, 38.

107. *The Works* (Jackson), xiii, 256.

108. Drew, *The Life of the Rev. Thomas Coke, LL.D.*, 64.

109. Lawson, *John Wesley and the Christian Ministry*, 139–141.

110. For the description of Wesley's ordinations see Simons, "Wesley's Ordinations," 145–154.

111. William Phoebus, *Memoirs of the Rev. Richard Whatcoat, Late Bishop of the Methodist Episcopal Church* (New York: Joseph Allen, 1828), 18.

112. Wesley, "Facsimile of Dr. Coke's Ordination Certificate," in *Journal*, vii, between 16 and 17.

113. Tyerman, *The Life and Times of the Rev. John Wesley, M.A., Founder of the Methodists*, vol. iii, 436; Norman W. Spellmann, "The Formation of the Methodist Episcopal Church," in *The History of American Methodism*, eds. Bucke and others, vol. i, 214–215.

114. Nygren, "John Wesley's Changing Concept of the Ministry," 273.

115. For an example of this, see *The Sunday Service of the Methodists in North America: With Other Occasional Services* (London: W. Strahan, 1784).

116. *Wesley in America: An Exhibition Celebrating the 300th Anniversary of the Birth of John Wesley*, 46. "The number of Methodists in the United States at Wesley's death was over 76,000—some four thousand more than in Great Britain. . . . A generation later, Methodists in the United States numbered over 184,000, while their British cousins claimed about half as many members."

117. Journal on August 1, 1785, in *Works*, xxiii, 371.

118. William Myles, *A Chronological History of the People Called Methodists, of the Connexion of the Late Rev. John Wesley; from Their Rise in the Year 1729, to Their Last Conference, in 1802*, 4th ed. (London: Conference-office, Thomas Cordeux, agent, 1813), 175.

119. *Works*, xxvi, 290–291.

120. Green, *John Wesley*, 91.

121. *Letters*, vii. 262.

122. Letter "To Samuel Bardsley," in *Letters*, vii, 321.

123. *Conversations between the Church of England and the Methodist Church; an Interim Statement* (London: S.P.C.K., 1958), 13.

124. Recited from Tyerman, *The Life and Times of the Rev. John Wesley, M.A., Founder of the Methodists*, vol. iii, 439.

125. Whitehead, *The life of the Rev. John Wesley*, 532–533.

126. *Letters*, iv, 149–150.

127. W. J. Townsend, H. B. Workman, and George Eayrs, eds., *A New History of Methodism*, 2 vols. (London: Hodder and Stoughton, 1909), vol. i, 387.

128. *Works*, iii, 428.

129. Stoeffler, "Tradition and Renewal in the Ecclesiology of John Wesley," 312.

130. According to the Toleration Act, "congregations declaring themselves to be 'Protestant Dissenters' might insure their meeting-houses against trespass and destruction, and dissenting ministers, on taking the oaths of allegiance, might obtain a license to preach and might protect their persons from arrest by the constable or from the violence of the mob." Thompson, *Wesley: Apostolic Man, Some Reflections on Wesley's Consecration of Dr Thomas Coke*, 36.

131. For the distinction between the ordination of deacons and that of priests in the Church of England, see "The Form and Manner of Making of Deacons" and "The Form and Manner of Ordering of Priests," in *The Book of Common Prayer, 1662 Version*, 400–422.

132. In his sermon "Prophets and Priests"(1789), saying that he received his preachers "as prophets, not as priests," Wesley associated prophets with the office "to preach" and priests with the office "to administer sacraments." *Works*, iv, 79. The distinction between "prophets" free to preach and "priests" commissioned for sacramental administration goes back to Richard Hooker and before. See Richard Hooker, "*Laws of Ecclesiastical Polity*," Book V, lxxviii. 6; also see Francis Paget, *An Introduction to the Fifth Book of Hooker's Treatise of the Laws of Ecclesiastical Polity*, 2d ed. (Oxford: Clarendon Press, 1907), 250–251. It was also an accustomed distinction, though differently nuanced, among the Puritans; for example see Leonard Trinterud, "The Order of the Prophecy at Norwich," in *Elizabethan Puritanism*, ed. Leonard Trinterud (Oxford: Oxford University Press, 1971), 191–201, especially the editor's introduction; William Perkins, *The Art of Prophesying*, rev. ed. (Edinburgh: Banner of Truth Trust, 1996). *The Art of Prophesying* was first published in English in 1606

133. John S. Simon, *John Wesley and the Advance of Methodism* (London: Epworth Press, 1925), 291.

134. Letter "To the Revd. Charles Wesley," on June 20, 1755, in *Works*, xxvi, 561.

135. *Letters*, vii, 179.

136. Letter "To William Thompson (?)," on February 21, 1787, in *Letters*, vii, 372.

137. Lawson, *John Wesley and the Christian Ministry*, 83.

138. Stillingfleet, *The Irenicum*, 133.

139. *Works*, iv, 79.

140. Letter "To Alexander Suter," on November 24, 1787, in *Letters*, viii, 23.

141. *Works*, iv, 75.

142. *Works*, iv, 77–78.

143. *Works*, iv, 79.

144. Wesley, "A Farther Appeal to Men of Reason and Religion," Part III, III, 15, in *Works*, xi, 300.

145. *Letters*, iii, 186.

146. Letter on October 31, 1755, in *Letters*, iii, 150.

147. *Works*, iv, 80.

148. Letter "To Mary Bishop," on October 18, 1778, in *Letters*, vi, 327.

149. Wesley, Sermon "On Attending the Church Service," in *Works*, iii, 477–478.

150. *Works*, iii, 466.

151. Baker, *John Wesley and the Church of England*, 137.

Chapter 7

Wesley's Ecclesiology in the Christian Tradition

Wesley himself once commented of the word "church" that "[a] more ambiguous word than this . . . is scarce to be found in the English language."[1] He never admitted that what he was building himself was a Church. The early Methodists were not a church in the beginning, but a group of societies belonging to the Church of England. They did not need their own doctrine of the church. In that sense, Albert C. Outler cautiously asserted that Methodists in the beginning "had no distinctive doctrine of the church."[2] Durward Hofler also observed, "There is no Wesleyan doctrine of the church as such, for John Wesley unlike John Calvin did not undertake a systematic compilation of his theology or ecclesiology."[3] Indeed, Wesley did not write a systematic theology as such with a proper place given to ecclesiology.

Nevertheless, it can't be rightly said that Wesley never possessed his own unique ecclesiology. In fact, there have been scholars who argue that Wesley had his ecclesiology. J. E. Rattenbury held that Wesley's ecclesiology, like his brother's, remained essentially Anglican, and that the Wesleys had the view of the Church of England as "a divinely instituted organization, endowed with a sacerdotal ministry, which received its authorization by direct succession from the Apostles."[4] John Deschner proposed that Wesley had one, but that it was basically the New Testament understanding of the church.[5] Howard A. Snyder suggested parallels between the Anabaptists and Wesley on the doctrine of the church as a functional or missional reality, and, in doing so, he stressed Wesley's free-church ecclesiology.[6]

k Baker believed that "throughout his adult life Wesley responded with varying degrees of enthusiasm to two fundamentally different views of the church": catholic and free church.[7] Colin W. Williams suggested that Wesley held together three interpretations of the church: the Catholic, the Classical Protestant, and the Free Church.[8] Interestingly enough passages can be found in Wesley's many writings which support either one or all of these interpretations.

John Wesley was a man of tradition. He appreciated his rich legacy he inherited from various traditions, and his indebtedness was broad. He read numerous works of a variety of the theologians, ranging from the early Fathers to the contemporary Pietists. In shaping his theology, he interwove a variety of strands from the numerous books of all preceding centuries and many traditions. He drew heavily on the early Fathers, on the Anglican divines of the previous century, on the Puritans, and on the Pietists. He drew, though not heavily, on the mystics of the Roman Catholicism and, indirectly, on the reformers. He drew on any Christian divines in whom he could find helpful thought. In a sense, understanding Wesley entails understanding the whole of the Christian tradition before and in his age.

The roots of Wesley's ecclesiology are not confined to one religious tradition. When one enumerates major traditions which were important for his ecclesiology, they include Scripture, the primitive church, Anglicanism, Puritanism, and Pietism. There were also other tributary streams such as Catholicism and reformers that indirectly influenced Wesley.

Primitivism offered a lasting influence on and a continuing model for his ecclesiology throughout his life. Wesley drew from primitive Christianity an ideal of what Christianity and the church should be. For him primitive Christianity served as a standard by which to measure the faith and practice of Christians. Primitive Christianity was a model for his Methodist movement as well as a standard of his personal faith.

From the beginning John Wesley's ecclesiology was formed from his desire to recreate the primitive faith community. In his childhood Wesley was taught to revere the primitive Christianity by his father and studied the classics at Charterhouse. At Oxford University, which was favorable for the patristic studies, he read much of the early Fathers. In Wesley's day existed there a considerable concern on the part of many High-Church Anglicans for primitivism. In particularly, through his exposure to the Anglican patristic revival and some direct reading of Eastern Fathers, Wesley became familiar with the Eastern patristic tradition and shared the early Eastern understanding of *theosis*. As a result, throughout his life Wesley often defined Christian salvation as "a recovery of the divine likeness" or "the renewal of our souls after the image of God." This soteriology that stresses the present human spiritual transformation led Wesley to affirm the essential role of the disciplinary function of the church in its proclamation of salvation in Christ.

At Oxford he devoted himself to the spiritual practices of the primitive church. For example, his practice of stationary fasts at Oxford was to follow the standard of the early church. During the last years at Oxford, Wesley's encounter with the High-Church nonjurors of the Church of England such as Thomas Deacon, John Clayton, and John Byrom, had an impact on his primitivism. They turned Wesley's interests to the liturgical and sacramental features of the early ecclesiastical tradition.

Wesley went out to Georgia as a missionary inspired with a vision of the primitivism, but his attempt to restore primitive Christianity in Georgia turned out to be a failure. During the Georgia period, however, he read Bishop Beveridge's *Pandectae canonum conciliorum*, which slightly corrected his views of the primitive church. Also, during that period, the encounter with the Moravians in Georgia invigorated his primitivism with evangelical features. Wesley recognized the evangelical primitivism of the Moravians as one which had recovered more of primitive Christianity than those like himself who had devoted themselves to ancient ecclesiastical practices. Furthermore, his contact with Moravians opened up new prospects for assurance of salvation, and upon his return to England those prospects became personally appropriated in his evangelical awakening. In short, the early Wesley in Epworth, Oxford, and Georgia was committed to primitivism, showing his serious attempts at holy living.

While returning to England from Georgia, Wesley was reading the works of St. Cyprian. His reading of Cyprian and his response during the reading indicate that till then he still maintained his sacerdotal and high view of the ministry. According to Cyprian, an unbroken episcopal succession is necessary to give efficacy to all religious exercises. Following Cyprian's teaching, Wesley believed threefold order of ministers (bishops, priests and deacons) to be of divine appointment. The early Wesley saw ordination, the laying on of hands, by a bishop who stood in the line of apostolic succession as the basic requisite for priesthood. On the whole, the early Wesley adhered to the sacerdotal view of the ministry and to the concept of the church as an institution, pursuing the ideal of primitive church.

Ironically, however, it is his attempts to pursue the ideal of primitive church that led the middle and later Wesley to change his views of ordination and apostolic succession. In 1746 Wesley read Lord Peter King's *An Enquiry into the Constitution, Discipline, Unity, and Worship of the Primitive Church*, and thereafter he changed his views of ordination and apostolic succession. King's work convinced Wesley that in the early church there was no episcopal monarchy comparable to what is to be seen in the Middle Ages and in modern times, and that the episcopal form of the church government is described, but not prescribed in the New Testament. Wesley found that till before the Queen Elizabeth's reign, the divine right of episcopacy had not been asserted in England. Above all, King's work, and also Stillingfleet's *Irenicum*, led Wesley to the conclusion that bishops and presbyters are the same order and consequently he had a right to ordain. For a long time Wesley was reluctant to exercise this right since he, as a conscientious, faithful and devout member of the Church of England, did not want to violate the established order of the Church to which he belonged. For the same reason, he did not also allow his lay preachers to administer the sacraments. However, circumstances forced him to seriously consider the change of his position. The situations in North America particularly accelerated the change. In 1784, Wesley finally consecrated Thomas Coke as a superintendent and ordained Richard Whatcoat and Thomas Vasey by taking the case of North America out of the circumstances of the primitive church. Edgar Thompson's suggestion is reasonable that in his ordinations Wesley followed the precedent of the Church of Alexandria in the first three centuries, where presbyters appointed and consecrated their own bishops without intervention from other sees.[9]

There is no evidence that Wesley received a direct influence from medieval Catholicism—except the mystics—as he did from Primitive Christianity. The early Wesley read many of the mystics and learned from them an emphasis on inward religion and inward relation to God. The mystics' stress on self-discipline was also influential upon the early Wesley. But he withdrew from mysticism from around the mid-1730s. At the heart of his reservations about mysticism was avoiding the mysticism as solitary religion and the mystics' tendency to privatize the revelation of God. Wesley was certain that Christianity is a social religion and that social holiness, the fellowship of believers, in the Christian life is necessary. Particularly, Wesley, in the controversy with Moravian Quietists, stood against the mysticism that ignored the use of all external means of grace in the Church by sinking into the divine mysteries. Against the Quietists, Wesley argued for the inwardness of religion mediated through means of grace, which was not his newly found idea for he had emphasized it even at Oxford earlier in the 1720s. It needs to be noted that the controversy with the Quietists provided Wesley with an opportunity to enhance and develop his own ecclesiology. In addition, Wesley's anti-mysticism did not persist even after he came to reject mysticism as the enemy of Christianity. The influence of mysticism upon Wesley remained throughout his life and was greater than he was aware.

With regard to ecclesiology, there seems to be no evidence of Wesley's direct dependence upon medieval Catholicism. While it is possible that he was influenced by Catholicism through the medieval influences on Anglicanism, there is no evidence of direct influence from medieval Catholicism that Wesley acknowledges—except the mystics. Nevertheless, the investigation of medieval monasticism is helpful to understand what Wesley's Methodist organization was like. Methodism was not designed as a substitute for the Anglican or any other church. Wesley's United Societies did not qualify for the designation "churches" since nothing about them approximated the meaning of church either in Anglican or in Roman Catholic usage or for that matter according to the broad and loose patterns of the free churches functioning in his day. In fact, the United Societies were designed to be auxiliary to the Anglican church, supporting her mission by enriching and deepening the spiritual life of the members who used their services. At this point, Wesley's Methodism most clearly resembled "Tertiaries" or "Third Orders" of High Medieval Western Catholicism which had been auxiliary to and not independent of the Catholic Church.

Some similarities and parallels between Tertiaries of medieval Catholicism and Wesley's Methodism are striking. Wesley's United Societies insisted on fasting, prayer, worship, and benevolence as did the Catholic Tertiaries, composed as they were of men and women engaged in ordinary occupations. Lay-persons played a pivotal role both in medieval monasticism and in the early Methodism. For example, Wesley's Helpers and the Little Poor Brothers of St. Francis were both originally lay-persons. The new place of the laity was emphasized by St. Francis in the foundation of his Tertiaries. Likewise, none would deny that the key to the influence of Methodism was its appeal to the laity. Deprived of its lay workers Methodism assuredly would not have survived.

St. Anthony, the founder of monasticism, and the earlier monks were generally laymen. Although in the course of time the monks joined the priesthood, the monks, at least in theory, were not necessarily priests. Likewise, the early preachers of Methodism were generally lay-persons. The lay preachers of Methodism were the itinerant persons who were Wesley's full-time lieutenants. They were used for what they could very well do. The justification of their vocation depends on their gifts, grace, and fruits necessary for the work regardless of their social status or education. The lay preachers were not simply preachers, but they also gradually came to function as pastors with due pastoral authority as did the monks.

Monasticism and Methodism were both in connexionalism. Cistercians, the Friars and Methodists had a similar conference. For instance, although each Cistercian monastery was an independent unit, Cistercians kept up the

connexional spirit by enforcing everywhere a unity of usage, and by an annual chapter or conference in September at Citeaux attended by the abbots
of all Cistercian foundations. Discipline was maintained not only by this
conference but by giving to the abbot of Citeaux a prevailing voice in the
congregation of which he was the president, with also the right of visiting
any monastery at will. Each abbot also had the duty of visiting the daughter
houses of his own foundation. In the organizational structure of Cistercians
one sees striking similarities with that of the Methodists. The organizational
similarities are also observed between the medieval friars and Wesley's
preachers. The Franciscans were divided into Provinces, over each of which
was a Provincial Minister, among the Dominicans elected for four years
only. The Provinces were again divided into Custodies, under the charge of
Custodians, who possessed general rights of supervision for their districts.
Every year Chapters-General were held. Among the Franciscans, as in
Methodism, it roamed about. In many of its powers these Chapters-General
corresponded with the Methodist Conference. The original purpose of both
the Franciscan Chapter-General and the Methodist Conference was the
same: the forgathering of brethren from far and near that they might gain
new enthusiasm by the communion of saints. As they grew, the Friars restricted the Chapter-General to the delegates of the Provinces. Wesley excluded all but a select band of preachers, the 'Legal Hundred.' Both Friars
and Wesley found that this common government by a central court united
the whole body into a compact effective instrument.

However, it must be noted that despite the striking similarities between
monasticism and Methodism, they do not prove Wesley's direct borrowing
from the historic monastic tradition. There is no evidence, at least Wesley
acknowledges, of direct dependence of the Methodist Church organization
upon the medieval Tertiaries. Since Methodism did not provide for goods in
common or encourage celibacy, there was no element of strict monasticism
about it. Of course, it is possible that Wesley derived some monastic ideas
from his contemporary context even though he never spoke of it. For example, the Church of England, even after the dissolution of the monasteries in
the English Reformation, retained the monastic ideal of morning and evening prayer in its prayer book. That practice clearly affected Wesley's rules
for Methodists. Also, Wesley read much of the church Fathers and possibly
from the sources he imbibed some monastic spirit such as the desire for
holiness, a rule of life, and the serious use of religious discipline of prayer,
scripture reading, fasting, and the like, while such spirit is not limited in the
monasticism.

Wesley seems to have read little of the reformers. The reformers do not
count as an influence on Wesley in any sense similar to that of the primitive

Christianity on him. In fact, Wesley does not seem to have had any distinct and functioning conception of "the Reformation" in the way that he had a distinct and functioning conception of "primitive Christianity." Of course, he did have a conception of "the Protestant," as opposed to "the Catholic"; and his stress on primitive Christianity is precisely one element of what it means for him to be Protestant. But he did not dwell or draw on the theologies of the so-called magisterial reformers in the way that the Lutheran and Calvinist traditions do. Often, when he encountered their theology—as when he read Luther on Galatians—he did not like it. But the reformers had an influence on Wesley on the sense that they introduced certain themes— particularly sanctification and discipline—into ecclesiology which were to have an impact on Wesley not through any encounter with the works of the reformers themselves, but primarily through the way in which those themes played themselves out in the Anglican and Puritan traditions.

The reformers first affirmed two great dimensions of the church: Word and Sacraments. And in the period 1559–1660, attention focused on a third dimension, "the discipline of Christ," which includes personal discipline, church order and ecclesiastical polity. The reformers, with the themes of sanctification and discipline they put stress on, had an impact on Wesley's ecclesiology indirectly through the traditions of English Protestantism (the Church of England and the Puritans). With respect to the emphasis on sanctification and discipline, Wesley was closer to Bucer and Calvin than to Luther. Wesley stressed the importance of a disciplined life as essential to the church being the church. A powerful theological support for his inclusion of discipline as an important element in the church is the place of sanctification in his soteriology. Sanctification would entail a call for the church to be a holy community. Wesley affirmed the essential role of the disciplinary function of the church in its proclamation of salvation in Christ. Certainly, one of the contributions Wesley's ecclesiology offers to the Christian tradition is its emphasis upon discipline. Many of Wesleyan scholars like Howard Snyder make much of the place of discipline in Wesley's societies and attribute the success of Methodism to it.[10] In this case discipline refers to the ongoing stress on moral accountability and the correction of the community in the life of the individual by members of the societies by the means of tickets, expulsions, General Rules, etc. Of course it should be added that Wesley's discipline was teleological in nature and not legalistic. Its purpose was to hasten one along in his pursuit of holiness.

Wesley was theologically conscious of the two Protestant marks of the church: Word and Sacraments. He accepted and valued them not as much as marks of the true church as divinely ordained means of grace. For Wesley, where the church is truly alive, there will be neither abuse nor neglect of either the Word or of the sacraments. Nor will one be displaced by the other as if there were a primacy of one over the other. Particularly in regard to the sacraments, Wesley believed that a due administration of the sacraments was necessary to the well-being of a Church, for they are the ordinary means whereby God increases faith.

As far as the Lord's Supper is concerned, Wesley accommodated a Calvinistic emphasis on the spiritual presence while his view was close to the Zwinglian "memorial" view. Wesley believed that although the bread and the wine are the figure or the symbols of Christ's body and blood, Christ is present through the mediation of the Holy Spirit in the Lord's Supper. Wesley further emphasized the sacrament as the means of grace by which one experiences the transforming presence of God. For Wesley, one in the Lord's Supper experiences prevenient, justifying, and sanctifying grace, which transforms her/his life. In a sense, while the reformers in the sixteenth century were interested in what, if anything, happens to the elements of bread and wine and how it occurs, Wesley had a more interest in what God is doing in the sacrament. In Luther's view, the sacrament is a confirming rather than a converting ordinance. And for Luther, the sacrament as the *verbum visibile* (visible Word) must be associated with the *verbum vocale* (preached Word) and therefore should be administered only to those who live under the preaching of the true Word. However, for Wesley, the Lord's Supper, because of the Spirit's presence bringing Christ's grace in it, has a power to arouse the participants' faith and therefore is a converting ordinance. Wesley's view that the sacrament is a converting as well as a confirming ordinance suggests that even where we are dissatisfied with the doctrinal standards of other bodies, we are called to see the sacrament as a place where God is calling together and offering to build up in unity those whom He has used as His church.

The reformers' ecclesiology indirectly had an impact on Wesley through the Church of England. Obviously informed by the Augsburg Confession, Article XIX of the Church of England defines the church as "a Congregation of faithful men, in the which the pure Word of God is preached, and the Sacraments be duly administered according to Christ's Ordinance, in all those things that of necessity are requisite to the same."[11] Throughout his life, Wesley continued to hold to this Article.

The Church of England was the initial and a lasting influence upon Wesley's ecclesiology. Both of Wesley's parents had left dissenting congregations to join the established church and they remained faithful communicants in the Church of England until their deaths. The young Wesley who had been reared in the Church of England was a faithful member of the Church and was enthusiastic to follow the teachings of the Church. One sees that to the young Wesley his religious self-understanding was tied up with the Church of England and his religious responsibility was centered in the Church of England. For the early Wesley, to be a good Christian was essentially to be loyal to that Church and its teaching, to share in its sacramental life, and to induce others to do the same. The High-Church Anglican churchmanship inherited from his background was working beneath his conscious mind throughout his life. At least up till the Georgia period, Wesley maintained the so-called "sacerdotal concept of the priesthood in the Church of England" and his High-Church Anglican zeal. In accordance with the high-church view, he in Georgia refused Holy Communion to all those who had not received baptism at the hands of an episcopally ordained clergyman. This action shows his high view of the sacraments and of apostolic succession. In short, the early Wesley was a High Churchman in the Church of England equipped with a formal ecclesiology and attached to the concept of the church as an institution though he on other side was developing his concern of practical divinity.

However, his High-Church views clashed with the evangelical conversion of 1738, and later insoluble tensions and difficulties remained in Wesley's theological development. The Aldersgate event gave Wesley an experience never to be forgotten throughout his after life, which was one of the most significant developments in his spiritual pilgrimage. The Aldersgate experience did not lead to a repudiation of the institutional church, but forced Wesley to consider, more than ever, the primacy of the soteriological mandate. After Aldersgate, Wesley, while remaining fond of the liturgy of the Church, was no longer bound by the formal ecclesiology. The experience of evangelical conversion sometimes clashed with his Anglican background, causing him to act and speak inconsistently at times, but in general Wesley's ecclesiology after Aldersgate was dictated by his desire for the salvation of souls or his highly developed sense of mission.

Wesley's view of ministry after Aldersgate was changing to meet the pragmatic needs of a developing work. While Wesley supported the authority of the Church of England in the ordination of persons to holy orders, it was clear to Wesley after Aldersgate that the power and gifts of the Spirit working within persons' lives could not be denied. Now Wesley recognized and supported a variety of ministries as legitimate responses to God's call regardless of the dictates of formal ecclesiology. Because of his conviction that God's grace and justification by faith are available to all, Wesley accepted, although sometimes reluctantly, the responses by laypersons to the movement of the Spirit within their lives. Wesley's ministry after Aldersgate became more in tune with the physical and spiritual needs of the persons. Wesley was eager to respond to God's saving grace and inward call with a social passion to care for one's neighbor. He accepted the forms of ministry shaped by the gifts that persons were given and the needs of the neighbor.

After Aldersgate, soteriology took a more central place in Wesley's theology, and all other doctrines, including ecclesiology, established their character and validity in relation to the saving work of Christ. Salvation was the heart of Wesley's understanding of church. Faith in Christ's redemptive work was the primary prerequisite for membership in the body of Christ. At the same time, the ongoing process of "faith working by love" resulted in a holy people who proclaimed to the world the reality of the transformation wrought by the Spirit.

This salvation-centered ecclesiology led Wesley to respond to the situations according to the needs of mission. Although he continued to respect the usages and ordinances, and the doctrine and the discipline of the Church of England, ecclesiastical authority in the deepest sense was now found in the needs of the mission. Where the salvation of soul is demanded, there is a necessity. If there is an absolute necessity, he was ready to follow even irregularities.

For a long time Wesley had disallowed sacramental rights to his preachers and ecclesiastical status to his societies. He did not want to violate the established order of the Church to which he belonged. But circumstances made this impossible. The lack of interest on the part of the clergy of that day in the preached gospel for saving souls led Wesley to preach to those willing to listen in any place, and to accept lay-helpers with no thought he was separating from the Established Church. The open-air preaching and lay preaching, however, were not a manner of the Church of England at that time. Moreover, as the Methodist movement grew up, Wesley could not help taking some crucial actions and steps for Methodism. In his later period Wesley came to approve some female preaching though not generally, and became acutely aware of the need for ordained Methodist clergy to administer the sacraments, administrate the Methodist societies, and perpetuate the movement. And he finally ordained two ministers for the ministry in America in 1784. This action transformed Methodism from an ancillary movement within the Church of England to an autonomous ecclesiastical body, and by the ordination, Wesley eventually established an independent Methodist ministry that needed to depend upon no other ministry including that of the Church of England than their own to satisfy the ecclesiastical needs of their people.

In short, since the middle period of his ministry, Wesley was dominated by the primacy of the soteriological mandate, and he moved from formal ecclesiology to a more practical and functional understanding of ecclesiology that is controlled and justified by the need of a specific situation. This pragmatic understanding of church, as Edgar Thompson suggests, became a principal of the Methodist ecclesiology: "Where is the Work, there is the Church."[12] Part of Wesley's genius lay in his pragmatism.

Although through his life Wesley suffered changes of emphasis in his ecclesiology and periods of recasting basic motifs, his understanding of the nature and meaning of the sacraments didn't suffer any considerable change through his life. Even when he left behind his insistence on apostolic succession, he did not leave behind the sacerdotal aspect for the administration of the sacraments. Wesley always held to the belief that only duly ordained men should administer the sacraments. Originally the Roman Catholic Church held this view, and the Church of England followed suit. In this view, only one ordained by a Bishop in the apostolic succession can be the celebrant, and only one confirmed by such a bishop can be a recipient. Following the Church of England, Wesley distinguished the call to preach from the authority to administer the sacraments. He never allowed his preachers to administer the sacraments without ordination, even after his eventual action toward an autonomous church by ordination. Even though Wesley in the middle and later periods of his ministry rejected the qualification of confirmation for the recipient, he gave real support to the view that true ordination is necessary to right administration. This fact is apparent, especially in his 1789 sermon on "The Ministerial Office." Frank Baker is right in noting that "Wesley never shook off his conviction that for the sake of decency and order, if not for validity and effectiveness, the Lord's Supper must be administered by an ordained clergyman."[13] Wesley, while on one hand developing his practical and functional understanding of church, on the other maintained his high sacramentalism. For his sacramentalism Wesley was most Anglican precisely.

Wesley did not want to separate from the Church of England, before and even after his ordinations. The influence of the Church of England upon Wesley continued through his life in relationship of tension with the sense of mission which came to be more prominent from his conversion. It is true that many of Wesley's views on the church were close to those of Anglicanism of the seventeenth and eighteenth centuries. However, Wesley's ecclesiology was not static. Throughout his entire life, Wesley developed his ecclesiology in reaction to changing circumstances. In particular, after 1738, Puritanism and Pietism exerted an increasing influence upon Wesley. The one was a main contributor to Wesley's unorthodox churchmanship after he became a field preacher in 1739. The other permanently influenced Wesley's doctrine of salvation which was most important in understanding his ecclesiology.

Wesley had a critical eye on the deficiencies and iniquities of the established Church, which in a sense led to his Methodist movement. Much of Wesley's criticism of the established church echoes Puritan concerns. The Puritans were an important and immediate impact on Wesley's theology and practices. There is clear evidence that Wesley read and used many Puritans and was to substantial extent influenced by them. Of course, it must be noted that Puritanism is a multifaceted tradition, not all of which was congenial or acceptable to Wesley as he worked out his own theological stance and packaged it as a resource for his Methodists. Nevertheless, it is undeniable that Wesley's image of the Christian life and his instructions in its practice reflect strong affinities with the Puritan ethos. His emphasis on a serious, circumspect, and disciplined daily life was driven from the Puritans as well as his High-Church asceticism in his early phase. There is affiliation between Wesley and the Puritans in many aspects such as experimental theology, ethics, pastoral ideals, and the concept of the church as a disciplined Christian community.

However, it would be an overstatement to suggest that Wesley was a Puritan. No claim can be made that Wesley was a reinvigorated seventeenth-century Puritan, nor that Methodism was an eighteenth-century form of English Puritanism. Wesley himself rejected the accusation that he had reinstated Puritanism with the Methodist societies. Wesley maintained a unique combination of intense dedication to the Church of England and affinity with and sympathy for some aspects of Puritanism, and he lived with the resultant tensions.

Pietism was instrumental in permanently influencing Wesley's soteriology on which his theology including ecclesiology was centered. The Pietists, together with the Church of England, exerted a powerful influence upon Wesley in their regard for the order and spirit of the primitive Church. Wesley seems to have derived the themes of religion of heart or inward religion and holy living from the Pietists—possibly also from the mystics. He learned from the Pietists the importance of the role and training of laity and was impressed by their discipline and enthusiasm for mission. Above all the particular influence of the Pietists was prominent in the creation and development of Methodist Church organization. Wesley admired the Pietists' organization and in some ways imitated it as seen in his import of "band" system from the Moravian Pietists. The Methodists' church-order, and even terminology, show the influence from the Pietists.

In sum, the sources of Wesley's ecclesiology run back from the Anglican and Pietistic to the primitive traditions. The religious self-understanding of the young Wesley was governed by a mixture of primitivism, Puritan legalism, and High-Church sacramental Anglicanism. Also, the

German Pietists significantly influenced Wesley in constituting his ecclesiology. Moreover, Wesley was impressed by the piety, or holy living found in the contemporary religious societies and examples of holy living found in Roman Catholicism. Wesley's indebtedness was remarkably broad, and he recombined many divergent Christian emphases and traditions. Indeed, the catholicity of his sources is surprising. Wesley was quite eclectic in his appropriation of traditional sources. This eclectic approach has frequently made it possible for many to claim Wesley as their own. Wesley apparently owed no allegiance to any particular school, though he remained an Anglican. His ecclesiology was "an interesting amalgam."[14]

This multifaceted feature of Wesley's ecclesiology makes it difficult to determine the place of Wesley's ecclesiology in the Christian tradition. In evaluating the place of Wesley's ecclesiology in the Christian tradition, Wesleyan scholars often have excessively stressed his relationship with the Church of England. In doing so, they unconsciously highlighted a classical Protestant color of Wesley's ecclesiology. This tendency was apparent from the incipient period of interpretations of Wesley's Methodism. For example, William Hobrow's *The Doctrines of the Methodists, Dedicated to the Preachers, in Connection with the Late Reverend Mr. John Wesley*, which was written right after Wesley's death, states:

> The general Question asked is, "*Why we go to hear the Methodists*, and do not stick to the Ministers and Places where we were brought up?"
>
> The Answer is clear, (in general) they do not preach the *ancient Doctrines of the Reformers*, nor the *Experience of the Christians, laid down in the New Testament*—Nor do they shew us the Way to attain Heaven—neither do they know it themselves.
>
> The Doctrines we mean are the Doctrines of the Church of England, contained in her Articles, and Prayer-book, and of all the Reformed Churches in Germany and other Nations.[15]

There is no doubt that Wesley argued for ecclesiology in an Anglican manner—that is, the church as "a Congregation of faithful men, in the which the pure Word of God is preached, and the Sacraments be duly administered according to Christ's Ordinance, in all those things that of necessity are requisite to the same." Obviously this interpretation was informed by the Augsburg Confession. In that sense, Wesley's ecclesiology was close to the classical Protestant interpretation which emphasized the preaching of the gospel and the administration of the sacraments as essential marks of the church. But this common explanation of Wesley's ecclesiology, if it ends at this point, would paint Wesley in too much of a classical Protestant color and does not really explore the depth of his thought. In formulating his ecclesiology, Wesley took the multiple traditions which he inherited and sought to appropriate them in a creative eclecticism.

Furthermore, Wesley's ecclesiology was always tempered by the appeal to reason and Scripture, as well as the traditions of the church. For Wesley, the church is subordinate to Scripture. No institution can be justified unless it conforms to scriptural teaching. "In all cases, the Church is to be judged by Scripture, not the Scripture by the Church."[16] But studying the biblical warrants for ecclesiastical practices, Wesley soon discovered that the Scriptures were not as explicit in this area as he had once believed. He came to realize that Scripture does not provide warrants for all the ecclesiastical practices he was exercising, and his decision was that "Scripture, in most points, gives only general rules; and leaves the particular circumstances to be adjusted by the common sense of mankind."[17] This decision, together with his soteriological concerns, allowed Wesley considerable flexibility in forming his ecclesiology.

Of course, almost from the beginning, there were well-reasoned critics who pointed out that Wesley was theologically confused and was developing a theological position that might well come to no good end. For instance, John Smith addressed a series of letters to Wesley, commenting on the instabilities in Wesley's teachings and the confusions they were creating.[18] Wesley knew such criticisms, analyzed them shrewdly, and chose his options and acted "in accordance with a self-chosen image he was willing for the world to see." It, as Outler asserts, is "the image of an Anglican folk-theologian, a mass-evangelist," and "a small-group therapist,"[19] whose goal was to spread the evangel and biblical holiness to the whole land and to save souls. This vision for Wesley was central and clear, and its exposition is richly nuanced in his life and his works. Everything creative in his theologizing has this practical, soteriological concern as its warrant.

Basically Wesley understood the nature of the church from the soteriological perspective. The church for Wesley is the agent of saving souls. He clearly speaks of the soteriological agenda of the church:

> men who did fear God and desire the happiness of their fellow-creatures have in every age found it needful to join together in order to oppose the works of darkness, to spread the knowledge of God their Saviour, and to promote his kingdom upon earth. Indeed he himself has instructed them so to do. From the time that men were upon the earth he hath taught them to join together in his service, and has united them in one body by one spirit. And for this very end he has joined them together, 'that he might destroy the works of the devil', first in them that are already united, and by them in all that are round about them.

... This is the original design of the church of Christ. It is a body of men compacted together in order, first, to save each his own soul, then to assist each other in working out their salvation, and afterwards, as far as in them lies, to save all men from present and future misery, to overturn the kingdom of Satan, and set up the kingdom of Christ. And this ought to be the continued care and endeavour of every member of his church. Otherwise he is not worthy to be called a member thereof, as he is not worthy to be called a member thereof, as he is not a living member of Christ.[20]

Accordingly, for Wesley, salvation is the essence of nature and function of the church. A personal experience of saving grace is essential to the incorporation into the church of Christ, and the mission is essential to the function and goal of the church. For that reason Wesley committed himself to making Methodism the most effective and efficient organization to meet its soteriological goal, "to spread scriptural holiness over the land."

Wesley himself once described his vocation in a letter to William Hervey: "I have only one thing to do, to save my own soul and them that hear me."[21] Wesley also confessed, "I think every day lost, which is not (mainly at least) employed in this thing [saving souls]. *Sum totus in illo.* [I am entirely occupied with it]."[22] For half a century he devoted himself to the vocation, traveling across the British Isles and offering Christ to any who would hear him.

For Wesley soteriology governs ecclesiology. Resisting pressure to form a new dissenting body of believers in England, Wesley died a faithful Anglican. His sympathies for the institution, however, were sometimes overshadowed by his concern for salvation. When the order of the established Church became restrictive to his evangelistic endeavors, Wesley affirmed the priority of his soteriology. Rather than withdraw from his commitment to the salvation of souls, Wesley pressed on with an ever-expanding movement, arguing, "We cannot with good conscience neglect the present opportunity of saving souls while we live, for fear of consequences which may possibly or probably happen after we are dead."[23]

When the spread of scriptural holiness was frustrated by ecclesiastical structures or leaders, he felt justified in deviating from accepted practices to form new means of maintaining the primacy of salvation in the church. In the Conference Minutes of 1747, he defined the limits of ecclesiastical authority: "We will obey the rules and the governors of the church whenever we can consistently with our duty to God: whenever we cannot we will quietly obey God rather than man."[24] The church as a God-ordained institution merited respect and obedience; but only insofar as it remained the means and not an end in itself. Wesley affirmed his allegiance to the Church and simultaneously the limitations of that allegiance: "I would observe every punctilio of order, except where the salvation of souls is at stake. There I prefer the end [salvation] before the means."[25]

What was vital to Wesley is the salvation of souls. This evangelistic commission was extended to all who called themselves Methodists. As Outler observes, Wesley "taught his Methodists to be martyrs and servants....They learned it from him and so became evangelists themselves, not many of them as preachers, but all of them as witnesses whose lives backed up their professions."[26]

Wesley's emphasis upon salvation is well represented in his oft-quoted description of the geographical boundaries of his ministry:

> God in Scripture commands me, according to my power, to instruct the ignorant, reform the wicked, confirm the virtuous. Man forbids me do this in another's parish; that is, in effect, to do it at all, seeing I have now no parish of my own, nor probably ever shall. Whom then shall I hear? God or man? 'If it be just to obey man rather than God, judge you.' 'A dispensation of the gospel is committed to me, and woe is me if I preach not the gospel.'
> . . . I look upon *all the world as my parish*; thus far I mean, that in whatever part of it I am I judge it meet, right, and my bounden duty, to declare unto all that are willing to hear the glad tidings of salvation. This is the work which I know God has called me to. And sure I am that his blessing attends it.[27]

What is significant in the context of this statement is the priority of mission over any institutional limitations. Wesley persistently declared, "I live and die a member of the Church of England."[28] In its beginning, Methodism was "a society in search of the Church [of England]."[29] But the soteriological commitment forced Wesley to ignore geographical boundaries, and had him declare that his vision was beyond parish boundaries. The same soteriological commitment permitted him to disregard institutional limitations as well.

For example, the soteriological commitment resulted in Wesley's ordinations. Receiving no help or sympathy from the established church, he acted "not by choice, but necessity" and ordained his preachers for the ministry in America in 1784. The ordination eventually offered an autonomous ecclesiastical body in the United States. Also, Wesley's subsequent ordinations for Ireland, Scotland, and England itself eventually made Methodism need to depend upon no other ministry than their own to satisfy the ecclesiastical needs of their people including the administration of the sacraments. Therefore, the denominational beginning of Methodism was the outcome of

Wesley's decision to place soteriological concerns above those of institutional commitments.

At this point, Colin Williams is at least partly correct when he observes that for Wesley, "mission is the primary mark of the church."[30] While there are distinctive features created by his peculiar circumstances, Wesley seems to have captured the central emphasis of the New Testament that the church is a community of people called into being by God for the purpose of carrying out His redemptive mission (in his words, "spreading scriptural holiness") in the world.

The original cause of most of Wesley's separatist actions was "spiritual need rather than theological conviction."[31] From the need of mission did originate his Methodist structures. It is difficult to argue that Wesley had a self-conscious ecclesiological plan from his many references to the serendipitous nature of the new structures. Rather, from the perceived need, Wesley and the early Methodists moved to experience, developing structures either by conscious design or fortuitous discovery. Therefore, the principle of *necessity* took a priority in Wesley's ecclesiology that was pragmatic. The experiential and pragmatic nature of Wesley's ecclesiology, with the multifaceted feature of his ecclesiology shaped by the various sources, makes it difficult to place Wesley's ecclesiology in a specific Christian tradition.

There were three major ecclesiologies by Wesley's day. First, there was the Catholic view which defines the church in terms of ministry and which sees the church in essence as a historical institution preserved through the apostolic succession. The Catholic view insists that the true church is in the apostolic tradition, and accordingly stresses the continuity of the apostolic tradition in history. It emphasizes the historical church as an institution, established through apostolic succession and vitalized through sacramental activity. This view also emphasizes the objective holiness of the church and the presence of Christ maintained in the church through the sacraments.

Secondly, there was the Classical Protestant interpretation which emphasized the preaching of the gospel and the administration of the sacraments as essential marks of the church. This view places priority on the fact that the church is continuously being called into existence from above through the preaching of the Word and sustained by the sacraments. Article VII of the Augsburg Confession says, "The Church is the congregation of saints [the assembly of all believers], in which the Gospel is rightly taught [*purely preached*] and the sacraments rightly administered [according to the Gospel]."[32] Obviously informed by the Augsburg Confession, Calvin, in the *Institutes*, also says: "Wherever we see the Word of God purely preached and heard, and the sacraments administered according to Christ's institu-

tion, there, it is not to be doubted, a church of God exists."[33] For these reformers, where is the Word, there is the church. The sacraments are that
Word made visible and enacted. While there were major differences in
these groups, the Lutheran, Reformed, Anglican, and Presbyterian churches
did have these facets in common with one another.

Third was the free church position where the emphasis was upon the
free response of the Spirit and the need to be open to whatever forms of
worship and mission Christ calls us. This position insists a large measure of
freedom and autonomy in congregational life. It also has tendencies to
stress the personal experience and holiness of the individual believers who
then constitute the church, and thus to stress the inwardness of the true
Church as a union of believing hearts in Christ. This position views the
church as *koinonia*, that is, a fellowship of believers validated by the apostolic experience and perpetuated by evangelistic zeal. Thus, in this position
is emphasized the importance of the church as a community, and especially
of the Christian cell, the small company of Christian meeting for prayer and
edification as a means of grace. In Christian history there had been many
corporate embodiments of the doctrine of "communion of saints." There
were premonitions of its revival among the Anabaptists, and among the
'gathered Churches' of the English separatists. But in Spener's Pietism and
Zinzendorf's Moravianism, the church as *koinonia* came into its own.[34]
Frank Baker notes that this free church position "sees the church in essence
. . . as a faithful few with a mission to the world."[35]

Interestingly, all of these three appear to find their appropriate place in
Wesley's thought. Frank Baker well analyzes such a characteristic of
Wesley's ecclesiology even though he speaks explicitly of only two when
he refers to the basic views to which Wesley seemed to give support:

> One was that of a historical institution, originally linked to the apostolic
> church by a succession of bishops and inherited customs, served by a
> priestly caste who duly expounded the Bible and administered the sacra-
> ments in such a way as to preserve the ancient tradition on behalf of all
> who were made members by baptism. According to the other view the
> church was a fellowship of believers who shared both the apostolic ex-
> perience of God's living presence and also a desire to bring others into
> this same personal experience by whatever methods of worship and evan-
> gelism seemed most promising to those among them whom the Holy Spirit
> had endowed with special gifts of prophecy and leadership . . . the first
> was a traditional rule, the second a living relationship. In the church as an
> institution Wesley had been born and reared and ordained: into the church
> as a mission he was gradually introduced, in part by his parents, but in-
> creasingly by a widening circle of colleagues, and especially by a growing
> awareness of God's calls upon him as an individual. In this process every

inch of institutional loyalty reluctantly yield at the challenge of providential openings led to the demand for another yard. Nevertheless, just as something of the Pietist sectarian approach was present in his youthful upbringing, so to his life's end he retained several Catholic convictions.[36]

As Baker points out, Wesley's ecclesiology was in general moving from a Catholic view to a free-church one, but it is true that he was subject to occasional fluctuation as one may see in his sacerdotal view of the administration of the sacraments.

No doubt Wesley, especially the later Wesley, emphasized a church understanding of 'the Christian fellowship of all true believers.' For Wesley, the essence of the church need not be sought in its visible institutions, not even some invisible elected numbers. The church for him is composed of all "persons in the universe whom God hath so called out of the world . . . to be 'one body,' united by 'one spirit'; having 'one faith, one hope, one baptism; one God and Father of all, who is above all, and through all, and in them all."[37] The church is "the *whole body* of men endued with faith, working by love, dispersed over the whole earth."[38] This definition makes a greater inclusion of the "fellowship of believers" than was generally accepted by the Church of England.

Wesley never claimed his Methodism to be the only true church. He saw it as "a religious movement with a particular mission among the broader body of Christian believers."[39] Methodists, for Wesley, "are not the *whole* 'people of God', yet are they an undeniable *part* of his people."[40] Furthermore, "Wesley saw Methodism itself as a means of grace by which God's presence could become more vital in the lives of individuals, in the fellowship of believers, in the Church, and in the Nation or the world."[41]

If the Christian fellowship of believers is central to Wesley's ecclesiology, how could he affirm the Catholic, "churchly" ecclesiology of sacerdotal episcopacy and sacraments? Wesley seems to have believed that the established church with its rituals and ministry and measure of continuity with the church universal, past and present, provides a stability that guards against the splintering of the body of Christ, and also that there is a sense in which objective holiness is maintained in this connection. Wesley emphasized imparted holiness as a true nature of the church and the goal he tried to accomplish through Methodism was "to reform the nation, particularly the Church; and to spread scriptural holiness over the land."[42] He seems to have thought that the churchly settings would provide a context within which he could find the possibility of the reform of the church. Schism from the church would limit the possibility of those with a "living faith" serving as leaven to influence the larger body.

Albert Outler suggested that the old distinction between "catholic" and "evangelical" is "no longer a fruitful polarity and the only conceivable Christian future is for a church truly catholic, truly evangelical and truly reformed."[43] Perhaps "truly" is not the best or most appropriate modifying term for each of these terms, especially the last two; we need a church "truly catholic, thoroughly evangelical, and continually reformed." Such an ideal of church may be found in Wesley.

Wesley was a distinguished figure to unify the spiritual heritages in Christian tradition, as shown in the catholicity of the sources he integrated to establish his ecclesiology. Although he wanted Methodist societies to be not independent on but auxiliary to the Church of England, his vision was not limited just to the Church. Wesley saw Methodism's ecclesiological pattern as designed to function for the universal Christian community, which includes all the other Christian traditions as well as the Church of England, united by one spirit, one faith, one hope, one baptism, and one God. "[T]he Methodist . . . are themselves no particular sect or party; but they receive those of all parties who 'endeavour to do justly, and love mercy, and walk humbly with their God'."[44] Wesley did not require subscribing any list of beliefs such as creeds, confessions, or articles of religion, to be a Methodist, except professing "a desire to flee from the wrath to come, and to be saved from their sins."[45] For Wesley, Methodism was an evangelical order to save the souls working in the encompassing catholic church.

Wesley was also an evangelist within the Church of England who thought out of and lived in the Scripture and Christian tradition. He committed himself to encouraging, training and resourcing the Methodists to fulfill their calling—to spread gospel and scriptural holiness over the land. His ecclesiology was subservient to evangelical needs. For Wesley, the church is an act, a function, and a mission in the world as well as a form and an institution. "Significantly, and at every point, Wesley defined the church as . . . the enterprise of saving and maturing souls in the Christian life."[46] He understood the church as a saved and saving community.

Wesley, moreover, was a reformer who exercised leadership through teaching and example and offered a vision of "building up the body of Christ until we all reach unity in the faith and in the knowledge of the son of God and become mature, attaining to the whole measure of the fullness of Christ" (Eph. 4:12). Wesley understood his enterprise as the effort to meet an emergency situation with needful, extraordinary measures. As with the eschatological views of the New Testament Christians, the emergency has lengthened and the emergency crew has acquired the character of an establishment. But Methodism originally was designed to be a continuously reforming agency within which to function as a proper evangelical order of witness and service, discipline and nurture.

Although over the course of the last two centuries, many scholars have stated the ecclesiology of Methodism, among the Methodists today lacks consensus in basic truths of Methodist ecclesiology. In this respect, concern for the original identity and authenticity of Methodism helps Methodists' ecclesiological self-understanding. What is the distinctive Methodist ecclesiology? It requires many further studies, but hopefully, Wesley's ecclesiology will provide our Church with a renewed understanding of Methodist origins and a model for moving toward truly catholic, thoroughly evangelical, and continually reformed church.

Notes

1. Wesley, Sermon "Of the Church," 1, 1, in *Works*, iii, 46.

2. Outler, "Do Methodists Have a Doctrine of the Church?", in *The Wesleyan Theological Heritage*, eds. Thomas C. Oden and Leicester R. Longden, 212. Outler further, in commenting of the sermon "Of the Church" (1785), the first written summary of Wesley's ecclesiology, evaluated Wesley's ecclesiology as "neither Anglican, Lutheran, nor Calvinist" but as "an unstable blend of Anglican and Anabaptist ecclesiologies." Wesley, Sermon "Of the Church," An Introductory Comment by Albert Outler, in *Works*, iii, 45–46.

3. Durward Hofler, "The Methodist Doctrine of the Church," *Methodist History* 6, no. 1 (October 1967): 25.

4. J. E. Rattenbury, *The Evangelical Doctrines of Charles Wesley's Hymns* (London: Epworth Press, 1941), 229.

5. John Deschner, "Methodism's Thirteenth Article," *Perkins School of Theology Journal* 13 (Winter 1960): 13.

6. See Snyder, *The Radical Wesley and Patterns for Church Renewal*.

7. Baker, *John Wesley and the Church of England*, 137.

8. Colin W. Williams, *John Wesley's Theology Today* (New York: Abingdon Press, 1960), 141f.

9. Thompson, *Wesley: Apostolic Man, Some Reflections on Wesley's Consecration of Dr Thomas Coke*, 30–32.

10. Snyder, *The Radical Wesley and Patterns for Church Renewal*, 57ff.

11. Burnet, *An Exposition of the Thirty-Nine Articles of the Church of England by Gilbert, Bishop of Sarum*, 233.

12. Edgar W. Thompson, *The Methodist Doctrine of the Church*, rev. ed. (London: The Epworth Press, 1944), 34.

13. Baker, *John Wesley and the Church of England*, 158.

14. Outler, "Do Methodists Have a Doctrine of the Church?", 214.

15. Hobrow, *The Doctrines of the Methodists, Dedicated to the Preachers, in Connection with the Late Reverend Mr. John Wesley, M. A. By Way of Question and Answer; Designed as a Catechism for them*, 11–12.

16. *The Works* (Jackson), x, 142.

17. *The Works* (Jackson), viii, 255.

18. See Wesley's letters to "Mr. John Smith," in *The Works* (Jackson), xii, 72ff. The person who sent the letters to Wesley under the assumed name of John Smith and to whose criticism Wesley replied defending himself was most perhaps Thomas Secker (1693–1768), at that time Bishop of Oxford, and afterwards Archbishop of Canterbury. *The Works* (Jackson), xii, 610, note 12.

19. Outler, "The Place of Wesley in the Christian Tradition," in *The Place of Wesley in the Christian Tradition*, ed. Kenneth E. Rowe, 29.

20. *Works*, ii, 301–302.

21. *Letters*, vii, 63.

22. *The Works* (Jackson), xii, 139.

23. *The Works* (Jackson), viii, 281.

24. Baker, *John Wesley and the Church of England*, 113.

25. *Letters*, iv, 146.

26. Albert Outler, *Evangelism in the Wesleyan Spirit* (Nashville: Tidings, 1971), 103ff.

27. *Works*, xix, 67.

28. *The Works* (Jackson), xiii, 274.

29. Williams, *John Wesley's Theology Today*, 216.

30. Williams, *John Wesley's Theology Today*, 209.

31. Baker, *John Wesley and the Church of England*, 2.

32. "The Augsburg Confession," in Philip Schaff, *The Creeds of Christendom with a History and Critical Notes*, vol. iii, 11–12.

33. John Calvin, *Institutes of the Christian Religion*, vol. xxi of The Library of Christian Classics, 1023.

34. Rupert Davies and Gordon Rupp argue that the "*koinonia*" gave something to the ethos of Methodism which it has never entirely lost. See Rupert Davies and Gordon Rupp, eds. *A History of the Methodist Church in Great Britain*, vol. i, xxxvi.

35. Baker, *John Wesley and the Church of England*, 137.

36. Baker, *John Wesley and the Church of England*, 137–138.

37. Wesley, Sermon "Of the Church" (1785), I, 14, in *Works*, iii, 50.

38. Journal on Feb. 19, 1761, in *Works*, xxi, 304–305.

39. Ted. A. Campbell, *Methodist Doctrine: The Essentials* (Nashville: Abingdon Press, 1999), 19.

40. *Works*, xxi, 305.

41. Richard Heitzenrater, "Wesleyan Ecclesiology: Methodism as a Means of Grace," The Källatad Lecture, Överås Metodistkyrkans nordiska teologiska seminarium, Göteborg, Sweden, May 24, 2005, http://www.metodistkyrkan.se/overas/pdf/Wesleyan_Ecclesiology.pdf (December 20, 2005).

42. *The Works* (Jackson), viii, 299.

43. Outler, "The Place of Wesley in the Christian Tradition," 32.

44. Wesley, Sermon "Prophets and Priests," 21, in *Works*, iv, 84.

45. Wesley, "A Plain Account of the People called Methodists," I, 8, in *Works*, ix, 257.

46. Outler, "Do Methodists Have a Doctrine of the Church?", 219.

Bibliography

Primary Sources

John Wesley Primary Sources

Wesley, John. *The Bicentennial Edition of the Works of John Wesley.* Edited by Frank Baker, Albert Outler, Richard Heitzenrater, and others. Nashville: Abingdon Press, 1984–

———. *A Christian Library: Consisting of Extracts from and Abridgments of the Choicest Pieces of Practical Divinity, Which have been publish'd in the English Tongue. In Fifty Volumes.* Bristol: Printed by Felix Farley, 1749–1755.

———. *Explanatory Notes upon the New Testament.* London: Epworth Press, 1950.

———. *The Journal of the Rev. John Wesley, A.M.* Edited by Nehemiah Curnock. 8 vols. London: Epworth Press, 1938.

———. *The Letters of the Rev. John Wesley, A.M.* Edited by John Telford, B.A. 8 vols. London: Epworth Press, 1931.

———. *The Poetical Works of John and Charles Wesley: Reprinted from the Originals, with the Last Corrections of the Authors; Together with the Poems of Charles Wesley Not Before Published.* Collected and Arranged by G. Osborn. 13 vols. London: Wesleyan-Methodist Conference Office, 1869.

———. *The Sunday Service of the Methodists in North America: With Other Occasional Services.* London: W. Strahan, 1784.

———. *The Works of the Rev. John Wesley, M.A.* Edited by Thomas Jackson. 14 vols. 3d ed. London: Wesleyan Conference Office, 1872.

Other Primary Sources

The Ante-Nicene Fathers: Translations of the Writings of the Fathers down to A.D. 325. Edited by Alexander Roberts and James Donaldson. American Reprint of the Edinburgh Edition. Revised and Chronologically Arranged, with Brief

Prefaces and Occasional Notes, by A. Cleveland Coxe. 10 vols. New York: Charles Scribner's Sons, 1908–1911.

The Arminian Magazine: Consisting of Extracts and Original Treatises on Universal Redemption. 20 vols. London: Printed by J. Fry & Co. and sold at the Foundery, 1778–1797.

Asbury, Francis. *The Journal and Letters of Francis Asbury.* Edited by Elmer T. Clark, J. Manning Potts, and Jacob S. Payton, 3 vols. London: Epworth Press; Nashville: Abingdon Press, 1958.

Bede. *The Ecclesiastical History of the English Nation, From the Coming of Julius Caesar into This Island, in the Sixtieth Year Before the Incarnation of Christ, Till the Year of Our Lord 731.* Carefully Revised and Corrected from the Translation of Mr. Stevens, by the Rev. J. A. Giles. London: E. Lumley, 56, Chancery Lane, 1840.

The Book of Common Prayer, 1662 Version (includes Appendices from the 1549 Version and other Commemorations), with an Introduction by Diarmaid Mac-Culloch. London: David Campbell, 1999.

Calvin, John. *Commentary on a Harmony of the Evangelists, Matthew, Mark, and Luke.* Translated from the Original Latin and Collated with the Author's French Version by William Pringle. Grand Rapids: Erdmans, 1949.

———. *Institutes of the Christian Religion.* vols. xx and xxi of The Library of Christian Classics. Edited by John T. McNeill. Translated by Ford Lewis Battles. Philadelphia: The Westminster Press, 1960.

Cassian, John. *The Conferences.* Translated and Annotated by Boniface Ramsey. New York: Paulist Press, 1997.

———. *The Institutes.* Translated and Annotated by Boniface Ramsey. New York: The Newman Press, 2000.

Canons and Decrees of the Council of Trent. Original Text with English Translation by H. J. Schroeder. St. Louis, Mo.: B. Herder Book Co., 1941.

Cranmer, Thomas. *The Works of Thomas Cranmer.* Edited for The Parker Society by Rev. John Edmund Cox. 2 vols. Cambridge: The University Press, 1840–.

Deacon, Thomas. *A Compleat Collection of Devotions, both Publick and Private, Taken from the Apostolical Constitutions, the Ancient Liturgies and the Common Prayer Book of the Church of England.* London, 1734.

The First Prayer-Book of King Edward VI 1549. Reprinted from a Copy in the British Museum. London: Griffith Farran Okeden & Welsh, 1888.

Herbert, George. *The Works of George Herbert in Prose and Verse.* Edited by Robert A. Willmott. London: George Routledge and Co., 1854.

Hooker, Richard. *The Folger Library Edition of the Works of Richard Hooker.* Edited by P. G. Stanwood. 6 vols. Cambridge: The Belknap Press of Harvard University Press, 1981.

Hooper, John. *Early Writings of John Hooper.* Edited for The Parker Society by Rev. Samuel Carr. Cambridge: The University Press, 1843.

Jewel, John. *An Apology of the Church of England.* Edited by John E. Booty. Ithaca, N.Y.: Cornell University Press, 1963.

King, Peter. *An Inquiry into the Constitution, Discipline, Unity and Worship of the Primitive Church, that Flourished within the First Three Hundred Years after Christ, Faithfully Collected out of the Fathers and Extant Writings of Those Ages*. New York: G. Lane and P. P. Sandford, 1841.

Lavington, George. *The Enthusiasm of Methodists and Papists Compar'd*. London: Printed for J. and P. Knapton, 1749.

Luther, Martin. *Luther's Works*. American Edition. 55 vols. General Editors, Jaroslav Pelikan (vols. 1–30) and Helmut T. Lehman (vols. 31–54). St. Louis: Concordia, and Philadelphia: Fortress Press, 1955–1976.

———. *D. Martin Luthers Werke; kritische Gesamtausgabe*. Weimar: H. Böhlau, 1883–.

———. "The Ninety-Five Theses," 265–275 in *The Prince by Niccolo Machiavelli. Utopia by Sir Thomas More. Ninety-Five Theses, Address to the German Nobility, Concerning Christian Liberty by Martin Luther. With Introductions, Notes and Illustrations*. Edited by Charles W. Eliot. Harvard Classics: The Five Foot Shelf of Books. vol. 36. New York: P.F. Collier & Son, 1910.

Methodist Episcopal Church. *A Form of Discipline: For the Ministers, Preachers, and Members (Now Comprehending the Principles and Doctrines) of the Methodist Episcopal Church in America, Considered and Approved at a Conference Held at Baltimore, in the State of Maryland, on Monday the 27th of December, 1784: In Which Thomas Coke, and Francis Asbury, Presided. Arranged under Proper Heads, and Methodised in a More Acceptable and Easy Manner*. Philadelphia: Printed by Joseph Crukshank, and Sold by John Dickins, 1791.

Minutes of the Annual Conferences of the Methodist Episcopal Church, for the Years of 1773–1828. New York: T. Mason and G. Lane, 1840.

Minutes of the Methodist Conferences, from the First, Held in London by the Late Rev. John Wesley, A.M., in the Year 1744. 5 vols. London: John Mason, at the Wesleyan Conference Office, 1862 –1864.

Pearson, John. *An Exposition of the Creed: With an Appendix, Containing the Principal Greek and Latin Creeds*. Revised by the Rev. W.S. Dobson. New York: D. Appleton & Company, 1851.

Perkins, William. *An Exposition of the Symbole or Creede of the Apostles: According to the Tenour of the Scriptures, and the Consent of Orthodoxe Fathers of the Church, Reuewed and Corrected by William Perkins*. Cambridge: Printed by Iohn Legat printer to the Vniuersitie of Cambridge, 1596.

———. *The Art of Prophesying*. Revised Edition. Edinburgh: Banner of Truth Trust, 1996.

Pseudo-Macarius, *The Fifty Spiritual Homilies and The Great Letter*. Translated, Edited, and with an Introduction by George A. Maloney. Preface by Kallistos Ware. New York: Paulist Press, 1992.

Ridley, Nicholas. *The Works of Nicholas Ridley*. Edited for The Parker Society by Rev. Henry Christmas. Cambridge: The University Press, 1988.

Spener, Philipp Jakob. *Philipp Jakob Spener Schriften*. Edited by Erich Beyreuther. Hildesheim: Georg Olms Verlag, 1979–.

————. *Pia Desideria*. Translated by Theodore G. Tappert. Philadelphia: Fortress Press, 1964.

Stillingfleet, Edward. *The Irenicum, or Pacificator: Being a Reconciler as to Church Differences*. Philadelphia: M. Sorin, 1842.

The Two Books of Homilies Appointed to Be Read in Churches. Oxford: The University Press, 1859.

The Two Liturgies, A. D. 1549, and A. D. 1552: with Other Documents Set Forth by Authority in the Reign of King Edward VI. Edited for The Parker Society by Rev. Joseph Ketley. Cambridge: The University Press, 1844.

Wallace Jr., Charles., ed. *Susanna Wesley: The Complete Writings*. New York: Oxford University Press, 1997.

Zinzendorf, Nicolaus. *Nikolaus Ludwig von Zinzendorf, Hauptschriften in Sechs Bänden*. Edited by Erich Beyreuther and Gerhard Meyer. Hildesheim: Georg Olms, 1962–1963.

————. *Twenty One Discourses or Dissertations upon the Augsburg Confession, Which is Also the Brethren's Confession of Faith: Deliver'd by the Ordinary of the Brethren's Churches before the Seminary. To Which is Prefixed, A Synodal Writing Relating to the Same Subject*. Translated from the High Dutch, by F. Okeley. London: W. Bowyer, 1753.

Secondary Sources

Aland, Kurt. *Kirchengeschichtliche Entwürfe: Alte Kirche. Reformation und Luthertum. Pietismus und Erweckungsbewegung*. Gütersloh: Gerd Mohn, 1960.

Allen, C. Leonard, and Richard T. Hughes. *Discovering Our Roots: The Ancestry of Churches of Christ*. Abilene, Tex.: ACU Press, 1988.

————. *Illusions of Innocence: Protestant Primitivism in America, 1630–1875*. With a Foreword by Robert N. Bellah. Chicago: University of Chicago Press, 1988.

Anderson, Floyd, ed. *Council Daybook: Vatican II, session 1–4*. Washington, D.C.: National Catholic Welfare Conference, 1965–1966.

Anderson, Neil D. *A Definitive Study of Evidence Concerning John Wesley's Appropriation of the Thought of Clement of Alexandria*. Lewiston, N.Y.: Edwin Mellen Press, 2004.

Anstadt, Peter. *Luther, Zinzendorf, Wesley: An Account of John Wesley's Conversion through Hearing Luther's Preface to the Epistle to the Romans Read in a Moravian Prayer Meeting in London, England: To Which is Added a New Translation of Luther's Preface*. York, Pa.: P. Anstadt, 18--?

Archer, Stanley. "Hooker on Apostolic Succession: The Two Voices," *Sixteenth Century Journal* 24, no. 1 (1993): 67–74.

Avis, Paul D. L. "'The True Church' in Reformation Theology," *Scottish Journal of Theology* 30, no. 4 (1977): 319–345.

Baker, Frank. "The Beginnings of the Methodist Covenant Service," *The London Quarterly and Holborn Review* 180 (1955): 215–220.

————. *Charles Wesley As Revealed by His Letters.* London: Epworth Press, 1948.

————. *From Wesley to Asbury: Studies in Early American Methodism.* Durham, N.C.: Duke University Press, 1976.

————. *John Wesley and the Church of England.* London: Epworth Press, 1970.

————. "Practical Divinity—John Wesley's Doctrinal Agenda for Methodism," *Wesleyan Theological Journal* 22, no. 1 (Spring 1987): 7–16.

————. *A Union Catalogue of the Publications of John and Charles Wesley.* 2d ed. Stone Mountain, Ga.: George Zimmermann, 1991.

————. "Wesley's Early Preachers in America," *The Duke Divinity School Review* 34, no. 3 (Autumn 1969): 143–162.

Beecham, John. *An Essay on the Constitution of Wesleyan Methodism, in Which Various Misrepresentations of Some of Its Leading Principles Are Exposed, and Its Present Form Is Vindicated.* London: John Mason, 1851.

Beetz, Manfred, and Giuseppe Cac, eds. *Die Hermeneutik im Zeitalter der Aufklärung.* Collegium Hermeneuticum 3. Cologne: Böhlau, 2000.

Bett, Henry. *The Spirit of Methodism.* London: Epworth Press, 1937.

Bishop, John. *Methodist Worship in Relation to Free Church Worship.* London: Epworth Press, 1950.

Bowmer, John C. *The Sacrament of the Lord's Supper in Early Methodism.* London: Dacre Press, 1951.

————. *The Wesleyan Doctrine of the Ministry: A Lecture Delivered on April 15, 1970 at Perkins School of Theology.* Dallas: Southern Methodist University, 1970.

Bozeman, Theodore D. *To Live Ancient Lives: The Primitivist Dimension of Puritanism.* Chapel Hill, NC: Published for the Institute of Early American History and Culture, Williamsburg, Virginia, by the University of North Carolina Press, 1988.

Bray, Gerald, ed. *The Anglican Canons 1529–1947.* Woodbridge: Boydell Press, 1998.

Brecht, Martin, et al., eds. *Geschichte des Pietismus,* 4 vols. Göttingen: Vandenhoeck & Ruprecht, 1993–.

————. "Probleme der Pietismusforschung," *Nederlandsch archief voor Kerkgeschiedenis* 76 (1996): 227–237.

Brockwell Jr., Charles W. "Methodist Discipline: From Rule of Life to Canon Law," *The Drew Gateway* 54, no 2–3 (1984): 1–24.

Brown, Dale W. *Understanding Pietism.* Grand Rapids: Eerdmans, 1978.

Bucke, Emory Stevens, et al., eds. *The History of American Methodism.* 3 vols. Nashville: Abingdon Press, 1964.

Burnet, Gilbert. *An Exposition of the Thirty-Nine Articles of the Church of England by Gilbert, Bishop of Sarum.* Edited by James R. Page. New York: D. Appleton and Company, 1866.

Butler, David. *Methodists and Papists: John Wesley and the Catholic Church in the Eighteenth Century.* London: Darton, Longman and Todd, 1995.

Campbell, Ted A. *John Wesley and Christian Antiquity: Religious Vision and Cultural Change.* Nashville: Abingdon, 1991.

————. *Methodist Doctrine: The Essentials*. Nashville: Abingdon Press, 1999.

Cannon, William R. "The Holy Spirit in Vatican II and in the Writings of Wesley," *Religion in Life* 37, no. 3 (Autumn 1968): 440–453.

————. "John Wesley and the Catholic Tradition," Paper delivered at World Methodist Council Executive Committee, Toronto, Canada, 24 September 1980.

Carter, Henry. *The Methodist Heritage*. Nashville: Abingdon-Cokesbury Press, 1951.

Cell, George C. *The Rediscovery of John Wesley*. New York: Henry Holt and Company, 1935.

Chilcote, Paul Wesley. *John Wesley and the Women Preachers of Early Methodism*. Metuchen, N.J.: Scarecrow Press, 1991.

Cho, John Chongnahm. "John Wesley's View on Baptism," *Wesleyan Theological Journal* 7, no. 1 (Spring 1972): 60–73.

Christensen, Michael J. "Theosis and Sanctification: John Wesley's Reformulation of a Patristic Doctrine," *Wesleyan Theological Journal* 31 (Fall 1996): 71–94.

Church, Leslie F. *The Early Methodist People*. London: Epworth Press, 1948.

Church of England. *Conversations between the Church of England and the Methodist Church; an Interim Statement*. London: S.P.C.K., 1958.

Clarke, Adam. *Memoirs of the Wesley Family*. New York: Lane and Tippett, 1976.

Clendenin, Daniel B. *Eastern Orthodox Christianity: A Western Perspective*. 2d ed. Grand Rapids: Baker Academic, 2003.

Collins, Kenneth. "John Wesley's Critical Appropriation of Early German Pietism," *Wesleyan Theological Journal* 27 (Spring-Fall, 1992): 57–92.

Collinson, Patrick. *The Elizabethan Puritan Movement*. Berkeley: University of California Press, 1967.

Coomer, Duncan. "The Influence of Puritanism and Dissent on Methodism," *London Quarterly and Holborn Review* 175 (1950): 346–350.

Cox, Leo G. "John Wesley's View of Martin Luther," *Journal of the Evangelical Theological Society* 7, no. 3 (1964): 83–90.

Davies, Horton. *The English Free Churches*. London: Oxford University Press, 1952.

————. *Worship and Theology in England*, 5 vols. Princeton, N.J.: Princeton University Press, 1961–1975.

Davies, Rupert, A. Raymond George, and Gordon Rupp, eds. *A History of the Methodist Church in Great Britain*. 4 vols. London: Epworth Press, 1965–1988.

Deanesly, Margaret. "The Capitular Text of the Responsiones of Pope Gregory I to St. Augustine," *Journal of Ecclesiastical History* 12, no. 2 (October 1961): 231–234.

Deeter, Allen C. *An Historical and Theological Introduction to Philipp Jakob Spener's Pia Desideria: A study in Early German Pietism*. Ph. D. dissertation. Princeton University, 1963.

Deschner, John. "Methodism's Thirteenth Article," *Perkins School of Theology Journal* 13, no. 2 (Winter 1960): 5–13.

Dieter, Melvin E., and Daniel N. Berg, eds. *The Church: An Inquiry into Ecclesiology from a Biblical Theological Perspective.* Anderson, Ind.: Warner Press, 1984.

Dimond, Sydney G. *The Psychology of the Methodist Revival: An Empirical and Descriptive Study.* Nashville: Whitmore & Smith, 1926.

Dix, Dom Gregory. *The Shape of the Liturgy.* London: Dacre Press, 1975.

Drew, Samuel. *The Life of the Rev. Thomas Coke, LL.D.: Including in Detail His Various Travels and Extraordinary Missionary Exertions, in England, Ireland, America, and the West-Indies: With an Account of His Death, on the 3d of May, 1814, While on a Missionary Voyage to the Island of Ceylon, in the East-Indies.: Interspersed with Numerous Reflections; and Concluding with an Abstract of His Writings and Character.* New York: J. Soule and T. Mason, 1818.

Dryer, Frederick. "John Wesley: Ein Englisher Pietist," *Methodist History* 40 (January 2002): 71–84.

Duffy, Eamon. *The Stripping of the Altars: Traditional Religion in England, c.1400 – c.1580.* New Haven: Yale University Press, 1992.

Dülmen, Richard van. *Kultur und Alltag in der Frühen Neuzeit.* Dritter Band: *Religion, Magie, Aufklärung: 16.–18. Jahrhundert.* München: C.H. Beck, 1994.

Edwards, Maldwyn. *This Methodism: Eight Studies.* London: Epworth Press, 1939.

England, Martha W., and John Sparrow. *Hymns Unbidden: Donne, Herbert, Blake, Emily Dickinson and the Hymnographers.* New York: New York Public Library, 1966.

Erb, Peter C. *Pietists: Selected Writings.* New York: Paulist Press, 1983.

Fitchett, W. H. *Wesley and His Century: A Study in Spiritual Forces.* New York: Abingdon Press, 1917.

Freeman, Arthur. "Gemeine: Count Nicholas von Zinzendorf's Understanding of the Church," *Brethren Life and Thought* 47, no. 1–2 (Winter-Spring 2002): 1–25.

Fries, Paul, and Tiran Nersoyan, eds. *Christ in East and West.* Introduction by Jeffrey Gros. Macon, Ga.: Mercer University Press, 1987.

Friesen, Abraham. "The Impulse Toward Restitutionist Thought in Christian Humanism," *Journal of the American Academy of Religion* 44 (March 1976): 29–45.

Fulbrook, Mary. *Piety and Politic: Religion and the Rise of Absolutism in England, Württemberg and Prussia.* Cambridge: Cambridge University Press, 1983.

Gibson, Edgar C. S. *The Thirty-Nine Articles of the Church of England.* 2d ed. London: Methuen, 1898.

Green, V. H. H. *John Wesley.* London: Thomas Nelson Ltd, 1964.

———. *The Young Mr. Wesley: A Study of John Wesley and Oxford.* New York: St Martin's Press, 1961.

Greyertz, Kaspar von, ed. *Religion and Society in Early Modern Europe 1500–1800.* London: George Allen & Unwin, 1984.

Grundmann, Herbert. *Religiöse Bewegungen im Mittelalter: Untersuchungen über die geschichtlichen Zusammenhänge zwischen der Ketzerei, den Bettelorden und der religiösen Frauenbewegung im 12. und 13. Jahrhundert, und über die geschichtlichen Grundlagen der Deutschen Mystik.* Darmstadt: Wissenschaftliche Buchgesellschaft, 1970.

Gunter, W. Stephen. *The Limits of 'Love Divine': John Wesley's Response to Antinomianism and Enthusiasm.* Nashville: Kingswood Books, 1989.

Hahn, Hans-Christoph, and Hellmut Reichel, eds. *Zinzendorf und die Herrnhuter Brüder: Quellen zur Geschichte der Brüder-Unität von 1722 bis 1760.* Hamburg: Wittig, 1977.

Halévy, Élie. *The Birth of Methodism in England.* Translated and Edited by Bernard Semmel. Chicago: University of Chicago Press, 1971.

Hamilton, J. Taylor, and Kenneth G. Hamilton. *History of the Moravian Church.* Bethlehem, Pa.: Interprovincial Board of Christian Education, Moravian Church in America, 1967.

Haugaard, William P. "Renaissance Patristic Scholarship and Theology in Sixteenth-Century England," *Sixteenth-Century Journal* 10, no. 3 (Fall 1979): 37–60.

Hawley, Monroe. *The Focus of Our Faith.* Nashville: 20th Century Christian, 1985.

Heitzenrater, Richard P. *The Elusive Mr. Wesley.* 2d ed. Nashville: Abingdon Press, 2003.

———. *John Wesley and the Oxford Methodists, 1725–1735.* Ph. D. dissertation. Duke University, 1972.

———. "John Wesley's *A Christian Library,* Then and Now," *American Theological Library Association Summary of Proceedings* 55 (2001): 133–146.

———. *Wesley and the People Called Methodists.* Nashville: Abingdon Press, 1995.

———. "Wesleyan Ecclesiology: Methodism as a Means of Grace." The Källatad Lecture. delivered at Överås Metodistkyrkans nordiska teologiska seminarium, Göteborg, Sweden. May 24, 2005, http://www.metodistkyrkan.se/overas/pdf/Wesleyan_Ecclesiology.pdf (December 20, 2005).

Herbert, Thomas W. *John Wesley as Editor and Author.* Princeton, N.J.: Oxford University Press, 1940.

Higgins, P.L. *John Wesley, Spiritual Witness.* Minneapolis: T. Denison and Co., 1960.

Hilderbrandt, Franz. *From Luther to Wesley.* London: Lutterworth Press, 1951.

Hirsch, Emanuel. *Geschichte der Neuern Evangelischen Theologie im Zusammenhang mit den Allgemeinen Bewegungen des Europäischen Denkens.* 5 Bände. Gütersloh: Bertelsmann Velag, 1951.

Hobrow, William. *The Doctrines of the Methodists, Dedicated to the Preachers, in Connection with the Late Reverend Mr. John Wesley, M. A. By Way of Question and Answer; Designed as a Catechism for them.* 4th ed. Liverpool, England: E. Johnson, 1793.

Hockin, Frederick. *John Wesley and Modern Methodism.* London: Rivingtons, 1887.

Hofler, Durward. "The Methodist Doctrine of the Church," *Methodist History* 6, no. 1 (October 1967): 25–35.

Hunter, Frederick. *John Wesley and the Coming Comprehensive Church.* London: Epworth Press, 1968.

———. "The Origins of Wesley's Covenant Service," *Proceedings of the Wesley Historical Society* 22 (1939–1940): 126–131.

———. "Sources of Wesley's Revision of the Prayer Book in 1784–8," *Proceedings of the Wesley Historical Society* 23 (1941–1942): 123–133.

Hutchinson, F. E. "John Wesley and George Herbert," *London Quarterly and Holborn Review* 161 (1936): 439–455.

Jay, Eric G. *The Church: Its Changing Image through Twenty Centuries.* Atlanta: John Knox Press, 1980.

Jones, Scott J. *United Methodist Doctrine: The Extreme Center.* Nashville: Abingdon Press, 2002.

Jung, Martin H. "1836—Wiederkunft Christi oder Beginn des Tausendjährigen Reichs? Zur Eschatologie Johann Albrecht Bengels und seiner Schüler," *Pietismus und Neuzeit* 23 (1997): 131–151.

Keefer Jr., Luke L. *John Wesley: Disciple of Early Christianity.* 2 vols. Ann Arbor: University Microfilms International, 1981.

———. "John Wesley: Disciple of Early Christianity," *Wesleyan Theological Journal* 19, no. 1 (Spring 1984): 23–32.

Kimbrough Jr., S. T., ed. *Orthodox and Wesleyan Spirituality.* Crestwood, N.Y.: St. Vladimir's Seminary Press, 2002.

Kissack, Reginald. *Church or No Church? A Study of the Development of the Concept of Church in British Methodism.* London: Epworth Press, 1964.

Knowles, Dom David. *The Monastic Order in England,* 2d ed. Cambridge: Cambridge University Press, 1963.

Knox, Ronald A. *Enthusiasm: A Chapter in the History of Religion, with Special Reference to the XVII and XVIII Centuries.* London: Collins, 1987.

Krause, Gerhard, and Gerhard Müller, eds. *Theologische Realenzyklopädie,* 36 vols. Berlin: de Gruyter, 1977–

Küng, Hans. *The Church.* Translated by Ray and Rosaleen Ockenden. London: Sheed and Ward, 1967.

Kurowski, Mark T. "The First Step Toward Grace: John Wesley's Use of the Spiritual Homilies of Macarius the Great," *Methodist History* 36, no. 2 (January 1998): 113–124.

Ladner, Gerhart B. *The Idea of Reform: Its impact on Christian Thought and Action in the Age of the Fathers.* Cambridge: Harvard University Press, 1959.

Lang, August. *Puritanismus und Pietismus. Studien zu ihrer Entwicklung von M. Butzer bis zum Methodismus.* Beiträge zur Geschichte und Lehre der Reformierten Kirche 6. Neukirchen, 1941.

Lawson, A. B. *John Wesley and the Christian Ministry: The Sources and Development of His Opinions and Practice.* London: SPCK, 1963.

Leach, Elsie A. "John Wesley's Use of George Herbert," *Huntington Library Quarterly* 16 (1952–1953): 183–202.

Lee, Jesse. *A Short History of the Methodists in the United States of America; Beginning in 1766, and Continued till 1808. To which is Prefixed, a Brief Ac-*

count of Their Rise in England, in the Year 1729, &c. Baltimore: Magill and Clime, 1810.

Lee, Umphrey. *The Lord's Horseman: John Wesley the Man.* Nashville: Abingdon Press, 1954.

Leff, Gordon. *Heresy in the Later Middle Ages: The Relation of Heterodoxy to Dissent, c. 1250 – c. 1450.* 2 vols. Manchester, Manchester U.P.; New York, Barnes & Noble, 1967.

———, "The Apostolic Ideal in Later Medieval Ecclesiology," *Journal of Theological Studies* 18 (April 1967): 58–82.

———, "The Making of the Myth of a True Church in the Later Middle Ages," *Journal of Medieval and Renaissance Studies* 1 (1971): 1–15.

Lemay, J. A. Leo, ed. *Deism, Masonry, and the Enlightenment: Essays Honoring Alfred Owen Aldridge.* Newark: University of Delaware Press, 1987.

Lewis, A. J. *Zinzendorf the Ecumenical Pioneer: A Study in the Moravian Contribution to Christian Mission and Unity.* Philadelphia: Westminster Press, 1962.

Lindberg, Carter, ed., *The Pietist Theologians: An Introduction to Theology in the Seventeenth and Eighteenth Centuries.* Malden, MA: Blackwell Publishing, 2005.

Maclaren, Alexander, ed. *The Ejectment of 1662 and the Free Churches.* London: National Council of Evangelical Free Churches, n.d.

Maddox, Randy L. "John Wesley and Eastern Orthodoxy: Influences, Convergences and Differences," *The Asbury Theological Journal* 45, no. 2 (Fall 1990): 29–53.

———. *Responsible Grace: John Wesley's Practical Theology.* Nashville: Kingswood Books, 1994.

Matthaei, Sondra Higgins. "Practical Divinity: Ministry in the Wesleyan Tradition," *Quarterly Review: A Journal of Theological Resources for Ministry* 12, no. 4 (Winter 1992): 57–68.

Matthias, Markus. *Lebensläufe August Hermann Franckes.* Kleine Texte des Pietismus 2. Leipzig: Evangelische Verlagsanstalt, 1999.

McBrien, Richard P. *Catholicism.* Minneapolis: Winston Press, 1981.

McDonnell, Kilian. *John Calvin, the Church, and the Eucharist.* Princeton: Princeton University Press, 1967.

The Message and Mission of Methodism: the Report of the Committee Appointed by the Methodist Conference, 1943, 'to Re-consider and Re-state the Message and Mission of Methodism in Modern Society.' London: Epworth Press, 1946.

"Methodist Petition, Oct. 28, 1776," *The Virginia Magazine of History and Biography* 18, no. 2 (April 1910): 143–144.

Meyendorff, John. *Byzantine Theology: Historical Trends and Doctrinal Themes.* New York: Fordham University Press, 1979.

Milner, Benjamin C. *Calvin's Doctrine of the Church.* Leiden: Brill, 1970.

Moede, Gerald F. *The Office of Bishop in Methodism: Its History and Development.* Zurich, Switzerland: Publishing House of The Methodist Church, 1964.

Monk, Robert C. *John Wesley: His Puritan Heritage.* Nashville: Abingdon Press, 1966.

———. *John Wesley: His Puritan Heritage*, 2d ed. Lanham, Md.: The Scarecrow Press, 1999.

Myles, William. *A Chronological History of the People Called Methodists, of the Connexion of the Late Rev. John Wesley; from Their Rise in the Year 1729, to Their Last Conference, in 1802*. 4th ed. London: Conference-office, Thomas Cordeux, agent, 1813.

Nagler, Arthur W. *The Church in History*. Nashville: Abingdon-Cokesbury Press, 1929.

———. *Pietism and Methodism, or The Significance of German Pietism in the Origin and Early Development of Methodism*. Nashville: M. E. Church, South, Publishing House, 1918.

Newton, John A. *Methodism and the Puritans*. London: Friends of Dr. Williams's Library, 1964.

———. *Susanna Wesley and the Puritan Tradition in Methodism*. London: Epworth Press, 2002.

Niesel, Wilhelm. *The Theology of Calvin*. Translated by Harold Knight. Philadelphia: Westminster Press, 1956.

Nygren, E. Herbert. "John Wesley's Changing Concept of the Ministry," *Religion in Life* 31, no 2 (Spring 1962): 264–274.

Oden, Thomas C., and Leicester R. Longden, eds. *The Wesleyan Theological Heritage: Essays of Albert C. Outler*. Grand Rapids: Zondervan, 1991.

Olsen, Glenn. "The Idea of the *Ecclesia Primitiva* in the Writings of the Twelfth-Century Canonists," *Traditio: Studies in Ancient and Medieval History, Thought, and Religion*, vol. xxv. New York: Fordham University Press, 1969: 61–86.

Outler, Albert C. *Evangelism in the Wesleyan Spirit*. Nashville: Tidings, 1971.

———. *John Wesley*. New York: Oxford University Press, 1964.

———. *Theology in the Wesleyan Spirit*. Nashville: Tidings, 1975.

———. "Towards a Re-Appraisal of John Wesley as a Theologian," *The Perkins School of Theology Journal* 14, no. 2 (Winter 1961): 5–14.

Overton, John H. *The Evangelical Revival in the Eighteenth Century*. London: Longmans, Green, and Co., 1907.

Paget, Francis. *An Introduction to the Fifth Book of Hooker's Treatise of the Laws of Ecclesiastical Polity*. 2d ed. Oxford: Clarendon Press, 1907.

Patrides, C. A., ed. *George Herbert: The Critical Heritage*. Boston: Routledge & Kegan Paul, 1983.

Paul, Robert S. *The Church in Search of Its Self*. Grand Rapids: Eerdmans Publishing Co., 1972.

Pelikan, Jaroslav. *The Riddle of Roman Catholicism*. Nashville: Abingdon Press, 1959.

Phoebus, William. *Memoirs of the Rev. Richard Whatcoat, Late Bishop of the Methodist Episcopal Church*. New York: Joseph Allen, 1828.

Piette, Maximin. *John Wesley in the Evolution of Protestantism*. London: Sheed and Ward, 1937.

Rack, Henry D. *Reasonable Enthusiast: John Wesley and the Rise of Methodism.* London: Epworth Press, 1989.

———. "Religious Societies and the Origins of Methodism," *Journal of Ecclesiastical History* 38 (1987): 582–595.

Rattenbury, J. Ernest. *The Conversion of the Wesleys: A Critical Study.* London: Epworth Press, 1938.

———. *The Eucharistic Hymns of John and Charles Wesley: To Which Is Appended Wesley's Preface Extracted from Brevint's Christian Sacrament and Sacrifice Together with Hymns on the Lord's Supper.* Edited by Timothy J. Crouch. Cleveland, OH: OSL Publications, 1990.

———. *The Evangelical Doctrines of Charles Wesley's Hymns.* London: Epworth Press, 1941.

Rigg, James H. R. *The Churchmanship of John Wesley, and the Relations of Wesleyan Methodism to the Church of England.* London: Wesleyan-Methodist Book-Room, 1886.

———. *The Living Wesley, As He Was in His Youth and in His Prime.* With an Introduction by John F. Hurst. New York: Nelson & Phillips, 1874.

Rowan, Steven, trans. *Religious Movements in the Middle Ages.* University of Norte Dame Press, 1995.

Rowe, Kenneth E., ed. *The Place of Wesley in the Christian Tradition: Essays Delivered at Drew University in Celebration of the Commencement of the Publication of the Oxford Edition of the Works of John Wesley.* Metuchen, N. J.: The Scarecrow Press, 1976.

Runyon, Theodore. *The New Creation: John Wesley's Theology Today.* Nashville: Abingdon Press, 1998.

Rupp, Gordon E. *John Wesley und Martin Luther: Ein Beitrag zum Lutherischen-Methodistischen Dialog.* Stuttgart: Christliches Verlagshaus, 1983.

———. *Protestant Catholicity; Two lectures.* London: Epworth Press, 1960.

———. *The Righteousness of God: Luther Studies.* New York: Philosophical Library, 1953.

Russell, Jeffrey B. *Dissent and Reform in the Early Middle Ages.* Berkeley: University of California Press, 1965.

Sasek, Lawrence A., ed. *Images of English Puritanism: A Collection of Contemporary Sources, 1589–1646.* Baton Rouge: Louisiana State University Press, 1989.

Sattler, Gary R. *God's Glory, Neighbor's Good: A Brief Introduction to the Life and Writings of August Hermann Francke.* Chicago: Covenant Press, 1982.

Schaff, Philip. *The Creeds of Christendom with a History and Critical Notes.* 3 vols. Grand Rapids: Baker Book House, 1966.

Schmidt, Martin. *John Wesley: A Theological Biography.* 3 vols. Nashville: Abingdon Press, 1962–1973.

———. "Philipp Jakob Spener und die Bibel," in *Pietismus und Bibel.* ed. Kurt Aland. Arbeiten zur Geschichte des Pietismus 9. Witten-Ruhr: Luther Verlag, 1970: 9–58.

———. "Spener und Luther," *Luther Jahrbuch* 24 (1957): 102–129.

Shepherd, T. B. *Methodism and the Literature of the Eighteenth Century*. London: Epworth Press, 1947.

Simon, John S. *John Wesley and the Advance of Methodism*. London: Epworth Press, 1925.

———. *John Wesley, the Last Phase*. London: Epworth Press, 1934.

———. *John Wesley, the Master-Builder*. London: Epworth Press, 1927.

———. *John Wesley and the Religious Societies*. London: Epworth Press, 1921.

———. "Wesley's Ordinations," *Proceedings of the Wesley Historical Society* 9 (1913–1914): 145–154.

Smith, George D., ed. *The Teaching of the Catholic Church: A Summary of Catholic Doctrine*. 2 vols. New York: Macmillan, 1949.

Snyder, Howard A. "John Wesley and Macarius the Egyptian," *The Asbury Theological Journal* 45, no. 2 (Fall 1990): 55–60.

———. *Pietism, Moravianism, and Methodism as Renewal Movements: A Comparative and Thematic Study*. Ph. D. dissertation. Notre Dame University, 1983.

———. *The Radical Wesley and Patterns for Church Renewal*. Eugene, Or.: Wipf and Stock Publishers, 1996.

Spellmann, Norman W. "Early Native Methodist Preachers," *The Duke Divinity School Review* 34, no. 3 (Autumn 1969): 163–187.

Stein, K. James. "Renewal: Philipp Jakob Spener's Parallel Word for Sanctification," *The Asbury Theological Journal* 51/2 (1996): 5–13.

Stephen, Leslie. *History of English Thought in the Eighteenth Century*. 2 vols. New York: Harcourt, Brace & World, Inc., 1962.

Stewart, Stanley. *George Herbert*. Boston: Twayne Publishers, 1986.

Stoeffler, F. Ernest. *German Pietism during the Eighteenth Century*. Leiden: E. J.Brill, 1973.

———. *The Rise of Evangelical Pietism*, Studies in the History of Religion 9. Leiden: E. J. Brill, 1965.

———. "Tradition and Renewal in the Ecclesiology of John Wesley." 298–316 in *Traditio, Krisis, Renovatio aus Theologischer Sicht: Festschrift Winfried Zeller zum 65. Geburtstag*. Marburg: Elwert, 1976.

Sträter, Udo, ed. *Pietas in der Lutherischen Orthodoxie*. Wittenberg: Hans Luft, 1998.

Telford, John. *The Life of John Wesley*. New York: Hunt & Eaton, 1888.

Thompson, Edgar W. *The Methodist Doctrine of the Church*. Revised Edition. London: Epworth Press, 1944.

———. *Wesley: Apostolic Man, Some Reflections on Wesley's Consecration of Dr Thomas Coke*. London: Epworth Press, 1957.

Tigert, John J. *A Constitutional History of American Episcopal Methodism*. 2d ed. Nashville: Publishing House of the Methodist Episcopal Church, South, 1904.

Todd, John M. *John Wesley and the Catholic Church*. London: Hodder and Stoughton, 1958.

Towlson, Clifford W. *Moravian and Methodist: Relationships and Influences in the Eighteenth Century*. London, Epworth Press, 1957.

Townsend, W. J., H. B. Workman, and George Eayrs, eds. *A New History* of *Methodism*. 2 vols. London: Hodder and Stoughton, 1909.

Trinterud, Leonard, ed. *Elizabethan Puritanism*. Oxford: Oxford University Press, 1971.

Tuttle Jr., Robert G. *John Wesley: His Life and Theology*. Grand Rapids: Zondervan Publishing House, 1978.

Tyerman, Luke. *The Life and Times of the Rev. John Wesley, M.A., Founder of the Methodists*. 3 vols. New York: Harper & brothers, 1872.

Vanderschaaf, Mark E. "Archbishop Parker's Efforts Toward a Bucerian Discipline in the Church of England," *Sixteenth Century Journal* 8 (1977): 85–103.

VanValin, Howard F. "Mysticism in Wesley," *The Asbury Seminarian* 12, no. 2 (Spring-Summer 1958): 3–14.

Wainwright, Geoffrey. "Methodism's Ecclesial Location and Ecumenical Vocation," *One in Christ* 19. no. 2 (1983): 104–134.

Wakefield, Gordon S. *Methodist Devotion: The Spiritual Life in the Methodist Tradition, 1791–1945*. London: Epworth Press, 1966.

Wakeley, J. B. *Anecdotes of the Wesleys: Illustrative of Their Character and Personal History*. With an Introduction by Rev. J. M'Clintock. New York: Carlton & Lanahan, 1870.

Wakeman, Henry Offley. *An Introduction to the History of the Church of England: From the Earliest Times to the Present Day*. Revised, with an Additional Chapter, by S. L. Ollard. London: Rivingtons, 1919.

Wallmann, Johannes. *Der Pietismus*. In *Die Kirche in ihrer Geschichte*, Bd 4, Lieferung O1. Göttingen: Vandenhoeck & Ruprecht, 1990.

———. "Eine alternative Geschichte des Pietismus. Zur gegenwärtigen Diskussion um den Pietismusbegriff," *Pietismus und Neuzeit* 28 (2002): 30–71.

———. *Philipp Jakob Spener und die Anfänger des Pietismus*, 2d ed. Tübingen: Mohr, 1986.

———. "Pietismus und Chiliasmus. Zur Kontroverse um Philipp Jakob Speners 'Hoffnung besserer Zeiten,'" *Zeitschrift für Theologie und Kirche* 78 (1981): 235–266.

———. "Was ist Pietismus?" *Pietismus und Neuzeit* 20 (1994): 11–27.

Ward, W. R. *The Protestant Evangelical Awakening*. Cambridge: Cambridge University Press, 1992.

Watson, David Lowes. *The Early Methodist Class Meeting: Its Origin and Significance*. Nashville: Discipleship Resources, 1985.

Watts, Michael R. *The Dissenters*, 2 vols. Oxford: Clarendon Press, 1978.

Wedgwood, Julia. *John Wesley and the Evangelical Reaction of the Eighteenth Century*. London: MacMillan and Co., 1870.

Wendel, F. *Calvin; the Origins and Development of his Religious Thought*. Translated by Philip Mairet. London: Collins, 1963.

Wesley in America: An Exhibition Celebrating the 300th Anniversary of the Birth of John Wesley, February 3 – April 11, 2003. Curated by Richard P. Heitzenrater & Peter S. Forsaith. Dallas, Tex.: Bridwell Library, Perkins School of Theology, Southern Methodist University, 2003.

Wettach, Theodor. *Kirche bei Zinzendorf*. Wuppertal: Theologischer Verlag Rolf Brockhaus, 1971.

Whitehead, John. *The Life of the Rev. John Wesley, M. A.: Some Time Fellow of Lincoln College, Oxford. Collected from His Private Papers and Printed Works; and Written at the Request of His Executors. To Which is Prefixed Some Account of His Ancestors and Relations; with the Life of the Rev. Charles Wesley, M. A . Collected from His Private Journal, and Never before Published. The Whole Forming a History of Methodism, in Which the Principles and Economy of the Methodists are Unfolded*. Boston: Dow & Jackson, 1845.

Williams, Colin W. *John Wesley's Theology Today*. New York.: Abingdon Press, 1960.

Williams, N. P., and Charles Harris, eds. *Northern Catholicism: Centenary Studies in the Oxford and Parallel Movements*. London: SPCK, 1933.

Workman, Herbert B. *The Evolution of the Monastic Ideal: From the Earliest Times Down to the Coming of the Friars, a Second Chapter in the History of Christian Renunciation*. Boston: Beacon Press, 1962.

———. *The Place of Methodism in the Catholic Church*. London: Epworth Press, 1921.

Wright, D. F., trans. and ed. *Common Places of Martin Bucer*. The Courtenay Library of Reformation Classics 4. Abingdon, England: Sutton Courtenay Press, 1972.

Index

absolution, 49, 53, 96, 147, 171; sacerdotal, 140, 170
Act of Supremacy, 63
Act of Toleration, 64, 67, 236, 247n130
Act of Uniformity, 9, 63, 64, 66, 67, 72, 236, 243n56
Adam, Thomas, 213
Aland, Kurt, 89, 113n1
Aldersgate, xviii, xix, 15, 27, 43n94, 49, 87n128, 100, 109, 125, 140, 151, 159–164, 165, 172–175, 187, 194n11, 257, 258
Alleine, Joseph, 72, 75
Alleine, Richard, 72, 75
Ambrose, Isaac, 75
American Revolution, 225, 228
Anabaptists, 8, 73–74, 121n99, 249, 266, 269n2
anachronism, 225
Anglicanism, 1, 9, 10, 16, 18, 19, 22, 23, 24, 33, 34, 37n17, 42n80, 54, 56, 57, 58, 60, 62, 71, 72, 73, 74, 77, 106, 113, 155n74, 168, 173, 183, 215, 250, 253, 255, 257, 259, 260, 261, 266, 269n2; Anglican(s), 9, 22, 37n17, 56–57, 59, 61, 70, 140, 141, 142, 145, 171, 173, 175, 183, 225, 245n91, 250, 259, 261,

262, 263. *See also* Church of England
Annesley, Samuel, 67, 75
Anthony, St., 30, 253
antinomianism, 29
Apostolic Canons, 129, 130, 151, 152n6
apostolic Christianity, 6–7, 15, 34n2; apostolic church, 5, 8, 10, 15, 65, 140, 141, 189, 214, 220, 266. *See also* primitivism
Apostolic Constitutions, 129, 130, 151, 152n6, 199
apostolic succession, 8, 21, 22, 30, 55, 60, 65, 83n63, 140, 143, 144, 193, 214, 215, 216, 231, 234, 236, 242n38, 249, 251, 257, 259, 265; episcopal succession, 145, 215, 221, 222, 251, 266; Presbyterian succession, 222; Wesleyan succession, 234
Archer, Stanley, 83n63
Arminian Magazine, 51
Arndt, Johann, 90, 91, 92, 93, 99, 100, 102, 114n6, 115n15, 124n135
Arnold, Gottfried, 90
Asbury, Francis, 219, 221, 223–230, 244n89, 245n91, 245n96, 245n97
asceticism, 24, 25, 68–69, 76, 260

assurance, 15, 49, 70, 71, 102, 138, 143,
    150, 151, 159, 165, 173, 174, 205,
    251
Augsburg Confession, 51, 52, 78n3,
    79n25, 103, 256, 261, 265
August of Braunschweig-
    Wolfenbüttel, Jr., 92
Augustine of Canterbury, 7, 36n7
Augustine of Hippo, 10, 11, 14, 15, 182

Bach, Johann Sebastian, 114n12
Baker, Frank, xvi, 42n80, 60, 72,
    87n133, 190, 226, 250, 259, 266,
    267
Balguy, Archdeacon, 73
band(s), 23, 93, 102, 107, 112, 124n134,
    179, 208, 210, 212, 254, 260
Bandhalter (or band leader), 107
baptism, 17, 21, 48, 49, 53, 77n2, 98,
    104, 121n101, 130, 140, 143, 144,
    146–148, 149, 150, 161, 164, 173,
    176, 177, 186, 187–193, 205, 216,
    224, 226, 229, 238, 257, 266, 267,
    268; infant, 129, 186, 189, 190,
    191, 192, 193; lay, 129, 143, 237
baptismal covenant, 101
Baptist(s), 66, 75
Basil of Caesarea, 11, 12, 15, 34n2
Bassett, Paul, 53
Baxter, Richard, 66–67, 70, 75, 85n87,
    86n110
Bede, 7
Bekehrung. See conversion
Bellarmine, Robert, 58
Benedict, St., 30, 31
Bengel, Johann Albrecht, 90, 118n60
Benson, Joseph, 237
Bett, Henry, 29
Beveridge, William, 14, 85n96, 130,
    251
Beza, Theodore, 84n73
biblical scholarship, 132, 136, 138
Binning, Hugh, 75
Bishop, John, 71–72
Boardman, Richard, 223
Boehm, Anton Wilhelm, 99, 115n18
Boehme, Jakob, 91
Böhler, Peter, 102, 108
Bolton, Ann, 244n89
Bolton, Robert, 63, 75

Bolzius, John Martin, 143, 155n90
Boniface VIII, 42n82
Book of Common Prayer, 58, 60, 61,
    64, 65, 67, 72, 83n60, 146, 147,
    148, 184, 190, 198n105,
    199n118, 205, 225, 247n131,
    261
Bosanquet, Mary, 211–212, 241n29
Bowmer, John C., 159, 169, 186,
    197n91, 215
Boyce, Gilbert, 192
Bozeman, Theodore D., 37n16
Brecht, Martin, 89–90
Brevint, Daniel, 181, 182, 183
Brockwell, Charles W., 24
Brown, Dale W., 101
Brown, John, 75
Bucer, Martin, 2, 8, 9, 37n15, 52, 53,
    80n31, 80n37, 81n46, 84n85, 89,
    255
Bücher vom wahren Christentum/
    True Christianity, 92, 115n15,
    115n18, 115n19, 124n135
Bullinger, Heinrich, 8, 37n15
Bunyan, John, 75
Burnet, Gilbert, 57, 58, 59, 82n59
Burton, John, 129
Busskampf (or penitential struggle),
    101
Byrom, John, 128, 251

Calamy, Edmund, 72
Calvin, John, 2, 8, 43n85, 52, 53, 57,
    58, 80n38, 80n40, 90, 146,
    198n102, 249, 255, 265; and
    Wesley, 49, 111
Calvinism, 22, 77, 91, 111, 152n13,
    177, 181, 187, 255, 256, 269n2
Campbell, Ted A., 10, 11, 12, 37n17,
    38n24, 39n32,
Cannon, William R., 24, 187
Carter, Henry, 187
Cartwright, Thomas, 63, 73, 74
Cassian, John, 6, 34n2,
catholic (universal) church, 23, 55, 56,
    57, 65, 71, 104, 105, 108, 121n101,
    204–205, 268, 269
Causton, Thomas, 152n13
Cave, William, 13, 14, 40n41
celibacy, 33, 79n21, 168, 254

About the Author

Gwang Seok Oh (1967, Ph.D. 2005) is a pastor of the Berlin Methodist Church in Germany. He is also a visiting scholar at the Humboldt-Universität zu Berlin where he is working on a project in German Pietists and John Wesley. He is an external consultant to the Center for the Study of the World Christian Revitalization Movements.

CPSIA information can be obtained
at www.ICGtesting.com
Printed in the USA
BVHW040208220920
589354BV00014B/709